AF478915

Amitié/ Friendship

An Investigation into Cross-Cultural Styles in Canada and the United States

J. BARRY GURDIN

Amitié/ Friendship

An Investigation into Cross-Cultural Styles in Canada and the United States

J. BARRY GURDIN

Austin & Winfield
San Francisco • London • Bethesda

Austin & Winfield, Publishers, San Francisco
Austin & Winfield, Publishers, London
Austin & Winfield, Publishers, Bethesda

Library of Congress Cataloging in Publication Data

Gurdin, J. Barry, 1947-
    Amitié/Friendship: an investigation into cross-cultural styles in Canada and the
United States / J. Barry Gurdin.

    Includes bibliographical references and index.
    ISBN 1-880921-51-0   –   ISBN 1-880921-52-9
    1. Friendship--Sociological aspects.   2. Friendship--Quebec (Province)--
Montréal--Sociological aspects.   3. Friendship--Cross-cultural studies. I. Title.
HM132.5.G87 1996
302.3'4--dc20   93-6060

To the loving memory of my mother, Estelle Thalheimer Gurdin,

and my father, Joseph Gurdin

Contents

Acknowledgments

When I chose a topic for my doctoral dissertation, I realized that friendship had been the most important social relationship that I had experienced. To my close friends my deepest gratitude is owed.

This work would not have been undertaken, if, as an undergraduate, I had not been inspired by the superb teaching and personal encouragement of Eve Michaelson, who stimulated my interest in anthropology. Then came the War in Vietnam which profoundly changed my life and much of the research on friendship found in this book. As a person who had chosen to dissent from the war for liberal and humanistic reasons, I was dependent on the hospitality of the peoples of Canada and Sweden. Without their strong support of higher education, I could not have afforded to continue my graduate studies as an anti-war activist. Nor without the intellectual excitement and nurture of Sandra Wallman and her husband, Wally Baker, could I have made it through a rigorous master's degree program at The University of Toronto while adapting on meager resources to a new country. I began my research on friendship as a doctoral candidate and lecturer in the Institute for Social Anthropology at the University of Stockholm. A small grant from The University of Stockholm permitted me to purchase a photocopy of the manuscript of the Harvard-based conference on friendship that had been directed by Cora DuBois. At the end of 1970 I delivered a talk to the scholars at the Institute on the progress that I had made in my research. I shall never forget the intellectually stimulating year I spent there. To its scholars I owe my hearty thanks.

When I returned to Canada, I decided to continue my doctorate in sociology at the Université de Montréal. When I told my thesis director, Robert Sévigny, of my interest in friendship, he pointed out to me Jean Maisonneuve's classic book on the psycho-sociology of the affinities, one of the major works of French psycho-sociology of the 1960s.[1] An important part of my doctoral dissertation was a replication of Jean Maisonneuve's study.[2] Besides directing me to this outstanding work, Robert Sévigny stood by me during this long project. I deeply appreciate his guidance.

While a lecturer at Concordia University's Department of Sociology on the Loyola Campus, I was provided with invaluable assistance in computer programming by Jeff Kurtzman and Danny Jensen, and with help in administrative matters by Iona Farrell. Horst Hutter of the Department of Political Science of Concordia provided me with a manuscript of his book, *Politics as Friendship,* insightful discussions, and personal support. He, along with Eyvind Ronquist of Concordia's Department of English on the Sir George Williams Campus, helped sound out some our common interests in friendship in a public seminar at Concordia. With them I have a community of dialogue, debate, friendship, and mentorship, that has continued to grow over the years. Sandra Rafman of the Department of Psychology of the Université du Québec à Montréal provided me with the emotion, cheer, and company to analyze the voluminous material reported on in this book. My college and university students, Michèle Verrette, who was my principal French-language interviewer, and thousands of Montrealers deserve special recognition for their hours of time spent conversing and writing about their friendships.

Since returning to the United States of America, I have discovered that the Sociological Practice Association: A Professional Organization of Clinical and Applied Sociologists (formerly the Clinical Sociology Association) has an approach most similar to my training in *psycho-sociologie.* Moreover, I feel a *gemeinschaft* of theory and practice within that quite heterogeneous group of which I am an active member. SPA members, it is a great satisfaction having people with whom I can dialogue.

My special thanks are due to my wife, Rita Jeruchimowicz Jeremy, who was Co-Director of The University of Chicago's Parent Health and Infant Development Project (and who is currently a child psychologist in the Department of Pediatrics at the University of California, San Francisco), who opened the door to my participation with the methodologically knowledgeable members of her research team, and particularly Louis Guttman, Leland Wilkinson, Ingwer Borg, Shlomit Levy, and the principal investigator, Joseph Marcus. My appreciation is also extended to Sandy Gruba-McCallister and Linda Henson, who have worked for the Chicago project, for their assistance in programming some of the multivariate analyses that I have added to this work. During the 1984-85 academic year, Claude S. Fischer sponsored my being a visiting scholar (research associate) at the University of California, Berkeley, Department of Sociology, and Victor Jones invited me to air some of the contents of this book before the University of California, Berkeley's Canadian Studies Group. Again in May 1987, Thomas Barnes, of the University of California, Berkeley's Department of History and School of Law, extended to me the welcome to read from my second book before the Canadian Studies Group, and Nelson Graburn was my sponsor as a research associate in the Department of Anthropology at the University of California, Berkeley, in the fall semester of 1987. To all of them I extend my gratitude for helping me to realize a dream.

I would like to thank my sociological colleague and friend, Stephen J. Morewitz, who carefully read my manuscript and offered helpful suggestions for revision and corrections, as did the original readers of McGill-Queen's University Press, which accepted an earlier version of this manuscript in 1987. I owe much appreciation to my friends who are professional psychologists, Michael Acree, of the Center for AIDS Prevention Sciences and the California Institute of Integral Studies, and practicing clinician, Barbara Levy, who have proofread this work. I thank my son, Boaz Nathaniel Gurdin, who assisted me in drawing a figure of a joint Multidimensional Scalogram Analysis plot which proved too costly to reproduce in this work and for taking the photograph which appears on the cover of the paperback edition of this book. He kept me thinking about friendship in infancy and childhood and how to foster friendship within the family. I express my gratitude to the graphic artist, Gideon Y. Kramer, who was able to reproduce, reduce, and refine the various multivariate statistical graphics in the appendices of this book. He made them more aesthetic and readable than the original computer-generated printouts. I also wish to thank the graphic artist, Diane Spencer Hume, who designed the beautiful and inspiring cover of the paperback edition of this book.

Finally, let me extend my appreciation to my editors at Austin & Winfield, Robert West and Carole Bosch, who believed in my manuscript and shepherded it into print.

Notes

1. Maisonneuve, Jean, *Psycho-sociologie des affinités* (Paris: Presses universitaires de France, 1966).

2. Gurdin, Joseph Barry, "*Amitié* / Friendship: The Socio-cultural Construction of Friendship in Contemporary Montreal." Ph.D. diss., Department of Sociology, Université de Montréal, 1978.

Introduction

Amitié/Friendship: An Investigation into Cross-cultural Styles in Canada and the United States is about friendship in a special place at a particular time. It is set in Montreal, Quebec, Canada, in the mid-to-late 1970s, but it can be any place on the Planet Earth at any time where human beings try to climb up to an authentic relationship called friendship through traditional or unconventional means. It is also Chicago, Illinois, and the Bay Area in California, where the lessons learned about the qualities of friendship were turned into an intervention that promotes understanding of and improvements in this human bond.

The book that you are about to read is a total revision of my doctoral thesis from which I have eliminated much statistical double-checking, to which I have added a few multivariate analyses, and in which I address questions raised in recent research.[1] Soon after completing my Ph.D., I worked up a small group exercise for the development of friendship based on my doctoral research.[2] The insight into friendship that I have gained from these groups affords the potential for psycho-social interventions that are spelled out in this new tome.

After finishing an academic dissertation devoted to a rigorous replication and advancement of Jean Maisonneuve's psycho-sociology of the affinities, I construct a new meaning of friendship as I mediate through these different sources. Like a good translator, I want to render the meaning of these sources as accurately as possible while capturing the dimension of the sublime found in much of my source material.

My dissertation raised several questions that required further clarification. The most pressing issue was the question of whether ethnicity was as salient a factor in friendship as it had appeared to be in my thesis. I subsequently framed a direct question about the ethnicity of Montrealers and of their closest friends and asked it of a randomly selected sample of 2,371 people listed in the Montreal telephone directory. This poll was carried out in 1977 by my students in several of my classes at the Loyola Campus of Concordia University as a semester project. Its actuarial results confirmed (replicated) what I had found in my thesis; ethnicity was, indeed, a salient factor in friendship. Part of these findings were reported in a paper presented at the national convention of the American Anthropological Association in 1980, and published as a chapter in a book.[3] But the heart of these findings was delivered at the annual meeting of The Society for the Study of Social Problems in 1983 in a paper which was subsequently published in part.[4]

That the social sciences are not uniform should be rather obvious to the scholar and informed citizen in an age of rapid international travel and communications. Their methods, techniques, philosophy, and content differ considerably among the various nation-states in which they are practiced. At the 82nd annual meeting of the American Sociological Association in August 1987--devoted to the theme "Cross-National Research in Sociology"--President Melvin L. Kohn reminded the ASA convention that "Today, U.S. sociology and U.S. sociologists have much to learn from the sociologies and sociologists of other countries."[5] Yet, often with a poor command or no knowledge of a language other than English, many American sociologists ignore or disparage overtly or covertly social scientific literature in other languages. It is important to bring up this point here because many of my basic references may be unknown to the American reader. In a similar vein, there was a gap in my own knowledge of some important American sources that I have tried to fill since returning to the U.S.A. During the period of my graduate education in Canada, there was a serious movement toward Canadian and European sources and a simultaneous distancing from the American social sciences in Canadian universities. While this trend may have been more noticeable in French-speaking institutions, it was a pattern in English-speaking ones as well. One of the works of American social psychology that I have read since my return to the U.S., *Intimate Relations*, has influenced this book in a roundabout fashion. In 1973, Murray S. Davis told us that although he used observations of his own intimate relations and those of the intimate relations of others he had known, he couched these in the words, phrases, experiences, opinions, or findings of others. In my dissertation and original revision I minimized my personal observations and experiences of friendship in Montreal. In this book, in contrast, I will draw upon them to clarify my other resources, but, unlike Murray S. Davis, I will identify them as my own.

Studying friendship in a unique city at a critical period of its history sets the contours of the meanings of this relationship. Therefore, the setting of Montreal in the mid-to-late 1970s is laden with associations, symbols, and special senses for the components of the cognitive field of friendship. In this chapter, I introduce the various definitions of friendship found in my bibliographic references and interviews. The answers to the question, "What is a friend?" make up the cultural norms of what people in different subgroups of Quebec value, believe, and perceive about their friends. These topics are dealt with in Chapter 1.

In the second chapter, "Styles of Friendship," I introduce the notion of styles of friendship, which includes what people do in and say about their closest friendships. Ten main styles stood out among the close friendships of Montrealers who were interviewed, and I sketch the main features of these styles here and support them with quotations of my interviewees' descriptions of their friendships in this and subsequent chapters. These styles are: 1) the family-oriented friendship; 2) the sibling friendship; 3) the remaining family friendship after the break-up of the family; 4) non-nuclear family friendship; 5) the best friend-neighbor; 6) the best friend-proximity; 7) the similar-interest-best friend; 8) the buddy-*copain-copine* phenomenon; 9) girl-friend/ boy-friend, *petit/e ami/e*; and 10) the best-friend-in-mind. A multidimensional scalogram analysis of my in-depth interviewees' styles of friendship reveals that these people were polarized along a {head-to-heart} facet which lay orthogonal to an {institutionalized-to-chosen similar-interest friend} facet.

When I carried out a smallest space analysis on Montrealers' definitions of friendship coded into the Maisonneuvean content analytical categories, I discovered that this space is polarized between a definitional facet of {steadfastness}, that seems to be manifested in the stylistic facet of {institutionalized-to-chosen similar-interest friend}, and a definitional facet of {communication} that is superimposed upon the stylistic facet of {head-to-heart}. These findings put into question the model of a regular process of social penetration and suggest that a model of varying friendship styles better fits the friendships that I studied. The particular spacial constellation of friendship styles described in this chapter may reflect a pattern that was supported by the macro-socio-cultural structures of the welfare state.

Ethnicity is important in comprehending configurations of friendship in Montreal. In applying the Chicago School's concentric circle theory of expansion to Montreal, Carl A. Dawson found that Montreal had been squeezed into "concentric kidneys" between Mount Royal and the St. Lawrence River. Marlene Shore is astute in observing that Chicago urban theory could not explain "the division of the city, straight through its centre, into French and anglophone groups."[6] How Montrealers think about and act toward their friends may be strongly influenced by their coming from a "French-," "English-," or "Other-" "Canadian" background. This ethnic factor penetrates the expectations in friendship and the various ways people interact with their friends. While most people have close friends from ethnic groups outside their own, the majority of Montrealers select more of their close friends from their own ethnic group. Belonging to an ethnic group influences the cultural norms and related styles of friendship in subtle ways, as we shall see in Chapter 3, "Some of My Best Friends Are ... ." However, a person is never a member of only an ethnic group; a person belongs to a particular class, is a certain gender, is of a certain age, is married or not, and has children or not.

In many parts of Montreal the class system can be seen readily by looking at how far up or down the mountain people live. Although not a perfect pattern, the wealthier live higher up and the poorer live further down from Mount Royal. Although the degree of homogeneity varied among the participants in my study along class lines, Montrealers' friends come in largest part from a milieu similar to their own from the point of view of resources and goods possessed; in second largest part from a higher social stratum; and in third largest part from a lower socio-economic level. Supporting this socio-economic pattern are many attitudes about the class element in their friendships about which people offered tales spiced with superior, regretful, negative, or matter-of-fact emotional overtones. I show how SES bears upon a general indicator of class likeness among friends and upon more specific indicators such as occupation and education and combined indices of wealth, education, and occupation. In addition, I summarize the different psychosocial traits which the different socio-economic groups attribute to friendship. The empirical findings lead me to question various inconsistent interpretations about the influence of class on friendship in sociological literature. I criticize some structuralist views of the influence of class on friendship by pointing out their partial or complete dismissal of people's experience of this relationship and their denial of the great variance within the extremely few class groupings they posit. I conclude by reporting on how a psycho-social intervention improved the interpersonal milieu of institutionalized underclass people. Chapter 4, then, takes a look at "Friendship: Up, Down, and in the Middle."

From Freud to contemporary family practice, the family has often been depicted as a battleground rather than a place of friendship. In Chapter 5, "Friendship and the Family," the loci of friendship in the family are examined. Which relationships are more or less conducive to friendships are reported in their empirical manifestations in contemporary Montreal and comparisons are made with the United States and France. In the social sciences today there is considerable disagreement over the different socio-economic groupings' experience of the intersection of kinship and friendship, particularly over the question of whether or not people of lower class backgrounds live in a world of kinship devoid of friendship. In my investigation of the relationship between kinship and friendship, I learn that much of the confusion is due to the overlap in the language and thought of these two important aspects of these individuals' lives. A review of the literature reveals that former research has tended to minimize the accounts of people studied to the profit of rigid analytical grids, and, thereby, to exaggerate the extent of class differences. While taking up the relationship between kinship and the family in the classics, modern social science, and my interviews, I will cite some examples of the style of family friendship and will contrast some of these family friendship styles evident in my interview material.

Intimately linked to the implications of civil status for close friendship are the effects of the aging process. Human development takes us through a series of passages that change our statuses and roles. Most people marry; many have children and others do not; increasingly more people are choosing a myriad of alternative intimate relations; and many more people are living to become "senior citizens." Many philosophers and social scientists have depicted radically different types of friendships at these different stages of peoples' lives. My data in Chapter 6, "Friendship over the Years," point to the human life cycle, mediated by culture and society, leading people to tend to become more selective among their friends and less deep in their communications with close friends. Among the oldest segment of my interviewees, the style of "friend-in-mind" is prominent in their psycho-social lives.

Male chauvinists have argued that men are particularly apt for close friendship, while feminists have put forward evidence that suggests that women's expressiveness makes them more suited to the type of communication found in friendship. Some male authors and speakers, particularly those influenced by feminist thought, contend that American males' instrumentality, combined with the competitiveness of American culture, make the American male a poor candidate for close friendship. Comparative data from Montreal show that most men and women have close friends of the opposite gender, but that the larger part of their close friends are of their same gender. More importantly, both men and women in Montreal do not differ in having friendships of quality. Although different data bases are inconsistent in this regard, women may stress communication and men steadfastness more than their sexual counterpart in their friendships. I examine the interviewees' beliefs about appropriate conduct vis-à-vis friends of the opposite sex and bring to light the cultural context in which these beliefs are changing. The "boy-friend/girl-friend, *petit/e ami/e*" style of friendship covered in this chapter typically unites sexuality, communication, and some forms of aid. This style evident in my in-depth interviews was consonant with my finding that around one-fifth of Montrealers who responded to my questionnaire displayed a component of *eros* with their six closest friends at minimally a low level. I note the evolution of this style from a primarily premarital, cross-sex, intimate relationship into one that can take place among singles of any age. So Chapter 7 is succinctly entitled "Women, Men, and Close Friendship."

In Chapter 8, "A Clinical Sociology of Friendship," I discuss the small group exercise I developed to help people better understand their own friendships and the relationship of friendship in general and summarize the possibilities for and limitations of friendship for maintaining and improving mental health and enhancing individual lives. My research on friendship in small groups illustrates the mutual feedback between theory and practice in the social sciences. My recent friendship development groups in underclass and middle class environments show that despite the tendency for external hierarchies to reassert themselves within these groups, some participants experience a peak and others a greater understanding of their own or others' friendships, or friendship in general. After I review my own attempts at friendship intervention, I outline my and others' empirical findings about maintaining and breaking up with close friends. In Montreal Maisonneuve's six degrees of friendliness were not replicated, and my own results pointed out that social forces in the real world may operate to disestablish close friendship regardless of the level of intimacy or range of activities between close friends. The great horizontal mobility afforded to urbanized, industrialized Montrealers proved to be the worst culprit in ruining close friendship. Moreover, each age of philosophy or social science recognized varying generative forces that build up or tear apart friendship. Serious illness can strengthen old and create new friendships. In the case reported here, new friendships proved even stronger than the marital bond. In today's literature the negativity of the self, collusion, connivance, and destructive interpersonal rhetoric have been identified as notorious killers of friendship. To illustrate these negative processes, I analyze the "buddy-*copain-copine* phenomenon," which is a substyle of the common interest friend. It is subject to easy strain and termination because it is very superficial, unstranded, non-broad, and emotionally shallow.

In Chapter 9, "The Meanings of Friendship," I summarize the major components of friendship. Different folk, social scientific, and philosophical explanations have interpreted the interplay of these components of friendship in divergent ways. In this chapter I will compare and contrast some diverse essential facets of friendship; referents of the friendship experience; friendship from within the relationship; the roles of fantasy, imagination, and unconscious in friendship; and the relationship between friendship and society. A complex interplay of social, cultural, personality, and situational factors brings about the significance of friendship, which is best described by investigations in particular historical, ethnographic, and personal settings, where new combinations and qualities give rise to new nuances of this human experience.

In Chapter 10, I recount how a few of my own friendships began and have changed over the years and how they fit in or differ from the general trends found in my research. I conclude by reviewing several of my principal findings about friendship and record a few judgments on the condition of friendship since I gathered my data.

Finally, I must make a few points on aesthetics and form. Although my publisher follows *The Chicago Manual of Style*, I find that the statistical tables in Jean Maisonneuve's book--many of which are replicated herein--are much more legible when printed with borders similar to those of the original *Presses universitaires de France* work. Thus, I have followed a style quite like *Psycho-sociologie des affinités*, but I have moved these tables to the note section of this book to avoid intimidating readers not enamored of statistics. Moreover, as some important, recent references in this book are to University of California Press publications, I have followed the California style, modified the Chicago one, or combined them depending on which form seemed to be the clearest and afford the reader the greatest accessibility.

The Many Methods Used in This Book

My assumptions and experiences while writing and doing analyses, relationships with significant others, and techniques all contributed to this present account of friendship.

Throughout this work I rely on a multi-method approach, but I give a special place to a phenomenologically inspired social science. While avoiding the absolutist notion of essences of friendship, I show that the current discussion of meaning in the social sciences has had to integrate a degree of naturalism and relativism to take into account the real world. In Appendix A, I summarize my methods in more detail and recall some of the personal experiences that influenced this tale of friendship.

The Period of My Material and Contemporary Social Theory

It is not unusual for there to be a significant gap in time between a study in the social sciences and when it is published. During this period, theoretical positions frequently change, new studies are done, and new interpretations are offered. For example, Jean Maisonneuve's "reasoned" sample for his study of friendship was gathered during the years 1954-55 and was published in 1966.[7] My main in-depth interviews and questionnaires were accomplished between 1973-76, and my large telephone survey was conducted in the spring of 1977 in Montreal. The friendship development groups discussed in this book were facilitated between 1979 and 1984 in Chicago and San Francisco, and this book is being published in 1995. Thus, while my theoretical framework is in the tradition of a sociology of meaning with a French accent, it developed before Barry Wellman's work in Toronto, Claude S. Fischer's in northern California, Rebecca G. Adams's and Rosemary Blieszner's in Chicago and North Carolina were published--to mention but a few of the new studies of friendship I cite throughout this revised work.[8] In 1993 a social science of meaning became popularized again through a heated public debate about the "politics of meaning." This controversy raged in the American media over First Lady Hillary Rodham Clinton's being inspired by the words of Michael Lerner.[9]

So too have the early 1990s brought a serious evaluation of the evolution of Quebec and of Canada from the points of view of the majority and minority and the insider and outsider during the last quarter century.[10] And the importance of the historical context for the study of friendship has been stressed.[11]

Although any serious scholar must note the great variance and serious disagreements in method, focus, and conclusions among the studies of friendship that have appeared in the period between the mid-1970s and the early 1990s, I believe it insightful to place them within a broader perspective of social theory. When the life course is focused upon, the friendships of the individual in infancy, adolescence, adulthood, and "older adulthood" depict very complex changes in development in which it is normal to take on new friends and leave some of the old as a person grows in an increasingly complex society. This view is characteristic of James Coleman's neo-Lockean perspective on human beings as being "rationally capable of calculating the most efficient means to their ends." However, its critics assess the neo-Lockean perspective as having "little sense of how human identity is shaped by linguistic and moral communities."[12]

In contrast, some observers, more rooted in a social science of meaning, have described the late sixties and seventies as having conceived of relationships, friendship included, as being "more short-term and disposable than had previously been the case. At that time there had been a hedonistic tendency to regard dissatisfaction with a relationship as a ground for breakup and a move to a new relationship."[13] While this more communitarian view also depicts there currently being a value on the preservation and continuity of relationships in part due to anxieties about relationship breakdown and AIDS, the opposite perspective--rooted in the self-help notion of co-dependency--remains widespread established truth in some therapeutic circles. More empirical, some writers are careful to distinguish friendship from other relationships such as benevolence, utility, and love more or less characteristic of certain stages in the life cycle.[14] Yet, there is a concern among pro-communitarians now that the communitarian literature fails to explain the main cause of the disposable attitude toward human relationships, which is the "new global capitalism" which threatens "to turn us all into unattached, disposable workers."[15]

Trying to remain objectively above this fray is a theoretical model incorporating "both sociological and psychological perspectives on friendship."[16] While commenting on the strengths and weaknesses of many studies of friendship, Rosemary Blieszner and Rebecca G. Adams stress that the elements of their model vary by structural, cultural, and historical context. For them:

> *Age* ... and other *social and individual characteristics* ... influence *friendship patterns.* Age is a proxy measure for *stage of the life course* and *stage of development,* which both affect one another. The effects of other individual characteristics, such as *gender* (or race, class, and so on), are conceptualized both in structural terms, as determining *opportunities for and constraints on friendship,* and in psychological terms, as predicting *personality traits and dispositions.* Stage of life course affects social

> structural opportunities for and constraints on friendship, and stage of development affects psychological disposition.
>
> Friendship patterns consist of the *structure* (the form of the ties linking an individual's friends such as the hierarchy and solidarity among them, the similarity of their social positions, the number of friends, the proportion of them who know one another, and the pattern of connections among them), *processes* (the thoughts, feelings, and behaviors involved in acting as friends), and *phases* (the formation, maintenance, and dissolution of friendship networks and of the friendships within them). ... Structure, processes, and phases influence one another as do the characteristics of *dyads* and *networks*.

Yet the language in which these authors ensconce their model suggests positivists' yearning for a meta-analysis that precludes asking the questions of value posed by the communitarians. Conceptualizing friendship as a dyadic structure consisting of *power hierarchy, status hierarchy, solidarity,* and *homogeneity* leads these authors to an entirely different line of questioning than that pursued by an interpreter of the meaning of friendship in secondary sources such as books and films who tells us about the meaning of the friendship between E.T. and Eliot, Tom Sawyer and Huckleberry Finn, and Narcissus and Broccadoro.[17] Defining solidarity as "the horizontal dimension or the degree of intimacy or closeness between the people involved ... [or] as a process variable ... [or] as a measure or the strength of social ties and of social distance" does not lead an inquirer to delve into the inner psycho-social state of activist friends who may have turned in rage upon each other when they were not able to bring about near perfect equality in their own lives or in the area of society they sought to change.[18] Nor would it lead such researchers to investigate the causal connection between the experience of such social actors for justice being filled with cynicism, lack of trust in others, and scepticism toward the possibility for collectively working for a better world and the blockage toward social change in developed democratic countries.[19]

If a neo-Lockean model of friendship helps us to locate the place of friendship within the social system, and to record its contours with some precision, it gives us less a feel for the experience of friendship for social actors within given historical and cultural contexts. It is for this reason that I prefer to replicate the social phenomenology of Jean Maisonneuve which is closer to the concerns of current communitarian social theory.[20]

Notes

1. Gurdin, Joseph Barry, "*Amitié*/Friendship: The Socio-cultural Construction of Friendship in Contemporary Montreal." Ph.D. diss., Department of Sociology, Université de Montréal, 1978.

2. Gurdin, J. Barry, "The Therapy of Friendship," *Small Group Behavior* 17 (November 1986): 444-457; Gurdin, J. Barry. "Groups for the Development of Friendship," *Small Group Behavior* 19 (February 1988), 57-66.

3. Gurdin, J. Barry, "Quebecer and *Québécois:* Same Meaning?" (Paper delivered at the Session on the Lexicon, 79th annual meeting of the American Anthropological Association, Washington, D.C., 6 December 1980); Gurdin, J. Barry, "Naturalistic Categories of Ethnic Identity in Quebec," Chap. 9 in *Culture, Ethnicity, and Identity: Current Issues in Research*, ed. Bill McCready (New York: Academic Press, 1983), 149-180.

4. Gurdin, Joseph Barry and Horst Hutter, "Some of My Best Friends Are ...: The Relationship of Ethnicity to Close Friendship." *Quebec Studies* 3 (1985), 101-112.

5. "Introduction," in *Cross-National Research in Sociology*, ed. Melvin L. Kohn (Newbury Park: Sage Publications, 1989).

6. Shore, Marlene, *The Science of Social Redemption: McGill, the Chicago School, and the Origins of Social Research in Canada* (Toronto: University of Toronto Press, 1987), 135 - 137.

7. Maisonneuve, Jean, *Psycho-sociologie des affinités* (Paris: Presses universitaires de France, 1966), 507.

8. Wellman, Barry, "Network Analysis," in *Sociological Theory*, ed. R. Collins (San Francisco: Jossey-Bass): 155-200; idem, "Men in Networks:

Private Communities, Domestic Friendships," in *Men's Friendships*, ed. Peter M. Nardi (Newbury Park: Sage Publications, 1992), 74-114; Fischer, Claude S., *To Dwell among Friends: Personal Networks in Town and City* (Chicago: The University of Chicago Press, 1982); Rebecca G. Adams and Rosemary Blieszner, *Older Adult Friendship: Structure and Process* (Newbury Park: Sage Publications, 1989); Rosemary Blieszner and Rebecca G. Adams, *Adult Friendship* (Newbury Park: Sage Publications, 1992).

9. Michael Lerner, "The Meaning of the Politics of Meaning," *The Wall Street Journal*, 3 June 1993, A15; Alice Kahn, "Hillary Clinton's Spiritual Adviser," *San Francisco Chronicle*, 1 June 1993, B3; B5; Fields-Meyer, Thomas, "This Year's Prophet: With *Tikkun*, His Magazine of the Jewish Left, and His Catch Phrase "the Politics of Meaning," Michael Lerner Has Become the Clintons' Norman Podhoretz," *The New York Times Magazine*, 27 June 1993, 28-32; 35-36; 61-62.

10. *Forces: Economic, Social and Cultural Quarterly*, ed. Marcel Couture. Montréal: la Société d'édition de la revue Forces, 100 (Hiver 1992-199); Lipset, Seymour Martin, *Continental Divide: The Values and Institutions of the United States and Canada* (New York: Routledge, 1990); Richler, Mordecai, *Oh Canada! Oh Quebec! Requiem for a Divided Country* (Toronto: Penguin Books, 1992); Ouellet, Danielle, "Bilan de société: Repères pour une société en mutation, avec le sociologue Guy Rocher," *Le Devoir*, 6 février 1993, A 11.

11. Hansen, Karen V., " 'Our Eyes Behold Each Other': Masculinity and Intimate Friendship in Antebellum New England," in Nardi, 35-58.

12. Bellah, Robert N., Richard Madsen, William M. Sullivan, Ann Swidler, and Steven N. Tipton, *The Good Society* (New York: Vintage Books, 1992), 290.

13. Gilmour, Robin and Tuvia Melamed, "The Repair and Maintenance of Relationships," in *Person to Person*, eds. George Graham and Hugh LaFollette (Philadelphia: Temple University Press, 1989), 156-157.

14. Francesco, Alberoni, *L'amicizia* (Milan: Garzanti s.p.a., 1984).

15. See: Derber, Charles, "Coming Glued: Communitarianism to the Rescue." *Tikkun: A Bimonthly Jewish Critique of Politics, Culture and Society* (Oakland, CA: the Institute for Labor and Mental Health), July/August 1993, 27-30; 95-99; Derber, Charles, Mary Edsall, Peter Gabel, Ruth Rosen, and Michael Sandel, "Roundtable." *Tikkun: A Bimonthly Jewish Critique of Politics, Culture and Society* (Oakland, CA: the Institute for Labor and Mental Health), September/October 1993, 19 - 26; 87- 89; Derber, Charles, "Clintonism: Beyond Left and Right?" *Tikkun: A Bimonthly Jewish Critique of Politics, Culture and Society* (Oakland, CA: the Institute for Labor and Mental Health), January/February 1994, 40 - 45. For a reply to Derber, see: Etzioni, Amitai, "On Communitarianism and its Inclusive Agenda." *Tikkun: A Bimonthly Jewish Critique of Politics, Culture and Society* (Oakland, CA: the Institute for Labor and Mental Health), September/October 1993, 49- 51.

16. Rosemary Blieszner and Rebecca G. Adams, *Adult Friendship* (Newbury Park, CA: Sage Publications, 1992), 4-5.

17. Ibid., 6-7; Alberoni, 92-94.

18. Blieszner and Adams, 6-7.

19. See: Michael Lerner, *Surplus Powerlessness: The Psychodynamics of Everyday Life ... And the Psychology of Individual and Social Transformation* (Oakland, CA: The Institute for Labor and Mental Health, 1986); also see: Eugène Enriquez, *De la horde à l'état: Essai de psychanalyse du lien social* (Mayenne: Editions Gallimard, 1983), 119-123.

20. When writing the letters of permission for this book, I discovered the existence of a replication of Jean Maisonneuve's original study. He requested that I add the following remarks: "The same author in collaboration with L. Lamy published with the same publisher in 1993 a *Psycho-sociologie de l'amitié* [*Psycho-sociology of Friendship*], where thirty years later he takes up again his investigations of the patterns of friendship and his hypothesis of the affinities of semantic style between intimates." Also see page 54, footnote 40.

Chapter One

What Is a Friend?

When human beings speak about their relationships, they employ words, like friendship, to encode their meaning. Often these words are related to other groups of words and may be regrouped into larger units, which social scientists have called cognitive fields. Sometimes these sets of words are explained in terms of underlying assumptions and principles that relate these words to one another. The sociologist of language usually looks at these words very differently from linguists because, for socio-linguists, the meaning of the words we use is constantly being modified in concrete situations of human interactions that are situated in particular historical and socio-cultural settings. Examining friendship by paying attention to its fields and contexts recaptures the framework of its etymology. Indeed, friendship is an ancient object of inquiry that has been traced back to the early Indo-European vocabulary and has been found at all levels of social organization from the simplest to the most complex.[1] Even though friendship flourishes in some social and cultural settings and withers in others, anthropologists have described it briefly in the major ethnographic areas of the world.[2]

Much has been written on the history, philosophy, theology, and philology of friendship.[3] Just go to *The Oxford English Dictionary, The Oxford Dictionary of English Etymology, Trésor de la Langue Française,* among many other standard works, to behold the detailed pages of the differentiation of the significations of friend and friendship.[4]

Miss Fitich, the venerable hag browbeaten by modern linguists, warned the boys and girls of Victorian classrooms that they ought not to compile "garbage lists"--long enumerations of words, strung together by commas, with few internal explanations. She would really have hated contemporary social scientists who pretend to understand the meaning of texts and other codable contents by jotting down strings of words, frequently preceded by a number. Like Miss Fitich, admirers of history and literature dislike the dislocated gleanings of reality presented in this fashion. Despite my agreement with their qualms about such prose, a "garbage list" helps us, nevertheless, to grasp readily the main components of friendship across time and space. In each age and place friendship takes on different components which interact in different ways, but some of these elements of friendship regularly reappear and are sometimes explained in a similar fashion.

A catalogue of these often repetitive parts of friendship centers around: 1) a contractual exchange; 2) hospitality; 3) confidence; 4) helpfulness; 5) freedom per se and freely instituted relationships based on custom, interest, or reason that aim for solidarity; 6) signs such as words labeling "the friend" and actions such as kissing; 7) a label for near and distant kin; 8) subjective feelings; 9) prudence in choosing and breaking with friends; 10) being constant and sincere in attempting to maintain friendship; 11) a human bond with everything dear to mankind and on which its existence depends; 12) a rational choice by which the values of sincerity and loyalty temper usefulness; 13) building on a similarity of nature and on equality of virtue, yet excluding being identical; 14) treating another on the same footing as oneself regardless of the other's social status; 15) tending toward durability which requires duties and circumspection; 16) harmony; 17) justice; 18) philanthropy; 19) availability in adversity; 20) the simple possessive; 21) a military companion or ally; 22) guarding against flattery; 23) goodwill; 24) a community joined in a cult of friendship; 25) the appropriation of objects to one's environment; 26) a moral relationship; 27) the pleasurable; 28) separating friendship from knowledge; 29) the reconciliation of generosity and discernment in doing good; 30) being spontaneously grateful; 31) being rule governed; 32) a friendship with God; 33) being necessary because the lone person is weak or because friendship fits in with mankind's nature; and 34) being impossible with a tyrant because people can only fear, not trust, such a person.

These varied elements suggest that prehistory, philosophy, and the social sciences were grappling with the questions of how friendship clarifies the relationship with the other; how friendship can explain objective and subjective manifestations of these relationships; how friendship explains the metaphysical meaning of these relationships; and how macro- and micro- social forces lead to the relationship of friendship.[5]

Without repeating a summary of the fascinating history of friendship, it remains important to stress that any one of its often recurrent components mentioned in our "garbage list" retains only a shell of significance outside its place in society, culture, and history.[6] Let us consider a few examples to make this point. Consider the twenty-first element of the list above, a "military companion or ally." The ancient vocabularies point to related lexical items which encompass the idea of the friend as the companion in combat. Evidence for this association is taken from the Germanic **drauhti-*, Gothic *ga-drauhts*, "soldier," and **drauhti-no* (Old Icelandic *drottin*, "chief, lord"). These words are related to the Slavic and Baltic ones meaning "friend, companion." Like the Latin *dominus* and *tribunus*, one can establish a link between a nominal term and its derivative in *-no*. **drauhti-* is a collective term designating company in the military sense such as Tacitus describes it in *Germans* 13 and in the sense of *drauhtino-*, the *principes*, in whom authority is incarnated. The Germanic specifies "company" by meaning a "warrior friendship." Old Slavic keeps a parallel expression, the collective term, *druzina*, "army companions." The Gothic term for "soldier," *ga-drauhts*, literally "he of the same *drauhti-*," means, therefore, "he who shares a companionship, a friendship." These are understood as collective terms for the group of people who are tied by common services in war. The abstract *drauhts* is "companionship or warrior. *drauhti-witop* is combat as the rule of the *drauhti*. Likewise in the Germanic legends of the Odin Herjan and in Tacitus' *Germans* 43 and Gothic *harjis*, German *Heer* appears as the name of a masquerade group occasionally united for expeditions of plunder. All of these friendships are exclusively man to man ones in a male society devoted to the practice of combat. *Harjis, drauhti*, and *traven* always go back to this set of ideas and institutions."[7]

Another illustration of the situatedness of friendship can be drawn from the Greek period. Jean Claude Fraisse informs us that the pre-philosophic Greeks had popular notions of friendship which formed the basis for their later philosophical reflection. He distinguishes two periods. From the time of the Homeric poems down to the period of the Pythagoreans, the Greeks appear to consider social life as a natural fact. They wanted to determine precisely what its rules were. To do this they used the notion of divine will. Although there lingered a concern for naturalist explanation around the fifth century B.C., a new position was developed. According to this new thought, man has an original place in the universe, even though his new situation might have been brought about by such different causes as his own invention, the gods, or pure luck. Reasoning in this manner, it would follow that thinkers should look at man himself to discover what explains and justifies social life. In this period, civil concord was most uncertain in most of the important states. In contrast to this public condition, the private status of *philia* was kept as a model, the rules of which the philosophers attempted to make ex-plicit so that they could find the source of its stability. Such a search had to reconcile agreement and usefulness. It could be said that the evolution of the idea of *philia* is tied to the discovery of liberty which comes before friendship. Fraisse wonders about the origin of the thought on friendship in this period. Does the will for friendship answer a need for feelings? Does it correspond to a rational requirement? Does it call for the intimacy of a common life or simply the codification of reciprocal duties?[8]

When documenting the socio-cultural and temporal rootedness of friendship, it is important to stress that in looking back in time we are dependent on the work of others in secondary sources. In reading these sources and selecting information from them, any author is necessarily making several mediations. In the case of friendship, various researchers have interpreted the same evidence quite differently. This point is evident in comparing the works of Fraisse and Hutter.[9]

According to Fraisse, the Greek philosophers began to distinguish between the human and natural worlds as they borrowed from an analysis of the material components of physical phenomena. They put forward the notions of resemblance, complementariness of opposites, and usefulness to explain relationships with the other. In the *Lysis* the idea of *oikeiotès*, of convenience, comes about from an inner, personal conversion that takes preparation.[10] *Oikeiotès* does not separate a person's happiness that is due to the other's presence from his pleasure that is due to his friend's indispensable part in his own personal progress. An individual's friend is the witness of the progress of his reason, the guide of his research, and the disciple of his teaching. For these reasons, a person and his friend are integrated to some extent in regard to the legitimate end of their conduct. In Platonic thought, relating to the person of an individual's friend brings about this integration.

For Fraisse, these are the core concepts of Plato. Although Hutter would not disagree with Fraisse's emphasis on the personal qualities of Plato's idea of friendship, Hutter sees love as the real key to understanding Platonic friendship. In Hutter's interpretation in "the Aristotelian system, and later in Stoicism and Epicureanism, love is seen as opposed to friendship."[11] According to Hutter, this is Aristotle's main difference with Plato. In contrast, for Fraisse, Aristotle's main contribution to understanding friendship lies in his analysis of human self-sufficiency and the psychological conditions of human happiness.

Aristotle demonstrates that the friendly community finds its meaning completed by theoretic activity. In Fraisse's interpretation of Aristotle, solidarities do not result from equating rationality and virtue or sensitivity and vice. Rather, ideally every virtuous, happy activity is necessarily common to several different solidarities. For example, contemplative activity is really carried out with partners. According to Fraisse's interpretation, if Aristotle had discovered a quasi-subjective form, then Epicurus' materialist and empiricist perspective transformed "human nature" into data. For Epicurus, the course of things is a chaos even when it is rationally explained. In this system, every individual and his friend independently order themselves to this nature.[12] While Hutter would agree with this individualistic interpretation of Epicurus, he points out that Epicurus' utilitarian framework is equally important in his view of friendship.

In Stoic philosophy *philia* is related to the whole process which ties man to his fellowman. All is well in a universe directed by providence or destiny. Therefore, nature is good as is the tendency which carries a person toward those like himself. But in another sense it is human nature to love his fellowman only as a being endowed with reason. Thus, a man must prefer the harmony of his own conduct to what he perceives immediately in this world such as friends.[13]

From all these historically situated ideas, a deep principle of friendship can be put forward. This core would include three main elements: desire; activity conscious of itself; and the pleasure of existence. *Philia* is seen as one of three ends: rational activity, happiness, and friendship. Even if Fraisse thinks that *philia* tends to be lost when it is regarded objectively as the result of interests, manifestations of tendencies, and an equilibrium of social forces, Hutter certainly provides an illuminating discussion of friendship in antiquity using these very sources.[14]

Before proceeding to the social, cultural, and temporal locus of my study of friendship, consider two documents that lend weight to the contention that the meaning of friendship changes tremendously in different places and eras. By the eighteenth century the ancient world's use of naturalism to interpret friendship gives very different senses to the generic terms and their subcomponents found in this discussion, and these arguments are framed in an entirely different package of concerns. The English and French philosophers of this period pictured friendship as "natural." Whether as "sympathy" or as rational egoism in which individual interests agree and in which people can help out one another in the pursuit of happiness, they highly regarded friendship. The utopian socialist writers saw equality, free communication, solidarity, and mutual trust of all members of society in friendship. François Marie Charles Fourier contrasted friendship with "materialistic" and "authoritarian" feelings. For him, friendship bypassed selfishness and family interests and united all people in a society of social harmony. Fourier thought that the principle of harmony among the passions was his greatest discovery, but to achieve this goal, society needed to be reconstructed into co-operative or united industry. For Fourier, every passion sought to satisfy a tendency. Five tendencies were sensual and individual (taste, touch, hearing, sight, and smell). Seven others were social. Of these, friendship and ambition were the two major tendencies. In criticizing capitalist society, utopians like Owen showed that religion and egoism which rule under capitalism discourage free contact between people. They linked friendship to eradication of incorrect ideas, unjust rule, and the establishment of a new social order.[15]

The exact opposite point of view has recently been espoused by Silver, who contends that with the development of impersonal markets in products and services a parallel system of personal relations emerges whose ethic excludes exchange and utility. Thus, in Silver's view, commercial society purifies personal relationships by distinguishing friendship from personal relations of instrumentalism and, instead, founds friendship on sympathy and affection.[16]

Just as it broadens our understanding of friendship to consider its variability in our own and others' cultural past, so is it informative to grasp what the meaning and experience of friendship may be for people living in a society and culture, in some ways quite similar to and in some ways quite different from our own. This reason underscores the rationale for reflecting on friendship in the Montreal of the latter half of the 1970s.

The Montreal and Quebec Settings

In comparing Canada to the United States of America, probably the most frequently repeated observation has been that the closer areas are to one another in both countries, the more they are alike than progressively more geographically removed regions in their same country. Thus, culture, geography, population, and political organization may be more similar in Vancouver and Seattle than is Vancouver like Montreal or St. John's, the capital of Newfoundland. There are aspects to life in Montreal and Boston that resemble one another more than life in Montreal and Winnipeg. Montreal displays many of the characteristics of a "Yankee City," yet it is sufficiently different to strike any American tourist from the Northeast as being a metropolis of a very different country. Like Boston, Montreal is seeped in history for a North American environment.

On the second of October 1535, as he was going up the Saint Lawrence River, Jacques Cartier saw land that was "more beautiful and better than one could imagine," and, in its middle was a mountain, to which he gave the name of Mount Royal. The first colonists arrived on the island on the seventeenth of May 1642. And on September 8, 1760 the English conquest put an end to the French Empire in North America. When England united Upper (English) and Lower (French) Canada, Montreal became the capital between 1843 and 1849. The island itself covers an area of 145,000 square acres (496 square kilometers), and is 35 miles (56 kilometers) wide. By 1980 the census revealed that there were 3,607,900 people in the standard metropolitan statistical area, and 1,020,900 in the city of Montreal itself.

In its center, Mount Royal rises 750 feet (230 meters) high. Evolving from its beginnings in fur trading and shipping, by 1967 Montreal could be described as the banking and financial center of Canada.[17] Although it was originally a predominantly English-speaking city, by this century it had grown to become two-thirds French-speaking, the second largest French-speaking city in the world, with over thirty other different ethnic groups.

As in other parts of the world, social movements working to promote greater social equality and ethnic mobilization set the tone of much of the climate of the 1970s in Montreal. In addition to these movements for social change, Montreal hosted the World's Fair of 1967 (Man and His World) and the Olympics of 1976, which left impressive architectural monuments, an excellent subway, an amusement park, several large sport centers, a velodrome, and underground shopping malls. As the famous author of *The Insolences of Brother Anonymous*, Jean-Paul Desbiens, explains, the act creating Quebec's Department of Education on May 13, 1964, had been significant in ushering in the Quiet Revolution.[18] Besides these happenings, Montreal acquired a franchise from the National Baseball League which turned into the Montreal Expos, a team which became almost as much a source of civic pride as its famous hockey team, the Canadians. These events, centrally orchestrated by Mayor Jean Drapeau, also left legacies of General Charles de Gaulle's "*Vive le Québec libre*," proclaimed from Montreal's City Hall, a billion dollar debt, and a variety of active civic opposition groups. By the mid-1980s these groups elected a civic government appealing to the newly educated and managerial classes which favor honest, rational decision-making and its symbolism. And on November 15, 1976, René Lévesque and his Parti Québécois were elected with a majority government to the Quebec National Assembly.[19]

Undoubtedly, like the other "frostbelt" cities in the north-central and and northeastern regions of North America, Montreal witnessed a considerable degree of economic decline and stagnation during the last thirty years; and, as in other "frostbelt" cities, the reasons for this decline have become the sources of acrimonious debates: federalists blame the rise of *Québécois* nationalism; liberals blame Mayor Drapeau's Roman-like circuses, infused with enormous graft and corruption, instead of sustained growth in modern economic sectors; conservatives blame socialism and powerful unions driving up artificially high wages;

and, until the mid-to-late 1980s, some economists claimed that French Canadians are good artists, writers, and lawyers, but poor businessmen. As the Quebec friendship patterns found in this book are those of the 1970s, I will not detail the cultural ambiance of the Montreal of the 1980s. Before the world stock market decline of 1987, that venerable bastion of centrist conservative thought, *Time Magazine*, wrote of "once troubled Quebec" as "a province of prosperity," a "Land of Hope and Hustle." It approvingly noted that higher education in Quebec produces a large part of Canada's M.B.A.s. *Time Magazine* seemed pleased that a tenth of the population invested in the stock-market and that exports to the United States had increased by 8.5 billion American dollars from 1976 to 1987.[20]

This *Time* article made no mention of the extent to which this economic activity had been generated by the Reagan Administration's military build-up. Jocelyn Coulon estimated that 100,000 people work for Quebec's military industry and that it is the most important sector of industrial manufacturing.[21] According to the federal government of Canada, military sales abroad reached $1.19 billion in 1985, of which 87% went to the United States. Eric Shragge, Ronald Babin, and Jean-Guy Vaillancourt have traced the more general contours of Canada's role in the armaments race of the 1980s.[22] Even though sociological findings usually received greater coverage in the Montreal press in the 1970s than in newspapers in American cities of comparable size, the sociological discussion of flight to the "Sunbelt" was not a media favorite. Despite the importance of sociological writings, the influence of superhighways, industrial automation, inexpensive, low-tax suburban industrial parks, nonunion Southern plants, low-density southern housing, the shorter period required to cultivate trees and other such factors on flight to the "Sunbelt" did not attract great interest in Montreal during this period. To the contrary, emphasis in the French-language media placed the blame for industrial flight on Quebec's and the rest of Canada's dependence on American multi-national companies' sole interest in immediate maximal profits and on the intolerance of primarily English-Canadian large enterprise to recruit qualified French

Canadians. By the winter of 1992, Jean Guertin, Director of the Graduate School of Business Administration (HEC) at the University of Montreal, continued to reflect a conservative bias by blaming the recent recession and slow, current growth on the Kennedy-Trudeau years, leading business and government to go into debt. Professor Guertin does not mention the leveraged buy-outs, the Bank of Credit and Commerce International, the Savings and Loan Scandal, the extreme reduction of corporate taxation, nor the enormous increase in the national debt to pay for the military spending that skyrocketed during the Reagan-Bush era.[23]

By the beginning of the great recession, even many anti-establishment Quebecers who had initially strongly criticized the James Bay Project--the largest hydro-electric adventure in the world--changed their position and began promoting it as a major economic asset to Quebec and a symbol of French Canadian know-how. Thus the beautiful pictures and celebratory descriptions of Richard Drouin and the James Bay Project vividly depict this new pride of a segment of Quebec bureaucrats and their intellectual defenders.[24] Despite their adulation, by the 1990s opposition to Hydro-Quebec's James Bay project became vocal in other segments of Quebec public opinion and elsewhere. Grand Chief Matthew Coon-Come of the Grand Council of the Crees (of Québec) expressed this sentiment in the following letter:

> Watchia:
> You and I have never met! We live in different countries. Our cultures are very different.
> But you and I are deeply connected. We share a common home: the vast and beautiful continent called North America. We live thousands of miles apart, but we may both see the same migrating whales, the same migrating birds, and we share the waters of the ocean. It is Mother Nature that connects us.
> I believe that you understand this and that you are a human being who is concerned about Mother Nature, a person who knows that we share a magnificent home that money can never replace.
> I write to you because a part of our home is in trouble. That place is called James Bay and my people, the Crees,

live there. You will probably never visit James Bay. That does not matter. I am asking for your help because the destruction of my home is the destruction of your home.

Let me tell you about the land where my family and I live.

I was born and raised on the shores of Lake Mistissini in northern Canada. I was raised in a wigwam in the wilderness where the winter temperature drops to 55 degrees below zero. The ice doesn't break up on the James Bay until mid-July. It is too cold to grow food, so my people have always lived from the moose, caribou, sturgeon, pickerel, whitefish, and all of the other animals that the creator has seen fit to put upon the earth in our homeland.

Our way of life depends on the continued survival of the animals. We have hunted and fished, in balance with nature, for more than 300 generations. Long before the Egyptian pyramids were built or the Bible written, we were hunting in this same way.

For 5,000 years we did not leave a trace of our having been in James Bay. What we had came from the land and went back to the land. The land is sacred to us. This land holds the graves of our ancestors.

But, now, Hydro-Quebec is destroying our sacred land and our way of life. If you were to fly with me today in a Cessna, starting from the first James Bay dam, we'd fly for four and a half hours, and all you'd see is land drowned by water, three major rivers destroyed. The graves of our ancestors now rest under Hydro-Quebec's reservoirs.

But it is the living who suffer. Many of my people living near the reservoirs are contaminated with methyl mercury poisoning. Our Cree language does not even have a word for mercury poisoning. We call it "nimass aksiwan"--fish disease. Can you imagine the dread this causes in people who depend on fish to live. Without hunting and fishing, our 5,000-year-old culture is dying.

We will not sit passively and accept this. We are a proud people. We want our children to be proud of who they are. We want them to develop in ways which sustain Mother Nature and do not destroy her.

We are now fighting to stop James Bay Phase II. Phase II of their project will cause so much mercury contamination that officials inside the Environment Department of Hydro-Quebec call it the "Frankenstein Project."

I am not asking for your sympathy. I am asking for your help--to stop Phase II, before all of James Bay and its wildlife is destroyed.

> You can play a special role in the fight for James Bay--
> by supporting NRDC (National Resources Defense
> Council), a group which knows how to use the law and win.
> Phase I of James Bay was exempted from Canadian
> environmental review. But, now, the government of
> Canada has agreed to review Hydro-Quebec's disastrous
> plans for Phase II before it goes forward. ... [25]

Before the Grand Chief of the Cree wrote this letter, William Nicholls, representative of the Grand Council of the Cree of James Bay, along with other spokespeople, had visited officials in Albany, New York, in June 1991, to plead with them not to buy 1.8 million kilowatts of power for $19 billion from the James Bay II project until a thorough environmental study had been undertaken. Then, on August 5 of that year, Mayor David Dinkins of New York City requested the state to delay the purchase of this Hydro-Quebec power until the environmental, social, and economic costs of this development had been calculated. It has been reported that the Mohawk resistance to the expansion of a golf course on their land in the summer of 1990 was a major factor empowering the Cree Indians to convince Hydro Quebec to scrap their expansion in northern Quebec. It also led to the creation of the Royal Commission on Aboriginal Peoples which is expected to call for self-government to promote self-esteem and economic self-reliance.[26]

In addition to these macro-societal changes taking place, the various liberationist ideologies found strong social support in the Montreal of the 1970s. In this atmosphere, there thrived active and diverse groups promoting women's and gays' liberation, organizations promoting third-world causes, movements in favor of green spaces and ecology, clubs in favor of rights for bicyclists, and activists who successfully lobbied for legislation forbidding discrimination on the basis of sexual orientation. Montreal throbbed during the 1970s as in earlier decades with high and popular culture. Singers such as Gilles Vigneault, Paul Piché, Pauline Julien, Robert Charlebois, and Diane Dufresne filled the nightlife of many concert halls with their different impassioned styles of music. Writers and poets such as Gerald Godin, Marie-Claire Blais, Leonard Cohen, Clark Blaise, and many others such as "the little" singer René

Simard captivated the speech and daily life of the exciting diversity of the citizenry of Montreal.[27] Film makers such as Georges Dor, Michel Brault, and many others captured the grievances, joys, and sorrows of contemporary Quebecers for Montreal audiences. Constant debates raged in the press over the laws controlling French-language and Canadian content in television and radio programming, and documentation proving or disproving that this or that communication bureaucracy was a "white elephant" seized the pages of newspaper copy.

The ministry for tourism launched various campaigns to get Montrealers and other Quebecers to "*faire le tour*" of the province. The very proximity and splendor of the parks and wilderness and the vastness of Saint Lawrence River enticed many to take a trip, especially of the Gaspé Peninsula. Many middle and upper-middle class Montrealers either own or rent summer and winter cottages in the countryside. The advertisers' call beckoned many working class Quebecers, especially the youth, who hitchhiked, camped out, or stayed with relatives , if other means were not available. It is within this socio-cultural ambience that the definitions and experiences of friendship in this book are framed. When people speak about agreeing or disagreeing with their close friends, they mean agreeing or disagreeing about these events, buildings, songs, plays, and issues. When people report sharing common activities with their friends, they refer to doing the types of activities that have been briefly outlined in this description.

Definitions and Perceptions of Friendship in Contemporary Montreal

Herbert Blumer reminds us that as human beings "we act singly, collectively, and societally on the basis of the meanings which things have for us." Friends are one of the innumerable objects which have meanings on the basis of which we act toward them. Blumer observes that in:

our activities we wend our way by recognizing an object to be such and such, by defining the situations with which we are presented, by attaching a meaning to this or that event, and where need be, by devising a new meaning to cover something new or different. This is done by the individual in his personal action, it is done by a group of individuals acting together in concert, it is done in each of the manifold activities which together constitute an institution in operation, and it is done in each of the diversified acts which fit into and make up the patterned activity of a social structure or a society.[28]

There are a variety of ways the sociologist and anthropologist can find out about the meaning of friendship at a given moment. Great methodologists, such as Louis Guttman, have stressed the value of replicating former studies. Jean Maisonneuve had formulated a question in his book on the social psychology of the elective affinities, and it seemed to me to be a reasonable place to begin an investigation of friendship in contemporary Montreal. "What is a friend? What is (or what are) the sign (or the signs) of a true friendship?"[29] While the social scientist conducts formal interviews with his sample of individuals, he or she can listen to the ways in which people in different milieu and social situations employ the words, friend and friendship. This method may entail eavesdropping on conversations, clipping quotes from printed matter, and jotting down or recording relevant quips from television, the radio, movies, and daily interaction. I followed this procedure as well while I was gathering the formal interviews for my study. Of course, the more empiricist and behavioral will demand a battery of objective questions to be responded to on a formal questionnaire that reveals what people really report about doing in friendship in their own lives. To satisfy this type of inquirer I administered the La Gaipa and Bigelow instrument but performed factorial analysis on the whole set of responses. Also, it may be helpful to use unabridged dictionaries and related literary references to examine how the often antiquated meanings have changed in relationship to life in today's world. Although this latter step is out of favor with the here and now consensus of a majority of social scientists, it, nonetheless, remains quite informative; so I have availed myself of this technique of classical literary analysis. Finally, the validity of the information collected needs to be checked by asking these same questions to the same people in another place or time or through different instruments.

Michael E. Roloff and Charles R. Berger provide us with a summary definition of social cognition as how people think about people, involving thought processes, thought focused on human interaction, and thought organized in some fashion, that vary in the degree to which they are true representations of self, others, and behaviors.[30] In applying this broad definition to how we think about friends, we first run into the problem of putting together our various data bases which give quite different nuances to people's definitions and perceptions of friends. As depicted by one recent model, these definitions are processes "which encompass cognitive, affective, and behavioral categories as well as proxy measures."[31]

Jean Maisonneuve categorized his French subjects' definitions of friendship into three large categories, each with their subcategories which he classified according to the "socio-professional" ("socio-economic") background of these respondents.[32] I was initially quite hesitant to "stuff" my Quebec data into these categories for content analysis designed for French data, so first I performed a protothematic analysis of data by breaking up how Montrealers had defined friendship into subcategories of response for each individual. These subcategories were then rewritten on new IBM cards and became the title for the related prototheme of friendship. In all my analysis sorted out 48 "protothemes" of which 16 were quite frequent.[33] After carrying out this protothematic analysis, I could be more assured that Maisonneuve's categories were appropriate for the Montrealers' definitions of friendship, so subsequently I also used Maisonneuve's classification system to analyze these same Montreal data. In the following discussion I will combine the common findings of these two methods with the results of the factor analysis of answers to Bigelow's and La Gaipa's questionnaire about friendship.[34]

It is reasonable to call the divisions into which the respondents' replies were categorized as social cognitions of friendship because they are a researcher's attempt at reporting as objectively as possible the apparent componential areas of people's thoughts about friends and friendship. Let us designate the first social cognition of friendship as *communication*. Communication is the most complex subfield of friendship thought, for it contains the most diverse subcategories. Communication includes reciprocal affection, which is expressed by such responses as "love, affection, feeling, tenderness, and distinctions between degrees of friendship." Communication incorporates the pleasure of being together, which is marked by "hitting it off, happiness, enjoying each other's company, and being someone with whom you can have fun." Communication implies sharing joys and sorrows like "sharing of experiences and feelings" while being comfortable in your friend's "presence." To communicate means confiding and being intimate together. These actions are recognized by confiding in, sharing secrets, openness, feeling free to talk with one's friends, counseling, and not talking behind your friend's back. Communication is noted by mutual understanding, "a mutual, deep knowledge, an acceptance" of your friend. Communicating is characterized by being frank, sincere, and not secretive. These traits are seen in a friend who is "a sincere, frank person," someone who is "truthful" and "responsible." This type of friendship is seen in the ability for friends to have differences of opinion and criticize each other without getting hurt. Communication is found in a community of ideas and tastes. This realm is demarcated by the similarity of friends' personalities, interests, tastes, and values and was often described in abstract language such as "someone who shares the same ideals and thoughts." A related subset of communication contains the elements of friends' resemblance to each other, of friends' being another self, and of friends' being kin like a brother or a sister. And communication subsumes friends' complementing each other and a physical side to friendship. The first factor suggests that communication between close friends operates on the levels of the spoken word and through the emotional feelings of openness, genuineness, and lack of defensiveness. Knowing that mutual aid is available leads to feelings of security and reciprocity, which contribute to friends' actually enjoying each other's company. This enjoyment is accompanied by consideration and respect, as seen in the items of factor six. Finally factor two emphasizes the positive character traits, interests, and likeness of closest friends.

Helping out is the second large cognitive subdivision of friendship. Helping out requires that we be able to count on and stick by our friends in all circumstances. Montrealers said that they can depend and rely on their friends, that they are always there. Such real friends were said to be rare. Friends show that they are helping out in three principal ways. They give material aid and services. "Helping out in time of trouble," "an experience which embellishes life during tough times," "mutual aid," and "chasing away one's enemies," were some ways in which Montrealers characterized this part of friendship. Equally important to this material aid is boosting morale that is often sought after in unhappiness. Also, on the same level as these other aspects of helping out are devotion, sacrifice, and disinterestedness. In combining the results of different methods of deciphering the definitions of friendship, it should be noted that independent judges found that the Bigelow-La Gaipa test focused on communication to a much greater extent than Maisonneuve's other supercategories of mutual aid and fidelity that were derived from spontaneous notions of friendship. Noting this difference in emphasis between the two methods, we can observe that the Bigelow-La Gaipa test portrays the sentiments of "helping out" as being quite well integrated into factors stressing communication. Factor three stresses that the intimate secrets, thoughts, advice, and problems which close friends talk about in an atmosphere of personal warmth and support leave one's close friend with the feelings of reliance and of being an important person. And factor five puts together the similarity of one's friend's characteristics, attitudes, and opinions with the feelings of concern, trust, support, dependability, and tolerance of differences. The major elements of factor seven focus on closest friends' building up and boosting ego's self concept and actions in a secure, relaxed environment.

And the eighth factor points to the responsibility and seriousness of closest friends which make it possible for them to be counted on and enjoyed at the same time.

Fidelity is the third main subfield in the cognition of friends and friendship. Trust and loyalty are its first set of components. Such honesty gives the friend an aura of being "a person in whom one can have confidence," "someone who admires you," someone with whom you have "mutual esteem," and someone with whom you have "no need of reassurance or guarantees." Fidelity is also marked by constancy and perenniality which give a holy quality to friendship. Montrealers claimed that a friend is a "person you are with a lot of the time" and that friendship is "something that should last a long time," and that it is a "relation cultivated over the years." The psycho-social traits that enable friends to be faithful are regrouped into factor four. These qualities are those of tolerance and strength of character, which permit differences of opinion in a basic emotional milieu of unaffected positive regard.

When we look at the relative weights of these supercategorical divisions of the definitions of friendship, we find that communication stands in first place, if we base ourselves on the number of times the elements of the definitions of friendship were encoded under this label. The theme of helping out comes in second place, and is followed by the field of fidelity. In comparing the results of the Montreal definitions from the mid-1970s with those reported on by Maisonneuve in France from the mid-1950s, we note a similar importance given to the major social cognitions of friendship between the France of the mid-1950s and the Montreal of the mid-1970s. This result suggests that Montrealers had not begun to view their friendships as more short-term or disposable, as thought to be a historical change by some scholars of interpersonal relationships.[35] In the next chapter a third, multivariate cross-validation of the definitions of friendship suggests that Jean Maisonneuve's three super-content-analytical categories should be reduced to two large facets, "communication" and "steadfastness."

Besides saying best friend, close friend, good friend, *meilleur ami, ami intime, de bons amis,* there are a host of other expressions by which

Montrealers indicate progressively lesser degrees of friendship, such as chum, buddy, *copain, copine, camarade, mes amis les Perrault, connaissance*, and acquaintance. When I studied these terms to determine whether or not major demographic variables produced any variance in their usage, I found no statistically significant differences.

However, all of these definitions and perceptions of friends and friendship are very much colored by the occupational, ideological, and situational factors of the interviewees. For example, a Catholic brother in his sixties, who lived in a residence for other brothers in the vicinity of The Oratory of St. Joseph, invited me back several times to clarify some points of the questionnaire. These sessions with him were not unlike prayer meetings. As he wrote and spoke, he replied in French:

> I speak in terms of "best" friends and "close" friends to whom you reveal not only your good side but to whom you show your weak points and faults, even pure being received by the other as you are and being healed and pardoned by His love that is stronger and greater than our flaws and misdeeds ....

Although this brother's response emphasizes that a close or best friend can accept his friend insofar as the Divine has forgiven and repaired the friend's sins and poor conduct, this gentleman's great emotionality and religious fervor that were witnessed in the interview help us to understand what he means about his vocabulary of friendship and related terms.

I carried out a content analysis of these definitions of a friend and friendship to discover if the interviewee stressed herself ("A true friend understands me, helps me, and remains loyal to me"), the other ("For a friend I'd (or you'd) be ready to go out of your way for"), or the reciprocity of the friend bond ("Among friends, you say any and everything; you help out one other"). Although most of the definitions mixed together all three relational orientations, they, nevertheless, tended to be ego-centered.[36] This finding lends support to Maisonneuve's interpretation that

> we tend to characterize our friends and preferred
> companions according to a model oscillating between the
> present image which we have of ourselves and that of our
> ideal personality but as a function of our own level of
> acceptance and self-esteem.[37]

When social scientists examine an interview, they look for the internal consistency in what the person said and reflect on their own impressions of the person's conduct and environment and how they relate to what was said. The resulting recorded accounts gathered leave precise texts of what was said. Making sense out of the interview is, however, a more complicated process. For instance, the componential units of the theme of communication may spatially occupy the largest part of a definition of friendship, and then suddenly the interviewee may interject that she thinks that a subtheme of helping out is the most important element of friendship. In such a case, the social scientist must decide whether to take her at her word, whether to rely on the frequency of the communication subthemes mentioned, or whether to employ some other criterion. In my hermeneutics of the friendship account, I have attempted to use several different methods and to explain my situated procedures of interpretation. Having reported on the more quantitative analyses of the definitions of friendship, let us take a brief look at how they are integrated into the larger whole of an account of friendship.

My chief French-language interviewer was Ms. Michèle Verrette, a native speaker of Quebec French, a Montrealer, educated in the schools of the Catholic School Commission, a holder of a degree in social science from the University of Montreal. Ms. Verrette is an emotionally intense, attractive female in her mid-to-late twenties at the time of the interviews. Driving to the addresses from our random sample that were located all over the city, we did many of the interviews together. One evening we drove to one of the addresses located in a working class neighborhood, in an ethnically mixed area, not far to the east of Saint Lawrence Boulevard, the traditional dividing line between the "French" and the "English" sides of the city. Having interviewers of both sexes eases the initial transition in a interview situation. Ms. Verrette accompanied me to the door and introduced us to a thirty-three year old woman, a former teacher of English, who was soon to be divorced. In this attractive apartment, furnished in modern Scandinavian with a colorful wall-to-wall carpet and a large piano, located in a rather modest building, we talked for a few minutes before Michèle had to leave for another appointment. This well-groomed, somewhat hefty, fashionably but conservatively dressed in tweed, French Canadian professional had come from a family of which her father, now deceased, had been a lawyer and her mother a housewife. She exuded a great deal of interest in the interview. Her heavy smoking seemed to indicate a general or situationally high level of anxiety, although she described her own personality as being very nervous and always on the move. In response to my question, "What is a friend? What is (or what are) in your opinion the sign (or the signs) of a true friendship?" she replied in French:

> I would say that a friend is someone who understands us, someone in whom you can confide, to whom you can tell everything, but also someone who knows how to listen. You really have to do it for her in my opinion.
> I would say that the sign of a true friendship is understanding. The real sign, in my opinion, is that when you are bad off, it's a question of helping out. It's always toward a friend that you turn, in my opinion, for whatever reason, whether because of a sickness, of something going wrong at work, in whatever area, when you are really bad off, you turn to friend. Then it is the person who comes to get us going, and who really does it out of a good heart, without asking anything in return. That is a true friend.

Then I asked her, "When you say 'get me going,' are you referring to something?"

She answered,

> I said that as being the most important. It's not at all simply that. It can also be people with whom you get along pleasantly, with whom you find yourself to have a good time. It's not just people you go to get out of a fix, to whom you go to say, "I'm in a bad way; come get me." First of all

it's people you chose. It's people with whom you chose to
live.

As we learn later in our conversation about her two closest friends,
the series of particular memories of acts, thoughts, and symbols, set in
a background of very different personalities, emphasize emotional
prestations, although some of this exchange of emotions and advice is
conceptualized as helping out.

Dictionary Definitions of Friend and Its Derivatives

The great unabridged dictionaries of the natural languages resemble
museum catalogues. When perusing their pages, the researcher can find
long listings of the various usages and varieties of words cited in literary
documents. Unlike the philosophical encyclopedias, dictionaries do not
address the underlying set of concepts, institutions, and beliefs that
marked a particular recorded entry. Despite this lack of a proper
context, these reference works provide the curious with striking
contrasts with how terms are used in other places or in the past in
comparison to how the notion is used in a particular place today.
Examining these dictionaries for friend, friendship, friendly, friendless,
and so forth, and their French equivalents, can help us trace the
parameters of the relationship we are studying.[38] For example, dueling
is no longer a custom, so "friend" is not "applied to duel," nor could I
record the items "heavy friend, small friend" to signify an enemy.[39] Nor
did the variants friendable, meaning friendly; ill or well friended;
friendess; friendful; friendism; friendlihood; friendman; friendrede; or
friendsome crop up in current Montreal speaking or writing. Likewise,
only a fraction of the enormous variety of the usages of "*ami, ie, amitié*"
in French dictionaries occur in the contemporary Montreal French I
recorded. For instance, I did not come across Montreal expressions
similar to Molière's usage of "*Ami de cours,*" meaning "he who only has
false appearances of being a friend" or "*ami du genre humain*" referring
to "a friend of everyone's and no one's." While I could systematically

describe each of the comparisons and contrasts between current and dead speech about friends, I will draw upon this resource only to throw light on the current words and expressions of friend and friendship as they appear in my interviews and observations.

Within the field of these cognitions of friendship, I can begin to sketch the dominant styles of friendship found in contemporary Montreal.[40]

Notes

1. Benveniste, Émile, *Le vocabulaire des institutions indo-européennes: 1. économie, parenté, société* (Paris: Les Éditions de Minuit, 1969).

2. Cohen, Yehudi, *Social Structure and Personality: A Casebook* (New York: Holt, Rinehart, and Winston, 1961); DuBois, Cora, ed., *Studies of Friendship* (Boston: Harvard University, 1953); Brain, Robert, *Friends and Lovers* (New York: Basic Books, Inc., Publishers, 1976).

3. Gurdin, Joseph Barry, "*Amitié*/Friendship: The Socio-cultural Construction of Friendship in Contemporary Montreal." Ph.D. diss., Department of Sociology, Université de Montréal, 1978, 1-161.

4. *Dictionnaire alphabétique et analogique de la langue française*, s.v. "Ami - amitié," ed. Paul Robert. Paris: Société du Nouveau Littré, 1960, 132-135; *Édition abrégée dictionnaire canadien français-anglais anglais-français*, s. v. "Ami, e, amitié." Toronto: McClelland and Stewart, 19; *The Gage Canadian Dictionary*, s.v. "Chum" and "friend - friendship." Toronto: Gage Educational Publishing Ltd., 1973, 203; 467; *Glossarium Mediae et Infimae Latinitatis*, Tomus 1. s. v. "amiabilis - amicus." Conditum a Cardo du Fresne Domino du Cange: Niort, L. Favre, 1883, 223-224; *Lexicon Totius Latinitatis*, Tom 1, s.v. "Amicabilis, e - amicus." AB Aeugidio Forcellini: Arnaldus Forni Excudebat Bonoiae Gregoriana Edente Patavii, 1965, 215-217; *Lipsiae in aedibus*, Vol. 1, s.v. "amicabilis, e - amicitia, ae," and "amicus - amicus," B. G. Tevbner, 1900, 1891-1914; *Littré dictionnaire de la langue française*, Tome 1, s.v. "Ami, ie - amitié." Monte Carlo: Édition du Cap, 1970; 191-193; *The Oxford Dictionary of English Etymology*, ed. Charles Talbut Onions.

Oxford: Clarendon Press, 1966, 37; *The Oxford English Dictionary Being a Corrected Re-issue with an Introduction, Supplement, and Bibliography of a New English Dictionary on Historical Principles Founded Mainly on the Materials Collected by The Philological Society*, Vol. 4, F-G, s.v. "Friend, friendship." Oxford: Oxford at the Clarendon Press, 1933, 545-547; OED, *The Oxford English Dictionary*. Oxford: Clarendon Press, 1961; *Trésor de la langue française. Dictionnaire de la langue du XIXe et du XXe siècle (1789-1960)*. Centre National de la Recherche Scientifique. Centre de Recherche pour un Trésor de la Langue Française-Nancy. Tome Deuxième: Affinerie - Anfractuosité, ed. Paul Imbs. Paris: Éditions du Centre National de la Recherche Scientifique, 1973, 754-771; 779-787.

5. Fraisse, Jean-Claude, *Philia: La notion d'amitié dans la philosophie antique: essai sur un problème perdu et retrouvé* (Paris: Philosophique J. Vrin, 1974).

6. Gurdin, 1978, 1-161.

7. Benveniste, 110; Ibid., 103; Ibid., 113.

8. Fraisse, *Philia*, 32.

9. Ibid., 1974. Also see: Hutter, Horst, *Politics as Friendship* (Waterloo, Ontario: Wilfrid Laurier University Press, 1978).

10. Fraisse, *Philia*, 450.

11. Hutter, 92.

12. Fraisse, *Philia*, 453.

13. Ibid., 454.

14. Ibid., 456.

15. Kon, I. S., "Druzhba - Friendship," in *Bol'shaia Sovetskaia Entsiklopediia* [*Great Soviet Encyclopedia*], (Moscow: Sovetskaia Entsiklopediia Publishing House, 1962), 76-77.

16. Silver, A., "Friendship in Commercial Society: Eighteenth-Century Social Theory and Modern Sociology," in *American Journal of Sociology*, 95, 1474-1504, cited by Rosemary Blieszner and Rebecca G. Adams, *Adult Friendship* (Newbury Park: Sage Publications, 1992), 30-31.

17. Sirois, Antoine, *Montréal dans le roman canadien* (Montréal: Marcel Didier, 1968), XIII-XXII.

18. Desbiens, Jean-Paul, "Looking to the Future." *Forces: Economic, Social and Cultural Quarterly*, ed. Marcel Couture (Montréal: la Société d'édition de la revue Forces), 100 (Hiver 1992-199), 54-55.

19. McKenna, Brian and Susan Purcell, *Drapeau* (Markham, Ontario: Penguin Books, Ltd., 1980).

20. Stoler, Peter, "Land of Hope and Hustle." *Time Magazine*, 5 October 1987.

21. Coulon, Jocelyn. "L'industrie militaire au Québec. Plus de 100,000 personnes travaillent pour ce secteur," *Le Devoir*, lundi, 2 fevrier 1987.

22. Shragge, Eric, Babin, Ronald, and Jean-Guy Vaillancourt, *Roots of Peace: The Movement Against Militarism in Canada* (Toronto: DEC Book Distribution, 1986).

23. Lejeune, Jean Paul, "The Economy--between the Boom Times and New Expansion: Interview with Jean Guertin, Director, École des Hautes Études Commerciales, Montreal." ed. Marcel Couture, *Forces: Economic, social and cultural quarterly* (Montréal: la Société d'édition de la revue Forces), 100 (Hiver 1992-199)], 78-81. Also see: Bartlett, Donald L. and James B. Steele, *America: What Went Wrong?* (Kansas City, Missouri: Andrews and McMeel, 1992).

24. Drouin, Richard, "Crown Corporations: An Original Contribution to the Economic, Political and Social Development." In Couture, 82-89.

25. I received Grand Chief Mathew Coon-Come's letter as a mailing from The National Resources Defense Council. That organization encouraged concerned citizens to write the Ambassador to the United States, Embassy of Canada, 501 Pennsylvania Avenue, N.W., Washington, D.C. 20001 and to the Chairman and CEO, Hydro-Quebec, 75, blvd. René-Lévesque Ouest, Montreal, Québec, H2Z 1A4, pointing out the environmental dangers and alternatives to the project.

26. Richler, Mordecai, *Oh Canada! Oh Quebec: Requiem for a Divided Country* (New York: Penguin Books), 213-219; Farnsworth, Clyde H. "An Uneasy Peace -- And No Peace of Mind: In Quebec, Indians Look back in

Anger at Oka Crisis," *San Francisco Sunday Examiner and Chronicle*, 6 February 1994, *Sunday Punch.*

27. Petrowski, Nathalie, *Notes de la salle de rédaction* (Montréal: Les Editions coopératives Albert Saint-Martin de Montréal, 1983).

28. Blumer, Herbert, "Sociological Analysis and the 'Variable'," in *Symbolic Interaction. A Reader in Social Psychology*, 2nd ed. by J. G. Manis and B. N. Meltzer (Boston: Allyn and Bacon, Inc., (1956) 1972), 96.

29. Maisonneuve, Jean, *Psycho-sociologie des affinités* (Paris: Presses universitaires de France, 1966), 512; 515.

30. Roloff, Michael E. and Charles R. Berger, *Social Cognition and Communication* (Beverly Hills, California: Sage Publications, 1982), 9-26.

31. Blieszner, Rosemary and Rebecca G. Adams, *Adult Friendship.* (Newbury Park, CA: Sage Publications, 1992), 61.

32. Maisonneuve, 191.

33. See Gurdin, Joseph Barry, 1978, 221-293. A prototheme indexes a respondent's definition of friendship. Thus, using TF to represent "Theme Friend," followed by a number representing which prototheme, I divided the first French Canadian respondent's answer to "What is a friend?" in the following way:

un ami:	*1. une personne en qui on peut avoir confiance* [TF4]
	2. qui ne nous laisse pas tomber au premier mauvais coup [TF5]
	3. mais qui nous aide à en sortir [TF7]
	4. même si on est un bon moment sans se voir on ne s'oublie pas [TF16]

Then on a separate computer card, I recorded all the components from respondents' definitions which were labeled as belonging to a certain prototheme, say *Prototheme 1*, which hinges around the cognitive field of "similarity of the personality, interests, tastes, and values of friends."

Protothematic analysis establishes a folk dictionary of the lexical items of {friend} and {friendship}. It reduces redundancy through grouping and regrouping of surface text. Each one of these protothemes was crosstabulated for presence and absence of twenty-two sociological categories taken (compared) two at a time in the following manner: 1) French Canadian Professional, French Canadian Blue Collar Worker; 2) French Canadian Professional, French Canadian White Collar Worker; 3) French Canadian White Collar Worker, French Canadian Blue Collar Worker; 4) French Canadian Male, French Canadian Female; 5) French Canadian Younger, French Canadian Older; 6) English Canadian Professional, English Canadian White Collar Worker; 7) English Canadian Professional, English Canadian Blue Collar Worker, etc. Note that in this book I use the term "White Collar Worker" to refer to the category I denoted as "Employee" in my thesis. In my dissertation I used the term "Worker" for the category I refer to as "Blue Collar Worker" in this book. Likewise, in my thesis I used the category "Youth" which I have renamed "Younger" in this work. For each of these comparisons two crosstabulations were run: the first is called the "grouping method" and the second the "item method." By the grouping method two entries from the same individual regrouped under the same prototheme count as "one" because they come from the same individual. For the item method two entries from the same individual count as "two" because they are independently divided as separate meaningful units of the same individual's answer and so forth.

More French Canadian Youngers as compared to English Canadian Youngers defined friend in a way that emphasized similarity of the personality, interests, tastes, and values of the friends. $\chi 2$ is significant at α .02 by the grouping method, and $\chi 2$ is significant at α .01 by the item method for this first prototheme.

More English Canadian Females' as compared to French Canadian Females' definitions of friendship were classified under the second prototheme that stressed "depending on, loyalty, counting on, relying on, sticking by, *sur qui l'on peut compter, on peut se fier, celle qui est toujours là.*" $\chi2$ is significant at α .05 by the grouping method, and $\chi2$ is significant at α .02 by the item method for this second prototheme.

More English Canadian Professionals as compared to English Canadian Blue Collar Workers emphasized "understanding and acceptance, *la connaissance mutuelle approfondie*," the third prototheme, in their definitions of friendship. $\chi2$ is significant at α .01 by the grouping method, and $\chi2$ is significant at α .05 by the item method for this comparison. Moreover, more English Canadian Females as compared to English Canadian Males stress this third prototheme in defining friendship. $\chi2$ is significant at α .05 by both the grouping and item methods for this comparison.

The fourth prototheme consists of such components of the definition of friendship as "confiding in, sharing secrets, openness, feeling free to talk with," modified by "*quelqu'un de pas bavard*." The English Canadians stressed "in providing guidance and counsel" and the French Canadians the aspect of secrecy of the communication, i.e. "*sans qui'il aille répéter aux autres ce qu'on lui a dit*." More White Collar Workers as compared to Blue Collar Workers are found in this category. $\chi2$ is significant at α .02 by the item method for this comparison, and $\chi2$ is almost significant at α .05 [$\chi2 = 3.832$ ($\chi2 = 3.841$ at α .05; 1 degree of freedom)] by the grouping method for this fourth prototheme.

"Sharing of experiences, feelings, in whose presence you feel comfortable, *être bien dans la peau avec quelqu'un, ceux avec qui tu peus partager*," form the core of the fifth prototheme. More English Canadian Professionals as compared to English Canadian Blue Collar Workers stressed these components in their definitions of friendship. $\chi2$ is significant at α .02 by both the grouping and item methods for this comparison. Similarly, more English Canadian White Collar Workers' as compared to English Canadian Blue Collar Workers' definitions fell into this prototheme. $\chi2$ is significant at α .05 by the grouping method, and $\chi2$ is significant at α .02 by the item method for this comparison. In general, more White Collar Workers as compared to Blue Collar Workers defined friendship in this manner. $\chi2$ is significant at α .02 by both the grouping and item methods for this comparison.

"Trust, honesty, *une personne en qui on peut avoir confiance, l'honnêteté*" are typical of items of the sixth prototheme. More French Canadian Professionals as compared to French Canadian Blue Collar Workers defined a friend in this fashion. $\chi 2$ is significant at α .05 by the grouping method, and $\chi 2$ is significant at α .01 by the item method for this comparison. Likewise, more French Canadian Professionals as compared to French Canadian White Collar Workers defined friendship in this way. $\chi 2$ is significant at α .01 by both methods. More English Canadian White Collar Workers as compared to French Canadian White Collar Workers defined friendship in this way. $\chi 2$ is significant at α .05 by the grouping method, and $\chi 2$ is significant at α .01 by the item method for this comparison.

"Helping out in time of trouble, *qui peut nous rendre service, une expérience qui embellit la vie durant les dures moments*" are the kind of items in the seventh prototheme, which accounts for boosting morale and material aid. There is a strong tendency--almost attaining statistical significance at α .05--for more English Canadian Males as compared to English Canadian Females to underscore prototheme seven in their definitions of friendship.

More English Canadian Youngers as compared to English Canadian Olders stress prototheme eight, which contains such responses as "giving; without thought of being paid; who'll do you favors without asking for one in return." $\chi 2$ is significant at α .01 by both methods for this comparison.

The ninth prototheme regroups items such as "concern, mutual feeling of wishing only the best for one another, *le désir de faire plaisir, quelqu'un qui nous veut du bien et à qui l'on veut du bien.*" More French Canadian Professionals' as compared to French Canadian Blue Collar Workers' responses were classified under this prototheme. $\chi 2$ is significant at α .05 by the grouping method, and $\chi 2$ is significant at α .02 by the item method for this comparison.

"Love, affection, *l'amitié est un ressentir, tendresse*" typify the items of the tenth prototheme. There is a strong tendency for more English Canadian Females as compared to French Canadian Females to define friendship in this manner. This result is significant at α .05 for the item method [$\chi2 = 4.211$] and approaches significance at α .05 [$\chi2 = 3.630$] by the grouping method.

"Respect; *quelqu'un t'admire*; *l'estime vis-à-vis l'un de l'autre*" fills the twelfth prototheme. There is a strong tendency for more English Canadian Olders as compared to English Canadian Youngers to use these items in defining friendship. At one degree of freedom by both methods, $\chi2 = 3.525$ and approaches significance at α .05 [$\chi2 = 3.84$]. There is also a tendency for more Male as compared to Female items to be classified under this prototheme. This result is significant at α .05 for the item method [$\chi2 = 4.252$; 1 degree of freedom] and approaches significance at α .05 [$\chi2 = 3.382$] by the grouping method.

The sixteenth prototheme is composed of such items as "something that should last a long time; person you are with a lot of the time; *relation cultivée avec des années, constant; fidelité*." More English Canadian Males as compared to French Canadian Males define friendship in this way. This result is significant at α .05 for the grouping method and at α .01 by the item method. There is also a strong tendency for more French Canadian Youngers as compared to English Canadian Youngers to have responses classified under prototheme sixteen. This result is significant at α .05 for the grouping method [$\chi2 = 4.055$; 1 degree of freedom] and approaches significance [$\chi2 = 3.702$] by the item method at 1 degree of freedom.

The physical side of friendship is dealt with in the nineteenth prototheme. More French Canadian Males as compared to French Canadian Females have answers grouped into this prototheme. This result is significant at α .05 for the grouping method [$\chi2 = 4.4339$; 1 degree of freedom] and is significant at α .01 [$\chi2 = 7.636$] by the item method at 1 degree of freedom.

"*Une personne sincère, franche; la sincérité*; truthful" are the core elements of Prototheme 25. More English Canadian Professionals as compared to French Canadian Professionals have elements of their definitions of friendship classified under this prototheme. This result is significant at α .05 for the grouping method and is significant at α .01 by the item method at 1 degree of freedom.

The significant differences which surfaced through protothematic analysis were not crossvalidated at a statistically significant level by the content analysis reviewed in the following paragraphs. Thus I cannot claim them to be reliable. However, some of the non-statistically significant trends in the content analysis point to similar statistically significant differences noted in the protothematic analysis, and I have integrated these correspondences in my tracing the cognitive field of {friend} and {friendship} in my main text. Therefore, I agree with Seymour Martin Lipset's methodological proposal that a sociologist can emphasize theoretical and logical consistency in connecting data. See: Lipset, Seymour Martin, *Continental Divide: The Values and Institutions of the United States and Canada* (New York: Routledge, 1990), *xvi*.

After much resistance, I forced myself to categorize my data from Montreal into the categories established by Jean Maisonneuve for his data from France. The correspondences are clear only in the cases of protothemes 3, 4, 5, 6 , 9, 10, 11, 13, 16, 26, 38, and 40. In several cases the categories cut up a prototheme, as is the case for protothemes 1, 7, 8, and 16. In the cases of protothemes 12, 14, 15, 17, 18, 19, 20, 23, 27, 28, 31, 32, 33, 36, 38, 40, 42, 44, 45, 46, and 47, the meaning of the response is practically absent or evident only after thin and complicated reasoning fit it into one of the categories of Jean Maisonneuve's content analysis. Protothemes 22, 24, 30, 34, 37, 39, and 48 could not be classified into Maisonneuve's categories. Nevertheless, the following rough correspondences may be drawn:

Communication	Prototheme
Reciprocal Affection	9, 10, 14, 29
Pleasure of Being Together	11, 17, 18, 26, 43, 44
Sharing Joys and Sorrows	5
Confiding (Being Intimate Together)	4, 32, 33, 45
Mutual Understanding	3
Being Frank, Sincere (Not Secretive)	25, 28, 38, 40
Community of Ideas, of Tastes	1, 13, 15
Friends Resemble Each Other (Friend Another Self: Friend-Brother)	1, 2, 23, 47
Friends Complement Each Other	1, 19
L'Entraide [Helping out Each Other]	
Count on the Friends in All Circumstances	2, 20
Material Aid, Services	7, 8, 31, 46
Moral Support (Sought after in Unhappiness)	5, 7, 8, 35
Devotion, Sacrifice, Disinterestedness	16, 21, 27, 36, 49
Fidelité [Fidelity]	
Trust, Loyalty	6, 12, 42
Constancy, Perenniality	14, 16, 41

In regard to the classification of the respondents' definitions into Maisonneuve's content analytical categories, none of the major demographic variables studied--ethnicity, class, age, and sex--produced statistically significant differences, although I did observe some notable trends. See Gurdin, 1978, 223-236.

In the following tables, Method "1" takes into consideration one count per all encoded occurrences within each of the three large categories per interviewee's definition, whereas Method "P" registers each subcategorical encoded occurrence per interviewee's definition and results in a regular cumulative summation for each of the three large categories.

Table 1.1 Method "1": A Content Analysis of the Definitional Components of Friendship by the Ethnicity of the Respondent

Count Column %	English Canadian	French Canadian	Total
Communication	89 40.5%	23 46%	112 41.5%
Helping out Each Other	73 33.2%	15 30%	88 32.6%
Fidelity	58 26.4%	12 24%	70 25.93%
Column Total	220 81.5%	50 18.5%	270 100%

$\chi 2 = .516$ Not Significant

As can be seen in Maisonneuve's results, the French data yielded very similar results to my Montreal sample analyzed by Method "1," the more common statistical procedure:

Count Column %	French
Communication	290 43%
Helping Out Each Other	233 35%
Fidelity	147 22%
Column Total	670 100%

Table 1.2 Method "P": A Content Analysis of the Definitions of Friendship by Subcategories of the Definitional Components of Friendship

Communication	Frequency of Encoded Responses	Percentage of Communication	Percentage of All Themes
Reciprocal Affection	42	15.11%	8.62%
Pleasure of Being Together	54	19.43%	11.1%
Sharing Joys and Sorrows	25	8.99%	5.13%
Confiding (Being Intimate Together)	51	18.35%	10.47%
Mutual Understanding	37	13.31%	7.6%
Being Frank, Sincere, (Not Secretive)	34	12.23%	6.98%
Community of Ideas, of Tastes	23	8.27%	4.72%
Friends Resemble Each Other (Friend Another Self)	9	3.24%	1.85%
Friends Complement Each Other	3	1.08%	0.0062%
Theme of Communication	278		57.08%
Helping out Each Other			
Count on the Friends in All Circumstances	60	47.24%	12.32%
Material Aid, Services	12	17.32%	2.46%
Moral Support (Sought after in Unhappiness)	22	17.32%	4.5%
Devotion, Sacrifice, Disinterestedness	33	25.98%	6.78%
Theme of Helping out Each Other	127		26.08%
Fidelity			
Trust, Loyalty	55	67.07%	11.29%
Constancy, Perenniality, (Friendship Is Holy)	27	32.93%	5.54%
Theme of Fidelity	82		16.84%
Total of the Encoded Responses	**487**		**100%**

34. The items of the Bigelow and La Gaipa instrument form the content of the factor analysis. When reading the factors, refer to the numbers to the left of the item that correspond to the number code given to the left of each factor loading. The following items that appear on that instrument refer to the interviewee's best friend or to the interviewee and his or her best friend:

1. Appreciates and praises what I do.
2. Like to spend a lot of time together.
3. Interested in my welfare and gives me his (her) moral support.
4. Puts his abilities to good use.
5. Cares about my feelings.
6. Can feel at ease to express my most intimate feelings with.
7. Supports and defends his (her) beliefs.
8. In time of need I could count on this person.
9. Have traits of personality in common.
10. Increases my self-worth.
11. Could reveal to him (her) my deepest experiences and ambitions.
12. He (she) is him- (her-)self with me.
13. Have similar attitudes and opinions.
14. Has serious goals and accomplishes them.
15. Doesn't try to take advantage of me.
16. Believes that my ideas are important.
17. Could divulge to him (her) some shameful things which I've done.
18. Does not permit differences of opinion.
19. Encourages me.
20. I feel free to be myself with this person.
21. Does things for me out of kindness and expects nothing in return.
22. Feels that our relation is important.
23. Recognizes his (her) duties as member of society.
24. Could speak with this person of my most intimate family problems.
25. Could spend an agreeable evening together.
26. Constantly protects me.
27. I feel relaxed and secure with this person.
28. Respects my convictions even if he (she) does not share them.
29. Have several interests in common.
30. Honestly gives advice when asked.
31. Has strength of character.
32. Can leave aside a defensive attitude and be myself with him (her).
33. Feels that I am an important and interesting person.
34. Can speak with this person about my personal problems.
35. More interested in me than the advantages he (she) can get out of me.

Varimax Rotated Factor Matrix after Rotation with Kaiser Normalization: Factors 1 - 4 (Bigelow-La Gaipa); Questionnaire data. F = Factor in the column headings.

	F1	F2	F3	F4
ITEM 1	-.11135	.51726	.16896	.07355
ITEM 2	.60332	.05727	-.08737	.03045
ITEM 3	.53250	.26947	.11239	.01348
ITEM 4	.11398	.73971	.04170	-.05023
ITEM 5	.57475	.19207	.13869	-.12948
ITEM 6	.70365	.10797	.44921	-.16243
ITEM 7	.42617	.43396	-.01270	.02659
ITEM 8	.74744	.04867	.13957	.03941
ITEM 9	.13284	.18570	.13416	.18954
ITEM 10	.22561	.29658	.05324	.10561
ITEM 11	.53404	.02123	.49256	.01650
ITEM 12	.30988	.24628	.20739	.35821
ITEM 13	.16485	.49593	.03367	.31767
ITEM 14	.24575	.59157	.06160	-.08170
ITEM 15	.62513	.13586	-.00860	.13196
ITEM 16	.15656	.39208	.17242	.25082
ITEM 17	.24256	.21271	.79385	.22381
ITEM 18	.09479	.00597	.07117	.53241
ITEM 19	.46893	.20864	.29200	.24680
ITEM 20	.85831	.09836	.02955	.12180
ITEM 21	.62470	.00099	.15637	.16390
ITEM 22	.72171	.04144	-.00709	.14920
ITEM 23	.03902	.08361	.00164	-.00204
ITEM 24	.63410	-.05070	.29821	.01223
ITEM 25	.63433	.09145	.11820	.22195
ITEM 26	.29636	-.04328	.28810	.25930
ITEM 27	.69371	.14899	-.09753	.25222
ITEM 28	.49734	.32912	.03311	.42419
ITEM 29	.07964	.44933	.03998.	.19252
ITEM 30	.54849	.16356	.19462	.25941
ITEM 31	.39480	.06175	.04945	.45314
ITEM 32	.72094	.06220	.12459	.18927
ITEM 33	.12461	.12579	.20879	.15841
ITEM 34	.75397	.10547	.35695	.06262
ITEM 35	.59989	.18590	.06561	.12851

Factor Matrix Continued: Factors 5 - 8

	F5	F6	F7	F8
ITEM 1	.11801	.19928	.39934	-.07709
ITEM 2	.08243	.30811	.13192	-.19483
ITEM 3	.18442	.22400	-.22083	-.00505
ITEM 4	-.04531	.06420	-.07417	.03028
ITEM 5	.21527	.23626	-.14208	.07819
ITEM 6	.08199	.11923	.06795	.03711
ITEM 7	.15625	.50710	-.09638	-.14015
ITEM 8	.08584	.09515	-.10923	-.14606
ITEM 9	.83958	.15456	.05109	.05419
ITEM 10	.00583	.67791	.23341	-.01394
ITEM 11	.08920	.37918	-.14942	-.20824
ITEM 12	-.25738	.17372	.04452	-.03523
ITEM 13	.47132	.04822	.33446	-.06771
ITEM 14	.32963	.15629	.03122	.19123
ITEM 15	.00437	.04444	-.19645	.07515
ITEM 16	.17534	.51692	-.05945	.21335
ITEM 17	.10605	.17016	.11144	.03546
ITEM 18	.16692	.13420	.05244	-.04645
ITEM 19	.22332	.13031	.40026	-.01767
ITEM 20	.03157	-.01738	.05265	-.01089
ITEM 21	.08902	.07979	.22594	.05749
ITEM 22	.06510	.19935	.14927	-.06151
ITEM 23	.00339	.08655	-.00194	.72602
ITEM 24	.15321	.21768	.16618	-.00147
ITEM 25	.10228	.00482	.24203	.10827
ITEM 26	.11524	.29768	.31255	.14964
ITEM 27	-.12127	.14844	.14669	-.06806
ITEM 28	-.03710	.05127	-.26202	-.08864
ITEM 29	.04658	.17052	.03204	.06467
ITEM 30	.04852	.07553	.00429	.11473
ITEM 31	.05797	.08312	.07806	.15390
ITEM 32	-.00629	.08041	-.06891	.20923
ITEM 33	.06547	.50942	-.01280	.17087
ITEM 34	-.02700	.07942	.14324	.15310
ITEM 35	-.00827	.19860	-.19254	.09340

Questionnaire Data from Bigelow-La Gaipa Instrument
Transformation Matrix

	F1	F2	F3	F4
FACTOR 1	.81397	.29595	.25966	.23322
FACTOR 2	-.52992	.62255	.10920	.15194
FACTOR 3	.11754	.52092	-.50068	-.26804
FACTOR 4	.06388	.12170	-.58304	.65747
FACTOR 5	-.15609	-.00701	.20172	.41442
FACTOR 6	.03661	.03463	.02111	.03051
FACTOR 7	-.03842	-.48716	-.37724	.21885
FACTOR 8	.10754	-.01003	-.38287	-.44478

	F5	F6	F7	F8
FACTOR 1	.16090	.30660	.07916	.04346
FACTOR 2	.36514	.34367	.19039	.09446
FACTOR 3	-.22416	.08677	-.57605	-.05190
FACTOR 4	-.01290	-.34819	.28395	-.08289
FACTOR 5	-.77582	.33081	-.07402	.21528
FACTOR 6	.14414	-.32984	-.18179	.91295
FACTOR 7	.34732	.59705	-.27897	.12675
FACTOR 8	-.21696	.29055	.65473	.28939

35. Gilmour, Robin and Tuvia Melamed, "The Repair and Maintenance of Relationships," in *Person to Person*, eds. George Graham and Hugh LaFollette (Philadelphia: Temple University Press, 1989), 156.

36. Gurdin, 1978, 238-240.

37. Maisonneuve, 193; Ibid., 378.

38. OED. *The Oxford English Dictionary* (Oxford: Clarendon Press, 1933)., 545.

39. Ibid., 546.

40. In his and Lubomir Lamy's 1993 study, Jean Maisonneuve notes that "This new research has permitted [the authors] to appreciate the persistence of the evolution of models concerning the representations and the practices of friendship; to validate the aforementioned hypothesis to a large extent; and to confront the French study with other American and European work. The second book is available. The first book is out of print and available only in the library."

Chapter Two

Styles of Friendship

Within the social scientific disciplines, Jean Maisonneuve wrote about "styles of friendship," and Sarah M. Matthews described independent, discerning, and acquisitive "friendship styles."[1] Indeed, "style" has many advantages over Max Weber's more explicitly defined "ideal-type." Adapting the notion to my investigation, I define a style of friendship as a set of action, social relationships, contexts, cognitions, and emotions having to do with friendship.

I established these contrastable styles of friendship after carefully replaying each of my in-depth interviews and composing a brief sketch of what appeared to me as the notable features of each person's different styles. Part of these contrastive styles is the different definitional components of friendship. Thus, the styles I identified in the fifty in-depth interviews encompass the categories of the content analysis of interviewees' definitions, their real behavior in, and their normative expectations concerning friendship. Doing a smallest space analysis of my respondents' definitions of friendship throws a different light, though decontextually, onto what my interviewees "think, feel, and do" about friendship. By triangulating all of these indicators of style from the in-depth interviews and from some of the open- and closed-formed items on my questionnaire, I arrive at my description of friendship styles in the Montreal of the mid-1970s.

If we recall my interview with the recently divorced, female, teacher of English, thirty-three years of age and of French Canadian background, whose definition of friendship was quoted in chapter one, we can get an idea of how difficult it is to rigorously demarcate one style of friendship from another. Referring to Maisonneuve, her definition stresses "confiding in (being intimate together)," "mutual understanding," "material aid, services," "moral support (sought after in unhappiness)," and "constancy, perenniality, (friendship is holy)."[2] As we listen to her description of her friendships, however, we learn of a much more complicated thematic pattern evident in her experiences of friendship. In telling about her closest friends, this interviewee told me in French:

> Let us say that these two people have received the same education as I. They were raised in the same milieu ... I was born in a little town out in the province ... and then we did a part of our studies together. Only they left school before me.... [My close friend] is a girl who was my neighbor as she grew up. I spent my entire childhood with her. ... At the age of sixteen I was directed some place else while she entered the world of the workplace. ... She is a girl who knows how to understand me. She is a girl for whom I have an enormous amount of respect and for whom I have an enormous amount of friendship.... We were born two months apart. We got to know each other as babies, ... On the other hand, there were other girls ... who lived near me without ever hitting it off-- ... there was never a true friendship among us. Listen, she is thirty-three; I am thirty-three. She was born in June; I was born in September. ... Afterwards I came to work here in Montreal. She always stayed in her own environment. She is married. Now she lives in a suburb of Montreal. Let's say that we have found one another again here. We see each other a little more often, well, not as often as before. You know, ... she has a little girl. Well then, she doesn't have the same type of life that I have living alone. It's different, but, nonetheless, you see ... She just got back from a trip. Well, she sent me a post card. That's not a big thing, but I know

that I am the only person to whom she sent one. We don't forget one another, even if we don't have the same kind of life. ... I know that she is a girl I can count on and she can count on me as well. ... She never evolved from a cultural point of view as I did because she was cut off, spoiled, and much more pampered than I ... She has brought me things that I didn't have. For example, I have a very nervous temperament. Perhaps I have gone crazy over something sometimes. If I call her, well, she is going to say, "Well, listen, slow down, heh, heh, heh." She is an unbelievably calm person. She is a girl who takes things slowly ... She never gets irritable. ... Then when a bomb falls on my head or something of that kind, ... I call her, and then she is always surprised. Heh, I calm myself down with her. And she has time to discuss with me. Then time goes by ... that lets me reflect. ... She hasn't talked about my studies; she has talked about me: "What am I doing? Am I happy?" I have always heard it said that between friends one tells them their faults. ... it's rather vague; ... we said rather brutal things, but coming from her it was never shocking. And it was the same thing for me. ... "When I speak with you, it relaxes me sometimes." I say, "Aren't you tired of listening to me?" She says, "No, I find that interesting. ... I try to understand you." It's just words of encouragement that she gives me: learning about my news. If I am ill, she will come.

The second friend is different. ... I have known him for about ten years. ... I met him through other friends. ... He is a very intelligent man. That's what attracted me to him at first. ... He just has to talk to me ... and he knows me just like he made me. Well, this is a man I can't get anything by. ... He is a man with whom I am not at all inhibited and who is not at all inhibited with me. ... He gives me an enormous amount of advice about work, even about personal things. ... I am sure that he is a man who, if I were really bad off, would get me going again, and it's for that reason that I chose him as a friend. ... You know that I can almost guess the answers to the questions that I ask him and ... vice versa ... . We have about the same scale of values, tastes, and all that. We both have the same ideas about religion. We both received the same education. ... We had a lot of taboos then. ... In the present context religion is rather practiced by indifference than by anything else. It's not to follow the crowd, but it was never a great need for me. My friends are non-observant. He is a man who adores nature ... [and] animals like me. He has a dog. I have one.

> Sometimes on Sundays we would walk the dogs together.
> We would go to the mountain and ... look at the trees and ...
> flowers, and it's a kind of rest. It's relaxing.

If we compare this interviewee's definition with her subsequent report of her experiences of her closest friendships throughout her life, it becomes evident that there are differences in emphasis, omissions, and details between them. Again referring to Jean Maisonneuve's analytical schema, her definition contains elements of all the components of communication except friends' resembling one another. She describes friends who complement her in many ways. Moreover, two components that she stresses--listening to one another and choice--are not readily codable under Maisonneuve's categories, unless we add some new subcategories under communication. However, in her account of her friendships, she gives ample information documenting how one of her friends resembles her while the other one complements her. In her definition, elements of "counting on the friends in all circumstances," "material aid, services" and "moral support (sought after in unhappiness)" are present as they are in her description of her friendships. On the other hand, her report on what her friendships have been like gives much more room to the theme of "fidelity." Her entire tale of friendships (only part of which is quoted here), her definition and her description, accentuate all three of Maisonneuve's main themes of friendship with, perhaps, more emphasis given to "communication" and "helping out" than "fidelity." The other part of her story of friendship goes into detail about her friendships with her mother, sister, and brother, whom we will encounter when treating the subject of friendships in the family.

In trying to identify her styles of friendship, I recognize quite different areas: that of the "best-friend-neighbor," touches of the "best-friend-in-mind," and that of friendship related to the family.

In considering the various kinds of family friendships, it is helpful to differentiate a generalized "family-oriented friendship [Style A1]," "the remaining family friendship after the break-up of the family [Style A2]," "a sibling friendship [Style A3]," and a "non-nuclear family friendship [Style A4]." It is important to underscore that a person often enacts several of these styles in the different friendships he or she experiences or has experienced.

The Family-Oriented Friendship [Style A1]

One of the styles of the friendship in the family is that of the "family-oriented friendship," which I will also cover in my chapter on "Friendship in the Family." In Montreal there are several styles of friendship based on the family. In the style of the family-oriented friendship, the entire nuclear family tends to display warmth, openness, understanding, acceptance, trustworthiness, love, helping, reliability, and sharing, in an atmosphere of enjoyment that permits differences of opinion and manageable conflict. Of course, this is an idealized depiction for which no one family attains all of its dimensions. In this style, there are distinctions of age, rights, and obligations of roles among husband/father, wife/mother, and children/siblings. One family might be linked in friendship with another family; usually the husband and wife introduce their children to each other or meet through their children. Or the friendship may be centered in the family itself with individual members of the family attaching their closest friends to it. The family is generally settled in an occupation with relatively low geographical mobility. As residence, food, and basic income for its members are provided, exchanges of goods and services take place toward their friend in the family to the extent that their own economic and psychological well-being are not endangered. The wife and husband may be each other's closest friend, although this "couple companionate" relationship was recorded less frequently in Montreal in comparison to the United States.

In Appendix D, we can see that this style is most frequent among married people with children, of a middle age stratum (between the ages of 31 and 60). English Canadians, professionals, and males displayed this style more often than comparative groups.

The Remaining Family-Friendship after the Break-up of the Family [Style A2])

As I illustrate and explain all the styles of family friendship in detail in my chapters on "The Family and Friendship" and "Friendship over the Years," I will not elaborate these styles here. The titles I have given these styles are sufficiently self-explanatory to enable the reader to follow the discussion in this chapter. However, for those who feel they need a better grasp of them at this point, I will briefly summarize some of their main features here.

A friendship formed in the family may remain intact after divorce, death, war or some other disruptive circumstances destroy the family. In my interviews, for example, the French Canadian teacher of English in her early thirties--whom we met earlier in this chapter--remains a close friend with a friend of hers and her former husband. She turns to this man to ask for advice on terminating her marriage, for especially emotional support, although financial and other kinds of aid would be offered if requested. Such a friendship may provide physical support as well in a period of difficulty such as during an illness. It is a relationship characterized by reliance, trust, acceptance, understanding, and sympathetic talk over and beyond love, enjoyment, and similarity.

The Sibling Friendship [Style A3]

The brother and sister, sister and sister, or brother and brother may form a relationship of discussion, support, or helping out through sharing of residence, money, and food, often in opposition to other siblings or parents. This pattern tends to start in the teenage years and lasts throughout some part of life. If it lasts throughout the adult years, the initial physical proximity may give way to infrequent, though extremely psycho-socially significant, exchanges of letters, cassette tapes or telephone calls, and visits in each others' new homes--all brought about by mobility. They may share discussion of problems through sympathetic, accepting listening and establish a relationship of trust, based on good communication and keeping of backstage, secret information. A love may develop between them which is not necessarily accompanied by high degrees of sharing of similar beliefs and lifestyles but which displays tolerance, reliance, and positive, sympathetic regard despite the differences. Nevertheless, this support may lead to feelings of over dependence towards the whole family, especially when confronted by the socio-cultural norm which demands open independence. Sometimes the sharing may be limited to material support but not extended to deep socio-emotive exchanges.

The "sibling friendship" style was more descriptive of English Canadians, males, younger people, and professionals than comparative groups.

The Non-nuclear Family Friendship [Style A4]

Non-nuclear family friendships may extend to cousins, uncles, aunts, grandmothers, grandfathers, sisters-and-brothers-in-law, sons-and-daughters-in-law, etc. In French Canadian folklore the brother- and sister-in-law relationships were recounted as particularly fertile grounds for friendship, although none of these categories was commonly associated with the friendships in my study. People with more traditional values and beliefs may have such friendships more frequently than non-conformists. Often these friends share a common activity such as hunting, bingo, family dinners, and gossip about others, especially other family members. This relationship is characterized more by similarities of interests and values than by high degrees of communication.

As we are informed in Appendix D, the "Non-nuclear Family Friend" was observed more often among people in the middle age stratum, French Canadians, males, and people who were married and had children as compared to other groups.

The Neighbor-Friend [Style B1]

To get a feeling for a somewhat different style of friendship come with me to the poorer part of Outremont. Here we can see how "the neighbor-friend" can have a different emotional and cognitive dimension to it than the last interviewee's tale of a friendship that began in her neighborhood. Her story stressed the long-enduring relationship with her childhood girlfriend who had given her moral support over the years, whose very different personality was capable of soothing her, and with whom she had communicated very well for a long time. In contrast, in the account of friendship we are about to consider, the neighbor, who has different ethnic and religious affiliations from those of our interviewee, still lives downstairs, and this neighbor has given her invaluable help and companionship since they got to know one another five or six years before the interview took place. In addition, we will meet other styles in this woman's other close friendships.

For years Outremont was considered the posh French Canadian equivalent of Westmount--once the heavily upper class, English Canadian municipality on the island of Montreal. Michel Tremblay depicted it as such in his play, *The Impromptu of Outremont*. At the time of the interview, in its transitional area are upper-middle class Jewish families and in its poorer section are ethnically mixed groups--Greeks, a few Chinese, West Indian Blacks, English Canadians, Polish Canadians, and others. Here we meet an English Canadian woman, fifty-eight years of age, married over a third of a century, a white collar worker for more than twenty years in a large Montreal store, the mother of a grown man and woman, and an observant Anglican.

Speaking to me, this woman defines friend and friendship:

> A true friend is someone who helps you when you badly need it; who doesn't look for a reward for helping you, or any recognition like that. Take for instance a lady I have, a neighbor downstairs. I had my mother living with me, and she was very sick. She was 98. And I used to have to stay

up nights and days with her. And a couple times at one o'clock in the morning, after she'd come home from work, and she'd come up and sit here with my mother 'till five o'clock in the morning, so that I could get some sleep. That's what I call a true friend, because family, as far as I'm concerned, they don't do these things. It's only a true friend that would do a thing like that.

There is a slight difference in age between this neighbor-friend and my interviewee. Her friend is a waitress of native Canadian Indian background, Catholic, not quite as well off economically, and lives with her daughter and grandson. I asked, "Did Jane get to know your mom?" She replied,

Oh, yes, she called her "Nanny," the same as me. Everybody called her "Nanny." ... The grandchildren used to come up here, and they were no relation at all. They were Jane's grandchildren. They used to come up, and ... they figured she was their grandmother too. And they'd do errands for her, anything she wanted. They'd bring her little things, packages of candy and stuff like that. They were very good.

When I inquired as to whether their relationship was just bound up around her mother, she explained:

No, we discussed certain things concerning our family life, different things that happened in our lives, not just about Mother--well, whether I was going to work and the different things my husband's doing at work, as you would talk to an friend, you know. Jane is exactly four months younger than I am, and when we'll go into a store, she'll open the door and say, "Old ladies first," for me to go in. Or sometimes we'll be getting out of the car, and I'll say, "Hurry up, I'm the oldest. Come on and get out." Or "don't cross the street against the light. Remember, I'm older than you are, so do as I say." We kid back and forth like that all the time.

When I asked if she got her friends together or separately, she answered,

> Well, Jane has been to different places with us like
> weddings and stuff like that. Not too many parties.
> Because she was at home when I was working; or I was at
> home when she was working, we couldn't get together too
> often. Well, now, more or less every second Saturday we
> can get together.

Jane is her second closest friend. Although she had lived in Outremont eleven years, it was only five or six years prior to the interview that she got to know her friend when she retired. Before, their work schedules prevented them from getting to know one another. Now she reports "I'm in and out of her house. She has a key to my house. I have a key to her house. We go in and out." As with her other friends and their husbands, they reserve overt signs of emotional expression, such as kissing, for special occasions as when they go away and come back or at Christmas and birthdays.

This tale of friendship exhibits many features of a style that can appropriately be called the neighbor-friend [Style B1]. In this account, the friendship was based on living above and below one another in a low-rise, two- or three-story structure adjoining other similar buildings. This ecology is typical of large sections of the City of Montreal. Unlike the first story, in which friendship was formed by living near one another, this relationship began late in life and was maintained by regular exchange of service, emotional support, and quasi-kinship. In the interview with the 33-year-old teacher of English, her style of neighborhood friendship was no longer dependent on living in the vicinity of her friend. In contrast, in that interviewee's tale, proximity in childhood created a wealth of learning and socializing. During this period, one learns similar games, goes to the same school, even the same church, graduates from the same school, and knows pretty much the same set of people. One passes through the emotional trials of adolescence together. After leaving school, our interviewee's friend entered the world of work and family of procreation while our interviewee went on to higher education, a marriage, and a divorce. These new experiences introduced the old friends to new ones with whom they share fewer common characteristics of background. Often in these tales, one of the friends explores intense relationships in a permissive culture that leaves the person without the same degree of affinities, reliance, trust, and acceptance of the childhood friendships. Such a gap frequently pushed people to their lifelong friend formed in their childhood. This renewed relationship is often diffuse, i.e., the friends can and do anything or nothing, whatever comes up. In several of the interviews, we will hear of a pattern in which the neighborhood friendship is cultivated by the neighbors who are also wives often in similar circumstances of life cycle, childrearing, community activities, church participation, book and social clubs. Such neighborhood-based friendships are focused on common situations, values, beliefs, acceptance, reliance, gossip, enjoyment, and talk and grow into relations of love, trust, sharing of joy and sorrows and mutual aid. Likewise, single, downtown, white-collar workers, who finding their work world all consuming of time and energy, turn to their neighbor dwelling in a large apartment building for close friendship.

In Appendix D, it is reported that the "Neighbor Friend" characterized English Canadians, married people with children, professionals, and interviewees of the middle age stratum more than comparative groups.

Best-Friend Proximity [Style B2]

There are a host of other circumstances that bring together people near in space, such as being near together at work, in a hospital, convent, preparatory school, dormitory, etc., which create a relationship close to that of the neighbor who dwells nearby presumably for a relatively long period of life. Being near creates the background for friendship where the nearby place is pleasant and permissive enough for relationship to arise. When it lasts, this situation sets the background for close friendship, as so much of a person's life is spent in sharing the day-to-day pattern of living which includes having to handle different and common problems. As we learn in Appendix D, this pattern is found more frequently among female, English Canadian, and younger interviewees.

An example of this style can be seen in one of my interviewees from the wealthiest section of Montreal. At the time of my interview this man was in his early seventies, had been married over a third of a century, and was without children. With twelve years of formal education, he had worked as a salesman for most of his working life. He and most of his closest friends are of English Canadian or American background. He told me that occupation was the most important factor in promoting his friendships. In describing one of his closest friends, he related to me,

> From a business point of view we were as friendly as could be; it was very rewarding--I'm not putting a price on the friendship. It was a mutual friendship. We shared a lot in business. Yeah, in selling, yes. This was in [the electrical field]. ... We naturally went away fishing and our wives met and we had a very close relationship in that way. John was a very fine, out-going fellow. He's, I guess, about eight years younger than I am, but we thought so much alike in business matters particularly. Well, we, for instance, ... in sales policy, he would appreciate our side of the business transaction, and we could appreciate his position. I'm talking about placing some very big business, and this was on a basis of mutual trust and mutual appreciation of not only myself but of our facilities. [We've known each other] about twenty years. We met on the job. ... It developed gradually. It grew and grew and grew into a friendship. ... It was a mutually rewarding friendship--not that we were looking for anything like that, but this was my work and he was a part of it.

Similar-Interest-Close-Friend [Style C1]

With an ever differentiating job market in the means of production, an individual finds the choice of a career setting her or him off in life situation from earlier-made close friends. Depending on how conducive the work milieu is to the establishment of friendship, the individual makes choices for new friends in this ever-expanding new world which forces the person, to some degree, beyond his or her framework of family, ethnic community, and language group. If this individual's work milieu promotes an atmosphere where relationships are filled with the most meaningful aspects of friendship, this relationship has a ground on which to build. Indeed, in some professions, discussion of the subject of work is the central theme of the common interest. Where the work milieu does not promote friendship, these close friendships are formed in off-the-job associations like music, sports-participation at public sports centers, hockey, church, union and political meetings, music, theater, cinema, folk dancing, nightclubs, bingoes, bars, taverns, public celebrations like St. Jean Baptiste, Man and His World, excursions in nature, and the like. Often these relationships are appended to other styles of close or best friendship.

As this relationship is often independent of or surrogate for other primary ties, it provides the individual with mutual help in residence, obtaining a job, finance, rent, food, sharing of enjoyment, mutual activities, and being together. It enables its participants to talk about a gamut of subjects of common interests, but not too close to each of its participants selves.

Usually this style is tied to other relations of more intense communication and love and can involve other friends. Often, when communication begins to take precedence over the common interest, this style of friendship translates into a more socio-emotively evocative style.

This style of relationship is especially prominent among males, married people with children, and professionals, as is evident from the statistics and item plot in Appendix D. It is frequently combined with "family-oriented" and "non-nuclear family" friendship styles. Among average-energy-level or more traditional families this style is more characteristic after the children are old enough to leave them time for extra familial activities, and among high-energy level or less traditional families, this style is observed all the time. This style can be entered into by one of the members of a couple before marriage and be preserved independently of the marriage partner and/or together with the marriage partner, varying for each particular close friendship.

The similar interest friendship was a style characteristic of several relationships engaged in by one of my interviewees whose many friendships evidenced a stylistic profile more varied than any other. Of English Canadian ethnicity, this man was a Protestant minister in his middle fifties. Telling me about his childhood friendships, he related:

> Henry, I have a closer reading on because I see him frequently. ... He was born [in the same province I'm from], but we didn't meet until [we were] at a Church-related school ... , and he's also a minister of [my same denomination]. At two different times Henry and I were on the staff of this school--not at the same time--and we each occupied the same position ... [at] this school. ... . He was then completing some graduate studies in [another country]. And I had something to do with bringing him to [that school]. We've sort of leap-frogged a bit. I had a parish in [a major city], and when Henry was ready to leave the position [at that school], he was looking for a parish, and a neighboring parish became open in [that city], and I had something to do with facilitating Henry's coming as minister to that parish. ... So then we became neighboring ministers [there], and we could develop our friendship then in the same time, in the same place. Before it was kind of long-range, and we would meet occasionally, but not being able to work together. ... but I left my parish there ... and went to [another country] to do graduate study, and, the year following that ... Henry left his parish ... and came to his present parish in Montreal. ... Then I completed my studies ... . And all of this time we'd been urging Henry and his family to come down for a visit ... and they were always going to come but something always prevented it. And then ... I completed my master's degree ..., and I was then looking for another parish [in another part of Canada] again. And so the telephone rang ... and it was Henry saying that they had some time, and "We're going to come down," and "So, great!" So we're discussing on the 'phone, and ... --knowing that I was finishing my studies--he said, "Where are you going?" And I said, "Matter of fact, I don't know, but, ... I've engaged the express company to haul my books ... and we're going back. So if you come down, fine, we'll still be here." And so he said, "Have you heard about [my present church]," and I said, "No." I hadn't. ... And he said, "Well, it's vacant." So I said, "Oh." So we concluded the conversation, and ... I was not at all thinking that I was going to stay [in this part of Canada], and I then went up and looked up the statistics on [this church], never having heard of the place before; so

the following morning I 'phoned him back to Montreal and said, "Say, we might be interested in [that church]." And he said, "Well, you better get off--I still laugh about this--the 'phone, because I think they're going to 'phone 'ya." So independently, you see, and I am moved about this obviously, independently after he had hung up the night before, he had on his own, without any further reference from me, contacted the lay officials in this church and had told them about me, and this church was looking for a minister, and I was looking for a church, but, for heaven's sake, expecting to go [to another part of Canada]. And, so sure enough, in a matter of minutes after the morning 'phone call, the 'phone rang, and it was this lay-official from [the church] inquiring if I was interested and invited me to come up here--this was a Saturday morning--to be interviewed on Monday. My wife and I came up on Monday, and it just went through like nothing. And so, if you would want a definition of a friend, I suppose, one might say that a friend is a person who will do for you sometimes beyond the call of duty, and, there was no obligation. I don't think anywhere along the line that he and I were sort of helping each other. There was never anything, whereby, we had some kind of a contract, you know, to say, "O.K., you help me, Henry, and I'll help you. You scratch my back, and I'll scratch yours." ... And so, ... when ... his daughter was to be married ..., the bride asked if I would marry them, so I certainly did. So I was very pleased, you know. [Henry is] quite unlike the first two [friends I described]. He's a quicksilver kind of person. He's vivacious. He speaks rapidly. He's ambitious. ... Henry is the kind of fellow who is very bright and ... quick with repartee. And he is a student. ... Also he has abilities in writing. ... He's achieved quite a lot ... .[3]

The Buddy-*Copain-Copine* Phenomenon [Style C2]

This sub-style of the similar-interest-friend can be distinguished by its participants' unwillingness or inability to maintain an in-depth relationship of give-and-take of relatively high degrees of back stage information. Often one of the parties practicing this style feels it to be deeper than the other party, but this condition is often recognized by both of them. There is a great deal of variance in this type of friendship as to the extent to which the communicative aspect to this relationship assumes a greater or lesser role and develops over time. When the common interest predominates over the communication, this style of friendship risks breaking up. As we will hear in a tale of two sportsmen who began their friendships as hunting *copains*, psycho-social forces work to undermine this style of friendship, as will be recounted in my chapter on the "Clinical Sociology of Friendship." This kind of similar-interest friend subordinates the communicative aspects of their encounter to their shared interest.

The Girl-Friend/Boy-Friend, or *Petit/e Ami/e* [Style D]

This style of close friendship is formed most often among people who are "single, never married," males, and younger interviewees, compared to other groups, as we see in Appendix D. It is a relationship often embodying several meaningful activities of friendship to which it adds love, physical attraction, and/or varying degrees of sexual involvement. It occurs between members of the opposite sex, and much less frequently among members of the same sex in this sample. It may assume the form of a style of practice for a love relationship, but may never reach the full degree of an intense love relationship. It is most frequent in late adolescence and early adulthood but also among urban non-marrieds of all age groups in Montreal. As we learn from a case in my chapter on "Men, Women, and Close Friendship," it is often tied to a person's other close friend relationships. This style can form an institutional continuum to a fiancé relationship.

Best-Friend-in-Mind [Style E]

In this style, a person experiences friendship more as a philosophy toward people than a deep, concrete relationship between real living human beings. If not as a philosophy, such friendships may rest as idealized or model relationships of an on-going, living past-present. This experience may manifest itself in thinking of a friend, but a few people who display this style may be unable or unwilling to single out any one person as a close friend. This style of friendship in some of my interviews is typified by a group affiliation of friends rather than an intense one-to-one personal friendship. In these ways, my in-depth interviewees' best-friend-in-mind style resembles the friendship style labeled as "independent" by Sarah H. Matthews, although this style was found in 20% (13/63) of her interviews in comparison to 16% (8/50) of my in-depth interviews.[4] However, I found that the latter attributes also cluster with extremely pleasant memories of past encounters with friends that do repeat themselves when these friendships are renewed intermittently over the years. From Matthews' description, it is difficult to rigorously classify the latter trait as typical of her "discerning" or "acquisitive" friend style, although it seems to be compatible with both of them.[5] However, the psychic realm of these not often re-enacted friendships may play an outstanding role in sustaining a person's on-going psycho-social balance and sense of entertaining intimacy. Depicted in the item plot in Appendix D, this style of friendship was more frequent in married people with children, between the ages of 31 and 60 (the middle age stratum), and professionals, as compared to other groups. It appears to be linked to forces in the post-industrial society that require the individual to undergo geographical displacement.

The style of the friend-in-mind stands out in my interview with a Protestant minister of a Montreal church, but it blends in well with his other styles of friendship: the family-oriented friendship, the sibling friendship, the neighbor-friend, and the similar interest close friend. At the time of the interview this man, of English Canadian ethnicity, was in his fifties and was a husband and father of several children. He held graduate degrees in his field and had been a minister almost half of his life.

He initially defines a friend as a person in:

> whom you have a high level of trust and confidence; a person to whom you might go if you were in trouble or had some confidential matter you wished to discuss; and some person that you enjoy being with; you like their company; need not have any financial component to it. ... I suppose that I might on some rare occasion use the word pal, meaning a person I enjoy being with ... a pal would be in my

view a more intimate relationship than a friend. A friend could be someone who's known to me, and we're mutually known to each other, but could be not much more than an acquaintance. I could say, "Here, meet my friend, Mr. Jones," meaning that this was some person I knew personally, but he might not be a personal associate of mine particularly.

After defining friend, he begins to hit upon a major cause for the style of the friend-in-mind. The reverend said,

I think that it's because of my occupation that I have to move a fair amount. For example, since I graduated ... and was ordained, I was four years in a town ... in [another part of Canada]; I was then five years in a village ... . I was then two years in a [city ...]. And then I was two years in a city [in another country]. And I've been five years in this [part of Montreal]. And that was unlike my childhood because I grew up and lived in one community and my family did not move until I was grown and in university, so that I think that I have to subdivide my life into sections, perhaps, because of my professional necessity to move. Perhaps I've not been able to develop the same depth of friendship because of this moving that I knew as a growing person; so when I would speak of pals from my younger years, this would mean a person I was habitually with; who I would go to movies with; go to sports occasions with; who I would go out to the country with; and of course, we had our boyhood gangs also, and some of these friendships have persisted throughout, so that I still have these friends, but they're separated geographically from me and most of them are nowhere within visiting distance ... but interesting, in the past week, I've had occasion to be seeing about the possible move of one of my long-term friends, and I think I described him to someone who didn't know him as "he's my pal," or something like that, but that's a very rare thing.

The element of abstractness of the style of the friend-in-mind can be readily seen in this minister's description of an inanimate object as a friend. This abstractness may refer to communicating through ideas:

Books are friends to me. Inside of the cover of some of those Everyman Series [it is written] "Books are friends,"

or something like this. There is a sense in which a book
becomes a friend, and then to part with an old friend, a
book which has been with me for life. I can be a friend with
a book somehow. Don't ask me to analyze that, please.
We'll just let that drop.

Later in the interview in telling me about one of his closest friends
who is a physician, he again refers to the place of books in his
friendships,

> Then I know we're friends still even though we're not
> corresponding because he will come across a book that is
> very meaningful to him so he'll mail me a copy of the book.
> It'll be for me--a hard-covered book, and I understand that
> ... he thinks it's important, and he'll mail it to me for myself.
> And then he'll get caught up in some social movement--
> which he inherits naturally from his father who was very
> much into social action-- ... and ... suddenly there'll be in my
> mail ... a big batch of material on [that social movement],
> and I'll know it's Dr. Doe who has sent me this or had it
> sent to me.

In describing the contact he has had with one of his life-long friends,
this interviewee touches on a common mode of communication in the
"friend-in-mind" style:

> We've had a letter from him just yesterday, which is a
> rarity because I write very few letters. Neither does he. I
> should say my wife wrote the letter to say that we were
> coming and wished to visit. ... It's perhaps an index of our
> friendship that, notwithstanding the fact that she's due for
> surgery and may have a malignancy, and this is to take
> place ... we would appear at their place in a few days.
> Nevertheless, the door is open, and, you know, we're
> welcome, no matter what the crisis is. ...Well I've seen him
> maybe three times in the last 25 years, which is three
> times as much as I've seen [the other friend I just told you
> about].

Moreover, we can see that he carries in his mind a rather vivid image of this friend's personality to which he has referred over the years. The pastor continues,

> He has a good sense of humor, ... and he tends to be a very deep kind of fellow. He's of a philosophical bent, and he's extremely well-organized. I was thinking of this just now because planning an organization is not easy for me, and John has been always extremely well-organized. I was just reading not very long ago ... in some popular magazine ... that a common denominator of successful people seems to be that they keep a daily memo of what they're doing, a list of things they intend to do, and this triggered my memory of John, who as long as I can remember him always had a list and was always crossing off his list what he had accomplished and what he still had to do; whereas, when I'm pressed for time as I am, I will do this, but only when I'm forced into it when I get myself into a corner. I organize but I prefer to keep it in my head, and it's not very efficient, but John is efficient. O.K.?

After this summary, he goes into the demographic characteristics of John and his family. Then we learn that friends-in-mind may be called upon for an important service or honor in a critical situation after a long period of elapsed interaction. In returning to a discussion of his friend, the medical doctor, the minister reports,

> When his eldest daughter ... became engaged to a [fellow from another country] who was trying to get landed immigrant status in Canada, and who was so honest he went to the Immigration Authorities and explained about how he was a deserter from the army [of his home country], and that he was kind of illegally in Canada, because I think he jumped a ship or something, ... then they had to canvass their friends across the country to put some pressure because there is an escape clause that if a natural from another country is in the country and can prove that if he were to return to his native country his life would be in danger, he may be given a special category, so, of course, then we were circularized to write to Ottawa, which I did on behalf of this boy, and they subsequently married. ... This is that kind of a friendship.

Important Variations of Expectations and Behavior within the Styles of Friendship

The styles of friendship are expressed, in part, by varying expectations about friendship as indicated by my interviewees' definitions of the term. We saw indicators of this variance in the major categories which were introduced in the last chapter. Jean Maisonneuve's study utilized a tripartite analytical scheme to perform a content analysis of his subjects definitions of friendship.[6] A smallest space analysis of the subcategories based on my data, which will be reported on later in this chapter, shows that these units of the meaning of friendship should be more accurately reduced to two main areas, which I label "communication" and "steadfastness."[7]

The spontaneous notions of communication in friendship, which came out in the interviewees' definitions of friendship, are cross-validated by the more behavioral question that we put to Montrealers. We inquired of them how often they discussed their most intimate problems and thoughts with each of their friends. In the combined in-depth, recorded interview and written questionnaire material, 51.3% report that they often discuss their most intimate thoughts and problems with their closest friends; 23.4% say that they do so rarely; 22.1% claim that they never do; and 3.2% were tied on at least two of their answers. The extent to which Montrealers discuss their intimate problems and thoughts with their friends is strongly influenced by their ethnic affiliation and socio-economic class, which will be delved into in considerable detail in later chapters. Here let it be summarily noted that English Canadians reported discussing their intimate problems and thoughts with their closest friends significantly less often than French Canadians. Blue collar workers were observed to discuss their intimate problems and thoughts with their closest friends much less frequently than white collar workers or professionals, and white collar workers seem to discuss intimate problems and thoughts somewhat more than professionals and considerably more than blue collar workers.[8] My data show that the interviewees did not communicate their intimacies as deeply to all their close friends. By far the majority of them related their deepest thoughts and problems to their four closest friends in descending order, which is to say that they shared most with their closest friend and down the line.[9]

There is also some cross-validation of the category of "helping out," and, particularly its subcategory of "devotion, sacrifice, disinterestedness," found in the questionnaire data. There I repeated Maisonneuve's question, "To what do you attribute the strength and the firmness of a friendship? ..." The most frequently coded answer--covering 20.0% of the coded responses--was "due to the fact of having the opportunity to be together quite often and easily." Such a reply is certainly an indicator that "devotion, sacrifice, and disinterestedness" are dependent on the real world factors of jobs, children, etc., but also that the majority of people interviewed chose to devote and even sacrifice time and certain other obligations to be with friends.

Finally the theme of "fidelity" is crossvalidated in two questions on the questionnaire. Almost ninety-two percent (91.8%) of Montrealers questioned said that they try to put some time aside for their friends even if their work is most time and energy consuming, while only about eight percent (8.2%) of them said that they did not. Moreover, 62.4% of our respondents claimed that they either had not sacrificed nor would they sacrifice their friend relationships for serious reasons of a family nature if the question were raised. Around thirty-eight percent (37.6%) of the people questioned either had or would sacrifice their friends under such circumstances. However, the smallest space analysis introduced later in this chapter offers strong evidence that the subcategories of fidelity should be regrouped into two other major variables, "communication" and "steadfastness."

The Styles of Friendship as Expressions of My Interviewees as Individuals and the Map of These Styles as a Collective Representation of Friendship

To get a view of how all of my interviewees compared in their styles of friendship, I carried out a multidimensional scalogram analysis (MSA-1) on my data.[10] Here the reader must turn to Appendix D to refer to the three dimensional SSA of the styles of friendship and the item plots of MSA-1.[11] For reasons of economy, I have had to present the MSA-1 as item plots of each friendship style taken separately. The reader may more easily follow this discussion by tracing all the item plots on the same transparent piece of paper, i.e. superimposing all the friendship styles onto the same space. Each friendship style should be drawn in a different color of ink or colored pencil lead.

I may now observe that two groups of interviewees seemed to be polarized by a {head-to-heart} facet along the east-west dimension.[12] Thus, to the lower-left (west), we see a group of interviewees to which I attribute a best-friend-in-mind style (certainly a "heady" one), and to the lower-to-mid-right-hand (east), we are struck by interviewees characterized by the "girl-friend/boy-friend, *petit/e ami/e*" style. Moreover, along the north-south axis, there appears to be polarization along an {institutionalized-to-chosen similar-interest friend} facet. Concretely, we note the region of "similar interest style of friendship," intersecting with all the other styles along the southerly part of the space. Similar interests have the common trait that they are chosen by people. In contrast, descending at an angle from the more northern and western direction is the region occupied by interviewees I classified as having a family-oriented friendship over whom is superimposed a somewhat larger region of the neighbor friend. Finally, descending at an angle from the northeastern part of the space is the region of "best friend-proximity" of a few individuals that intersects several other regions. In the more northern part of the space there appear to be those individuals whose friendship styles are tied to institutions. There seems to be a gradient in the degree of institutionalization. Those people toward the northwestern area display friendship styles more institutionalized, in that neighbors are less institutionalized than family relations. Individuals in the north central space show greater leeway in the pool of friends; while those people in the more northeastern area, in choosing their friends from other propinquitous people, such as co-workers, have an ever greater degree of freedom, while still limiting themselves to such an institutionalized sphere as the world of work.

This interpretation of the styles of friendship becomes even more strongly supported when I performed a smallest space analysis (SSA), on the styles of friendship.[13] Whereas the MSA mapped my interviewees in space, the smallest space analysis maps out the styles of friendship-- the "items"-- in space.[14]

In the SSA diagram of the friendship styles in three dimensions presented in Appendix D, it is possible to see the emergence of the family-oriented friendship [Style A1], the remaining family friendship after the break-up of the family [Style A2], the best-friend-in-mind [Style E], and the neighbor-friend [Style B1] arising from the northeast, bottom plane of the plot. This diagram points to a main polarity in the styles that seems to pull them along an east-west dimension on the bottom side of the plane between the "heady" friendship rooted in institutionalized contexts as opposed to the friendship of "heart" toward the left or west side of this bottom plane. It is striking that this polarity replicates the central opposition in friendship interpretations between Aristotelian ("heady") and Platonic (of "the heart" or "eros") poles, which Hutter formulated and I reviewed in the first chapter.

Moreover, on the MSA-1 item plots, it is notable that the overlapping regions of the more "heady" styles of friendship intersect, thereby creating a stylistic basis for the socio-emotive traits of fidelity and helping out, which are characteristic of these more Aristotelian styles of friendship. In the southeast, bottom plane of the plot loom the highly "hearty" styles of friendship. This style is associated with the more passionate types of communication, including sexual and erotic encounter. This polarity--south of the X-axis, emanating from the bottom plane--is modulated by the north-south region of the similar-interest-friend, which varies depending on whether the content of the similar interest is more freely chosen or institutional.

The Socio-emotive Traits Associated with the Styles

Having analyzed the Montreal in-depth interviewees' styles of friendship, I may now focus on my questionnaire respondents' conception of this relationship. These conceptions are indicators of a wide range of cognitions, experiences, and emotions of friendship, also associated with the styles of friendship among my in-depth interviewees. It is informative to recall the relative frequencies of the respondents' definitions coded within Maisonneuve's nominal rubrics that I summarized in the first chapter.[15]

Maisonneuve's trichotomous, content analytical categories--communication, helping out each other, and fidelity--for dealing with the definitions of friendship were not perfectly replicated on my Montreal data. One of the subcategories of "fidelity," "constancy, perenniality," falls much more clearly into the space of "helping out each other," while the other aspect of "fidelity," "trust, loyalty," falls clearly into the region of "communication." Likewise, one of Maisonneuve's subcategories communication, "sharing joys and sorrows," is found more precisely in the region of steadfastness. Thus, I can more accurately identify two facets rather than three among the interviewees' coded definitions of friendship. I will call these facets "communication" and "steadfastness" because they are close but not identical to Maisonneuve's original cut.[16]

Is Friendship More an Intimate Relationship of Stylistic Variation or Social Penetration?

Montrealers' friendships are most accurately depicted by a model of stylistic variation. Summing up their most significant friendships reveals a complex diversity in these Montrealers' different stylistic profiles. Still, we have seen that a third of the in-depth interviewees have stylistic profiles identical to at least one or two other interviewees, although this overlapping is spread among six different styles. Moreover, multidimensional scalogram analysis and smallest space analysis have enabled me to identify two polarities that hold together the constellations that arose in the Montreal of the 1970s. These polarizing facets appear to pull the space orthogonally between a {head-to-heart friendship} facet and an {institutionalized-to-chosen similar-interest friendship} facet. It would not be inappropriate to describe these as psycho-social force fields which underlie the relative positions in space of the friendship styles that characterized the Montrealers of this period.

Yet, these empirically derived styles of friendship would seem to put into question some aspects of important descriptions of friendship and theories about the psycho-social process that gives rise to friendship.

First of all, it turns out that the forces of culture and society, operating in particular, contextual circumstances and through individual personalities, impose real limits on the friendships in the lives of the Montrealers in my sample. Seen in another light, my interviewees' styles and definitions mapped out into a rather clear constellation in the 1970s, which necessarily suggests that other patterns were left unrealized. From either examining the profiles in the raw data or in their multivariate interaction, it becomes clear that none of my in-depth interviewees enacted all the styles of friendship identified, and, indeed, most people experienced a few of these styles through one or another of their various close friendships. On a different level, my interviewees' definitions of friendship, reflecting their norms, expectations, and experiences of this relationship, fall into two facets, those of communication and steadfastness, which seem to overlay the facets of the styles of friendship on a psycho-social plane. By this statement, I mean that the stylistic facet of {institutionalized-to-chosen similar-interest friendship} seems to be manifested in the definitional facet of {steadfastness}. Likewise, the definitional facet of {communication} is superimposed upon the stylistic facet of {head-to-heart}.

The notion of styles of friendship emphasizes the content of the most important friendships in the lives of the Montrealers who accepted to be interviewed in depth. When they dialogued with the interviewers, filled out questionnaires, and wrote essays on friendship, they were able to grasp to some degree "the overt and behavioral events and the covert cognitive and affective responses that occur when people interact" as friends.[17] In brief, my study helped its participants deepen their understanding of process in their friendship. However, this current definition of process is broader and more flexible than the great emphasis on changes in an interpersonal process of social penetration that still influences the thinking of many social psychologists.[18] In this somewhat older sense my interviewees were often able to identify changes in their friendships but did not experience them as process. Moreover, Montrealers' accounts, questionnaires, and essays on friendship provided information on "proxy measures of process" such as multiplexity and directionality, but these were not the aspects of their friendships which were most meaningful to them.[19]

If we examine the content areas of the MSA of the friendship styles of my in-depth interviewees, we see that in the western half of the map are those individuals whose intersecting styles of friendship tend to be rooted in more traditional bonds of family and neighborhood. We have already heard some of the highly complex explanations of how friendship became possible in such relatively confined circumstances. Often the forces that initially promoted the friendships among the interviewees in this area have to do with affinities that were supported by the rather predictable social groups of family, neighborhood, school, club, and church. Although these affinities collect over time, this socio-emotional baggage was not necessarily experienced by my interviewees in a deep way. While knowing more about a friend's action over time may be "deeper" in the sense that more of an aspect of the person becomes known to a friend, it may not be the kind of knowledge that conveys with it the affective warmth, indeed, the mysterious fleeting fusion, that activates a bond felt as deep friendship. The mere collection of such knowledge may be a sign that a deep friendship is felt by the gatherer.

Part of the trouble with the idea of an interpersonal penetration process, even with a notion of breadth, is that it implies one essentially ideal form of friendship in which "as people continue to interact and maintain a relationship, they gradually move toward deeper areas of their mutual personalities through the use of words, bodily behavior, and environmental behaviors."[20] Friendships in the real world in Montreal were not nearly so neat! The female teacher of English in her thirties of French Canadian background told me that she does not know why she made friends with one childhood neighbor and not the others and then later tells me that this friend relaxes her though sympathetic listening and emotional nurturing, while she provides her friend with exciting stories of adventure outside her very domestic world. Am I to conclude that their complementary personalities are the key to their friendship or that they had built up a deep exchange though a gradual communication process over the years. Or are these two facts just part of the larger process? Perhaps Altman and Taylor would argue that their initial affinity of complementary personalities provided them with a base upon which to refine a deeper process of communication over the years which inserted their "pin" deeper and deeper into the layers of their "onion"? But from what she told me she did not discuss her pending divorce in detail with this friend but with another friend who knew her husband as well. Could it be that she did not want to threaten this close friend who had always lived such a sheltered life? For whatever reason, she, like many my other in-depth interviewees, chose not to communicate in-depth with a close friend about *some* major life events but instead chose another friend or kept it for themselves. The point is that most of my Montreal interviewees did not seem to place *progressively* a "pin" into the deeper parts of their friends' selves. Some may have done so, or even jumped into a "breadth" extension which "stuck in" deeply from the very beginning--due to varying initial affinities. But others varied in the degrees of depth they interacted with their friends all along as they added new or maturing experiences to their initial ones. Often their feeling of the "depth" was a rare but specially remembered moment.

Even if I were to try to cram my data into the categories of Altman and Taylor's theory, where would the various styles of friendship be ordered along their breadth and depth dimensions? It would be easy to place "the Buddy *Copain-Copine* Phenomenon" on the outer layer of the circle, but what happens in the next inner layers of the circle? Would we place the similar-interest style of friendship on the next level proceeding inward? For many of my interviewees, this similar-interest was deeply felt, and for some was the key to getting an excellent job, certainly the *Arbeiten* of Freud's formula for mental health. And if the Aristotelian and Platonic debates on whether the deepest part of friendship is a reflective *philia* or an impassioned *eros* still go on, who am I to decide which is to be placed at the core?

The model of varying friendship styles is more tolerant and relativistic towards the wide variety of ways of being friends. If a person called and defined a relationship a close friendship and was able to recount its content, present, development, and make-up, then I am satisfied that it should be considered a friendship. In a certain sense the more styles that characterized any particular friendship may indicate that it is at least a richer, if not deeper, relationship. Therefore, if two friends are neighbors, are integrated into one another's families as close friends, and share a variety of similar interests, and when they are separated, are often in one another's thoughts; then, if we also knew that they felt extremely close to one another, we would think that they had a very deep friendship. Or would an individual who experienced one or two different styles of friendship with four or five close friends be a person who had a greater capacity for friendship than a person who limited herself or himself to the same styles of friendship with one or two persons? Probably so, but we would need to know much more about the specific contents of the friendships compared before we could make such an assessment.

Furthermore, the content of the styles of friendship and the definitions of friendship cover a large part of social penetration theory's notion of breadth. Unlike the notion of breadth, they are rooted in a historical and ethnographic context. To remove them from that context strips them of what is most meaningful to their shared field. The map which locates that field shows that a large area of Montreal friendships was bounded within fairly traditional spheres of family, neighborhood, and, to a lesser extent, other propinquitous life areas like work. Each of these institutions places definite constraints on the breadth to which a close friendship could be cultivated but provides other psycho-social supports, such as predictability and security. By offering a wide variety of new alternatives in the realm of intimate relationships, the Montreal of the 1970s also exerted social control over a majority of my in-depth interviewees by providing satisfying friendship bonds within traditional institutions. The differences in breadth and depth are matters of a particular context, which confers meanings upon particular friends. Giving your keys to your neighbor-friend downstairs is seemingly a sign of trust, but it takes on very different meanings for the person who has most of her precious life possessions in her apartment and one who has little or nothing of value to steal. If my interviewee did not tell her neighbor-friend of the depth of her grief on the death of her mother, does it mean that their friendship was shallow? Hardly, if she had been socialized in a group where overt expression of grief was not encouraged.

Yet, the kinds of tradition that emanate from the friendship styles of a majority of my in-depth interviewees reveal an unstated process of irregular testing in real life circumstances for the quality of the friendship. The little words, the unspoken gestures, the silent deeds, all helped construct the close friendships Montrealers shared with me. A better analogy to describe becoming friends than Altman's and Taylor's "onion with a pin sticking through it" would be that of an old treasure chest in which very carefully selected jewels are stored.

Individuals and groups tending toward one or more friendship stylistic profiles may have difficulty understanding or appreciating the expectancies or behavior of others with different friendship styles. This is true for those with a prominently communicative friendship stylistics interacting with those with a predominantly steadfast stylistics. The person with a communicative style may not feel heard, appreciated, or emotionally touched, while the person with a stylistics of steadfastness may feel that she or he is encountering a "flake" who is all talk and no dependable action. For such a conflict, an intervention based upon a thorough knowledge of all the interacting friends and all their friendships-

-upon which a change strategy may be built--is more likely to succeed than an intervention based upon a universally applicable process.

Macro-Socio-Cultural Structures and the Styles of Friendship

Is the map of friendship styles relevant to the larger macro-socio-cultural structures? In my judgment the social democratic policies that the Canadian federal, provincial, and municipal governments pursued, to a greater extent than in the United States and to a lesser extent than in northern Europe--from roughly the Quiet Revolution to the late 1970s--eased the extent to which intimates, including friends, had to depend on each other in extreme situations brought on by poor health, natural, or economic disaster. Such policies as family allowances, socialized medicine, and urban planning set the contours of maintaining intact an individual in his or her family and neighborhood by encouraging basic protection against ill health, unemployment, and urban blight. In this sense, the more traditional relationships from which many of my in-depth interviewees' friendships were chosen were supported by the macro-socio-cultural structures. Furthermore, the policies of subsidizing urban transportation and parks opened up access to the urban space available for friends' mutual enjoyment and reduced the rigidity of class barriers blocking meeting people of different groups. I use the term "socio-cultural" rather than social because the value milieu made possible the enacting of these "structures." Such policies incorporate all citizens into the same community by putting them into a similar position in terms of rights and obligations vis-à-vis the state. But the value milieu of the Quebec of the 1970s framed these structures with unique tones of particularism, particularly new nationalistic or ethnic forces, that may have facilitated the acceptance of these policies, but, at the same time, rooted them in a long tradition of Quebec's special status. This unique history put friendship in a special position, being pulled strongly between forces of particularism and universalism, which will be documented in subsequent chapters.

Yet, because these programs were in place or being extended at the time of my study, it is difficult to measure their impact on friendship with the tools of a positivistic methodology, except by documenting how some friendships are enhanced by facilities made available by these policies. For example, when the teacher in this chapter said how much she and one of her friends enjoyed walking and talking on the Mount Royal, and how much this relaxed them, we could say that park maintenance, as an indicator of social democratic policy, had indirectly contributed to their quality of their friendship by providing them with a beautiful and restful environment. Similarly, these welfare state policies may have made family life a bit more secure by providing a bit more money, and a bit more happiness, thereby slowing other forces for family change emanating from the international arena, and, thereby making family life a bit more fertile for friendship. In another realm, urban planning and renewal have helped stabilize neighborhoods, and, thereby make them loci for the choice of friends. The metro, public plazas, sport centers, parks and spectacles, provided free or at very low cost to the public, enabled a larger part of the citizenry to meet and possibly make friendships with more of the other subgroups of the culture and society. So too did these facilities expose a large segment of all social groups to larger areas of the urban space.

Many outsiders think of Montreal as a "wide-open" city, where almost anything goes. From the perspective of a small town New Englander, Ontarian, or upstate New Yorker, this observation may seem true, but many life-long residents still liken it to a little village or one big family. Sociologists like to compare cities of similar size and make-up, and when the Montreal of the 1970s is compared to another city in this fashion, its political culture was more nationalistic and left-leaning. While nearly all of the alternative lifestyles in other North American cities could be found, Montreal was rather conservative in this regard in comparison to the largest North American megalopolis. Within this context, the styles of friendship found in my interviews frequently were sheltered under the umbrella of these other institutions.

Notes

1. Jean Maisonneuve, *Psycho-sociologie des affinités* (Paris: Presses universitaires de France, 1966), 191; Also see: Matthews, Sarah H., *Friendship through the Life Course: Oral Biographies in Old Age* (Newbury Park: Sage Publications, 1986), 33-58. Also see: Gurdin, J. Barry. "Styles of Friendship." Paper presented at the eighty-fourth annual meeting of the American Sociological Association, San Francisco, August 1989 [available from *Sociological Abstracts*, paper number 89S21438/ASA/1989/5254]. In addition, consult Cohen, Theodore, F., "Men's Families, Men's Friends: A Structural Analysis of Constraints on Men's Social Ties," in ed. Peter N. Nardi, 1992, 117.

2. Maisonneuve, 1966, 191.

3. Recall that all proper names have been changed throughout this book. Words in brackets [ ] are my substitutions that give the interviewee's general meaning but which assist in guarding the interviewee's anonymity.

4. Matthews, 1986, 34.

5. Ibid., 45-58.

6. Maisonneuve, 1966, 191.

7. Gurdin, *Amitié / Friendship*, (see Chap. 1, n. 33, p. 50, Table 1.2 Method "P": A Content Analysis of the Definitions of Friendship by Subcategories of Definitional Components of Friendship).

8. Question #12. The Relationship between the Frequency of the Interviewees' and Respondents' Discussing Their Most Intimate Problems with Their Close Friends and the Socio-economic Status of the Interviewees and Respondents

Socio-economic Status	Often Count & Col %	Rarely	Never	*A Tie	Row
Blue Collar Worker	18 22.8%	6 16.7%	16 47.1%	0 0%	40 26%
White Collar Worker	35 44.3%	18 50%	7 20.6%	3 60%	63 40.9%
Professional	26 32.9%	12 33.3%	11 32.4%	2 40%	51 33.1%
Column Total	79 51.3%	36 23.4%	34 22.1%	5 3.2%	154 100%

Raw χ^2 = 13.53438 with 6 Degrees of Freedom.
Significance = .0353 Number of Missing Observations = 21

9.

Interviewees' and Respondents' Communicating Intimacies to Close Friends, from Closest, Friend 1, to Least Intimate, Friend 10.

Closeness of Friend	Percentage of Interviewees' Communicating Intimacies to Friend 1 through Friend 10
Friend 1	28.7%
Friend 2	21.9%
Friend 3	19.3%
Friend 4	14.0%
Friend 5	9.0%
Friend 6	6.4%
Friend 7	0.2%
Friend 8	0.2%
Friend 9	0.2%
Friend 10	0.2%

10. Zvulun, Eli, "Multidimensional Scalogram Analysis: The Method and Its Application," in *Theory Construction and Data Analysis in the Behavioral Sciences*, ed. Samuel Shye (San Francisco: Jossey-Bass Publishers, 1978), 237-264; Lingoes, James C., "The Multivariate

Analysis of Qualitative Data," in *Geometric Representations of Relational Data: Readings in Multidimensional Scaling*, eds. James C. Lingoes, Edward E. Roskam, and Ingwer Borg (Ann Arbor, Michigan: Mathesis Press, 1979), 575-608.

11. To carry out this analysis, I first had to translate my clinical data into quantifiable units of presence ["2"] and absence ["1"] of the ten possible styles for each of my fifty in-depth interviewees. These formed a "profile" for each of these people. During the course of the analysis, I learned that only three people were classified as having Style A2, "The Remaining Family Friendship after the Break-up of the Family," and only one displayed Style C2, "The Buddy-*Copain-Copine* Phenomenon." These styles were, therefore, eliminated from the final analysis, although retained in the original data file. This left a maximum number of eight styles of friendship to describe any individual. For example, the first subject possessed the style of friendship encoded by "2" and lacked those styles encoded by "1" in the following manner:

Friendship Styles:	A1	A3	A4	B1	B2	C1	D	E
Interviewee 1:	2	2	1	2	1	1	1	2

After the item plots for each of the eight friendship styles were processed by MSA-I, six item plots yielded clear areas of presence and absence of these various styles. The coefficient of contiguity for five iterations for these item plots was .989101E+00.

12. When all of these regions are superimposed onto the same two dimensional space, we can see the joint partition of the space for fifty interviewees (structuples) into six regions of contiguity.

Examining the color-coded regions enables us to see how the individuals overlap in their friendship styles; however, attention should be paid to remembering that regionality is rarely pure, and, therefore, the regions represent the best fit of the data.

Attention should be paid to the areas demarcated by the color-coded partition lines. The numbers appearing in the space are the identification numbers of my interviewees. When these numbers are separated by a comma, it means that they are to be mapped onto the same space.

I wish to express my gratitude to Mrs. Linda Hanson, of The University of Chicago's Laboratory for Methodology in Child Development, who ran the MSA program and made several helpful suggestions for data analysis. Also I thank my wife, Rita J. Jeremy, Ph.D.--former Senior Researcher of the same project--for suggesting a way to numerically code my data and to design color-coded overlays.

13. Shye, Samuel, ed., 1979, 11-15; Levy, Shlomit and Louis Gutttman, "On the Multivariate Structure of Wellbeing," in ed. Ingwer Borg, 1981, 125-152; Guttman, Louis, 1968, "A General Nonmetric Technique for Finding the Smallest Coordinate Space for a Configuration of Points," *Psychometrika*, 33, 469-506; Wilkinson, Leland, *System Systat Statistics*. (Evanston, Illinois: Systat, Inc., 1984), 227-239.

14. In the analyses that follow that refer to the styles of friendship and in the subsequent series that have to do with the definitions of friendship, I will present the Guttman/Lingoes coefficient of alienation, the SSA in three dimensions, and the coordinates in three dimensions for my data. The following matrix is associated with the plot of the friendship styles in three dimensions displayed in Appendix D. For a discussion of the $\mu2$ coefficient, see Samuel Shye ed., 1978, 277.

Monotonic Multidimensional Scaling

Minimizing Guttman/Lingoes Coefficient of Alienation in 3 Dimensions

Iteration	Alienation
1	.259
2	.202
3	.180
4	.171
5	.160

Stress of Final Configuration Is: .16035

Similarities

Coordinates in 3 Dimensions

Note that the variables A1 - E refer to the styles of friendship which are abbreviated here from their full labels used throughout this book.

Variables	Dimension		
Styles of Friendship	1	2	3
A1=Family-oriented	-.64	.02	-.45
A2=after the Break-up	-.90	-.09	.13
A3=The Sibling Friendship	.19	.87	.05
A4=Non-nuclear Family	.03	-.24	.69
B1=The Neighbor-Friend	-.59	.05	.58
B2=Best-Friend Proximity	.77	.25	.58
C1=Similar-Interest Close	.45	.13	-.81
C2=*Buddy-Copain-Copine*	.35	-1.49	-.33
D=*Petit/e Ami/e*	1.15	.25	-.09
E=Friend-in-Mind	-.80	.25	-.35

15. See Gurdin, *Amitié/Friendship*, (Chap. 1, n. 39, Table 1.2 Method "P": A Content Analysis of the Definitions of Friendship by Subcategories of Definitional Components of Friendship).

16. Matrix of $\mu2$ Coefficients for the Maisonneuvean Content Analytical Categories. The Column and Row Headings Stand for: RA=Reciprocal Affection; PBT=Pleasure of Being Together; SJS=Sharing Joys and Sorrows; CBIT=Confiding (Being Intimate Together); MU=Mutual Understanding; BFSNS=Being Frank, Sincere, (Not Secretive); COIOT=Community of Ideas, of Tastes; FREOFAS=Friends Resemble Each Other (Friend Another Self); FCEO=Friends Complement Each Other; COTFIAC=Count on the Friends in All Circumstances; MAIS=Material Aid, Services; MSAIU=Moral Support (Sought after in Unhappiness); DSD=Devotion, Sacrifice, Disinterestedness; TL=Trust, Loyalty; CPFIH=Constancy, Perenniality, (Friendship Is Holy) .

	Reciprocal Affection=RA	Pleasure of Being Together= PBT	Sharing Joys and Sorrows= SJS	Confiding (Being Intimate Together= CBIT	Mutual Under-standing=MU
RA	1.000				
PBT	0.186	1.000			
SJS	0.106	0.283	1.000		
CBIT	-0.383	0.467	0.204	1.000	
MU	0.163	0.209	0.328	0.156	1.000
BFSNS	0.484	0.162	0.571	0.264	0.302
COIOT	0.256	0.233	-0.092	-0.405	0.150
FREOFAS	0.634	0.274	0.083	-0.456	0.536
FCEO	-0.006	0.468	-1.000	0.481	0.667
COTFIAC	-0.254	-0.115	0.061	0.051	0.070
MAIS	-0.466	-0.613	-0.111	-0.197	-0.125
MSAIU	0.236	-0.113	0.623	0.026	0.108
DSD	0.205	-0.230	-0.040	-0.121	-0.151
TL	0.392	-0.148	-0.024	0.154	0.132
CPFIH	0.197	0.143	0.350	0.164	-0.361

	Being Frank, Sincere, (Not Secretive)= BFSNS	Community of Ideas, of Tastes= COIOT	Friends Resemble Each Other (Friend Another Self)= FREOFAS	Friends Complement Each Other= FCEO	Count on the Friends in All Circum- stances= COTFIAC
BFSNS	1.000				
COIOT	-0.030	1.000			
FREOFAS	0.583	0.112	1.000		
FCEO	0.152	-1.000	0.939	1.000	
COTFIAC	-0.141	-0.208	-0.310	-0.295	1.000
MAIS	-0.059	-0.467	-1.000	-1.000	-0.131
MSAIU	0.181	0.008	0.171	0.424	0.002
DSD	0.037	-0.304	0.183	0.173	0.067
TL	0.532	0.333	0.274	0.468	0.019
CPFIH	0.390	0.486	0.003	0.283	0.295

	Material Aid, Services= MAIS	Moral Support (Sought after in Unhappi-ness)=MSAIU	Devotion, Sacrifice, Disinterested ness=DSD	Trust, Loyalty= TL	Constancy, Perenniality, (Friendship Is Holy)= CPFIH
MAIS	1.000				
MSAIU	0.260	1.000			
DSD	-0.304	0.206	1.000		
TL	-0.215	-0.233	0.200	1.000	
CPFIH	-0.190	0.208	-0.412	0.048	1.000

Number of Observations: 122

In the discussion in the text, I will present the Guttman/Lingoes coefficient of alienation, the SSA (Smallest Space Analysis) and the coordinates in three dimensions for my data on the definitions of friendship in Montreal.

Monotonic Multidimensional Scaling
Minimizing Guttman/Lingoes Coefficient of Alienation in 3 Dimensions

Iteration	Alienation
1	.239
2	.207
3	.205
4	.205
5	.204

Stress of final configuration is:　　.20383

Similarities Coordinates in 3 Dimensions

Letter Representing Maisonneuve's Content Analytical Category in SSA	1	2	3	Maisonneuve's Content Analytical Categories for Encoding Respondents' Definitions of Friendship and Their Abbreviations
A	.49	.73	.03	Reciprocal Affection=RA
B	.42	-.62	-.64	Pleasure of Being Together=PBT
C	-.48	-.22	-.36	Sharing Joys and Sorrows=SJS
D	-.30	-1.04	-.19	Confiding (Being Intimate Together)=CBIT
E	.40	-.66	.22	Mutual Understanding=MU
F	.18	.09	-.04	Being Frank, Sincere, (Not Secretive)=BFSNS
G	.40	.77	-.89	Community of Ideas, of Tastes=COIOT
H	.86	-.08	.24	Friends Resemble Each Other, Friend Another Self=FREOFAS
I	.59	-.59	.46	Friends Complement Each Other=FCEO
J	-1.14	.13	-.56	Count on the Friends in All Circumstances=COTFIAC
K	-1.41	.21	.73	Material Aid, Services=MAIS
L	-.56	.02	.45	Moral Support (Sought after in Unhappiness)=MSAIU
M	.11	.44	1.12	Devotion, Sacrifice, Disinterestedness=DSD
N	.70	.50	.19	Trust, Loyalty=TL
O	-.25	.33	-.77	Constancy, Perenniality, (Friendship Is Holy)=CPFIH

Now consult Appendix D for the three-dimensional smallest space analysis of Montrealers' definitions of friendship.

17. Rosemary Blieszner and Rebecca G. Adams, *Adult Friendship*, 1992, 12. borrowed their definition of process from (Kelley, Berscheid, Christensen, Harvey, Huston, Levinger, McClintock, Peplau & Peterson, 1983).

18. Altman, Irwin and Dalmas A. Taylor, *Social Penetration: The Development of Interpersonal Relationships* (New York: Irvington Publishers, Inc.), 1973, 27.

19. See Blieszner and Adams, *Adult Friendship*, 14-15. Citing the definitions of others, they define multiplexity as "The number of different activities in which friends participate" and directionality as "whether friends behave reciprocally, a particular friend gives more, or that friend receives more."

20. Altman and Taylor, *Social Penetration,* 15; Also see: Ibid., 27.

Chapter Three

Some of My Best Friends Are ...

We have just considered ten relatively different experiences of being friends. These styles of friendship are set in the context of a city in which ethnicity plays a very important role in nearly all aspects of life. Whether a Montrealer is English Canadian, French Canadian, or a member of one of the "Other" Canadian ethnic groups strongly delimits the boundaries of his or her friendships and what he or she will think about close friendship and do with close friends. The enormous importance of ethnic affiliation in determining the character of friendship in Montreal is revealed through such varying sources as questionnaires, in-depth interviews, a survey of public opinion, film, plays, newspaper articles, history, and participant observation. In depicting the relationship between ethnicity and friendship in Montreal, I will draw on all these various sources.

The Frequency of Friendship across Ethnic Groups

First of all, let us consider how frequently Montrealers cross ethnic lines in forming close friendships. Cultural artifacts such as literature portray the incidence of intimate interethnic contact as rather rare. Thus, specifically referring to ethnic relations between English Canadians and French Canadians, Hugh MacLennan coined the poetic description of "two solitudes," and the eminent Canadian sociologist, John Porter, described the degree to which ethnicity acts as a determinant of social stratification in Canada with the phrase, "the vertical mosaic."[1]

After gathering the data for my doctoral thesis, for which I had, in part, engaged in participant observation of close friendship in a bi-lingual Montreal college, I directed my students in two classes in the spring of 1977 at the Loyola campus of Concordia University in designing and carrying out a public opinion survey that looked into this issue.[2] The other concern of that survey aimed at learning about Montrealers' definitions of and distinctions between the words, Quebecer and *Québécois*.[3]

In our public opinion poll, we attempted to operationalize our concepts in part by asking people in the general population to report their own ethnicity and that of their six closest friends. Two questions from that survey help us to shed light on the relationship of ethnicity to close friendship. Question two asked: "To which ethnic group do you belong?" Question four asked: "To which ethnic group do your six closest friends belong?"

As can be seen in Appendix C, these data lead to the conclusion that most people chose more of their closest friends from their own ethnic group, although people from all groups chose close friends from groups outside their own as well. In good sociologese, it could be stated that a very high degree of ethnic homophily in closest friendship choice characterizes all ethnic groups in Montreal. This evidence supports my more qualitative findings based on participant observation in a small college that I will summarize in this discussion.[4]

As I have dealt elsewhere with the other areas concerning ethnic identity in this smallest space analysis, here we need to pay attention only to the items which refer to ethnicity.[5] The ethnicity of the subject is highly correlated with the ethnicity of his or her six closest friends, as can be seen in the semi-strong monotonicity coefficients of the items and of their closeness in space.[6]

Occupation exerts the only consistent influence for all three ethnic groups, and this influence is at a low to moderate level. In general, the background characteristics do not seem to have very much influence on how universalistic or particularistic a judge's ratings of an interviewee's definition of or distinctions between Quebecer and *Québécois* were. As Professor Louis Guttman and Shlomit Levy have noted often before,

> Indeed, this phenomenon of small correlation with background characteristics has been widely observed and is common to many research topics. Such static characteristics usually do not serve as very good predictors of attitudes and values.[7]

Occupation is just one indicator of class in the stratificationalist conception. Education and income are usually the other combined indicators of socioeconomic class. Although these criteria are usually rather highly correlated, I cannot assume that one produces the same effect as the other. Whatever the case, I must note a possible cross-cultural difference in the degree to which class conditions the relationship of friendship in comparing the Bay Area around San Francisco with Montreal. Claude Fischer found that education more than any other characteristic seemed to affect respondents' networks, and his discussion of networks overlaps considerably with my discussion of friendship. "In general, education meant broader, deeper, and richer networks."[8]

In Montreal while interviewees with higher status occupations have friends from a somewhat less ethnically homogeneous group than do individuals with low or middle class occupations, this difference is not large. Ethnicity seems to exert considerably more influence on the formation of close friendships in Montreal in comparison to the Bay Area. Yet, as in the Bay Area, it is somewhat attenuated by class. As we see later in this chapter, attitudes toward outgroups may be a stronger explanation for this phenomenon than Fischer's subcultural theory.[9] Fischer writes that "Urban ethnics may be less self conscious and formal about their membership and yet seem to be more immersed in an ethnic social world than their small-town cousins."[10] If anything, the opposite is true in Quebec, for the competition with other ethnic groups is greatest in the urban area, especially the metropolis of Montreal. Moreover, the decline of religion and greater contact with different language-groups, particularly English-speaking, North Americans, may be less notable in Rimouski, Quebec, than in Montreal. The effects of ethnic stratification in Montreal's economy and "urban economic competition ... organized among ethnic lines" more adequately explain boundaries between friendships across ethnic lines in Montreal.[11] The highly stratified nature of ethnic groups in Montreal's economy creates a barrier in the chances for people to form cross-ethnic friendship on an equal footing, or, if the status-role positions of potential friends be similar, competition for scarce positions may put them in conflict, thereby reducing their chances for becoming close friends.

Factors Inhibiting Close Friendship Across Ethnic Lines

What brings about this situation in which the greatest number of one's friends come from a similar ethnic background? First we can look at ecology. As in other North American cities, Montreal is spatially divided into geographic areas that contain high concentrations of various ethnic groups. In the local folklore, St. Lawrence was said to be the dividing line between the "French" and "English" parts of the city, but as in other North American cities, the geographic locus of ethnic concentration has changed as waves of occupation and succession have followed one another.[12] One reminder of this trend is that Quebec's cities were overwhelmingly English-speaking in the last century. With the influx of the French Canadians into the city, Montreal's "East End" became the French Canadian working and lower class and side of town while Outremont, after overtaking St. Joseph's Boulevard, became the upper and upper middle class French Canadian area. Stratification could strike the eyes with examples of, for instance, heavy concentrations of the Irish Catholic working class living in the plain below the cliff of the once solidly English Canadian, upper class, Protestant Westmount. After the

Second World War with the expansion of suburbanization and economic differentiation, parts of the middle class moved to the suburbs or *banlieux* which appear to be characterized by a greater degree of ethnic mixture.

A second factor contributing to the high degree of ethnic similarity in close friend choice is the denominational affiliation of education in the Province of Quebec. The Protestant, Catholic, and English-speaking and French-speaking lines of education in Quebec further attenuate the chances for making friends of other ethnic groups, especially for school aged citizens, and particularly on the French-speaking Catholic side.[13] Although the schools have lost much of their specifically religious content, many commentators have noticed that the religious element has been replaced by or substituted with a heightened degree of nationalism or ethnic consciousness of kind. This is not to argue that school years are the only or even particularly better for producing close friends. Rather, I am arguing that this factor acts as a salient constraint on making close friends from other ethnic groups over a significant period of the life cycle when attitudes toward out-groups are forming that may be less malleable in later years. Again, this is not to claim that cross-ethnic contact will be positive either for education or positive regard for out-groups.[14] Indeed, the violent confrontations that took place between French Canadian and Italian Canadian teenagers in Ville St. Laurent over the language of instruction evidence that ethnic group contact in and around the school may result in hostile and negative feelings and polarize and politicize the groundwork for interethnic contacts. Such a case illustrates an outcome of the contact hypothesis, where the groups interacting assume dissimilarities in attitudes, values, and beliefs that would probably disappear if members of the two groups could experience social interaction under favorable conditions.[15] On the other hand, "If the outgroup members are found to possess characteristics that lead to dislike," the contact "will exacerbate a poor relationship." Yet inter-group contact within the same school environment can provide the common ground of shared interest, age grade, activities, discussions of ideas, and personal information that contribute to close friendship in a favorable environment.[16] A complementary, functional, attitudinally conflictual situation can fall in between an atmosphere conducive to friendship and enmity. Such were the observations I made in a Montreal college.[17]

When I began the analysis of my dissertation material, I was working first part-time for one semester, then one year full-time as an instructor of sociology, philosophy, and English as a second language at a bilingual college which had been a private secretarial school which had recently become affiliated with the CEGEP (junior or community college) system. Approximately half the school was French-speaking and the other half was predominately English-speaking. The French-speaking half was almost exclusively of French Canadian ethnicity with a few individuals of Italian Canadian background who were studying in the French-speaking classes of the college. On the English-speaking side, the ethnic background was reflective of the highly heterogeneous ethnic make-up of Montreal. I taught both the French and English-speaking groups, although most of my classes were taught to the French-speaking division. The faculty was also divided between English and French-speaking sides, although faculty desks were housed in one L-shaped room. The head and owner of the college is half English and half French Canadian and is a perfectly bilingual male of middle age. The head of courses is a bilingual English Canadian female in her thirties who speaks French with a marked English Canadian accent. This social setting provides some interesting insights into the working of ethnicity as a social mechanism in friendship formation.

It was "common knowledge" to all insiders that there was an "English" and a "French" division in the college. The general tone of interaction between all groups was cordial and polite with occasional exchanges across ethnic lines, for example, in physical educational classes and, to a lesser degree, at school dances. Among most individuals there was a certain tension expressed in cross ethnic group communication, and there was a handful of individuals who crossed into the other group. The lowest level of ethnic segregation was found among the faculty members in whose room the ecology of the desk arrangement was not laid out on ethnic lines. Each group maintained images of each other, although this backstage information was mainly provided by the students. Among faculty and administrators this topic was to be avoided except in rare episodes of spoken incidents of frustration. The perceptions of each group at the college, as expressed in their behind-the-back or out-of-sight verbal exchanges, were essentially negative. Nearly all of the students were young women studying to become various kinds of secretaries or travel agents. In this situation, the French-speaking French Canadians saw the English-speaking English Canadians as being sloppy and ill-mannered. The English Canadians saw the French Canadians as being showy and complainers. These images were reported to individual teachers but not exchanged, for instance, in the mutually shared cafeteria where all the young women come to smoke, or have a snack at the food machines in the locker-community room. What stands out in my personal observations as being relevant for this discussion is that no very close or "best" friendships were observed over one year and a half between the English and French Canadian students across the anglophone/francophone administrative divisions of the school. A handful of close friendships were observed across ethnic lines within the English-speaking side of the school, and one close friendship was seen between a French-speaking Italian Canadian and a French Canadian. Several friendships, but not "best" or "closest" friendships, were seen between English-speaking (ethnically mixed among English, Jewish, Italian, Irish, and Polish Canadians and Americans) and French-speaking Canadians in the faculty room. As a general rule, this college was very traditional and family oriented. Most of the young women returned home traveling rather long transit distances daily, and they reported that most of their close friendship took place out of the school setting.

The low volume of close friendship that I observed in this institution can be explained by its character of being a rather socially and culturally conservative school, whose students and faculty members tended to be strongly oriented to their families, and whose career choices were primarily as secretaries or travel agents, many for large scale organizations. In this environment the college was viewed as a good place to get excellent training for an assured job in an office of quality. Such imagery was symbolically exemplified in its promotional audio-visual show and recruitment program, and the college's director expressed these values to whole families assembled in the audience of potential recruits. In this setting, social relationships were implicitly downplayed to the content of its course material, and close friendships, while not overtly discouraged, were constrained by the motivations of the students in choosing this college. The social occasions which did take place were mainly events to meet members of the opposite sex for possibly serious relationships, whose first aim was reproduction of the marriage and the family.

A third major factor contributing to the high degree of ethnic homophily in close friendship choice is attitude. There exists a norm in Montreal that one should have friends regardless of a person's ethnic background, race, or creed. Many interviewees in my dissertation phrased this norm in quasi-religious tones.[18] Yet both in my thesis study and present data, respondents report having more of their closest friends from their own ethnic background. Two attitudinal factors influence this seeming contradiction. First of all, despite the norm that one should have friends from all ethnic backgrounds, my participant observation of a small bi-lingual college in Montreal suggests that ethnic group members hold essentially negative stereotypical opinions of out-groups, and this is especially noted when it is cross-cut along English- and French-speaking lines. It could be that these negative attitudes are held alongside positive ones, but are not commonly articulated unless particularly elicited.[19] Furthermore, the negative outgroup images observed may be more strongly felt by the cohort of CEGEP age. Together with this observation, the higher nationalistic overtones of the historical period of the mid-1970s, when these observations were collected, could have heightened the degree of tension in cross-ethnic relations in Montreal.

In Montreal, as elsewhere, "the idols of the tribe" include a name, history, and origins of a group, national, regional or tribal affiliation language, religion, value system (inherited clusters of mores), ethics, aesthetics and the attributes that come out of geography or topography of a birthplace, but a generalized world view and pure chance are the factors which are perceived as mainly determining these ethnic worlds which reinforce barriers to close friendship.[20] Listen to the way in which a public school teacher in her mid-to-late thirties, a married woman with one child, who lives in a middle- to upper-middle class west-island suburb, tells us about the effect of her ethnicity on her and her husband's closest friendships:

> We are very Anglo-Saxon. We are somewhat musical. It makes us have a lot of acquaintances. Our musical activities do help tremendously. Say, we do Scottish country dancing, and I sing, so in both of these activities I make a lot of acquaintances. I don't really know how deeply I know these people, but I think being Anglo-Saxon we have a tendency to be reserved in our outgoing expressions towards other people which has nothing to do with depth because you can show very little towards other people and yet have very deep feeling ... .

Speaking in French, a French Canadian senior citizen of working class background reminisced about her people and her feeling of belonging to her ethnic group to Ms. Michèle Verrette, a younger native Quebecer who strongly identified as being a *Québécoise* at the time of the interview:

> When you travel a bit, well that lets us get to know other milieu, and then other mentalities, {and} to be in contact with other people, the public and all that. And frankly, that does you good. And sometimes, you make other friendships. You meet other people from our country, but who only do not stay in the same province ... It's funny how you feel tied among people of the same race.[21] When you go elsewhere, when you go to the United States, you know, the few trips that we have made there, we meet French Canadians. It's funny how you feel attracted right away ... then ... even if we didn't know them a long time, it's like we knew them for a long time ... I don't know if it is the blood that speaks, but right away we become, we help out each other, we tend,

you know, if there is something, sometimes, you feel a bit
helpless ... We are used to, for example, ... to help out one
another, to take them in our car, you know, we French
Canadians have, how could I say it, the best mentality in
the world, I think ... It's hospitable, you know, touching, we
are always brought to, it seems to me--not always in the
same province, in the same country; it is always said that
French Canadians are awkward to deal with, then, yes, ...
but it's funny when you see that it isn't true when you go
elsewhere--we meet people of our race; it's unbelievable;
you see that the blood does speak; if we go away as we
have taken several trips, when you go out in the street, you
see a license plate from Quebec. It's not deceiving. We
honk. And then the others, it's the same, you know. It's "hi
there" ... really I am really happy to be a type of the kind
because there are so many other races, other mentalities,
you know, they're haughty, but we ... right away are like a
family and then everybody gets together and then ... we
tend to tell what's happening, and then there are memories;
frankly, we have a good mentality ... .

These beliefs of particularly good qualities embodied in one's own
and/or other groups are also supported by a symbolic base, expressed in
images of dressing, grooming, and institutional signs evoking loyalty.
Consider what the following male university student eighteen years of
age, who lives with his family in the northern part of the island of
Montreal, told me tongue in cheek. His father is a textile salesman and
his mother has held down a variety of part-time jobs:

> ...As I said before, we're all WASPS in one way or another.
> ... Well, no, no, no, we just throw anything together,
> because myself, I can't afford clothes. I have three pairs of
> pants, and we all feel, well most of us feel the same, if we're
> just going out for a day on the street, we'll just wear a
> purple tie and a white shirt and black pants. And that will
> be our wardrobe for the day.

Most of the persons whom I interviewed disclaimed that ethnicity
formed any stumbling block to forming close friends across ethnic
groups despite the fact that their own friendships were ethnically
homophilous. Often this condition is described in patriotic or quasi-

catechismic style. Hear what these following two men have to say, even though all of their friends are of their same ethnic group. The first is a middle aged, married carpenter with children, and is an English Canadian, who said:

> ...He makes friends with anyone. Myself, I'm the same. I don't care where you're from...what language you speak. I can make a friend just the same...

Then I asked, "What do you think about the Monarch? Is that a tradition that's important to you?" He replied,

> Well, I think it should be important to all Canadians really, the monarchy, the Queen.

Then I inquired, "Do your friends feel similarly to you about this? Do you discuss this, for instance, with them?" He answered,

> No, the only time you might have something to say is, "Well, I heard the Queen speak Christmas Day over the T.V. She made quite a speech." That's about all. There's no details or anything.

Again, I wanted to determine, "What do your friends feel about this?"

> They're thinking of moving out, that's it. It don't bother me at all. If they want me to move out, I'll move out, but they're gonna have to pay me the price of my house.

A security guard, fifty three years of age at the time of the interview, a married man with three children, who, although he had had only five years of formal education, had traveled all over the world during the Second World War, confided his thoughts on ethnicity to Ms. Verrette, my principal French language interviewer:

> ... I find that the question of political party, whether they are "blue" or "red," no matter what color, it's like race, whether you are Canadian, Chinese, Italian, no matter what, I say that we ought to all get together, that's my own goal, I am good, I am in my way.

When asked about the apparently obvious discrepancy between claiming that ethnic difference makes no obstacles for forming close friends while at the same time not having close friends across ethnic boundaries, most individuals explained this fact due to the existence of a linguistic barrier or due to the chance of just not being in a place where there were persons of different ethnic groups.

The following young French Canadian male, who is a high school graduate with some college education, has held down various odd jobs from being a community organizer to working in surveying. In reflecting about how ethnicity has imposed limits on his making friends, he related to me in French:

> It's pretty much a question of verbal communication. That's what is lacking rather a lot. Sometimes I am able in the end to speak it. I am incapable of doing it ... In English I don't have the vocabulary to do it. I don't have the expressions.

Then there is an intermediate group of persons who come into contact with another ethnic group in on-the-job activities and for whom the experience is enjoyable at the level of being an acquaintance but for whom close friendship does not result. Listen to these two older male Montrealers. The first is a middle-middle class English Canadian. I asked him, "Were you close to any French Canadian?" He replied,

> Uh, not really close, but at one time I knew more French-speaking people that I did English people. Well, I belonged to a motorboat club for a good many years, and I knew quite a few French-speaking people there. And ... I got to know them. They got to know me, and we're acquainted, heh. Because we're together in the summertime. I like boating. They like boating and so on. Because there's so many French people that are so nice. They're good. They're good people. 'Course there's good and bad in any race of people. There's good and bad Englishmen. There's good and bad Frenchmen.

The next fellow, an upper-middle class French Canadian felt he needed to clarify his life experiences of cross ethnic friendship when he realized in the course of the interview that all the closest friends of whom he had spoken were of his same ethnic background. He interjected:

> Now you just said to me that my intimate friends are all French Canadians, but among my good friends, I have several English, yes, I have at least a dozen of them, but who are not intimate friends.

One encounters negative stereotypes which form attitudes in ethnic group character which would certainly tend to block any attempt at making friends unless a person were consciously or subconsciously propelled to seek out traits which he or she did not value. However, Hans Peter Dreitzel has pointed out that collusion may bring together two persons in an unconscious play interaction on the basis of a similar unresolved basic personality conflict. Thus collusion would at least explain two holders of negative impressions of each other's group coming into contact as close friends, not in order to share the same conflict, but to produce polarization along the same constant. It could be expected that one friend would overcompensate and the other friend would manifest regressive behavior.[22]

In one of my in-depth interviews with an upper-middle class, English Canadian health-care professional, a woman in her late thirties, demonstrates some of these forces operating in her attitudes.

> Well, you know, a lot of it depends on personal experience. My friend, and certainly her husband has this company and he feels that everything is just beautiful. They are probably the one couple we are friendly with who are very pro-Quebec in a way we're not.

I asked her, "What do you mean by pro-Quebec?"

And she replied,

> Well, they, I don't know, are just not as critical of, let's say,
> the French Canadian mentality ... as we are.

I inquired, "How are you critical? What do you see?"

She answered,

> We just find if we look around, it's a different mentality. It's
> not really something I can even describe. I just know it
> when I see it. And I've felt it when I go to meetings. The
> English way or the American way, or whatever you want
> to call it, it's very different from the French way, which is
> more like the French Canadian way. They talk a lot, but
> they don't have the same practical approach to problems
> as we do. They build lousy roads. They build lousy indoor
> parking complexes, but they don't have the same kind of
> engineering minds as we do. They're very good in the arts.
> They're very good in music, in medicine, in philosophy but
> to me, this isn't what makes a city run well. And I feel
> having lived in Ontario that Quebec is just not as stable a
> province economically because, and I think in many ways
> this is a French influence.

The complicated interplay of these interactive images of ethnicity is
abundantly manifest in Canadian literature and film. Consider Roch
Carrier's novel in which the only citation on the colorful cover-jacket of a
Quebec village in autumn is "The Others forbid him everything that a
free man has the right to do. What remains for him, in his cradle, if not
to think?"[23] Carrier's text goes on to depict the elements that symbolize
the chief characteristics of English and French Canadian interrelations
as felt in the experience of a French Canadian grandfather:

> It isn't altogether true that he wasn't afraid of anything.
> Hadn't he confided to Jean-Thomas that the Village of the
> English terrified him? A man does not speak of his fears.
> There were several houses close together around the road,
> like a trap. None of these houses had ever heard a single
> word of the *Québécois* language. Never a single French
> Canadian had entered into one of these houses. In any
> case, Thomas knew of none who had dared even pass in

front of [them]. Those who lived there were pure English. These English by their religion were all Protestant. Not a single French Canadian Catholic had ever crossed this village either during the day or night. In the olden times, some French Canadians, who weren't afraid, had themselves taken the risk in the road of the Village of the English. The English unleashed their dogs, big English dogs who barked in the language of their masters. The French Canadians who didn't get cold feet, had tried to pacify the beasts with words which made French Canadian dogs lie down, but these English dogs did not understand a word of *Québécois*, and they smelled French Canadian meat for the first time. They barked to high heavens, and they showed their cutting teeth like hunting knives. The French Canadians were off, happy to not leave a mouthful of their flesh or bones in the throat of the dogs. Since that story was told, no one had ventured forth into the Village of the English. Thomas wasn't afraid of anything. When in his youth he frequented his deceased (wife) who lived in the plain on the other side of the Village of the English, Thomas got down from his cart, took his horse by the bridal-harness, and across brushwood, the alder trees, over the obstacles, he guided his horse toward this other road which the French Canadians had traced in the forest in order to avoid the damned village. The day of his marriage, especially that day, he twisted around these dangerous houses well protected by the spruce planted close to one another. The English didn't see this girl, prettier than a queen in her long, white dress, and they would not be able to, in their bad Protestant plans, take over his wife as they had taken over the country of Quebec. Each year he returned to the village of his dead wife with the children who were packed more harmoniously in his cart. Thomas avoided the Village of the English. He made the children stop singing, to be quiet as soon as he saw the gray pile of houses on the horizon. The children no longer had the right to be happy. He threatened to hit them. The children were not happy any more. They had no more laughter, but tears. Could he say to them that he was afraid? Guiding the horse, he could not help his hand from trembling on the bridal-harness in his hand. He would have wished that his horse and cart glide through the mud and on the stones with the silence of a bird which passes in the sky. Behind the spruce, in the shadow of their branches, the English were perhaps lying in wait. The English of the trails in the forest endured the French Canadians: without them their

sawmills would have had no wood and they would have had
no arms to roll the logs ...

In her short-story, "The Doctor," Mavis Gallant, the English-
language Montreal writer, describes the exclusive social psychology of
the rare French- and English- Canadian Montrealers who mixed as
friends in the earlier part of this century:

> This overlapping in one room of French and English, of
> Catholic and Protestant--my parents' way of being, and so
> to me life itself--was as unlikely, as unnatural to the
> Montreal climate as a school of tropical fish. Only later
> would I discover that most other people simply floated in
> mossy little ponds labelled "French and Catholic" or
> "English and Protestant," never wondering what it might
> be like to step ashore; or wondering, perhaps, but weighing
> up the danger. To be out of a pond is to be in unmapped
> territory. The earth might be flat; you could fall over the
> edge quite easily. My parents and their friends were, in
> their way, explorers. They had in common a fear of being
> bored, which is a fear one can afford to nourish in times of
> prosperity and peace. It makes for the most ruthless kind
> of exclusiveness, based as it is on the belief that anyone
> can be the richest of this or cleverest of that and still be
> the dullest dog that ever barked. I wince even now
> remembering those wretched once-only guests who were
> put on trial for a Saturday night and unanimously
> condemned. This heartlessness apart, the winter circle
> shared an outlook, a kind of humor, a certain vocabulary of
> the mind. No one made any of the standard Montreal
> statements, such as "What a lot of books you've got! Don't
> tell me you've read them," or "What do you really *do*?"
> Explorers like Dr. Chauchard and Mrs. Erskine and my
> mother and the rest recognized each other on sight; the
> recognition cut through disguisement of class, profession,
> religion, language, and even what polltakers call "other
> interests."[24]

Related to attitude as a factor inhibiting the formation of close
friendship across ethnic lines is that different groups may construct
somewhat different expectations of friendship. For example, in a
contingency table analysis of the items of the La Gaipa Instrument

concerning the psychological basis of friendship, ethnicity produced ten statistically significant differences out of the thirty-five items. These indicators suggest that English Canadians stress sticking by friends and related psycho-social characteristics such as strength of character, defense of beliefs, seriousness of goals, etc., more than French Canadians. This finding does not mean that English Canadians do not enjoy spending time together with their friends; in fact, the opposite is true. However, such time which they enjoying spending together may be more wrapped up in pursuits which leave them with a feeling of steadfastness. Two ideal typical patterns for friendship expectations are suggested by my data: "the steadfast friend" and "the friend as confidant." The friend as confidant is more marked among the white collar workers, French Canadians, younger, and, to a lesser extent, female respondents. The steadfast friend better characterizes the professional, English Canadian, older, and, to a lesser degree male respondents. These ideal typical configurations were derived from my cognitive data, although to some extent they reflect the behavioral realm of close friendship. English Canadian Montrealers' real behavior in close friendship is best described by a small group of persons quite similar to the respondent in educational and occupational background and political beliefs; these people tend to be chosen from outside ego's family (47.2%) or from inside and outside the family (44%); these friends tend to meet together more often; these friendships face high risks of breaking due to occupational changes. In contrast, French Canadian Montrealers' real behavior in friendship is typified by a large group of persons more diversified in educational and occupational background and political beliefs; these friends can be chosen from inside and outside one's family; French Canadians tend to meet some of their close friends separately while meeting others together: these friendships risk breaking from changes in private life such as marriage or divorce.[25]

I must stress that these subtly different ethnic nuances in friendship behavior and attitudes produced only one trend in the multidimensional scalogram analysis of the styles of friendship. In Appendix D in the item plot of the style of the "Family-Oriented Friendship," we note that 60%

were French Canadian [12/20 who were classified as such or 12/50=24% of all in-depth interviewees]. In contrast, 40% were English Canadian [8/20 who were classified as such or 8/50=16% of all in-depth interviewees]. This trend among the in-depth interviewees supports the general contour of the statistically significant contrast I report in chapter five, note 31, on the basis of the combined results of the respondents to my questionnaires and in-depth interviews. There I observe that 47% of English-Canadian in contrast to 22% of French-Canadian Montrealers report that their friends are "outside" their family. 70% of French-Canadian, as opposed to 44% of English-Canadian, Montrealers said that their friends came from inside and outside of their family. Only 4% of French and about 5% of English Canadian Montrealers stated that they had friends only inside the family. However, rather than contradicting these contrasts of the different degrees to which English and French Canadian Montrealers drew their close friends from within their own family, the MSA underscores the somewhat greater development of the particular traits of the style of the family-oriented friendship among French Canadian Montrealers.

As I have outlined, differing political opinions between close friends is an element that distinguishes French Canadian from English Canadian friendships. Quebec had been portrayed as a relatively closed society in a variety of social scientific accounts. It was the French colonial society that had not experienced the Enlightenment and the French Revolution and the one that had been dominated by the Church, which had collaborated first with the English and then with the American bourgeoisies. Moreover, according to many authors, such a history had left its mark on the mentality of Quebecers. They were said to possess a vengeful-siege mentality toward outgroups while not permitting real dissent within the in-group--not unlike the Afrikaaners. Moreover, other critics had claimed the "French from France" trait of taking out political issues on an interpersonal level was also present in French Canadian national character. This scenario of French Canadian history was strongly attacked as a caricature during the 1970s. *Québécois* politicians resented lectures from the English-speaking community about their lack of appreciation of the institutions and customs of the Anglo-American enlightened, liberal tradition. In reference to this matter's bearing on close friendship, my data, contrary to this stereotype of French-speaking Quebecers, indicated that the French Canadians in my sample were much more open to political differences of opinion among their close friends than were the English Canadians.[26]

It could very well be that the heightening political drift toward pro-separatist and left-wing causes in the political culture of Quebec of the 1970s pushed members of the English Canadian community, already relatively quite occupationally and educationally homogeneous in their friendships, into more "ideologically pure" close friendships. If you were liberal or conservative, you would no longer let yourself be politically and materially threatened by social democrats, anarchists, and communists. If you were radical, you would no longer listen to the self-serving, exploitive points of view of namby-pambies. Reflecting on my own experience and listening to my interviews suggest such a social psychology underlying and producing the behavioral pattern in the table on the influence of ethnicity on political attitudes held by close friends.

When it comes to breaking with close friends, more English Canadian than French Canadian friendships were broken due to changes in occupations, while more French Canadian than English Canadian friendships ended due to a change in a person's private life such as marriage and divorce.[27]

These behavioral results are the opposite of what one would predict to be the ethnic difference on the basis of expectational or definitional notions of friendship. The steadfast friend is more typical of English Canadian interviewees' definitions, while the friend as confidant is more descriptive of the French Canadian interviewees' answers to the question, "What is a friend? What is or what are, in your opinion, the sign or the signs of a true friendship?"

Yet, if Quebecers of English Canadian extraction must move or do move more often than Quebecers of French Canadian background, this difference should not seem unusual. To an extent, greater geographical mobility would seem to be a structural concomitant of being stratified at a higher level of socio-economic class, for those groups in society closest to the growth sector of the political economy demand greater degrees of shifting residence and job location as a function of horizontal and vertical mobility. In addition to this factor, Quebec has been the geographical heart of the French Canadian culture, and with the rise of nationalism there has been a tendency to shift the ethnic identity from *Canadien français* to *Québécois*, providing a lesser ideological and identificational incentive to move outside the province. Even though these macro sociological processes help us understand these patterns of breaking friendships, they do not explain away the evident inconsistencies of one group's expectancy to remain steadfast with a close friend, yet breaking the friendship when, for example, moving, or the other group's stressing the communicative aspects in friendship, yet breaking this close relationship during the intensely emotional rights of passage of marriage and divorce. In brief, breaking with close friends is just one indicator of the relative lack of congruence in the human relationship of friendship.

One source of tension in friendship that could lead to breaking up is that not all of the same individual's friends might get along with one another. In a highly differentiated society with people from many different value, lifestyle, gender, class, age, ethnic, sexual orientational, civil status, political, religious, and personality sets, only in the most tolerant environments appreciative of diversity would it be expected that all of a person's friends would like one another. One way of handling this problem is to meet friends separately or together if two individuals are not expected to get along. The English Canadians and French Canadians in my sample handled this problem differently, as is clear from the data presented in the following table. More English, as compared to French, Canadians said that they met their friends together. Clearly more French, compared to English, Canadians said that they met some of their friends separately and others together. This pattern does seem consistent with the French Canadian "friend as confidant" style in that if a person were particularly keen on the communicative aspects of friendship, he or she would take particular care to insure that his or her close friends hit it off. If they did not, the tactful, considerate thing to do would be to meet them in different places at different times. Such appears to be the motivation behind this pattern.[28]

These beliefs, attitudes, and behaviors are probably indicative of macro-societal forces at work. Professor Jacques Dofny surveyed English and French Canadian engineers on what they regarded as the strong and weak points of one another's groups.[29] He found that:

> French Canadian engineers value English Canadian engineers mainly on two levels: the level of work (hard-working, conscientious, responsible, good organizers, etc.) and the personal and social level (exuberant, sincere, calm, optimistic, jovial, adapt well, etc.). When they describe French Canadians, English Canadians mention above all their personal and social qualities. Only 10.7% define them in terms of work value.

Judging solely on the basis of my written questionnaire, French Canadians see having close friends with the same ideas and opinions as a less primary base of close friendship in comparison to English Canadians. French Canadians report experiencing an unexplainable attraction between close friends in a much higher rank than do English Canadians.[30]

English Canadians initially claimed more friends than they actually ended up reporting on, while the number of friends French Canadians' claimed and reported on were similar. Moreover, when the number of friends really reported on is counted, French Canadians more frequently said they had "4, 8, 9, or 10" close friends while English Canadians said they had "2, 3, 6, or 7" close friends.[31] This finding suggests that English Canadian compared to French Canadians tend to have fewer close friends.

The fourth factor that accounts for the high degree of ethnic similarity among close friends in Montreal is the long history of de facto segregation of the ethnic groups which the famous novelist Hugh MacLennan described as the *Two Solitudes*. A document published by the Montreal *Gazette* from a major commentator on Quebec, Lord Durham, described their relationship in the 19th century in the following words:

> They rarely meet at the inns in this city, the principal hotels are almost exclusively filled with English and with foreign travellers, and the French, are for the most part, received at each other's houses, or in boarding houses, in which they meet with few English.[32]

Commenting on this separation of ethnic groups and its effect on possibilities for forming close friends in contemporary Montreal, a letter-to-the-editor in *Le Devoir* bemoaned the state-of-affairs in 1977:

> How do you make a people understand, an extraordinary [people] because it has survived an isolation of several centuries, and an original [people] because it is the only [one] to reconcile the advantages of a Latin society (enthusiasm, independence of spirit, joy of living) and of an Anglo-Saxon society (rigor, collective confidence, spirit of enterprise), so how do you make it understand that it is extraordinary and original?
>
> All of the immigrants that I know complain of having had a lot of difficulty in developing relations of friendship that go beyond superficial social contact with the "true" *Québécois*. Our friends are almost all colleagues. What a difference from the United States, where one made friends for life in several months despite the barrier of language. Here it takes years as in Europe: the open society and the closed society about which Peyrefitte speaks.[33]

In Montreal the concentration of entertainment in the downtown area--readily available from any point in the city by comfortable, relatively inexpensive, and readily accessible metro (subway) and bus service--brings together many teen-agers, young adults, older singles, and married couples to discotheques, restaurants, movies, and businesses where people from different ethnic groups meet, enjoy, partake, or participate in one another's different languages and ethnicities. The metro plazas joined to large and some even huge malls connecting with modern stores of various kinds and qualities, are often equipped with benches, rounded or rectangular coffee bars, or large steps where citizens may sit and look at strangers in safety in a public space. While rue St. Denis is definitely mostly French-speaking and French Canadian, and Crescent Street more English-speaking and English Canadian and "Other" Canadian ethnic groups, on both streets and especially in the downtown area in between, many "English," "French," and "Other" Canadian contacts occur in a variety of leisure time activities from simply looking through curious to intimate interaction. Furthermore, this meeting ground seems to be dependent on the existence of a commonly shared type of "culture of narcissism" that plays down ethnic and racial differences. Indeed, when this subculture notices differences, it appears to accord a positive value to the differences as being exotic, titillating, stimulating, and, thereby valued within the limits of having fun.

Particularly concentrating on the differences that set apart English Canadians from French Canadians, Marcel Rioux has found Ruth Benedict's national character dichotomy of Apollonian versus Dionysian useful. Although he notes that anthropologists do not agree on how to classify the *Québécois*, he finds some explanatory value in seeing the French Canadians as tending toward the Dionysian, ecstatic, given to excesses and free expression of their emotions, while English Canadians are measured, prudent, mistrustful of their emotions and are self disciplined. In short, French Canadians are warm and English Canadians are cold.[34] Ashley Montague would translate Rioux's contrast into a strong behaviorally based statement. He writes:

> ... Canadians of Anglo-Saxon origins perhaps even outdo the English in their non-tactility. On the other hand, French Canadians are as tactilly demonstrative as are their counterparts in their land of origin.[35]

During my almost decade of residence in Canada, I watched countless scenes of encounters between English and French Canadians that would suggest that this difference in tactility and proxemics inhibited or promoted friendships with the other ethnic group depending on the preference of the social actor. Those who preferred the dominant style of their own ethnic group would tend to seek out friends who displayed the tactile and proxemic style of their own group. Those who preferred the modal style of the other ethnic group would tend to seek friends with those who displayed the other group's style.

I tried to crossvalidate these field impressions through an objective item on my written questionnaire and an open-ended question on my in-depth interview, the results of which I report in detail in a later chapter on "Men, Women, and Close Friendship." When I inquired into the extent to which close friends hold hands, embrace, kiss, and make love without or with orgasm, I was not able to confirm the significant differences between French Canadians and English Canadians which the literature and qualitative observations suggested. These findings offer some support to the observation that both English Canadians and French Canadians were highly influenced by the general North American evolution of sexual and tactile behavior to a much greater openness in the 1970s which the electronic media and modern transportation pushed from center to periphery with great rapidity. Moreover, the reserve and coolness which is often attributed to English Canadians and the emotional effusiveness which is often attributed to French Canadians may be limited to the public sphere of interaction; their behavior with close friends reveals a quite similar realm of private tactile and sexual behavior.[36]

Regardless of the differences in socio-emotive styles among Montreal's ethnic groups, the facts that Montreal's urban center is still very much alive and that relatively inexpensive, attractive, and safe public transportation is present and expanding contribute to the possibilities for interethnic contact. Even though ethnicity has been depicted as crosscutting social class in North America in very significant ways, the subculture of leisure and transportation infrastructure manifestly undercut some of the bases for the class differences in friendship patterns noted in the English village of Shelton Hey.[37] The pattern which Allen recorded would certainly be exaggerated

in a small, relatively homogeneous village. In Montreal one can observe
the same positive interethnic contacts occurring on an expanding scale--
and perhaps attracting even a larger segment of the working class and
families at the sport centers which were the by-products of the Montreal
Olympics. Likewise one can see similar contacts at Man and his World,
the amusement park remains of the Montreal World's Fair, the large
park on Mount Royal, and in the Old City's central plaza, Place Jacques
Cartier. These places are the contours of where friends from different
backgrounds can be made. For example, in my dissertation sample I
found that 16.3% of the respondents claimed that their adult friendships
came about from "having similar pastimes or off-the-job activities" and
11.5% arose by "chance."[38] In addition, 21.1% said that their friendships
manifested themselves most often "through conversations and meetings
outside their homes, for example, in the street, etc."; 20% reported "in
activities and communal get-togethers away from the job, political or
social activities"; 17.7% noted "artistic or sports activities" and 20.3%
claimed "others."[39] There were no statistically significant differences
found for ethnic groups in this regard.

There are a number of secular groups whose norms promote or even
encourage meeting people from other ethnic groups. In Montreal as in
other large North American cities, groups like Unitarians, Humanists,
Humanist Psychologists, Moscow-oriented Communists (in Montreal,
members of the Communist Party of Canada), social democrats (in
Montreal, The New Democratic Party), Trotskyites, and other more
ideologically-diffuse groups like non-observant people of all religious
backgrounds, gays, feminists, and, perhaps to a lesser degree, Liberals,
health, sports, film, and game enthusiasts, all draw people from many
different ethnic groups together in a new belief system frequently at
odds with the one in which they were raised. The specific content and
intensity of beliefs of these various groups create the grounds for the
probable occurrence of one or another of the friendship styles enacted by
close friends coming from different backgrounds. For example, there is
tendency for political activists to view particular ethnic and national
groups as liberators or progressive and others as exploiters or

reactionary. People who are members of a favorably-viewed group would tend to be sought out as friends, and people who are members of groups held in disrepute would tend to be avoided; however, these propensities are tempered by the perception of a person's ethnic group in the power hierarchy of Montreal society and culture.

Summary and Conclusions

It has been pointed out that:

> the mere categorization of persons into in-group and out-group members...even in the absence of negative attitudes (prejudice) [is] sufficient to produce behavior that favors the in-group at the expense of the out-group. This categorization and other "normal" cognitive processes such as "illusory correlations" serve to prevent friendships and positive behavior from developing between members of in-groups and out-groups.[40]

Such seems to be the case in Montreal in the mid-1970s. In Bliezner's and Adam's neo-Lockean model, an interviewee's ethnicity and the ethnicity of her or his six closest friends constitute individual characteristics which determine opportunities for and constraints on friendship.

I found that the ethnicity of the respondent and that of his or her six closest friends are strongly associated with one another. This finding holds true when one controls for occupational status (an indicator of socio-economic class), although there is a trend for respondents to be progressively more open to outgroups in their world of close friends as one goes from lower through middle to higher occupational groupings. All ethnic groups in Quebec are characterized by this tendency for ethnic homophily (homogeneity) among closest friends, even though all groups have a considerable proportion of their close friends from other ethnic groups.

The principle of similarity or of like attracting like as a social psychological explanatory device explains only one aspect of this phenomenon. The contact hypothesis offers another explanation. In the neo-Lockean model, this configuration indicates that ethnicity acts as a structural constraint on friendship. So too, my finding that English-Canadian Montrealers' friends were more similar in educational and occupational characteristics when compared to French-Canadian Montrealers' friends demonstrates the operation of a component of structure on their friendships.

My contrast between the cognitive or expectational ideal type of the friend as confidant being more descriptive of French-Canadian Montrealers and of the steadfast friend as more descriptive of English-Canadian Montrealers points to an element of process within friendship.

My discovery that French Canadian Montrealers' friendships risk breaking because of a personal change such as marriage and divorce in contrast to English Canadian Montrealers' breaking friendships because of occupational change is framed as contrasting phases of friendship in Bliezner's and Adam's model.

English-Canadian Montrealers tended to meet their friends together more often while French-Canadian Montrealers tended to meet some of their friends separately and others together. This contrast may have been structurally produced by French Canadians' having a larger number of close friends. Hence they would need to accommodate to the greater educational and political diversity among their close friends to a greater extent than English-Canadian Montrealers. Despite the greater degree of diversity among French Canadians' friends, English Canadians felt pulled among their different friendships more frequently.[41]

Even though English-Canadian Montrealers' friendships appeared more "multistranded" in the network analysts' sense, I am suggesting that the importance of ethnicity in determining the strength of a social bond at the level of process impacted particularly strenuously upon social action in the realm of the marketplace. Thus ethnic solidarity appears to have significantly restricted the opportunity for forming friendships where the personal qualities inherently valued in friendship became ordered in secondary importance in the sector of economic competition.

Unfamiliarity and lack of experience in interacting on an intimate basis across ethnic lines would certainly tend to produce a high level of anxiety when dealing with individuals whose rules of interaction, customs, and etiquette may be based on very different expectancies than those to which one is accustomed.

Despite these difficulties, the world of work and the mass media bring most Montrealers into contact with individuals from outside their own ethnic group. Yet, interacting on a level of close friendship is far different from coming into contact with someone over a counter, desk, or a TV screen, or seeing someone on a relatively ethnically segregated factory floor or in a complex organization. In a society highly conscious of ethnic stratification, closest friendship may serve as a refuge from the competition of the market place, where outgroups are seen as competitors or exploiters. Despite these cultural and social constraints, many individuals manage to overcome them and form close friendships across ethnic boundaries. Certain secular subcultures in which ethnic differences are either played down or appreciated in a positive way for their diversity may promote building close friendships across ethnic boundaries.

Notes

1. MacLennan, Hugh, *Two Solitudes* (Toronto: Macmillan Company, 1945); Porter, John, *The Vertical Mosaic: An Analysis of Social Class and Power in Canada* (Toronto: University of Toronto Press, 1965).

2. This project could not have been done without the work of students in J. Barry Gurdin's "Individual and Society" and "Sociology of Quebec" classes in the spring semester of 1977. I wish to thank each one of them: Philippe Williate Battet, André Bourassa, Eleine Campbell, Carole Chartrand, Phil Coleman, Joan Fuller, Mike Gilbey, Michel Guay, Rena Halickman, Collen Hillock, William Dale Hoffman, Bankole A. Komolafe, Diana Kosyzycki, Claude Lafrenière, France Lalande, Sukdeo Latchman, Emanuel M. Lima, Tom Litchfield, Pamela Man-Yee Lo, Phemie London, Charles Montpétit, Colleen Moody, Bernard Nzo-Nguty,

Julie Owade, Denise Paré, Greg St. Laurent, Ann Raimondo, Ana Maria Rodrigues, Claude Séris, Nancy Scholefield, Terri Sternklar, Toni Studer, Louise Sullivan, Alexander Szuba, Robert Théoret, and Renée Tyberg. Thanks go to the Department of Sociology of the Loyola Campus of Concordia University, Montreal, Quebec, Canada, for paying for the printing of the questionnaires and to Marcel Douek for helping with many hours of transcription. Many thanks go to the members of the University of Chicago's Parent Health and Infant Development Project and to the late Professor Louis Guttman, who let me participate in his consultation and didactic seminar in the spring and winter of 1980. Thanks to Rita J. Jeremy for suggesting a cutting of the SSAs and for noticing a problem with the scoring system. Special thanks go to Sandy Gruba-McCallister for her computer programming.

3. See: Gurdin, J. Barry. "Quebecer and *Québécois:* Same Meaning?" Paper presented at the 79th annual meeting of the American Anthropological Association, Session on The Lexicon, Washington, D.C. That paper was published in a revised version as chapter nine, "Naturalistic Categories of Ethnic Identity in Quebec," in a book, see: Gurdin, J. Barry in McCready, William C., 1983, 149-180. Also see: Gurdin, J. Barry and Horst Hutter, "Some of My Best Friends Are ...: The Relationship of Ethnicity to Close Friendship." Paper presented at the 32nd annual meeting of the Society for the Study of Social Problems, Detroit, Michigan (available from *Sociological Abstracts* as S15531/SSSP/2081). That paper was published in a revised version, see: Gurdin, J. Barry and Horst Hutter, 1985, 101-112.

4. Also see Gurdin, J. Barry and Horst Hutter, 1985, 104.

5. See Appendix C: Three Dimensional Smallest Space Analyses for the Respondents and Their Six Closest Friends' Ethnicities.

6. As the "Other Canadian" category in our sample is so general and lumps together 103 subgroups, we need to take a look at the breakdown of this composite category. To make this manageable with so many subcategories or attributes, we can look at some of the most frequently occurring groups.

The "Other Canadian" category is a label given to a regrouping of the following categories of countries of national origin taken from *Canada Year Book* for 1976: Austria, Belgium, Czechoslovakia, Denmark, Finland, Italy, Malta, Netherlands, Norway, Poland, Portugal, Spain, Sweden, Switzerland, Turkey, U.S.S.R., Yugoslavia, Other Europe, The Republic of South Africa, Tanzania, Uganda, Zambia, Other Africa, Other Australasia, Bangladesh, China, Cyprus, Hong Kong, India, Indonesia, Iran, Iraq, Israel, Japan, Jordan, South Korea, Lebanon, Malaysia, Pakistan, Philippines, Singapore, Sri Lanka, Syria, Taiwan, Vietnam, Other Asia, Antigua, Bahamas, Barbados, Bermuda, Grenada, Haiti, Jamaica, Mexico, St. Kitts, Nevis, St. Vincent, Trinidad and Tobago, Other South America, Argentina, Bolivia, Brazil, Chile, Colombia, Ecuador, French Guiana, Guyana, Paraguay, Peru, Surinam, Uruguay, Venezuela, Fiji, Mauritius, Other Oceania, Eskimo, and Native Indian.

Likewise, when doing the computer analysis for this book, a problem arose about what to do with the 12% of the sample which responded that their own or some of their six closest friends' ethnicity is "Canadian."

As is usually the case when doing social research, we came across some answers that did not fall into these categories established beforehand for the answers to question two. These unexpected replies included the following: "Canadian, Quebec, French Canadian, names of specific towns, mixed ethnic backgrounds, and province." Sticking as closely as possible to the *Canada Year Book* for 1976's procedures, we defined "English Canadian" as being of British Isles origin. Thus, this category is made up of those individuals responding that they belonged to an ethnic group from "England, Northern Ireland, Scotland, Wales, Lesser Isles, Republic of Ireland, Australia, and New Zealand." The category of "French Canadian" includes respondents saying that they belonged to an ethnic group from "France or province" or being a Quebecer or French Canadian." Finally, we established a category, "unclassified," for those respondents who identified their ethnic group as "the U.S.A. (2% of the sample), the name of a specific town (2% of the sample), and mixed ethnicity (2% of the sample)." Please take note that the "unclassified category" was omitted from the table on page six because of the lack of clarity of the responses in that category.

The response of "Canadian" poses special problems. When "Naturalistic Categories of Ethnic Identity in Quebec," (Gurdin, J. Barry, 1983) was written, the operational decision to exclude this response category was made because this unanticipated marker of identification refers to the name of a national group or national state. It could be that some respondents chose to emphasize their being citizens of Canada over being members of any particular ethnic group. This type of response would be found among the "marginal" new Canadians who play up their hard earned new citizenship. To others, *"Canadien"* in French was a former ethnic identity label for French Canadians especially prevalent in the last century and early part of this century. Likewise, English Canadian Quebecers who stress their belonging to Canada as a whole or their opposition to separatism employ this tag as do the "Other Canadian" ethnics beyond the first generation. Of these, the students recoded 123 of these respondents as "English Canadian," 58 as "French Canadian," 39 as "Other Canadian," and 1 as "missing."

When the ethnic identity of the interviewee was missing or unclassified, 234 of their closest friends' ethnicities were, nevertheless, given. Of these 35 were English Canadian, 43 were French Canadian, 15 Other Canadian, 72 Canadian, 62 remained "unclassified," and 7 missing. On those questionnaires where the ethnicities or regrouped ethnic affiliation of the respondent's six closest friends were missing, the respondents' ethnicities included: 17 French Canadians, 12 English Canadians, 25 Canadians, 2 Greek Canadians, 1 Polish Canadian, 16 people of "Other national origin groups of Canadians," and 7 people whose ethnicities were unclassified and missing.

7. Levy, Shlomit and Louis Gutttman, "Structure and Level of Values for Rewards and Allocation Criteria in Several Life Areas," in *Multidimensional Data Representations: When and Why*, ed. Ingwer Borg (Ann Arbor, Michigan: Mathesis Press, 1981), 171.

8. Fischer, Claude S. *To Dwell among Friends. Personal Networks in Town and City* (Chicago: The University of Chicago Press, 1982), 251.

9. Ibid., 214-215.

10. Ibid., 215.

11. See Sales, Arnaud, *La bourgeoisie industrielle au Québec* (Montréal: Les Presses de l'université de Montréal, 1979), 107-153. Also see: Nagel, Joane and Susan Olzak, "Ethnic Mobilization in New and Old States: An Extension of the Competition Model," *Social Problems* 30 (1982), 131.

12. Wallace, Samuel E., *The Urban Environment* (Homewood, Illinois: The Dorsey Press, 1980), 168-184.

13. See Gurdin, J. Barry and Horst Hutter, 106-107.

14. Schofield, Janet W., "Complementary and Conflicting Identities: Images and Interaction in an Interracial School," in *The Development of Children's Friendships,* eds. Steven Asher and John M. Gottman (Cambridge: Cambridge University Press, 1981), 53-90.

15. Allen, Vernon L., "Self, Social Group, and Social Structure: Surmises about the Study of Children's Friendships," in *The Development of Children's Friendships,* eds. Steven Asher and John M. Gottman (Cambridge: Cambridge University Press, 1981), 189.

16. Schofield, Janet W., 1981, 68.

17. Gurdin, Joseph Barry, "*Amitié*/Friendship: The Socio-cultural Construction of Friendship in Contemporary Montreal," Ph.D. diss., Department of Sociology, Université de Montréal, 1978), 484 - 487.

18. Ibid., 476.

19. Dofny, Jacques, *Les ingenieurs Canadiens français et Canadiens anglais à Montréal.* Documents de la Commission royale d'enquête sur le bilinguisme et le biculturalisme 6, 1970, 101-102.

20. Issacs, Harold R., "Idols of the Tribe: Group Identity and Political Change," in *Ethnicity: Theory and Experience*, eds. Glazer, Nathan and Daniel P. Moynihan (Cambridge, Mass.: Harvard University Press, (1975) 1976), 29 -52.

21. In the contemporary French vernacular of Quebec, "race" has both the meanings of ethnic group and relatively distinct gene pool, similar to the earlier usages of the term in American English.

22. Summer lecture notes from a course on Love and Friendship with Professor Hans Peter Dreitzel, Boston University, 1977.

23. Carrier, Roch, *Il n'y a pas de pays sans grand-père* (Saint-Lambert, Québec: Editions internationales Alain Stanké, 1979), 74-75.

24. Gallant, Mavis, "The Doctor," in *The New Yorker*, 20 June 1977:33-42

25. Gurdin, Joseph Barry, 1978, 554, 559, 560, 562, 563-565, 568-569, 764.

26. *Question #19: "Have You Cultivated a Real Friendship with a Person Having Political Opinions Deeply Opposed to Your Own? A. Yes B. No." The Relationship between Differences in Friends' Political Opinions and the Ethnicity of the Interviewees and Respondents*

Question 19:	Count Column %	Ethnicity		
Friends' Political Opinions Different from Yours?		French Canadian	English Canadian	Row Total
Yes		30 / 63.8%	53 / 42.7%	83 / 48.5%
No		17 / 36.2%	71 / 57.3%	88 / 51.5%
Column Total		47 / 27.5%	124 / 72.5%	171 / 100%

Corrected χ^2 = 5.25277 with 1 Degree of Freedom. Significance = .0219
Number of Missing Observations = 4.

27. Question #22 On How Friendships Were Broken. The Cause of Break Cross-classified by Ethnicity of the Interviewees and Respondents

Count Column %	Ethnicity		
How Friendships Were Broken:	French Canadian	English Canadian	Row Total
Moving	14 26.4%	63 28.6%	77 28.2%
Changes in Occupation	2 3.8%	36 16.4%	38 13.9%
Changes of Position on Same Job	2 3.8%	8 3.6%	10 3.7%
Changes in Private Life	20 37.7%	31 14.1%	51 18.7%
Changes in Ideas	6 11.3%	25 11.4%	31 11.4%
Tiring of One Another's Company	4 7.5%	21 9.5%	25 9.2%
A Real Fight	3 5.7%	21 9.5%	24 8.8%
For No Particular Reason	2 3.8%	15 6.8%	17 6.2%
Column Total	53 19.4%	220 80.6%	273 100%

Raw χ^2 = 19.27822 with 7 Degrees of Freedom. Significance = .0074

28. *Question #21: "Do You Try to Get Several of Your Friends Together As Often As Possible or Rather Do You Meet Them Separately? A. Together B. Separately." [In the Analysis It Became Necessary to Add a Third Category to Account for Some Respondents' Meeting Some of Their Friends Together and Others Separately]. Cross-classification of Place of Meeting Close Friends by Ethnicity of the Interviewees and Respondents*

Count Column %	Ethnicity		
Place of Meeting Friends	French Canadian	English Canadian	Row Total
Together	17 35.4%	65 53.3%	82 48.2%
Separately	22 45.8%	53 43.4%	75 44.1%
Meet Some Together and Others Separately	9 18.8%	4 3.3%	13 7.6%
Column Total	48 28.2%	122 71.8%	170 100%

Number of Missing Observations = 5; Raw χ^2 = 13.10544 Significance = .0014

29. Dofny, Jacques, 1970, 100-102.

30. Gurdin, Joseph Barry, 1978, 673-676.

31. Ibid., 559-560.

32. Durham, Lord, *The Montreal Gazette*, Saturday, 4 December (1839) 1976, 5.

33. Devroede, G., "Le Québec de 1977 vu par un immigrant en quête de racines." *Le Devoir*, lundi, 20 juin, 1977, 5.

34. Rioux, Marcel, *Les québécois. Le temps qui court* (Bourges: l'Imprimerie Tardy Quercy Auvergne, 1977), 87-113.

35. Montagu, Ashley, *Touching: the Human Significance of the Human Skin* (New York: Columbia University Press, 1971), 308.

36. *The Incidence of Tactility and Sexuality by Closeness of Friends in Urban Montreal of the Mid-1970s Controlling for Ethnicity*

Count Col %	French Canadians' Friends				English Canadians' Friends			
Extent of Tactile and Sexual Behavior among Close Friends	High	Medium	Low	Absent	High	Medium	Low	Absent
My Friend and I Hold Hands	24 48%	47 38.8%	34 9.6%	145 20%	25 21%	20 23.3%	104 19.8%	851 19.9%
My Friend and I Embrace Each Other	7 14%	26 21.5%	72 20.3%	145 20.3%	36 30.3%	22 25.6%	92 17.5%	850 19.9%
My Friend and I Kiss Each Other	11 22%	41 33.9%	53 15%	145 20%	31 26.1%	22 25.6%	95 18.1%	852 20%
My Friend and I Make Love without Orgasm	1 2%	3 2.5%	101 28.5%	145 20%	8 6.7%	13 15.1%	122 23.2%	857 20.1%
My Friend And I Make Love with Orgasm	7 14%	4 3.3%	94 26.6%	145 20%	19 16%	9 10.5%	113 21.5%	859 20.1%
Column Total	50 4%	121 9.7%	354 28.3%	725 58%	119 2.4%	86 1.7%	526 10.5%	4269 85.4%

Zero   Order $\gamma =$ .03058   ; First-   Order   Partial $\gamma =$ .03434

37. Allan, Graham, *A. Sociology of Friendship and Kinship* (London: George Allen & Unwin, 1979), 82-84.

38. Gurdin, Joseph Barry, 1978, 573-575.

39. Ibid., 587-589.

40. Allen, Vernon L., 1981, 188-9.

41. *Question #20: "Do You Experience Certain Pullings among Your Different Friendships? A. Yes, Often; B. Yes, Sometimes; C. No, Never."*

The Relationship between the Ethnicity of the Interviewees and Respondents and the Frequency of Their Experience of Certain Pullings among Close Friendships

Count Column %	Ethnicity		
Experience of Certain Pullings among Close Friendships	French Canadian	English Canadian	Row Total
Yes, Often	2 4.3%	23 18.5%	25 14.7%
Yes, Sometimes	16 34.8%	61 49.2%	77 45.3%
No, Never	28 60.9%	40 32.3%	68 40%
Column Total	46 27.1%	124 72.9%	170 100%

Raw χ^2 = 13.00616 with 2 d. f.; Significance = .0015

Number of Missing Observations = 5; The results for this question were also significant for civil status (.0163). People who were married with children experienced the least pulling among their friendships (54.2% "No, Never") as compared to singles (36.7% "No, Never") or married people without children (22.2% "No, Never"). Hence the common life circumstance of raising children bonded married parents with a strong solidarity.

Chapter Four

Friendship: Up, Down, and in the Middle

A Play on the Effect of Class on Close Friendship

In David Fennario's play, *Nothing to Lose*, class and ethnic group intertwine into the mesh of the components of close friendship. Set in a tavern near a Montreal trucking depot, the play introduces the audience to its characters. Of working-class Verdun, Italian, English-speaking background, Jerry returns to the environment of his upbringing to have a beer and a chat with his closest friends, Jackie, the once tough, single stud, now married, and Frank, the less illustrious but steady, loyal buddy, who is working with Jackie.

While a strike looms in the background, the center of the play's action depicts the struggle between the workers' revolutionary take-over of the trucking business, symbolized by Jackie, or the evolutionary compromise of getting as much out of the job through smaller material gains, represented by the hard-working, dedicated fixer, the young union cadre, Murray, who is Jewish. Meanwhile, Claude, the French Canadian bartender, keeps the old alcoholic, Chibougamou, in line and serves the other middle-aged, family-men truckers, the Forman, Gros Gas, and Fred. They are all discussing the troubles on the job and the prospects for a strike. English Canadian and French Canadian stereotypes are depicted through the conservative English Canadian, Fred, who sees all the eventual problems of the strike, and Gros Gas, the radical French Canadian, promoting the strike.

Jerry is the star who has made good, and his friends, Jackie and Frank, are curious about what it was like in the world of Toronto show business. Ostensibly, Jerry wants to talk about the family difficulties that the impetuous, adventurous Jackie is having with his wife. In this setting, Jerry begins preaching for revolutionary change as the only way to overcome the boring, meaningless daily frustrations and conflicts which the present system imposes on its working class. Uptight, sensitive to his friends' plight, and hateful towards the system which has washed away his friends' personalities, Jerry argues for revolution.

While the characters of this play often become shells to the ideology they portray, *Nothing to Lose* sheds light on how class touches on intimate friendship. It shows that Jerry's social mobility as a playwright bestows upon him greater wealth and prestige than his friends. Because his profession as a playwright encourages him to think about the world, and more particularly because he has adopted a revolutionary ideology toward that world, his chosen occupation gives him a different outlook and position in life in contrast to his friends, Jackie and Frank, who have come to accept the world of marriage, the family, and an everyday job. Educationally, Jerry has gone beyond his friends as well. Ethnically they are one English and two Italian Canadian anglophones who work side by side and drink but stay socially separate from French Canadian francophones.

These friends care about the friendships of their youth, and they are willing to deal openly with the frustrations of their adult world together. This pathos, revealed at a tavern, is crosscut by these various currents, as are their friendships. Their friendships remain solid by being renewed through the common activities of beer drinking and pool playing and in mutual acceptance of each other's life situations. At the same time the playwright wants to alleviate the frustrated, unfulfilled lives of his worker friends. Even if Fennario's imaginary realism does not exactly mirror friendship in the real world, it does provide a simulation of real factors in larger-than-life Montreal friendships.

Class manifests itself in these friendships by putting the friends in different work, income, prestige, and power situations which influence their generalized world views. Yet in this play, as in the real world of Montreal, people frequently interpret a scene or human interaction as being brought about as much by ethnicity as by social class. Even though Fred and Gros Gas are both of similar class positions, it is implied that Fred's conservatism or moderation is due to his being English Canadian while Gros Gas's radicalism comes from his French Canadian background. In sociologese, it would be suggested that ethnicity intervenes in the construction of friendship by class in Montreal.

Sociologists' Understanding of How Class Bears on Close Friendship

Within sociology the concept of class has been understood very differently by different sociologies. In mainstream American sociology the stratificationalist point of view predominates. It looks at "how individuals are distributed whether by income, prestige, influence, education, or some other dimension," particularly in the consequences of class on "life-chances and life-styles of individuals." In the contrasting Marxian perspective, "Social classes are seen as group formations and as dynamic forces in history; group interest and power are the major themes."[1] To complicate matters, there are huge divisions in each of these two large camps. Among the theorists of stratification there are big differences between the reputational and objective approaches and their varied combinations, and among the Marxists there is a wide variety of structuralist, historicist, and humanist interpretations of class that are cross-cut among the other ideological subdivisions of social democrats, and Moscow-, Peking-, and Trotskyite-oriented communists.

Friendship has been seen to be affected by class primarily by the differentials it creates in resources, education, and life-style, which, in their turn, produce a communality of interest and a feeling of belonging to a community among people of similar class. In Jean Maisonneuve's explanation, three major factors bring about this phenomenon. People who work in the same line of work tend to have common plans of action, perceptions, and information because they meet the same problems, go through the same steps, and have the same movements. Economically, their incomes are similar, which eventually leads them to defend their financial interests against the management of their own firm or against other private or professional sectors. Certainly belonging to the same unions or professional associations can forcefully strengthen the affinities. For Maisonneuve, the most decisive elements of the community or profession are without doubt due to axiology, i.e. values, ethics, aesthetics, or religion. Colleagues feel like companions in the full sense of the word. Being interested in the same task, they fight on the same side in the same party for profit, status, and career. However, being a colleague can present some obstacles for the affinities, such as seeing too much of each other. Or, for example, being promoted can bring a colleague to break off a former friendship due to rivalry, tension linked to hierarchical inequalities, and relations of authority.[2] But for Marxists the class system is the underlying impediment to close friendship. In his *Manuscripts of 1844*, Karl Marx pointed to capitalism as the cause of the alienation that destroys friendship and other social relationships. Under the alienated labor of capitalism, mankind comes to feel that separation from other people is its true life.[3]

Accounting for the Influence of Class on Close Friendship

So much for the forces that affect friendships within the same class. When people cross class lines, they encounter enormous barriers to forming close friendships. In England, these boundaries have been described in the following passage:

> Certainly it is true that many people find that trying to socialize across class barriers can be a strain because of ingrained habits, outlooks, tastes, and interests, especially if they are people of low curiosity ... When people find themselves in a cross-class situation, they are likely to put on their best behavior and strain to make pleasant conversation.[4]

Generally Americans have been thought to be less class conscious than the English, and Canadians have been seen to lie in between, probably somewhat nearer the American pole. How does this class consciousness bear upon friendship? In heeding Maisonneuve's appeal for further differential and comparative studies, I put these same questions to Montrealers about the influence of class on friendship that he had asked the French of France.[5] On the written questionnaire, I inquired: "Among these friends which belong to: a) a milieu like your own, from the point of view of resources and goods possessed; b) a milieu more prosperous; c) a milieu less prosperous." Although I divided up the question to fit in the flow of conversation in each interview, I had composed formal items for the in-depth interview asking, " ... How do different factors like urban or rural environment, education, occupation, income, ethnicity, age and talent help or distract from your making or maintaining close friendships?" and "Can you objectively define class and meaningful work in your own society and in the world at large? Do you really feel that there is such a thing as class and meaningful work in your society and in the world at large? Do these facts enter into your best friendships?" Besides these more reputational or subjective questions, I had a number of formal inquiries about the "objective" attributes of class for each person interviewed. In this vein, each person who participated in my study was asked to specify his or her major former, present, and future trade, job, or occupation, and the number of years he or she had been in that occupation. I also asked for the income, occupation and estimated capital assets of the person interviewed and of his or her parents.

All the people in my study reported that the greatest number of their friends came from a milieu like their own from the point of view of resources and good possessed. My interviewees and respondents from all classes had the next greatest number of their friends from a milieu more prosperous than their own and had the fewest friends from a milieu less well-off than their own. Many fewer professionals than white and blue collar workers indicated that their closest friends came from a higher class. Likewise, professionals, then white collar workers claimed more, and blue collar workers claimed fewer, friends from a milieu less well-off than their own.[6]

The sentiments which underlie these structural findings are complex. Many people interviewed had negative evaluations of the life-styles of people in other classes. Yet, there was no up-front admission of pride of belonging to a particular class, as is quite clearly depicted in Michel Tremblay's *The Impromptu of Outremont*. However, speaking in French, a student of archeology in her early twenties, whose father is a civil servant, told me how class had affected her friendships. Her complaints stress how the different language, the emotional quality of, and the ostentation with which her friend's family display their worldly possessions disturbed her:

> ... I think what kept me from making friendships a lot is the milieu in which I went around ... My friend comes from the East End, from Rosemont ... which is so different ... It took me time before I got used to his milieu ... For example, the expressions that they used -- and then when those people there; they had a lot of family reunions, ... and then the language that was used was *joual*.[7] They cursed and all that. You see the kind of people ... and they are people who do not talk ... his father and mother do not talk ... Their values are something else too: superconsumption, color television, all kinds of unbelievable electrical appliances.

Some of my questions about social factors in friendship irritated people. When this single, male, service manager in his early twenties, who had fifteen years of formal education, was asked how class had affected his friendships, he replied rather cockily:

> I can define class in the sense that there are two ways. Do you want it upper, middle, lower, upper middle, upper lower, or whatever the hell you want. Anybody can read it out of a book. But in simpler terms, there is definitely a class. The majority of people in the world, they just don't relate. If you're in the $20,000 income group, you're not going to relate to someone in the $4,000 or $5,000 income group. You don't see them if you're working at the same company.

You won't be working with them because, you take the president of the company. How many times do you see him if it's a big company? And you go right down the scale. You take a large company, or a small company; let's take a big one, where you've got the president, the vice presidents, the managers, the assistant managers, the workers, right down to the night watchman, the laborers, whatever. Each one will see his boss, but how many employees actually go out with the boss, even for lunch? They don't even see each other, especially at night. Just even at lunch time, how many will go out for lunch, and that's one simple definition on how class breaks down. The foreman won't go with the worker, the manager definitely won't go with the president, or the vice president for lunch, or a party, unless it's a party at work. Do they enter into my friendships? Yes, in the sense that some nights I want to go out, to go out to the Playboy Club, the Holiday Inn, discos; I just can't afford to bring them every night. But I don't like to do that because I sound like the complete reverse of what I said earlier about simplicity. And what I really enjoy doing most of the time is just walking down by the beach, going up to my cottage, going for a ride in my car. But you just want to go out sometimes; and you want to go to a nice place; you want to go out for dinner, and in a sense, it will inhibit your relationship with some people because they just can't afford it.

While professional people seem to demean the language communicativeness, material, and familial values of the workers, the workers see a certain cliquishness and unhappiness among the well-off that works against friendship among them or with people of other classes. A married woman of fifty, who had been a housewife her entire life, and who has a working class, French Canadian background answered my question in French:

> ... Yes, well you want to say social level? That's it. Well, there are those who don't mix with others, who are a little group, and then who always stay together, and then who don't even speak to others. ... I would say that these people who maybe think that they are happy, but, who deep down are not, because in general it's people who have money, heh? ... There are two classes in society: the rich and the poor. ... There are those who are poor, poor, poor who are

really bad off, who don't have any money, but I think that they are as happy as the rich.

Among the white collar workers friends serve as a role model for desired social mobility. I noticed this observation when I interviewed a married woman with two children in her mid-twenties, of English Canadian background, who was working as a clerk-typist. Referring to her friend's socio-economic class, she said:

> And she wants a lot from me, more than what I, you know, like sort of. It's because she's well-off. It's what she is. I look up to her, and she wants a lot from me, more than what I have, so she'll help me out in that way, you know. Like I could be just satisfied with, um, living in the, living here, which is really a slum part of Montreal. And like, you know, I could live, well actually, I'm going to. She just wants me to come up and live where she is, she's living. And just, like a heart of gold, like I would think, "What I'm doing is fine, and just enough," and she talks to me and says, "You can really get a lot more out of life than what you're getting, you know." She'll talk to me and tell me how I can go about it and how to live, you know.

To determine the elements of class in friendship, the Montrealers in my study were asked to respond to questions concerning their close friends' education levels in relation to their own. In my sample 48.4% of Montrealers' friends' had educational levels the same as their own. 27.2% of my subjects' friends were better educated, and 24.4% were educated to a lesser degree than my interviewees and respondents.[8]

Education seems to specially create a barrier in getting people of different levels to understand the language, thought processes, and mannerisms of people with more or less education than their own. The aspect of professionals' having difficulty communicating with non-professional people, touched upon in the student of archeology's remarks, is made more explicit by a medical intern in his early-to-mid twenties, a single, French Canadian male, from the Eastern Townships, whose father is an industrialist. Replying to Ms. Verrette in French, he stated frankly:

> Contacts with the less educated classes are difficult for me. The contacts that I make with the less educated classes are between a medical doctor and his patient, and those contacts are very specialized, and I try to keep it that way, moreover, for the moment, because I believe that I am more honest with myself and, then, I give a much better service to the patient, ... , if I am like that because the patient does not himself understand the professional service that I give to him. The people with whom I hang around generally are people of the same level of education as myself, if you like, and in this sense, that hurts friendships. Then I don't have time to look for friends anyhow. I don't want to say that I don't want to do it. It's that same thing when it comes to the question of socio-economic level. It's with a certain class of people; it's undeniable. You have to be realistic. 99.9 percent of the time I am with a certain class of people.

Some more empirical Marxist-influenced sociology has accorded more importance to occupation as an indicator of socio-economic class or of class itself. To find out to which extent close friends are found among the members of a person's own occupational groups, interviewees were asked on the questionnaire: "Among these friends which are: a) in the same trade or occupation as you; b) in different trades or occupations (Please indicate which other trades and occupations or persons without trades or occupations in the respective columns referring to each of your best friends)." Montrealers informed us that about 52% of their friends were in the same trade or occupation as their own and around 48% were in different trades or occupations.[9]

More English than French Canadians had friends in their same occupation. If a group strongly values work, its members would spend much time on the job. Their choice of friends would be more restricted to co-workers. A middle aged, married, female, elementary school teacher, who reported having capital assets of between $100,000 and $249,000, emphasized the centrality of the work ethic for English Canadians:

> ... The English work ethic is very, very strong, you know. Ah, middle class English people feel very strongly about work, very strongly! One has to work. It's very, very

important that all the boys, not so much the girls, but that
all the boys get job openings to provide for their families.

It might be thought if a group valued work so strongly that its
members would find themselves seeking out friends on the job. In
Montreal, only 19.8% of the interviewees had made their close friends by
coming into contact with them on the job. If it is true that the greater
the person's occupational commitment greater will be the likelihood that
his or her friends will be colleagues, then this rather low figure suggests
that Montrealers may draw fewer of their friends from the world of work
than Americans, for whom work is reputed to be so central to the
national character.[10] As the young sales manager stated in an
interview earlier in this chapter, the status hierarchy on the job can
prevent people from becoming close friends. But also a corollary of the
work ethic pushes people to put their work before other people. Besides
this impediment, making friends on the job has been discouraged in
business managers' publications.[11] Yet, regardless of these forces
working against too friendly a job milieu, and despite directors' wishes,
close friends are to be found at work, as Homans recorded in *The Human
Group*, and as we learned from our interviewee who had made close
friends working in a large Montreal store. Yet, whether friends are made
on or off the job, a person must devote mental energy and time to
cultivate friendship. Jean Maisonneuve designed a question to probe into
this matter. In my translation this question asks, "Even if your work is
most time and energy consuming, do you try to put some time aside for
your friends at any cost? a. yes b. no." As it is a strongly valued cultural
norm to be with friends even if it means detracting from work or profits,
it is not surprising to learn that 91.8% of the people in my sample
responded affirmatively and only 8.2% negatively to this question.

In trying to measure as accurately as possible the extent to which
close friends come from similar or different socio-economic classes, I
combined the answers based on the criteria of the interviewee's close
friends' wealth, education, and occupation. This step led me to define
three conceptually discrete categories: *strict homophily*, in which one

has close friends only of one's own wealth, educational, and occupational levels; *mixed*, in which one has close friends of one's own and other levels of wealth, education, and occupation; and *strict heterophily*, in which one has close friends only of different levels of wealth, education, and occupation. When all the demographic characteristics were controlled for, 86% of the Montrealers in my study had closest friends from groups of mixed class components. 12.8% of these people had closest friends with strictly the same indicators of socio-economic class. No more than 1.2% of their closest friends were characterized by strictly different indicators of socio-economic class.

Of the background variables that I researched, only ethnicity brought about statistically significant contrasts. Although both the French and English Canadian Montrealers in my sample had most of their close friends characterized by several different elements of class, more French than English Canadian Montrealers had close friends of varied class backgrounds. Many more of the English in comparison to the French Canadian Montrealers studied had friends with strictly the same class make-up. Both groups had very few friends with strictly different socio-economic attributes.[12]

These findings suggest that while the principle of homophily--of like attracts like--is demonstrable for any one criterion of socio-economic status, when wealth, education, and occupation are taken together as indicators of class, only a small segment of the population chooses close friends on the basis of similarity on all these attributes. In a highly complex urban and industrial society under growth, a rapidly changing market values different educational, occupational, and wealth characteristics at different times. During periods of economic growth, recruiters may selectively choose various combinations of class criteria for newly expanding economic organizations. In such a society, only the super-rich and the unemployables remain untouched by this process. Under these conditions, people may give less emphasis to some desired attributes but demand certain others in selecting close friends. Beyond the structural realities of a highly urbanized and industrialized society, the greater secularization of Montreal society from the Quiet Revolution onwards, manifested first in the liberal, and then the left-of-center politico-cultural ideology of the 1960s and 1970s, produced a dominant set of values that gave at least lip-service to egalitarianism. The revival of a conservative economic ethos in the 1980s may have reversed this trend somewhat. Yet, overall in the period from the 1960s onwards, the normative context seems to have eased the formation of friendships across socio-economic classes.

My Montreal sample did not include any representatives of the "Canadian Establishment" or the "Canadian Corporate Elite." The literature on them gives ample evidence of their tight links of friendship. Their closest friendships appear to reveal a very high degree of class homophily based on several criteria of class. In *The Canadian Establishment*, Peter C. Newman sketches the friendship patterns of the upper class:

> Members of this business Establishment touch and greet each other on a wide spectrum of intimacy depending on the commonality of their objectives at any given moment. But no matter how much their goals may temporarily conflict, *they always take one another into account.* They accept, understand, and protect each other. "Make certain you see him before noon," runs the gentle admonition about one of the establishment's most distinguished power holders who has a drinking problem.[13]

In a less critical tone, Professor John Porter describes how upper class Canadians are socialized to their friendship patterns :

> The second important social mechanism for the co-ordination of elites of the various institutional orders is friendship, resulting from living together or having common experience of the same kind of social life.[14]

Even if the members of the higher socio-economic status group constantly refer to one another when it comes to making important decisions and in making their most intimate friends, research finds that they are "much more accepting of all ranks of immigrants than are respondents with lower occupational status, i.e. those for whom competition with immigrants for work is the sharpest."[15]

Different Interpretations of the Juncture of Class and Friendship

Two crucial issues arise in dealing with the subject of class and friendship. The first issue raised is the extent to which people of different classes become close friends. The second issue centers around the patterns, character, and quality of the friendships that typify different classes. Up to this point my results show a high, but varying degree of similarity, of close friends' wealth, educational, and occupational characteristics, and a rather low degree of strict similarity among close friends when all three of these statuses are put together into one indicator. While the thrust of my confirmation of Maisonneuve's and others' work on the homophily of social characteristics of close friends is reassuring, it is not the crucial issue for recent friendship theorists. Since much of the recent research on friendship comes out of vastly different theoretical concerns, readers should not be surprised to learn that many of their theories and findings are inconsistent, particularly in regard to the question of the content and a judgment about the quality of the content of different classes' friendship patterns.

In the genre of network research, Claude S. Fischer found for Bay Area residents, other things equal, the higher his respondents' education,

> the more socially active they were, the larger their networks, the more companionship they reported, the more intimate their relations, and the wider the geographic range of their ties. In general, education by itself meant broader, deeper, and richer networks.[16]

With other factors held constant, Fischer found that with more household income, his interviewees named more non-kin respondents and received more practical and companionable support. He comments that these results challenge the romantic notion of working-class or lower-class sociality.[17]

Jacques Bonin and Jules Duchastel of The Research Collective in Urban Sociology at the University of Montreal dealt with the influence of class on friendship in a chapter entitled, "Private Life and Public Life." Their discussion is rooted in the sociology of everyday life, inspired by the structuralist Marxism of Nicos Poulantzas's 1968 book, *Political Power and Social Classes*. They stress that their conclusions, based on a study of forty informants, cannot be considered representative either of Quebec francophones or of the population of the five neighborhoods studied in *Alienation and Ideology in the Everyday Life of French-speaking Montrealers* in which their work appears as a chapter. With this caution they put forward several hypotheses. The first two have to do with the private life of their informants and are stated in the following words:

> The closer one gets to the privileged pole, the closer friends and colleagues at work get to the nuclear family. The closer one gets to the underprivileged pole, the more kinship is the only universe which surrounds the family. At the middle of this dimension, one makes friends, but at the same time one tries to pick up kin when making friends; 2) The closer one gets to the privileged pole, the greater is the distinction between intimacy and private life. The closer one gets to the underprivileged pole, the more are intimacy and private life mixed together.[18]

They also specified two hypotheses about the public life of the informant:

> The closer one gets to the privileged pole, the more public life spreads out and is diversified. The closer one gets to the underprivileged pole, the more public life and work are superimposed upon one another. 4) The closer one gets to the privileged pole, the more one organizes his work ("Work is life"). The closer one gets to the underprivileged pole, the more one is organized by his work ("Work is a way of earning one's living). 5) The closer one gets to the privileged pole, the more relationships and conversations with people

> met at work become complex. The closer one gets to the
> underprivileged pole, the more relationships and
> conversations with people met at work take the following
> turn: opposition of relationships and conversations in the
> family and at work; opposition of relationships and
> conversations between superiors and colleagues at the
> same level of work.[19]

Most of their discussion is at this highly abstract level of analysis, and there are scarcely a few phrases from their informants to let the reader know whether or not the analysts' tight scheme of categorization so neatly fits their informants' actual responses.

However, Fischer's book and Bonin's and Duchastel's chapter both agree that the upper classes' world of friendship contrasts with the lower classes' almost entire exclusion of friendship from their worlds' of intimacy. In this vein, Colette Moreux recorded a similar configuration for the Quebec countryside:

> Sixteen persons out of 90 declare that they do not spend
> time with anyone outside of their family. Even for the
> others, friends are rare. At the most, when it is necessary
> for the husband's occupation, will one have acquaintances.
> "Friends, they're sincere for a year, and then they're of no
> meaning, and they fall back down on top of you."[20]

Likewise, in the American literature in the sociology of the family, some research points to a pattern devoid of friendship for the traditional family in contrast to the kinship of the non-traditional family in which friendship is incorporated.[21]

My own research and that of other social scientists writing on Quebec and Canada lead to somewhat different conclusions about the relationship of class to friendship. I found that all classes have considerable numbers of close friends both inside and outside the family at the same time. Thus 52% of the blue collar workers, 49% of the white collar workers, and 66% of the professionals reported having friends both inside and outside of the family simultaneously. Of these 28% of the blue collar workers, 24% of the white collar workers, and 18% of the professionals reported having 0,1, or 2 friends outside the family, and 72% of the blue collar workers, 76% of the white collar workers, and 81% of the professionals had 3 or more friends outside of the family. Many more detailed statistics on this matter will be presented in my chapter on friendship and the family. Moreover, as we will see later, counting the number of close friends is not as simple a procedure as these other studies would imply. In addition, when I carried out a series of contingency table analyses of the La Gaipa instrument regarding the psychological basis for friendship, eight statistically significant chi-square correlations pointed to white collar workers being more exacting in and holding a purer image of their close friendships than blue collar workers or professionals. Besides my finding, research on French Canadian youth in Quebec City would also suggest that friendship patterns are not so greatly dictated by socio-economic class.[22] And a study in Toronto found that both blue and white collar workers have more informal association with peers than with family, even though people in Toronto with less education and blue collar occupations have more family relations than white collar and more educated people.[23]

On the basis of the Toronto investigation, it has been observed that higher education, job status, and income put a person in touch with a wider variety of people. In turn, a person's broad contacts lead to further opportunities for advancement. Once entrance is secured to social groups and situations favoring upward mobility, the social milieu continues to lead upward in a spiral. However, this pattern occurs to a greater extent among non-British immigrants than among native Canadians migrated from central Canada or from the East Coast.[24]

The results from Toronto samples of English-speaking and English Canadians contrast with samples of English Canadians in the Montreal area, where working and lower middle class interviewees have been found to have active kinship exchange. It could be that the Quebec English Canadian population is influenced by being more highly stratified and by the more conservative trends in the family patterns of the majority French Canadian culture in the Province of Quebec.

These empirical results leave us with two rather differing pictures of the frequency of close friendship within and among the different classes. The more structuralist view both of the Marxian and non-Marxian variety tends to look at lower class individuals' entire lives wrapped in family and members of the upper classes enrobed in friendship with the middle classes putting on some family and some friends. Although a totally random, representative sample of Montrealers and Quebecers could clarify which of these descriptions is more empirically true, it could be so only if a highly sophisticated quantitative and qualitative methodology were carefully combined to explore this question. Most of the structuralist interpretations do not delve into the highly complex cognitive processes by which a person gets classified as a friend or a relative. The discourse of what interviewees say, their non-verbal messages, and their accounts of their experiences regarding this matter are either absent or barely cited. When their accounts are rarely quoted, the citations are selectively chosen to back up the position that kinship, not friendship, is characteristic of the lower classes. Secondly, the categories of the theorists of everyday life are not always mutually exclusive. For example, they have defined "network" to include acquaintances, colleagues, close friends at work, and intimate friends. To network they have opposed kin, and kin-made-friends.[25] When an informant thinks and acts toward a distant relative or close relative more as a friend than a relative--indeed, informants often exclude or have no knowledge of a large part of their kinship networks when talking to social scientists--to base a major part of an argument on the difference between these categories creates an image of the society's and culture's patterns of friendship more reflective of the analysts' framework than the lifeworld of friendship.

When dealing with the subject of class and friendship, the second salient issue involves the patterns, character, and quality of the friendship constellations of the different classes. Here, while the structuralist Marxian and non-Marxian orientations paint an essentially negative view of the private lives of the members of the lower classes, they do so for very different reasons. Some less rigidly encoded descriptions, including some Marxist ones, do not depict such an abrupt difference between the friendship patterns of the different classes.

For Bonin and Duchastel:

> There are two major ways to define intimacy. Either one attributes to it the quality of a sentiment, that is, an aptitude to be recognized, or as being a relationship to another, or one attributes to it the quality of a behavior, that is family life or the life of a couple ...

> Therefore, intimacy does not have for us the ideological meaning that culture gives to it, that is this appearance of privileged relationships among beings, relationships which some observers believe to recognize universally among all human beings. To the contrary, intimacy becomes a sentiment, unequally distributed according to one's class position which lends itself to being put in a relationship. In its occurrence, intimacy permits the passage of the network in the private life of the dominators. Therefore, it carries out the work of putting into special relationships people who thereby maintain their position of dominance while covering up this breach of the ideology of the private act or under the cover of a "state of the soul." Concretely, the dominator does not say "my privileged relationships are first of all those which I maintain with the dominators, in order to dominate and perpetuate my position of dominator." Rather he says "my special relationships with my friends reveal a natural affinity and a need for communication." It is this second way in which things are experienced, but it is the first in which the analysis must be expressed.[26]

While such a view emphasizes the structural boundaries drawn between friends by class, it denies, dismisses, or utterly shrinks their experience of friendship. Like other structuralist views of class, it is subject to criticism for putting all people into only two categories of people, dominators and dominated, while completely neglecting or minimizing the experience of their friendships and intimacy that it purports to explain. Certainly there are differences in some aspects of the qualities of the classes' friendship patterns and of the interpersonal relationships of people at various positions in the class hierarchy. The small owner of an East End *restaurant*--often a type of mom-and-pop store carrying everything from food to domestic supplies--is certainly different in his or her degree of being a "dominator" from the owner of a small clothing manufacture, to the owner of a large bus company, to the principal stock holder and possibly director of a large insurance or banking consortium. And most certainly the qualities of the friendships of these people in these different class positions can be expected to be influenced by their class position. But to claim, as Bonin and Duchastel do, that people's talk of intimacy is simply an ideological mask or cover for their class position, denies the image of intimate speech of the lower, middle, and upper classes portrayed in French Canadian, English Canadian, and "Other Canadian" literature, film, and common experience.

Here I must speak from the voice of experience. I lived for almost a decade in Canada, a year and a half in Toronto, and over eight years in Quebec. During that time I worked in a factory, libraries, a large hotel, several universities, and colleges; I volunteered at the University Settlement House in Toronto, where I ran recreation programs for working and underclass youth; I ran the American Refugee Service's hostel in Montreal, where I worked mainly with working and lower class young adults. In both Toronto and Montreal I went out socially and was active in politics and community service activities with people of solid working class background. When I taught in Canadian universities, I later had the opportunity of meeting and associating with people of middle and upper middle class background. Moreover, I lived in mostly lower, some middle, and two upper class neighborhoods for extended periods of time. Getting to know people well in these various different "walks of life" leaves me skeptical of the sharp differences in friendship versus kinship described by some authors. Indeed, the most familialistic people whom I got to know well in Montreal were some of my students at the college described in the last chapter, not the underclass of the extremely poor central southern part of Montreal. Coming into their homes and going out on an intimate basis with lower class Montrealers left me with the impression that they were touched in many ways more by the same cultural cross-currents I experienced. In some important ways, they seemed more open to me, because they felt less overtly nationalistic than many middle class Montrealers. A final weakness in the structuralist Marxist account of class and friendship should be underscored. I could tell many anecdotes and cite interviews of lower class people for whom friendship is very important and upper class people for whom family came before friends. Some people who would be objectively labeled as "dominators" in Poulantzas's sense have values which are more in favor of better distribution of society's goods and resources, of more peaceful international policies, and of less formal interpersonal relations than are some people who would be objectively labeled as "dominated," who may harbor racist attitudes, be extremely chauvinistic, rigid in interpersonal conduct, and in favor of fewer welfare state policies.

Jacques Bonin's and Jules Duchastel's view of the central southern section of Montreal--representing the patterns in the city's poorest part-- may exaggerate the degree of familialism and downplay the saliency of friendship and other forms of extra-familial sociability. In painting this picture of *Centre-Sud*, its normalcy is played up and its degree of social disorganization is played down. Anyone who has often walked through and lived near this area, as I have, could not help being struck by a variety of small stores, bars, and street corner life in which friendship appears to stand out more than family life. Besides these institutions, *Centre-Sud* is crosscut by relatively inexpensive public transportation which enables its denizens to get out of their neighborhood, and many of its children and young adults venture forth from its boundaries on bicycles and in motor vehicles. Like other extremely poor areas of North America, *Centre-Sud* displays higher than average forms of deviance, except perhaps very frequent, extremely violent crime. This condition would generally indicate a breakdown of the family, and thereby contrast to the case made for its great family solidarity.

Relevant to this discussion is a very different, but also rather negative, picture of friendship in another lower-class North American setting, that of the African American street corner men in Washington,

D.C., studied by Elliot Liebow in *Tally's Corner*. Using an ethnographic approach to describe friendship in this underclass world, Elliot Liebow wrote:

> Friendship is sometimes anchored in kinship, sometimes in long-term associations which may reach back into childhood. Other close friendships are born locally, in the streetcorner world itself, rather than brought in by men from the outside. Such friendships are built on neighbor or co-worker relationships, or a shared experience or other event or situation which brings two people together in a special way.[27]

In this lumpenproletarian world, Liebow observed that:

> Friendship is at its romantic, flamboyant best when things are going well for the persons involved. But friendship does not often stand up well to the stress of crisis or conflict of interest when demands tend to be heaviest and most insistent. Everyone knows this. Extravagant pledges of aid and comfort between friends are, at one level, made and received in good faith. But at another level, fully aware of his friends' limited resources and the demands of their self interest, each person is ultimately prepared to look to himself alone.[27]

This question of the empirical and theoretical importance of the effect of class on friendship is central to the issue of friendship's quality. The complexity of the underclass language of friendship recorded in Liebow, in some of my Montreal interviews, in some of Michel Tremblay's depictions of lowerclass life in Montreal's East End, and in Fennario's play discussed at the beginning of this chapter, dispute the lack of complexity attributed to lower class conversations by Bonin and Duchastel.[28]

When generalizing about the impact of class on the quality of friendships, researchers have often noted that class makes itself felt through a person's job. In summarizing his discoveries of how the patterns of friendship differ among the different classes, Graham A. Allan found in the English village of Selden Hey that the working-class people contained "relationships within specific contexts" which allowed them:

> a greater control over their relationships through limiting the demands others can legitimately make ... Similarly not using the home for non-kin sociability means that quite large areas of one's life are defined as irrelevant to these relationships and consequently also allows a greater control to be exercised over them.[29]

In my own study, civil status and age made more of a difference than socio-economic class in explaining how friendships were made and lived.[30] These differences will be considered in discussing the influence of age and civil status on friendship. Both the greater relative material wealth of contemporary Quebec in comparison to England and the different notions of proper giving rooted in the English Protestant and French Canadian Catholic religious traditions can help account for this variation. Still, Allan's observations help explain why taverns, church festivals, balconies at the back of many inner-city Montrealers' apartments, public parks and recreational facilities serve as the places where much of contemporary Montreal friendship takes place.

Although the workplace has been lauded as a locus of many close friendships and much sociable interaction, only approximately 20% of my interviewees reported that their friendships began at work and only about 14% said that their friendships broke off with a change of occupation.[31] This behavior is reflected in the norm inquired about in Jean Maisonneuve's sixteenth question,

> Do you think that one must leave off certain friendships sometimes for reasons of social responsibility or on account of new occupations?

Regardless of the age, civil status, ethnicity, gender, or socio-economic class of the interviewees and respondents, 63.5 percent replied "no" to this question. That 36.5 percent answered "yes" may indicate that social and cultural realities force people to give up friends owing to social responsibility and new occupations during the course of their lives.[32]

In Montreal a host of pleasant places to meet and socialize with friends exist outside of the workplace. Many an evening the streets or underground passages and covered malls, adjoining the subway system, are filled with citizens of many different classes interacting together. As the socialized medical system provides basic medical assurance, medical insurance and other critical forms of psycho-social support are not as directly linked to a person's place of work as they are in the United States of America, so a person's real dependence on the presence of co-workers' aid is lessened. Finally, many a commentator has noted that the pace of work in Canada as a whole and in Quebec in particular is not as frenetic as in the United States. Thus the centrality of the workplace as a principal institution for making and maintaining close friendship, while notable, appears to be less prominent in comparison to the United States.

Even though I am reluctant to accept the portrait of lower class people in Montreal as rather friendless, my clinical work among underclass Americans in a convalescent center in an extremely disadvantaged neighborhood in Chicago confirmed that many "mainstreamed" adults have a low level of trust of their fellow residents.[33] Without effective psycho-social intervention, friendships for the majority of them remain at best in the realm of fond or bitter memories.

Notes

1. Broom, L. and P. Selznick, *Sociology. A Text with Adapted Readings. Fifth Edition* (New York: Harper & Row, 1973), 197.

2. Maisonneuve, Jean *Psycho-sociologie des affinités* (Paris: Presses universitaires de France, 1966), 141-142.

3. Ibid., 151.

4. Salaman, G., *Community and Occupation: An Exploration of World Leisure Relationships* (Cambridge: Cambridge University Press, 1974), 167.

5. Maisonneuve, *Psycho-sociologie des affinités*, 188.

6. *Question #5:*

The Relationship between the Interviewees' and Respondents' Socio-Economic Status (SES) and the SES of Their Closest Friends

Count Column %	Interviewees' and Respondents' SES			
Friends' Milieu in Resources and Goods Possessed	Blue Collar Worker	White Collar Worker	Professional	Row Total
Friends from a Similar Milieu	41.00 61.20%	57.00 52.8%	55.00 61.10%	153.00 57.7%
Friends' Milieu More Prosperous	22.00 32.8%	33.00 30.60%	16.00 17.80%	71.00 26.80%
Friends' Milieu Less Prosperous	4.00 6.00%	18.00 16.70	19.00 21.10%	41.00 15.50%
Column Count Column %	67.00 25.30%	108.00 40.8%	90.00 34.00%	265.00 100.00%

Raw χ^2 = 10.84936 with 4 Degrees of Freedom.
Significance = .0283   Number of Missing Observations = 5

7. The French Canadian patois. *Joual* comes from a phonetic distortion of the voiceless sibilant, ch, in the French word for horse, *cheval.*

8. *Question #6.*

Relationship between the Interviewees' and Respondents' Education and the Educational Attainment of Their Close Friends by Ethnicity

Count Column %	Interviewees' and Respondents' Ethnicity		
Educational Level of the Interviewees' and Respondents' Friends	French Canadian	English Canadian	Row Total
Friends at about the Same Level of Education	42.00 43.30%	109.00 50.70%	151.00 48.40%
Friends Better Educated	26.00 26.80%	59.00 27.40%	85.00 27.20%
Friends Less Educated	29.00 29.90%	47.00 21.90%	76.00 24.40%
Column Count Column %	97.00 31.00%	215.00 68.90%	312.00 100.00%

Raw χ^2 = 2.53827 with 2 degrees of freedom; Significance = .2811

9. *Question #7.*
  Relationship between the Interviewees' and Respondents' Occupations and Those of Their Close Friends by Ethnicity

Count Column %	Interviewees' and Respondents' Ethnicity		
Occupational Similarity or Difference between the Interviewees and Respondents and Their Close Friends	French Canadian	English Canadian	Row Total
Friends in the Same Occupation	35.00 43.20%	89.00 56.30%	124.00 51.90%
Friends in Different Occupations	46.00 56.80%	69.00 43.70%	115.00 48.10%
Column Count Column %	81.00 33.90%	158.00 66.10%	239.00 100.00%

Corrected $\chi2$ = 3.18498 with 1 degree of freedom; Significance =.0743

10. Brenton, Myron, *Friendship* (New York: Stein and Day Publishers, 1974), 114.

11. Packard, Vance, *The Status Seekers: An Exploration of Class Behavior in America.* London: Longmans, 1959), 167-178.

12. *The Relationship between the Degree of Similarity of the Interviewees' and Respondents' Socio-Economic Class, Based on Three Combined Indicators of Wealth, Education, and Occupation, That Vary from Strict Similarity (Homophily) to Strict Difference (Heterophily)*

Count Column %	Ethnicity of the Interviewees and Respondents		
Similarity or Difference of Friends on Three Indicators of Class	French Canadian	English Canadian	Row Total
Strict Similarity (Homophily)	1.00 2.00%	21.00 17.20%	22.00 12.80%
Friends with Mixed Components of Class	48.00 96.00%	100.00 82.00%	148.00 86.00%
Strict Difference (Heterophily)	1.00 2.00%	1.00 0.80%	2.00 1.20%
Column Count Column %	50.00 29.10%	122.00 70.90%	172.00 100.00%

Raw $\chi2$ = 7.65371 with 2 d.f.; Significance = .0218; Number of Missing Observations = 3

13. Newman, Peter C., *The Canadian Establishment* (Toronto: McClelland and Stewart Limited, (1975) 1977), 447.

14. Porter, John, *The Vertical Mosaic. An Analysis of Social Class and Power in Canada* (Toronto: University of Toronto Press, 1965), 527-528.

15. Lambert, Wallace E., in *Readings in Social Psychology. Focus on Canada*, eds. D. Koulack and D. Perlman (Toronto: Wiley Publishers of Canada Ltd., 1973), 33-48.

16. Fischer, Claude S., *To Dwell among Friends. Personal Networks in Town and City* (Chicago: The University of Chicago Press, 1982), 251.

17. Ibid., 252.

18. Bonin, Jacques and Jules Duchastel, "Vie privée vie publique," in *Aliénation et idéologie dans la vie quotidienne des Montréalais francophones*, Vol. 2, eds. Yves Lamarche, Marcel Rioux, et Robert Sévigny, Montréal: Les Presses de l'université de Montréal, 1973, 562.

19. Ibid., 563.

20. Moreux, Colette, *Fin d'une religion? Monographie d'une paroisse canadienne-française.* Montréal: Presses de l'université de Montréal, 1969), 133.

21. Gagnon, N., "Un nouveau type de relations familiales," in *Recherches sociographiques* 9 (1968): 60-66.

22. Delude-Clift, C. and E. Champoux, "Le conflict des générations," *Recherches sociographiques.* 14 (1973): 157-201.

23. Crysdal, S., "Family and Kinship in Riverdale," in *The Underside of Toronto*, ed. W. E. Mann (Toronto: McClelland & Stewart Ltd., 1970), 104, 97-108.

24. Ibid., 104.

25. Bonin and Duchastel, "Vie privée vie publique," in *Aliénation et idéologie dans la vie quotidienne des Montréalais francophones*, 570.

26. Ibid., 584-585.

27. Liebow, Elliot. *Tally's Corner: A Study of Negro Streetcorner Men* (Boston: Little, Brown and Company, 1967), 180. Here it is important to stress that very recent research indicates that "Because working-class black males experience greater isolation from mainstream society than

upwardly mobile black men, they may not internalize the same taboos against male same-sex friendships, which result in non-self-disclosure, competitiveness, and nonvulnerability." See Clyde W. Franklin II in Peter M. Nardi (1992), 203; 201-214. Yet, it is important to remember that Liebow's study was of the lower-class, not the working or upwardly mobile classes of African Americans.

28. Liebow, Elliot. *Tally's Corner,* 161-207; Bonin and Duchastel, "Vie privée vie publique," in *Aliénation et idéologie dans la vie quotidienne des Montréalais francophones,* 563.

29. Allan, Graham A., *Sociology of Friendship and Kinship* (London: George Allen & Unwin, 1979), 119.

30. Gurdin, Joseph Barry, *Amitié*/Friendship: The Socio-cultural Construction of Friendship in Contemporary Montreal," Ph.D. diss., Department of Sociology, Université de Montréal, 1978, 575; 589.

31. Ibid., 575.

32. *Question #16:The Relationship between the Interviewees' and Respondents' Socio-Economic Status (SES) and Their Belief That One Must Leave off Certain Friendships Sometimes for Reasons of Social Responsibility or on account of New Occupations*

Count Column %	Interviewees' and Respondents' SES			
Leave off Certain Friendships Sometimes?	Blue Collar Worker	White Collar Worker	Professional	Total
Yes	17 37%	19 29.7%	26 43.3%	62 36.5%
No	29 63%	45 70.3%	34 56.7%	108 63.5%
Column Count Column %	46 27.1%	64 37.6%	60 35.3%	170 100%

Raw χ^2 = 2.49524 with 2 Degrees of Freedom;
Significance = .2872   Number of Missing Observations = 5

33. See: Gurdin, J. Barry, Janet Reohr, Deena Nardi, and David Schroder, "The Influence of Propinquity on Urban and Underclass Convalescent Center Residents," 1984.

Chapter Five

Friendship and the Family

In reading the literature relating friendship to the family, it strikes me that in the 1970s the place of class was central to many of the debates of the period. By the late 1980s and early 1990s much of the variability within the institutions of friendship and the family is now being explained in terms of gender.[1] Yet, even when researchers saw class as causing different constellations of family and friendship, they frequently disagreed about the influence of class on friendship. Their main debate centered around the question of whether or not people of lower class backgrounds are mainly involved in a world of kinship devoid of friendship. That debate was not new to either the social sciences or philosophy.

In modern societies Arlene Skolnick noted:

> Unlike kin relations in traditional societies, ... kinship in America and other industrial societies is much more like friendship--people often interact with their relatives according to how they feel about them. Good (1963) calls such kin relations "Ascriptive friendship."[2]

It was difficult for Montrealers to relate friendship to kinship and vice versa in large part because the language, thought, and emotions of friendship and kinship are experienced as intersecting and complementary, often at the same time. Even though the evidence portrays a large cleavage in the different social classes' experiences of friendship and kinship, this work has tended to minimize the accounts of the people studied to the profit of rigid analytical grids and, thereby, to exaggerate the extent of class differences. In this chapter I will record how my interviewees, the classics, and modern social science explain their similar and different grounds. I will cite examples of some styles of friendship in the family and contrast these to a family infertile for friendship.

The Difficulty in Calling Family "Friends" and Friends "Family"

The majority of people whom I interviewed were hesitant and unsure when asked to classify members of their family into being friends or not. When I taught at the Montreal college described in the chapter on ethnicity, I asked my students to write essays about the relationships in their families. I asked them if they would call these relationships friendship or something else. These mostly female students in their late teens were sensitive and uncertain about labeling family members by a particular relational term other than the common cultural name for that relationship. At a large university in Montreal, one of my twenty-year old students, an English Canadian male, whose father had been in the Canadian military for many years initially rejected describing his family as friends but ended up relating some family friendships. He wrote:

> ...The love in a family grows from being around them most of your life. As each new member in a family is born, the love is brought on by the caring and raising of the children together. ... Trying to talk about your family in terms of liking them is completely different from talking about loving them. It is like talking about your family as if they

were just friends. ... I shall ... talk about my family and then how I relate to each of them in terms of their being my friends. What I am going to do now is to give you a definition of what a "friend" is to me, and try to show how each member of my family comes as close as possible to my definition. A friend to me is a person who takes me for what I am now, not what I will be or what they think I should be. They should recognize the mood I'm in and then decide if they should help me, console me or leave me alone. Most of my friends know this about me, and know what I expect of them, so consequently, they stay my friends. To put my family in this position is hard because I see them as family and not friends.

In both my interviews and essays the discussions around this point were highly nuanced. When my interviewees were pressed into classifying one or more members of their family as friends or something other than friends and explaining their reasons for doing so, twice as many people chose to describe at least one member of their kin-group as friends rather than not. Yet, more interviewees claimed that they had close friends in their family than actually described such friendships. Their "claimed" number of friends refers to their initial responses to my replication of Jean Maisonneuve's questions,

> With how many persons are you presently linked in an active (best) friendship? Excluding the members of your family? _____ Including the members of your family? _____.[3]

People often told or wrote about fewer friends than they had claimed at the beginning of the questionnaire or interview. I consider the "real" number of friends to be the explicitly mentioned number of close friends described or written down in detail.[4] Montreal society values having friends in the family, even though socio-economic classes do so to somewhat different degrees.[5]

The Language and Thought of Family versus Non-family Friendships

Part of the difficulty that Montrealers expressed when speaking about friendships in the family has to do with language. Their vocabularies and cognitive sets used to describe kin and friends overlap. This fact can be traced back to ancient philosophy.

In the Greek classics the adjective, *philos*, could be used to refer to the father, mother, children, spouses, and near and dear ones. Its meaning was extended even more clearly to the gods and to the dead, thereby showing even more clearly its religious or sacred significance.[6] The ancient Greek philosophers as the contemporary sociologists put forth explanations--sometimes at odds with one another--to explain why friendship should be felt and conceptualized among the different relationships in the family. Family friendships are evident in the plays of Euripides, and Aeschylus uses *philos* to refer to kinship bonds. The Greek notions of *philia* and *philotès* first designated the bond of man with everything that is dear to him and on which his existence depends in some way. Gradually these terms evolved and their meaning became more restricted. They were integrated into the idea of a rational choice or into the values of sincerity and fidelity which question mere utility. According to Jamblicus, although Pythagoras clearly taught the friendship of everything towards everything else, his conception includes the friendship of man towards his wife, children, brothers, and near and dear ones.[7]

In many languages this association between similar attributes of kinship and friendship is noteworthy. Moreover, this confusion is compounded by the French verb, *aimer*, signifying "to love" and "to like." Rare was the interviewee, regardless of her or his socio-economic stratum, who so squarely distinguished his family from his friends, as did this middle-aged Montreal carpenter of English Canadian background. In reply to my questions, "Are you more intimate with your family or friends? Do you or do you not express this intimacy in the form of commitment of goods, services, emotional support, etc.? In other words, can you count more on your family or friends?" he responded:

> [I count] more on the family, anyone in the family ... I don't consider my wife as a friend; I consider her to be my wife.

I interjected, "What is the difference?" And he answered:

> A friend is a friend that lives across the street, a couple of streets over, or something like that. You pick up the phone and say "Hello. It's a nice day today." I go to bed with my wife .. the same thing. The daughter is married now. If I want to talk to her, well, I pick up the telephone. I phone her like a friend, but I don't consider her as a friend. I consider her as my daughter. That's it. The same thing with the son. He's not my friend. He's my son. ... I have helped my daughter in a way, and my son, I've helped my son financially .. I would go to my sister, if I had to.

Family-oriented Friendship with a Couple Companionate Nuance

This carpenter's implied distinction of a sexual bond with his wife and obligations toward his daughter and son distinguish why he thinks of them as kin rather than friends. His criteria vividly contrast to an upper class, 67 year of age, English-speaking Canadian woman and mother of seven children, who was one of the few Montrealers in my sample who so clearly demonstrate the couple companionate relationship commonly described by sociologists for the American middle class. Of her family members she says:

> My husband and I are friends apart from being husband and wife. I feel my children are friends. I forget that they're my children. I like them as people, heh. They can't forget I'm their mother because I'll talk to them as people, heh. After all, you've met Hal. He's 40 now, heh, so I mean my family's pretty well grown up. And it'll suddenly come on me they can't forget. They're my friends, heh. And one of the greatest compliments I had, Hal gave it several years ago [when we were visiting him in another country] ... He promised to see some friends of his. And he didn't say who

> we were. He said, "I'd like you to meet my very good friends." He wasn't trying to be funny. It was the nicest compliment one could get. ... This is my mother and dad, heh, but the first thing was "my very close friends." Do you follow? It meant so much to me, and I know it meant a lot to him. ... And I can discuss things with my sons, or we can get into arguments, and when we get involved with an idea, and then occasionally, [they'll say] "but, Mum, you're taking advantage." I wasn't taking any advantage, but they couldn't forget that I was their parent, but I could forget that they were my children. ... because they're people, heh. ... I mean they're friends apart from being, you know, relationships of mother and daughter. I have five sons and two daughters, heh. ... I'd rather count on my family. If you want an honest answer, ... if I needed help, I'd perhaps go to my husband. He'd be the first one I'd go to.

Please remember that this woman's cognition of the relationship with her husband and children represents a small minority of my respondents. As we shall see later in this chapter, it is striking that only 3.4% of the wives and 4.0% of the husbands were called close friends by their spouses. This finding suggests that the couple-companionate friendship is not as widely spread, especially in the middle-class milieu, as it is thought to be, or that there was a significant difference between Montreal and Chicago of the same period in this regard. This report does not suggest that there is a lack of positive affect between spouses in Montreal, but rather that this positive affect was packaged in different categories more frequently. On the other hand, this woman's description is representative of a version of a style of "family-oriented friendship." In this style the whole family is characterized by a warm, open, understanding, accepting, trustful, loving, helping, reliable, sharing, enjoyable atmosphere with varying degrees of high similarity in values, beliefs, and attitudes. There are distinctions of age, rights, and obligations of traditional roles among husband and wife and siblings and/or grandparents.

One family might be linked in friendship with another family. Usually the husband and wife introduce their own children to the other family's offspring. Or the friendship may be centered in the family itself with individual members of the family attaching their closest friends to it. This bond can last even after the termination of the original marriage bond in which it was begun.

The family is generally settled in an occupation. There is a residence, food, and basic income for its members and prestations of goods and services that take place toward their friend in the family to the extent that their own economic and psychological well-being is not endangered.

The wife and husband may be each other's closest friends. Those whose style approximates this couple-companionate arrangement may have higher degrees of geographical mobility and probably have met other same-sex friends in other parts of their life cycle. Indeed, other close friends may have facilitated their meeting and maintaining their friendship. They tend to have a traditional role-separation of the wife's and husband's activities. These traditional expectations provide a need to discuss traditionally tabooed subjects to same-sex friends with whom they maintain bonds through correspondence, telephone, vacations, and visits.

Love, sharing of values, experiences, durability, enjoyment, trust, and acceptance of the other's self take precedence over maximal understanding and discussion in "family-oriented friendship."

The 67-year-old mother and wife interviewed above had taught school a year and a half before her marriage and later for a few years as well as having volunteered for various community service activities. Unlike Stacey J. Oliker's interviewees of a few years later, this woman emphasizes that telephone calling was not an important aspect of her friendships.[8] In her language, "I don't have to phone people up and talk to them ... everyday or anything like that. I can get along beautifully on my own." Also, with lesser salience of the car culture as compared to the Bay Area, Montreal has neighborhoods which are more accessible by foot and public transportation, as this interviewee reports in the following words, "When my children were growing up then, Annette could say, Frannie, would you come on over. And I could go over. It was in walking distance." Closely rereading this long interview again just after completing *Best Friends and Marriage: Exchange among Women*, I did not find this woman's status as a mother and wife leading her close friendships with women to become a locus of "reflection and action to achieve or sustain the stability of a marriage or a sense of its adequacy."[9] Rather, for this Montreal woman of retirement age in the mid-1970s, the importance of religion in her thoughts and her positive recollections of ethnic images of her family of orientation and on-going ethnic commitments throughout her life's closest friendships had occupied the place that Bay Area women of the 1980s needed to devote to emotion work regarding their marriages with their husbands in order to accommodate to that institution.

The well-known Quebec sociologist, Guy Rocher, has noted that the contemporary Quebec couple "inwardly accepts the fact that the relationship may not be permanent. This instability may be a source of richness or difficulties, just as the stability was."[10] He also observes that whereas for his generation a religious education was a requirement, "Today we see that in families, parents generally allow their children complete freedom in this area," and that young people's anxiety "derives from the flexibility of having to choose. Some end up by going back to religion courses, which they prefer over moral studies courses, in order to find out more about religions and be able to make choices later." He also notices that, "The presence of the Catholic church is much more discreet and hidden now. I would say that the Québec mentality remains a Christian mentality which is still open to Christian teaching. This obviously cannot be measured by religious practices."[11] With the great changes in the status of women in Quebec since the 1970s, it could be that the type of structure of friendship for married women observed by Oliker currently is becoming a more prevalent pattern in Quebec as well. In short, it seems that "emotion work" may be occupying much of the former space of prayer and religious teaching in the realm of communication of married women friends.

Themes in the Language and Thought of Family versus Non-Family Friendships

Often the world view of family members who tell about close friendships in their families is hidden in the concepts of the social scientists or therapists who attempt to understand them. When a person speaks or writes about his or her family friendships, language, emotion, and behavior are generally co-present in the text of the recalled relationship. Often the social scientist may have information in the account that will permit him or her to substantiate, refute, or qualify the different way in which the family friendships are elaborated. By paying attention to the shading of these qualifiers derived from my participants' vocabularies and experiences of family friendships in comparison to their other family relationships, I can come to appreciate the particular basis upon which family friendship is built and lived.[12]

In this fashion let us examine some of the recurring themes in family friendship that are documented in my college student essays and interviews among many other Montrealers. In these compositions students attempted to examine and explain friendship or its absence in their own families. For most of them it was the first time to try to analyze in a systematic way their own families socio-emotive life. Most likely because they were novices at this kind of investigation and because they were under the constraint of a grade, these essays tend to be somewhat stilted. They often begin with a formal definition applied to the various relationships in their families with whom they were friends. Their vocabularies and sentence structures distinguished the nature of their relationships with these persons. For example, in some cases they pointed out differences in the degrees of confidence and quality of friendship in a very general language that avoids any reference to any particular circumstances.

Communication

For some the growing ability to communicate feelings and problems overrides the status differentials that become less prominent as both children and their parents approach their relationship with greater degrees of openness. A single, young adult of English Canadian background, whose father, a manager of product research and development for a large firm, and whose mother, a former nurse, now a homemaker, tells us:

> My parents are very complex people, but I love them for what they are, and I'm not going to try to change them, and they accept me for what I am, although they don't, like I said before, completely understand the things I do, but I love them very deeply because they've helped me a lot this year. We're like friends. It's no longer like a mother-daughter, father-son relationship. We've friendships now. Now if I've got a problem, I know I can go to them now instead of one of my other friends who can't really help me out. They can just talk to me, and that's about it. In ranking my friends from the most to the least intimate, ..., I'd have to say that I'd have to put my family at the top because of this year, the way we've grown that much closer, and the way I know we'll stay close.

This attitude of friendship on the part of children toward their parents was noted in 40.8% of my combined questionnaire and interview data. 19.5% of family friends were fathers and 21.3% were mothers. As in the quote above, most of these children had already grown up. But only 10.9% of the relative friends were children. Of these friends, who also held the status of family members, 4% were sons and 6.9% were daughters. Clear feelings of friendship of parents toward their children are spelled out in only 13.8% of the in-depth interviews, and very lucid dialogues in which children are discussed in detail as close friends are extremely rare. However, this feeling marks a complex process in which behaviors spoken of elsewhere as friendships are considered as kinship, not as friendship.

Status Differences, Particularly Age, Block Family Friendship

Plato put forth a developmental explanation of the rarity of reported friendship between parents and their children which would imply that parents would withhold the linguistic qualifier of "friend" in addressing their offspring until they are mature. In Plato's *Lysis* Socrates observed that saying that parents love their son means that they wish for his happiness and hope to confide in him. Yet, while educating him, they take away his freedom to some degree, subjugate him often, and refuse to confide in him. They do not let him act the way he wants until his knowledge is beyond question. Nevertheless, a day will come when the father of Lysis will hand over to him his household and eventually will confide in him if he judges him to be superior in knowledge. Even those whom nature destined to love, remain mistrustful and apparently hostile towards those who know nothing. They are not able to show *philia* towards him until he has shown himself useful to others. At that time all men become friends and act towards him as a near one. In Jean-Claude Fraisse's interpretation, Plato means that nature yields to a rational acknowledgment of competence in determining *philia*. This alone can bring on objectively friendly attitudes from different quarters.[13]

For others, status differences bring impediments to calling a family relationship friendship. In trying to determine whether or not her mother is her friend, one of my student essayists, a female in her late teens, came up with some reasons that are found explicitly or implicitly in many of my college students' papers that explain a close friend as well. The age differences, the cognitive and emotional expectations perceived of as natural to the status of a close relative, are of a different holistic quality from that of friendship. Hear what one French Canadian female in her late teens wrote about her relationship with her mother. Written in French, her essay was her term paper for my class in philosophy:

> To make her a friend on the same grounds as a girl of my age is not to recognize her worth. Maybe it's a feeling of

> affection based on blood ties, for it is to her that I owe my life. ... Open to dialogue, she is interested in my future, in what I am, and it's mutual. It's a sentiment of sympathy and admiration towards this woman who exudes strength, light, life, and love. She silently shaped my early infancy with her heart, her goodness, her intelligence, and her love. In response to all that she has done for me, I cannot avow that it's friendship that I feel towards her; it's perhaps a little more. ...

This student is coming to grips with the sacred and biological character of the rights and obligations that her mother has enacted toward her that have left her as a daughter with a different feeling from that she has for her friends.

In a different situation, the older Quebec Francophone high school teacher of English, whom we have met earlier, defines her relationship to her mother as one of friendship. Her language reveals more of her self and includes qualifiers which also hold for some of her non-family friends. She identifies real-world factors that underlie her friendship with her mother which could also explain some of her other friendships. Answering my question about family friendships, she responded:

> My mother has grown [to become] an understanding woman. She is 65 years of age and an only daughter who married and who always lived with relatives. First she lived with my grandparents. My grandparents died. Then my father, the husband of my mother, died. My mother realized that she had only her children in life. She had always lived surrounded by her husband and relatives. You see, it's like a kind of community, if you will, then, because my mother had always been spoiled. She's a spoiled woman who felt a little lost. Then I'm sure she found that really, really hard to wake up all alone ... one fine morning. We were children then ... She had always counted on her parents and my father; then to wake up alone like that made her get even closer, and then she had to fight for certain things, and then she wasn't used to a lot of things in life, and then, that made her come closer to us a whole lot. Perhaps she understood us better than before. ... My mother is an expansive woman, really happy. ... She's a joker in a sense. ... She's a woman with a good sense of humor, very optimistic, ..., one who opens herself up to new things. ...

She's an extraordinary woman. She knows very, very well
how to understand us. When I separated, my mother took
that very, very well.

When contemporary social scientists write about rights and
obligations expected as proper behavior for a particular status, they
address similar topics raised in Aristotle's ethics. When Aristotle dealt
with family friendships, he focused on the issues of equality and justice
as being central to understanding family friendships. He discussed
family friendships when writing about "Friendship between unequals."
Aristotle points out that equality does not mean the same in friendship
as in matters of justice. About this question, he philosophizes:

> There exists another kind of friendship, which involves the
> superiority of one of the partners over the other, as in the
> friendship between father and son, and, in general, between
> an older and a younger person, between husband and wife,
> and between any kind of ruler and his subject. These kinds
> of friendships are different <not only from those which
> involve equality, but> also from one another: the friendship
> which parents have for their children is not the same as
> that which a ruler has for his subjects, and even the
> friendship of a father for his son is different from that of the
> son for his father, and the friendship of a husband for his
> wife differs from that of a wife for her husband. For in each
> of these cases, the virtue or excellence and the function of
> each partner is different, and the cause of their affection,
> too, is different. Therefore, the affection and friendship they
> feel are correspondingly different. It is clear that the
> partners do not receive the same thing from one another
> and should not seek to receive it. But when children render
> to their parents what is due to those who gave them life,
> and when parents render what is due to their children, the
> friendship between them will be lasting and equitable. In all
> friendships which involve the superiority of one of the
> partners, the affection, too, must be proportionate: the
> better and more useful partner should receive more
> affection than he gives, and similarly for the superior
> partner in each case. For when the affection is
> proportionate to the merit of each partner, there is in some
> sense equality between them. And equality, as we have
> seen, seems to be part of the friendship.[14]

> In matters of justice, the equal is primarily proportionate
> to merit, and its quantitative sense, (i.e. strict equality) is
> secondary; in friendship, on the other hand, the
> quantitative meaning (of strict equality) is primary and the
> sense of equality proportionate to merit is secondary. This
> becomes clear if there is a wide disparity between the
> partners as regards their virtue, vice, wealth, or anything
> else.[15]

Interacting in a Certain Way Promotes Friendship in the Family

One of my student-essayists focused on the particular kind of
interaction process among family members which lays the ground for
friendship.

> To determine the criteria for friendship is to describe in
> some way prerequisites for friendship. But there seem to
> be several of them ... In the first place, it is the "ego." There
> will be friendship towards another person according to my
> "ego," that is my personality, my character, and the like.
> Therefore, I must want to bond myself in friendship with
> another. In the second place, it's the other ... who will share
> the same decision, namely whether or not he wants it.
> Thus, as in all communication, the "wish" of the two
> persons can start a certain approach to friendship. For it is
> not claimed that even with the agreement of the two
> persons will there be friendship. Therefore, there exist other
> factors .. Behavior [and] attitude toward the other will play
> a predominant role in this approach to friendship. Thus,
> certain obliging words, certain gestures will prove to the
> other, before all else, a certain interest manifested in her
> behalf. Then this aroused interest seems to be transformed
> over time by a certain friendliness, which from then on, in
> its turn, [becomes] a mutual attachment.

Another college essayist in her late adolescence was not lost for
words when analyzing why she is not friends with two of her cousins.
This late teen, Francophone Quebecer, young woman's descriptions are
somewhat intermediate between a social status and interactional
interpretation of what prevents friendship. They are status-oriented in

the sense that age and socio-economic differences set the stage for blocking friendships with these relations; yet, at the same time, they are interactional in that they focus on why acting in a certain manner-- given these status differences--prevents the formation of friendship. In describing her relationship with a female cousin about her age, she writes:

> Eighteen years of age, she and I have nothing in common. We have never gotten along. She is a jealous and egotistical girl. In her family they don't have much money. That's why she has always been jealous of me. She is mean too. We haven't spoken for two or three years. Personally, I don't know if she has any good qualities, but I don't find any in her.

Of her somewhat younger male cousin she records:

> Fourteen years of age, he is rather flighty. He loves to be taken notice of by everyone. He is rather dislikable. Nevertheless, he has some good points. He has a good heart. He loves to discuss with people older than himself. He doesn't have the character of a boy of fourteen years of age but rather of a boy of seventeen.

Feelings towards Friends and Family Depend on the Circumstances

For many others, there is a less abrupt, more situationally dependent flux between depending on friends or family. A single, English, upper-middle class young adult put it this way:

> In some circumstances I feel closer to my family and can count on them more than I can count on my friends, and in others, I feel closer to my friends and feel I can count on them more. It all depends on the situation. I'll make commitments to both friends and family depending on what the commitment is.

Specifying the different areas of action expected from family and friends, a single lawyer, twenty-five years of age, hit upon a widely-held evaluation. Speaking in French, he told me:

> To be positive, let's say that I can count on ... from the monetary point of view--support, service--a lot more on my parents than on my friends. On the other hand, for bolstering my morale, I can count on my friends a lot more than on my parents. Now the reason for that is perhaps the way in which I was raised. ...

I asked, "How were you raised?"

He replied,

> I was brought up so severely, and in a way to not reveal my feelings a lot. While with friends, I am rather free. That does not keep me from having a family life.

Sibling Friendship

The situational expression of commitment about which this young man spoke is concretized by the French Canadian high school teacher of English whom we met when discussing styles of friendship. She replied in French to my question about friendships in her family:

> ... But my sister is really important for me. She is a girl younger than I. She's 26. I'm 33. She evolved in the same work setting as I. I taught at a kindergarten. And, then, only she had a different upbringing from mine at home ... even if we had the same parents, because she grew up in a totally different school environment from mine. She is a girl who has huge differences of opinion [and] who doesn't share my ideas all the time. Perhaps there are things which I wouldn't tell to her which I'll tell to the two other [friends] because of her age ... for example, when I spoke about my separation at a certain point. I spoke about it a little. She was really nice, ugh, let's say, but I say that it got on her nerves. ... She told me that it did: "That is a problem that I don't know about; it gets on my nerves." And, then, my husband didn't like her. ... It's better that I don't speak about it. Let's say that she had not experienced those

things. [My brother] is 30 years of age. He is younger than I. He studied some years ago and then decided ... to go back to school to study something else because he's in a different field from the one in which he started out. You see, he's a really super guy. He's an extremely generous guy. It is his greatest quality. If I have problems, little things that happen ... then he would speak to me about my problems, but he'll tell me, for example, "Come, let's go for a beer some place." He feels it. He's really available.

In this teacher's and other interviews I can identify a style of sibling friendship. In my entire sample, only 7.5% of the family friendships were with brothers and 13.8% with sisters. With such a bond, the brother and sister, sister and sister, or brother and brother form a relationship of discussion, support, helping out often through the sharing of residence, money and food, and not infrequently in opposition to other siblings or parents. This relationship may start in the teen-age years or earlier and last throughout life. They share discussion of problems through sympathetic, accepting listening, and establishing a relationship of trust based on good communication and keeping of backstage, secret information. A liking or love develops between them which is not necessarily accompanied by high degrees of sharing of similar beliefs and life style, but which displays tolerance, reliance, and positive, sympathetic regard despite the differences. Nonetheless, this support may lead to feelings of over dependency and ambivalence, especially when confronted by the cultural norm which demands open independence. Often these differences lead them to be bonded to other non-family best friends with whom they share common beliefs, experiences, interests, and activities.

As we see in Appendix D, I found the "sibling friendship" more common among English Canadian [9/15 = 60%] than French Canadian in-depth interviewees [6/15 = 40%], although as we learn later in this chapter, the opposite trend is true when the questionnaire data are combined with the results from the in-depth interviews. Among my in-depth interviewees, the "sibling friendship" was more frequent among males [9/15 = 60%] than females [6/15 = 40%]; among professionals

[7/15 = 46.67%] than white collar [5/15 = 33.33%] or blue collar workers [3/15 = 20%]; slightly more frequent among those between 15 and 30 years of age [7/15 = 46.67%], compared to those between 31 and 60 [6/15 = 40%], and much less typical of those 61 to 76 years of age [2/15 = 13.3%]. The "sibling friendship" was about equally characteristic of those who were single and had never been married [7/15 = 46.67%] as those who were married with children [6/15 = 40%], but it was much less descriptive of those who were divorced [1/15 = 6.67%] or married without children [1/15 = 6.67%].

The Relationships in which Family Friendships Are Found

Having touched upon some of the facets of the cognitive complexity of how a relative gets classified as a friend, I can come back to the more objective question of which categories of relatives really get chosen as friends. As we can see, close friendship is primarily focused in the nuclear family regardless of the age, socio-economic class, or ethnicity of the interviewee.[16] By an overwhelming majority most of the family friends in urban Montreal are found among the members of the nuclear family. Yet, this outcome contrasts markedly with the data from France, where "near relatives" (uncles, aunts, first cousins, and grandparents) and affinal relatives (father-in-law, mother-in-law, brother-in-law, and sister-in-law) are very similar in numbers as close friends. This contrast is not so amazing if one takes into consideration that the Montreal data are urban while the data from France come from small and large towns as well as cities, and that my data were gathered during the mid 1970s while Maisonneuve's were collected in the mid 1950s before the progressively great changes in family life that came to characterize the late 1960s and 1970s. One would expect the extended family to furnish larger numbers of close friends in a rural milieu where the kinship system covered large parts of a geographically located population. In contrast one would expect urbanities to associate only with kin whom they considered to be friends. In his discussion of kin, Claude S. Fischer found:

> Core (i.e. central urban) respondents were more likely to
> consider the kin they did name as "friends" than were Town
> or Semi-rural residents; that is, they were less likely to
> include kin who were only kin. In fact, in terms of the kin
> "friends" respondents named, there were barely any
> community differences. ... Urban residents were also more
> likely, as we saw, to discriminate between nuclear and
> extended kin and to be selective with respect to which
> interaction they called upon kin for.[17]

The urban trends that I identified in Montreal also contrast to some expectations derived from field work in smaller towns in Quebec and from some passages of French Canadian literature where the importance of affinal relations for friendship, particularly the relationship of sister-in-law, could be deduced.

In their study of how kin are differentiated, Firth and Djamour emphasize that the intensity and frequency of interaction among relatives, which varies from strong to weak, will determine their classification from being "intimate kin" through "effective kin," to "nominal kin."[18] Piddington describes a similar phenomenon by noting that friendships fall mainly within the priority and secondarily within chosen effective kin categorizations.[19] Likewise, Maisonneuve distinguished among "immediately near," "near," and "distant cousins and relatives," on the basis of a difference in closeness of friendship tied in with these structural differences of relationship. Maisonneuve's own work, confirmed by my study, shows that much more friendship is situated in the immediately near category, which is followed considerably behind by the "affinal relatives," which in turn is tagged after by the "near" label, and lastly by "distant cousins and relatives." In Montreal "immediately near" relatives stand a much greater chance of becoming "intimate kin"; "affinal relatives" are more likely to be "effective kin"; and "near" and "distant" relatives are most likely to be nominal kin.

The basis for regulating conduct among friends in the nuclear family was seen to arise from nature in the literature of antiquity. Cicero succinctly summarized this argument:

> For it seems evident to me that our nature is such that there must be a certain fellowship between all men, and that this fellowship is the more perfect the nearer each individual unites himself with his fellows. So our fellow citizens have a greater claim to our affections than foreigners, and relatives than strangers. For among relatives nature herself has begotten friendship, though this friendship is of no great strength. Friendship has this advantage over mere relationship--that goodwill may be removed from the latter but never from friendship. For if goodwill be taken away, the very name of friendship is destroyed while relationship remains.[20]

Long before Cicero touched upon family friendship, Xenophon in his *Memorabilia of Socrates* relates the story of Socrates' discourse with his son, Lamprocles, about his mother, Xanthippe. In it the reasons for the rights and obligations of children toward their parents and brothers toward one another are spelled out, and, again, the closeness of these relationships to nature are emphasized. When Socrates came upon two quarreling brothers he knew well, Chaerophon and Chaerecrates, he reminded them "Common parentage and common upbringing are strong ties of affection, for even brute beasts reared together feel a natural yearning for one another."[21]

Plutarch saw friendship as an imitation of brotherhood, a relationship found more in nature. Plutarch believed that in dealing with friendships among brothers, nature takes the initiative and lets judgment confirm the friendship. Against Hesiod's dictum, Plutarch thought that a friend can be treated on equal footing with a brother only to the extent that the friend is shared by the two brothers and their relationship is strengthened by all parties to it.

Why Not *Homonoia?* or Parents and Their Children's Difficulties of Thinking Alike

In the Alcibiades, Socrates leads Alcibiades to realize that to run and maintain a state, friendship must be brought about among all its citizens. In reasoning with Alcibiades, Socrates clarifies that friendship is identified with concord or identity of thought. Alcibiades replies to Socrates by saying: "I suppose I may say that friendship and thinking alike is that, by which a father and a mother think alike, in loving their son, and a brother with his brother, and a man with his wife."[22]

Nevertheless, concord does not exclude radically different activities such as those that are found in real society between a husband and wife. Nor does *homonoia* depend upon the manner in which each person carries out his function. Diversity and even complementarity of tasks can engender *philia* which transcends particular functions. In Fraisse's view of the *Lysis*, Socrates is incapable of determining the nature and place of such *philia* and agreement. For Fraisse the notion of *oikeiotès* refers to a common inner-requirement for friendship whose fullest realization would be adhering to the Good. Yet, in Fraisse's opinion, *oikeiotès* does not solve the problems of the place or nature of *philia* and agreement.

Just as Plato identified *homonoia,* or thinking alike, as contributing to good friendship in the family, there were a series of issues that arose in the Montreal family of the 1970s that greatly affected relations among family members, particularly between parents and their teenage children. In most modern societies differing generations are socialized to a different set of salient symbols and historical events that orient them in differing directions. Jacques Bonin and Robert Laliberté analyze several of these areas which were key to understanding the problems of French-speaking parents in the Montreal of the 1970s. They take up their informants' experiences with young people's abandoning religion, mainly Roman Catholicism in the case of French-speaking Montreal Catholics; boys' wearing their hair long; the usage of drugs; pop festivals; dropping out of school; and the sexual freedom of young people; the independence of Quebec; the nationalization of the mines; the politicization of the unions; the laicisation of the Church; and implanting a true democracy. However, we can see the potential for conflict between parents and their children in learning that young people on the whole were more open to changes of a private kind, a kind of change aimed at solving problems of a normative order--the use of drugs, the place of married women, the use of birth control pills, and sexual relations before marriage. These trends are more notable among young people of the "dominant classes."[23] Most of the people interviewed from all classes were, with varying degree of nuance, negative towards these "cultural trends of youth."[24] Another potential impediment to friendship between parents and children lies in the finding that young people, regardless of their social class, were less favorable to constant renewal of public organizations than were adults. To the contrary, adults were significantly more open to change, particularly when it has to do with the laicisation of the Church.[25]

The Influence of Gender on Friendship in the Family

Over and beyond thinking alike, similarity along certain background variables such as age, sex, ethnicity, and civil status may increase the chances for friendship among family members. Within these categories of friendship, Jean Maisonneuve found that there was a tendency for family friends to be of the same gender. Sociologists term this "gender homophily." Montreal interviewees seem to balance the forces of homophily and heterophily when they chose friends within their own families. In Montreal slightly more male interviewees (5%) reported having female friends in the family, and somewhat more female interviewees (11.8%) reported that their family friends were also females, but the difference is not great. Here I must stress that thinking alike and sharing common interests may override gender and age status differences. The following English Canadian woman, between 36 and 40 years of age, has taught nursery or elementary school over seven years.

She feels that she has not become closer to her brother or sister-in-law because they do not share a common religious belief. She thinks that their different religious world views pervade other areas of their lives, particularly the way in which they raise their children, and these different beliefs lead to practices in these areas that have kept them from becoming close friends:

> I have one specific example of how my religious beliefs have influenced one set of close friendships which would be with my brother and his wife. Now my brother comes from one traditionally religious side of the family, which has a much more authoritarian view, and much more traditional views of God, and they're the kind of people that just would never miss a day of church, and do think of God as being a specific being, a Father, but I do see that their attitudes in raising their own children are colored by their beliefs that human beings are born not whole; they are born with original sin, even though I'm sure my brother and his wife would not say it ... , but I see it in [that] they are always training their child to be right; they are always training their child to be good. They haven't stood back and seen than the child was born good to begin with, and that he doesn't need to be changed; he just needs to be guided. That's one specific attitude I see which I do think is influenced by what I consider a too rigid religious belief, and, therefore, because I don't follow this preconceived idea that children are born under a cloud, but I do believe that a child is good to begin with, then again, my training of my child is so different from their attitudes with each other and their family that we have not become ... the close friends that we might have.

Such strong cultural norms as these different religious beliefs inhibit friendships regardless of gender.

Non-nuclear Family Friendships

Gender does seem to help explain one family relationship among Montrealers. Males tend to have brothers-in-law more frequently as close friends than sisters-in-law, and females tend to have sisters-in-law more frequently as close friends. Of all other family relationships, this is the only one that attained statistical significance. Several of my professors at *l'Université de Montréal* expected me to find that the relationship of sister-in-law was particularly conducive to friendship in Quebec culture. Yet, only 3.4% of my respondents were close friends with their brother-in-law and only 4.6% with their sister-in-law. My professors' anticipation may have been influenced by the imagery of the Quebec playwright's, Michel Tremblay's, now classic play, *Les Belles Soeurs (The Sisters-in-Law)*, that was, perhaps, the showcase of recent French Canadian theatrical literature.

In the *ouvrièrisme* (working-classism) genre of much of Quebec film and literature of that period, through the image of women socializing as they were hanging out their clothes on the lines in back of inner-city Montreal's ubiquitous backyard-facing wooden balconies, it was frequently implied that these women were kin, often sisters-in-law. Although the differences were not great, males more frequently chose male relatives as friends and females chose other females as friends more often.[26] From this more general pattern it would follow that a person's brothers- or sisters-in-law chosen as close friends would more likely be of the same sex.[27] The late or post-industrial trends of higher divorce rates, serial monogamous marriages, cohabitation, communes, greater tolerance of homosexual relationships, and a low birth rate began to assimilate Quebec in a salient way by the 1970s. In becoming more like a generalized North American pattern in this respect, Quebec affinal kin became much less important as a source of primary relations because the various family functions became progressively truncated. Now a person chooses his or her brother- or sister-in-law as a friend, not because he or she is the spouse of a brother or sister, but because that person likes or enjoys doing something with that other person. A shared pastime or hobby was a frequent explanation given for being friends with their in-laws, and this pattern seems particularly true of people who are bound by close family ties.

Among the in-depth interviewees, the non-nuclear family friend style was most frequently observed among people who were between 31 and 60 years of age [9/13 = 69.23%] and much less frequently among those who were between 15 and 30 [2/13 = 15.39%] or between 61 and 76

[2/13 = 15.39%]. The non-nuclear family friend style was more often characteristic of French Canadian [8/13 = 61.54%] as compared to English Canadian [5/13 = 38.46%] in-depth interviewees. Similarly, this style of friendship occurred more often among male [8/13 = 61.54%] than female [38.46%] in-depth interviewees. The style of the non-nuclear family friendship was seen more frequently among people who were married with children [7/13 = 53.85%] and less frequently among in-depth interviewees who were single [23.08%] or married without children [3/13 = 23.08%]. Class appears to exert the least influence on the style of the non-nuclear family friendship with 38.46% [= 5/13] professional, 30.77% [= 4/13] white collar, and 30.77% [= 4/13] blue collar in-depth interviewees displaying this style.

The Influence of Class and Ethnicity on Friendship in the Family

Popular culture in Quebec is full of portraits of friends from outside of the family brought into it or of family members in their various roles, one of which could be that of friends. Often the shades of family friendships are colored by their class origins. *La Famille Plouffe* (*The Plouffe Family*), a novel, remade into a popular film, and a former television series, shows Denis, a fervent teenage friend, being brought into the hearts and lives of all the family members of a working class neighborhood.

In the Quebec "soap," *Les Bergers*, the family and friends are integrated into their small travel agency. All of them have character flaws, and their trials and tribulations make up the content of this program.

Music, too, is another medium that frequently encodes friendship and kinship in class tones. Claude DuBois's 1967 ballad, "Like a Million Other People," depicted a working class man who married "without, for that, asking himself, if at least he could [love/like] her." This man had "to grit his teeth and clench his fists" to just enable his children to subsist.

DuBois' song above and the Quebec social science literature with a similar ideology led me to expect that, like in Jean Maisonneuve's French work, around two-thirds of his working-class subjects would have no family friends. But, in contrast to France, I found that even older and working class Montrealers tend to have both family and non-family friends at the same time. They really told about more family friends than they revealed at the beginning of an interview, as can be seen in the comparison between the "claimed" and the "real" number of family friends in the tables in the notes of this chapter. While the initial comments of the older and working class Montrealers suggest that they are less demonstrative of friendship in the family, their own full reports evidence ample family friendships. As in France, about as many white collar workers in Montreal have friends in their family as those who have none.[28]

Only ethnicity exerted some observable influence on the number of close friends.[29] Claiming to have more friends than they actually have, English Canadians appear to have somewhat fewer friends than French Canadians whose claimed and real numbers of close friends are similar.[30] There are more English Canadians whose close friends are chosen exclusively from outside of the family in comparison to French Canadians. In contrast, French Canadians are more likely to draw their close friends both from among their own family members and from people outside of their own family at the same time.[31]

Of course, having no friends in the family does not mean that one cannot have friends outside the family. People without family friends can have non-kin friends. Very few people have more than three family friends; whereas quite a large number of people have five or more non-family friends.[32]

The Research Collective in Urban Sociology (CRESU) of the University of Montreal reached conclusions on the interrelationship of kinship and friendship very different from mine. While respecting and reviewing many of their observations and insights, in comparing their informants' experiences of childhood and adolescence in their families of orientation and procreation, I must note that they interpret the Montreal family primarily as a tool to socialize its members to reproduce the class system.

Their research suffers from stuffing its data into a rigid structuralist, Marxist analytical mold. Their theoretical discussion provides so few citations from their informants to support their points that one is left wondering if their account is their image or the way Montrealers experienced the juncture of friendship and kinship. Despite this serious drawback, their work provides certain insights into class differences that would influence friendship in the families of French-speaking Montrealers. In the following paragraphs, I will summarize their findings that complement my work and that are suggestive of structural factors that would constrain or promote friendship in the French-speaking Montreal family.

Their findings would imply that friendship among certain family members would be promoted or hindered by their structural relations toward one another. Thus, older children are often "sacrificed" by having to do certain chores around the house and the youngest get more attention and education.[33] Therefore, you would expect that this unequal arrangement would not lead to friendship between older and younger siblings.

In Bonin's sketch of French-speaking, Montreal family life, he pointed out that his underprivileged informants believed in traditional Catholic values, one of which promotes a climate of good understanding between mother and father, whereas his privileged informants could break with Catholic values and identify with English-speaking, Protestant values without formally converting to a Protestant denomination.[34] In a related finding, people in the upper strata viewed family conflict as necessary in contrast to people in the lower strata, who either would forget about conflict or think it should not have happened. Such family conflict often centers around moral values. Those at the unfavored end of the social scale were concerned with individual moral values expressed in such admonitions as "don't drink," "be chaste," "behave well," while people at the favored end valued social success.[35] The values were expressed in parents' concern over their children's selection of a marital partner. His lower class informants were more preoccupied with the moral qualities of the future spouse, such as his use of alcohol, respect for his future partner, and honesty, while his upper class informants were more concerned with their future son- or daughter-in-law's socio-economic position.

According to Bonin, in the privileged class, bringing up children gives place to discussions with a public content: of the choice of a learning institution, a language, and a career. Moreover, these discussions are based on a differential analysis of the personality of each child. In the underprivileged classes, raising children evokes the transmission of moral principles such as honesty and temperance which guide private life.[36] Bonin's lower- and middle- class informants told him that they were less strict with their children than their parents were with them and that they are going to regret the benefits of this former strictness. They feared that they were now spoiling their children. The lessening of parental influence is experienced as the "letting go" (*laisser-aller*) of modern child-rearing. This process touches on the informants of upper class less brutally, for they still keep their role of placing their children in the dominant public networks.[37] In determining where his informants got their knowledge about childrearing, Jacques Bonin discovered that the upper class people refer more to public sources such as books, discussions with friends, etc. while at the lower end of the latter, people refer more to tradition, i.e. their knowledge came from relatives.

CRESU's study hypothesized that in the upper strata the influence of the socio-economic position is mediated by the mother's relationship to culture; in a middle class milieu by both the mother and the father; and in the lower strata by the father. They hypothesized that among families stratified at the upper-end of the social scale, the influence of the mother has a wide range of implications that order information of more subtle knowledge, sentiments of a relational kind, and openness to changes in the public domain. They hypothesized that in families stratified in the middle of the social scale both the father and mother enact roles that have a wide range of implications which order the relationship of a person to society, and his or her openness to total change. Finally they hypothesized among families stratified at the lower end of the social scale that the influence of the father would have a wide

range of implications that order information of "more familiar"
knowledge, sentiments relating to personal functioning and openness to
change.[38] In regards to the relationship of a person to society, they
proposed that the transmission of feelings of a relational kind is
experienced in the families of different social classes respectively under
the modes of opposition, dependence, and independence as you go from
higher to lower levels of stratification. In the families as a whole, there is
little relationship between the degree of psychological balance and of
authenticity felt by members of the family. Nevertheless, children feel
more psychologically balanced the more their father displays a strong
feeling of psychological equilibrium.[39]

Generalized Conditions Conducive to Family Friendship and Examples of Family Friendships in Contemporary Montreal

During the 1970s a host of models and typologies of good to bad,
functional and dysfunctional families were proposed by social scientists,
and marriage and family therapists attempted to apply these to family
practice. But in considering what these frameworks have to say about
friendship in the family, we should heed Philippe Garigue's admonition
that it is not really possible to separate four levels of causality--
biological, psychological, social, and cultural.[40]

Indeed, until the 1960s anthropologists usually conceived of
friendship and kinship in two different realms, even though a few
sociologists touched on their mutual occurrence. In the French psycho-
sociologist's, Eugène Enriquez's, analysis, the consequences of the action
of Eros thwarts the advance of civilization. Love makes the individual
dependent on the loved one. The person in love submits to the moods of
the lover, is anxious about the lover's future, is invaded by the fear of
losing the lover, and becomes fragile in this situation. For Enriquez,
"Succeeding in transforming the drives into 'a goal inhibited sentiment'
and into loving human beings in an equal measure is the condition of the
formation of the bonds of friendship which reinforce the bonds of
community."[41] Enriquez postulates that a group of brothers really got
together and killed their father, and that this crime was a result of their

pact, their first homosexual oath, and first and most serious strike against the bond of love.[42] Evidently Freud was not as much a true believer in this scenario as Enriquez, for he confided to Kardiner that this particular theory was not to be taken very seriously, and called it a hypothesis and a "Just-So-Story."[43] Even before Freud introduced the notion of the Oedipal complex, the contempt which family intimacy breeds has been recorded across the globe throughout history and must be dealt with in explaining how friendship is possible amid such family aggression.

The ancients who spoke of friendship in the family also recounted tales of bad feelings, conflict, and even fated murder. Some of the Greek philosophers such as Democritus (460 - 370 B.C.) preferred relationships of friendship to those with family, and, in his opposition between friendship and the family, friendship is seen as a means of preserving tranquillity if the friends exchange services. Democritus does not have words harsh enough to denounce the confusion engendered by the conjugal bond and by the presence of children to raise.[44] This classical portrait of the lack of friendship in the family is mirrored in the documentation of violence in the family that has captured attention in the sociology of the family in the late 1970s and early 1980s. Such aggression may vary according to situational factors as mood, stress, available time, health, presence of demands from third parties, especially spouses, the attitude of the interacting partner himself, and macro-sociological forces such as unemployment and the level of welfare, dependent on the electorate's changing opinion. Yet, such behavior may be described as more general attitudes corresponding to personality traits and class characteristics.[45] In critically summarizing the existing body of socialization research, Hans Peter Dreitzel sketched the adult-child relationship as a system of mutual demands:

	demanding (restrictiveness)	undemanding (permissiveness)
satisfying (warmth)	TYPE I [lower-class childrearing]	TYPE II [middle-class childrearing]
unsatisfying (hostility)	TYPE III [self-defense reaction]	TYPE IV [indifference that leads to deviance in working- and middle-class]

Dreitzel's summative review in the chart above is close to the image of the influence of class on the family that Bonin and Laliberté derived in their study. While all classes claimed and told about friends in the family, people of working class background did so less frequently than people of white collar and professional backgrounds, and they and older Montrealers claimed to have fewer family friends than they actually ended up reporting throughout the interview. This finding does not imply a stronger family structure among professionals than among blue and white collar workers. A family system may be equally functional whether its sentimental and behavioral base be respect, authority, friendship, or love. Nonetheless, in a society which has produced large sectors of thought-based economic activities, those parts of the population who question the largest part of their everyday activity can also turn their mind to the analysis of their personal relations including the family. As these thought-related economic bases are more pervasive among professionals, one would expect them to question their interpersonal relations more frequently than blue or white collar workers. In questioning interpersonal relations, family relationships come to have to face similar universal criteria of all other relationships. If conflict arises, few legal constraints exist to control an adult to keep up family relationships. A normative constraint that one should get along with and love the members of one's family exists, but this norm is tempered by another norm which asks everyone to meet the same standards of fair treatment, even though they vary among social and subcultural groups.

In traditional society family relationships were characterized by generalized reciprocity, which is to say a non-specific altruistic attitude of giving without expecting to receive in return. While this attitude lingers on in post-industrial society, it is challenged by the attitude that family members must fulfill their family roles in a manner which would be judged as fair and equitable by basic standards applied to any other relationship, although unconditional support is expected at the same time.[46] These two somewhat conflicting norms put extra pressure on family relationships in modern society. By linking close friendship to family relationships, such unconditional support may be demanded when a more universalistic ethic would require censure or restraint towards the family member in need.

At an extremely high level of abstraction, Horst Hutter identifies the best social basis for friendship which applies to friendship in the family. He came to the conclusion that friendship seems to flourish best in societies which "combine patterns of symmetrical and complementary differentiation." These societies, like ancient Greek society, tend to lie between the ideal types of mechanical and organic solidarity. His argument would see a moderately strong family system as conducive to close friendship. Hutter writes:

> Friendship is a relationship which implies both symmetry and complementariness. It is simultaneously diffuse and specific. It depends on a symmetry of affection but may develop from a complementariness of personalities, needs, and desires. It is diffuse in the sense that it covers the entire range of an individual's personality, all his joys, sorrows, hopes, and fears Yet it may also be specific in the sense that only certain specific individuals can become an individual's friends.[47]

Because Hutter's quote points to a very abstruse level of the social system, it is difficult to apply his formulae for the analysis of family friendship in any particular society or family. Indeed such broad generalizations have been scoffed at as being practically useless, particularly when they are used to analyze role relationships.[48] Other more applicable theories such as those of the exchange theorists imply that the equality between the most powerful social agents within the family, particularly the spouses, will set the tone of friendliness among all the family's members.[49] In their typology of husbands and wives, the degree of possible friendship would run from highest among those who practice an equal partner-equal partner arrangement; next conducive to friendship would be the senior partner-junior partner pattern followed by the head-complement type; and friendship would be predictably least among spouses whose relationships could be characterized as "owner-property." In the exchange model, friendship is achieved through equalization of power among the statuses in the family, which is based upon a rational evaluation of competence in regards to the constitution of civil society.

In this manner friendship in the family could be depicted as a scale with little weights representing sights, sounds, language, tastes, new experiences, ideas, a balance between eye contact and avoidance, listening, touching, inquiring, attitudes, and opinions exchanged between the various family members. When the scale is heavily loaded, friendship among family members is high. When the scale is lightly loaded, friendship is not plentiful among family members. In this model, rigid adherence to traditional patterns felt to be sacred would hinder making friends among family members because modern society values the free expression of ideas and feelings which are defined as inappropriately expressed by tradition. The stress and ambiguity caused by these ideals of a free society is felt most keenly in the relations between parents and their children, particularly adolescents. When a child reaches the age of being fully responsible toward obligations and rights in civil society varies enormously. Yet it is this sharing of full rights and obligations that encourages the equality characteristic of friendship.

Perhaps because it is inherent in the open market-place analogy of the exchange model, many exchange theorists have tended to minimize what Erving Goffman has called "backstage information." Such an emphasis puts the exchange model at opposite ends from the earlier popular Freudian explanation of family psychology which built up a plausible model that plays up secrets, subtle gestures, hidden and double meanings in its interpretations. Backstage information interferes with the sharing of cognition and affection that promotes family friendship. During the history of a family's interactions it becomes known that sharing particular beliefs or events will hurt another family member or produce feelings of shame and embarrassment. Because it is assumed that family relationships will be on-going over a long period of time, hiding such dangerous information may seem to make conflict more manageable in day to day interaction. Given the complexity of modern society, the risk that such backstage information may be exposed may remain at an acceptable level. Besides cutting itself off from the interference of backstage information, the exchange model masks the biological roots of family relationships, which unalterably erect inequality in the distribution of competence *vis-à-vis* the rights and obligations of civil society. The long period of socialization of the human being means that parents and elders are privy to unequally shared information, emotion, and experience which are essential to shape the experience of deep friendship. Thus, the biological roots of the family and the presence of backstage information in it assume an enormous saliency in the psycho-social life of the individual.

In reminding ourselves of the primacy of this intense emotion in family life, of the inculcation of love and hate, we recall that friendship in the family may exist alongside of, but be totally different from, love. Yet in his mechanistic explanation of group psychology, Sigmund Freud portrays identification as the groundwork of both love and friendship in the family. While we are more than aware today that the social agents and forms of family life vary tremendously in different cultures, Freud's discussion of identification still has much to offer as a process by which friendship in the family may be brought about. Sigmund Freud wrote:

> The individual in the relations which have already been
> mentioned--to his parents and to his brothers and sisters,
> to the person he is in love with, to his friend and to his

physician--comes under the influence of only a single person, or of a very small number of persons, each of whom has become enormously important to him.[50]

For Freud, identification is the earliest expression of an emotional tie with another person.[51] In discussing this identification, Freud distinguishes between an identification with the father and the choice of the father as an object.

> In the first case one's father is what one would like to <u>be</u>, and in the second he is what one would like to <u>have</u>. The distinction, that is, depends upon whether the tie attaches to the subject or to the object of the ego.[52]

Freud identified three sources of identification:

> First, identification is the original form of emotional tie with an object; secondly, in a regressive way it becomes a substitute for a libidinal object-tie, as it were by means of introjection of the object into the ego; and thirdly, it may arise with any new perception of a common quality shared with some other person who is not an object of the sexual instinct. The more important this common quality is, the more successful may this partial identification become, and it may thus represent the beginning of a new tie.[53]

I may now show how these elements become intertwined into contrastive styles of friendship in two contemporary Montreal families. At this point we may return to take a deeper look into the family friendships of my 20 year old male student whom we met near the beginning of this chapter. This young man is of medium stature, rather physically well-built, and is dressed simply but neatly in blue jeans and a flannel shirt. While not the purest example, his tale, nevertheless, displays many features of the generalized "family-oriented" friendship style. Listen to what he has to say:

> The most logical place to start off ... is at the top, with my father, Charles Doe. My father was born in Montreal, and has seen his share of war. He has always talked of war

because there was never anything more important than wars when he was growing up. He joined the Royal Canadian Air Force, and after his time in the force was up, he went to work for [some banking institutions]. He then went to work ... in the Canadian Arctic ... for as long as I've been born, twenty years. As long as I can remember, we (the rest of the family) would see him about twice a year, for about a month each time. Now, being raised by only my mother, my two brothers and I had the greatest upbringing a family could ask for. When Dad was away, we would hardly notice, because it's been like that for so long. Whenever Dad was home, to me the house and the family took on a new look. Most children would be happy to see their father, but I was happy for Mum and Dad, not for me. Dad was always around when someone needed help. He was always giving me money, buying gifts, and taking the family places. All this was great, but when all you want is for your Father to rest and enjoy his vacation, it was hard for me to "love" him, so I "liked" him. When my father became angry with us, I never took him seriously because I was never used to his authority. Oh, I did what I was told, but I took my time doing it. I would stop my day to day lifestyle so I could be with my father. As I was the youngest, Dad was taking me to places my other two brothers had no interest in going. As I was growing older, my father would still take me to places he thought I'd enjoy. I went with him, but I began to get bored, so I acted as if I was interested. I enjoyed being with my father, but going to the same places was really not interesting. I always wanted Dad to be with Mum most of the time he was home. I felt he should be with her because I knew he loved me, but he didn't have to spend his time with me. As I said before, just being home was good enough for me. Mom would tell me later on when I was older, that this was Dad's way of enjoying himself, by taking us places, spending money on us. Dad always wanted the best for his family and most of the time he got it. We repaid my father by doing what he asked of us when he was at home and when he wasn't. To me, my father was like seeing a friend you hadn't seen in a long time, and you asked to stay for a couple of days. My father is a father figure, and I love him, but I like him even more.

His father's infrequent visits led him to spend a lot of time with his sons, entertaining and giving them presents. However, the young man feels guilt in taking his father's time on leave away from his mother. In addition, we are left with the impression that the father's perpetual absence has led to a weakening of his authority *vis-à-vis* his sons, who set limits on his control by playing at passive resistance.

My student's mother was born in another country where she had also served in the military. Analyzing his friendship with his mother, this young man writes:

> ... Mum, or as everybody in the family calls her, Jane, was very strong willed, tough, overly generous, kind, and had a right hand like Mohammed Ali. Any other kind of mother wouldn't do for our family. People are amazed at how a woman, alone, could raise three boys who had different interests, all at the same time and keep us clean, respectable and happy. I can tell you easily. We did what we were told or else she used the strap. Man hath no fear greater than the fear of "getting the strap." Talking about my mother as a friend is hard because Mum was always around. I think the reason I can is because she had rules for each one of my brothers and me. As each of us got older more rules were set, and other rules were taken away as we grew up. When it got to a certain point in our lives, when Mum thought we didn't need anymore rules, she simply said, "That's your problem. You figure it out." Jane knew she could still help us, but she didn't, so that we could learn about making up our own minds about what is good and what is bad. To know and experience good, you have to have experienced bad. We did and were hardly ever punished for it because now she knew we probably wouldn't do it again. Either way we learned and Jane was right there to say "I told you so." I think a mother is the best friend a child could have. A mother knows her children; she knows how they will turn out later in life even when they leave the family. Call it instinct, upbringing, or anything else you want, mothers know. I still tell my mother where I'm going each night, and I sometimes ask permission to go and I'm twenty years old. Some friends I know would call that stupid or dumb, but I call it respect. Also, it's good for me to know that somebody knows where I am in case trouble arises. Doesn't everybody tell their friends what they have done or where they are going? My mother is my friend, but she's also my mother, and has been that for all of my life. How many friends do you have for life? What I do and what

I hope to do is how I show my mother I love her, but I tell
her I like her.

From the information he provides about his mother it appears that
their relationship lies in between TYPES I and II, between demanding-
restrictiveness and undemanding-permissiveness, both characterized by
satisfying (warmth) in Dreitzel's analytical scheme. It appears that this
middle way position on the dimension of demanding to permissiveness,
concurrent with the dimension of warmth, sets the stage for the
friendship he feels with his mother.

Although my student does not come out directly and say that his
brother, John, is not his friend, nor does he write of any overt conflicts
with him, he does not identify John as a friend as such. This brother
joined the military forces of another country and fought in its war. Of
this brother, my student writes:

> I can't really remember my brother, John, until after he
> returned from the war. All I know is that he did one year of
> University; he didn't like it; then he went to work for a
> while; and then left to join the army. My brother obviously
> needed some excitement in his life, and the army gave it to
> him. My brother always liked authority; it appealed to him.
> After he left the army, his life really changed. He had a
> good job, wife, money, and he has traveled all over the
> world. Since then he has changed to another position,
> equally successful. But, he carried his authority from the
> army back home. He is bossy, self-assertive, and he
> couldn't really be depended upon. He has become somebody
> who is so sure of himself. I can't really remember him
> helping me. He had his friends. He would just be there to
> boss me around. The last nice thing he did for me was to
> take me hunting with him. He is just a brother. I couldn't
> say I love him because he hasn't done anything for me. He
> appears to be more the friendly type, although I wouldn't
> call on him for help too often because he isn't reliable.

It is notable that my student does not see the possibility that this
brother had identified with the present military occupation of his father
or the former position of his mother. He feels sympathy for the plight of
this brother's marriage difficulties with his spouse, but does not
associate his brother's authoritarian character with his marital

problems. Nor does he seem to see a relationship to his family's "teasing" his sisters-in-law and their reaction to the other family members. We are also left in the dark about the nature of this teasing. In part, could it be that my student is expressing a generalized norm of family solidarity over and beyond any lack of friendship he feels toward this brother?

The next person whom my student introduces in his second brother, Peter. Even though we do not learn how frequently or infrequently his brother's helping him out had occurred, it stands out that he is perceived as having come through when called upon, to the best of his ability. The references to physical fights with this brother are alluded to in an almost endearing and respectful way:

> Peter, my other brother, I like better than John. Pete and I had similar interests, namely sports. We both played hockey, and John also played baseball, while I tried football. Anyway, we got along great except when it came to watching television. Man did we fight. Pete has always had a short temper. He would help you if you asked him, but only if you asked him. He didn't get in anybody's way. He did the most work around the house. Peter was always bringing girls home. John and I never did, too scared I guess, but Pete was the lady killer of our household, but once he met the right girl, he never went after any other girl. The last girl Pete met is now his wife, whom you'll meet later on. Pete wasn't always around when I needed him, but I didn't need him that often, but he tried to help me out as best as he could. He is that way with everybody. One thing though: don't get on the bad side of him. He is a small guy, but he's a fighter. I've seen him take on bigger guys. If he's provoked enough, he'll beat you bad. To look at him, one hardly sees an aggressive guy, but to me he is a brother and a friend. He has helped me out a number of times, and only asks for little, if nothing, in return.

In the next passage of his tale of family friendship, we are confronted with a picture of a sister-in-law, his brother, John's wife, who is initially portrayed in favorable terms, but whose withdrawal into her role of motherhood is identified as the source of conflict with his brother and the rest of the family of orientation. He uses the verb, "like," and the adverbial modifying phrase, "as a friend," in an almost ritualistic, begrudging tone, quickly intimating that he does not really feel this way: "I hope I never have to tell her how I really feel about her.'" Here we see the importance of the indexicality of the data. It seems that the author is bound by the subject of his essay on family friendship to call her a friend. Although his brother, John, is not his friend, he clearly sides with him in this conflict. He seems to be extending his sister-in-law a familial *noblesse oblige* for a possibly transitory period of conflict; he wants to keep her, his brother, and their child under the cloak of a family solidarity. The implied sympathy towards his brother's plight could very well derive from his role as a male and potential father who would resent his future wife acting in the current manner of his sister-in-law. Now my student's comments:

> I am now going to tell you about my two sisters-in-law because they are family to me, though not in the strict sense of the words. My first sister-in-law, Susan, is married to John. She became a part of our family about seven years ago. She was shy, pretty, and worried about how we were going to accept her. Well, we gave her the traditional Doe welcome. Pete, myself, and even John would pick on her and tease her to see her reactions. Susan knew we were only kidding and put up with us by insulting us right back. This is our way of saying "you're O.K." Over the years she became more self confident with herself, and we noticed the change. The big shock came when their baby girl was born. Susan started acting as if she was the only person who knew how to handle a baby. Nobody else knew how, only she. She began to tell John what to do and became increasingly demanding. She lived in a world of just the baby and herself, closing everyone out including John. This led to almost a break between John and her. They never bothered to call or visit like they used to, and when Susan did call it was always to say something bad about John. The family began to feel that, if they couldn't be bothered to call, then we would not call them. As it stands now, I could care less about Susan and what she does. To me, Susan went from a nice woman to an overly-confident woman. She never did anything for me. I like her as a sister-in-law and as a friend, but only that far. She has never given me cause to tell her what I really think of her, and I hope that day never comes.

In the next description of his second sister-in-law, my student gives us clues as to why so many men who chose to present a macho self-image find pleasure in establishing a friendship with a member of the opposite role constellation, e.g., someone who can cry, initiate questions about one's emotional state and problems, and give one a feeling of being heard. Although he and his sister-in-law are near to one another in age, it is her psycho-social characteristics of being supportive, yet tough--like the role model of his idealized mother--to which he attributes the basis of his friendship. This configuration frequently corresponds to a female role cluster, and for men like our informant who value family, these characteristics may frequently be found in the occupier of the status of sister-in-law, particularly when there are no sisters. Unlike sisters, sisters-in-law have not been subject to the same backstage information of siblings, and although still subject to social control by the extended family, the main person they must please is their spouse. Therefore, the relationship with in-laws becomes more voluntary, more one of choice one of the main components of friendship. Our informant describes his sister-in-law in the following passage:

> Norma, John's wife, is the greatest sister-in-law to have. If I had a real sister, I wish it was her. From the day I met her, I liked her. She is only a few years older than I, but she is closer to me than anybody, except Mum. Norma is a very sensitive girl. The slightest thing could set her crying. That's why I like her. She has feelings for everybody. She is the first to offer help if I have a problem. She is a strong girl and doesn't give up easily. I can see a lot of my mother in Norma. She is strong and tough when she has to be and gentle and kind at other times. Norma comes from a big family, so our teasing game didn't work on her. She's the kind of sister-in-law who helps, but also tells you what to do. Sometimes I resented her telling me off, but I never told her that. The real truth is I needed to be told off. Norma is the perfect friend. She is there if you need her, and if she can't help, she doesn't interfere. Sometimes when I'm alone, I call her on the 'phone just to say "Hi," and then she'd say "what's wrong." This is only a joke for her, because she always teases me about being with different girls. Norma is someone I need to have around. If I know

that she is there, then I can call her for advice or just to talk to. Norma doesn't need me to call her a friend, or a sister-in-law; she is in a class all her own.

An informative contrast to my student's understanding of friendship in his family was that of another young adult male who matched him on several social characteristics except ethnicity. At the time of the interview this fellow was 21 years of age, had sixteen years of formal education, and had worked at various odd jobs from being a handy man to being an organizer in a federal-governmentally sponsored program to help disadvantaged people. He spent most of his formative years in various upper-working and middle-class neighborhoods in Montreal. His father is an accountant, and his mother a housewife. Although his social class resembled my student's, his physical type, dress, and personality were quite different. He was well over six feet tall, very thin with pale skin and hair down to his shoulders. At first glance he seemed passive, but during the interview he really opened up and took the initiative in exploring his relationships. He described himself as being a manipulator of people and very dominant, but to me he seemed rather calm, relaxed, and non-aggressive. Although he smoked throughout the interview, he did not seem particularly anxious. He laughed at several places during our session. Even though I met him for the first time at his and his sister's randomly chosen address where he shares an apartment, he asked to come to my apartment to be interviewed at a later appointed time. Let us refer to him as "Jean-Claude." He described the atmosphere at his parents' home in French:

> My sister and I have struggled against our parents because they are afraid of life. It's because my parents lived through the Depression of 1929. And they experienced the times of war, rather difficult times I imagine ... It can also depend on how they were raised, what my grandparents did to them to make them afraid. I have the impression that, at times, things go too fast for them, that they are rather out of contact with what goes on. Also the fact of reading newspapers, *Le Journal de Montreal*, which puts cadavers on the front page. Murder is what life is. It's thefts. It's accidents. This is disgusting. They practically

never go out of the house because they are afraid, because they're afraid they'll be hit. It's terrible.

Best-Friend-Neighbor

In speaking of his childhood when he developed his closest and life-long friendship with a neighbor who lived "two minutes" from him, Jean-Claude tells of the effect of this atmosphere on the family members.

> At that time there were family problems at home. Then my sister fell into a severe depression ... She's eight or nine years older than I. She had a real nervous breakdown. For a long time, in fact for six years, she went back and forth from [a mental hospital] to home. Three months there; six months there; constantly like that. Now I have a little more exact idea ... Then I thought she was crazy. Now I think she had problems which were caused by the family milieu in general.

Regardless of the lack of trust which Jean-Claude implies, his parents were not indifferent towards their children, for they "encouraged" their children to study and left them with the feeling that they would be ready to help financially, even though their offspring did not want their help.

Jean-Claude spoke of his family problems with his closest non-family friend, Pierre, and their mothers were in touch. These conversations led to an invitation for Jean-Claude to live with Pierre's family. In his friend's family taking him into their own, we can see that friends may be substituted for family.[54] Jean-Claude imparts his story of how this happened to him.

> ... I was at their home a lot. [Pierre's] mother figured out, that things were not going very well at our home, which led her to say that she would be happy for me to stay at their home. Even then [Pierre's] mother and mine talked rather often. Then slowly, not fast, we finished secondary school and started junior college. [Pierre] thought it better for me to go to his home instead of hanging out in a park. His mother thought that if I hadn't known him, I'd have probably become a "bum." I think that they have helped me practically. At the same time they hurt me too because

there was a kind of explicit, rather implicit, morality, finally, which was in the air at their home ... I spoke like that with his mother. I spoke about sexual relations with girls among other things. [I was seventeen then]. Around that time I started to go out ... with Pierre's sister whose name is Francine. She was younger than I. She was about 15 years old then.

I interrupted, "You discussed sexuality with his mother?"

He replied,

Before, but especially after. In a certain way I want to say I was fixing it up to make it more relaxed at their house. In any case neither she [Francine] nor I had any money. Then around 18 or 19 years of age, in fact, we had known one another for two years, well, we wanted to make love. And we didn't have any place. At that point we succeeded in convincing her mother. I think that she let herself be convinced in any case. You know, to make it accepted or to let it be admitted that we had sexual relations at their home, then, ugh. I think that it bothered her quite a lot. It's funny because, in fact, for her mother, Francine's mother, I was her future husband. ... Then she liked me a lot. She had known me ... since I was a little guy. I had been with Pierre all of that time. I liked the way she spoke a lot. ... I called her Mrs. DuBois. Things were going poorly between Francine and me. ... And then there was friction. ... at that time ... I put the blame on sexual tensions which were not expressed, which were sublimated constantly. Then it was in this manner that I took up the subject with her mother. .... We were ... never really alone, really at ease. Then, ... to constantly have the fear of being surprised and all the guilt that is tied up with that. ... She had her own room, but her oldest brother in the family had his room. ... It's a double room. And he was in the room next door. Well, you know that really prevents you from being intimate, I think. ... At that point we really needed a lot more intimacy for a number of reasons. ... There was no way we could go to my home.

I asked, "How did Pierre take all this?"

Jean-Claude answered:

It was fine with him. He found that it was very simple. Yes, with him, too, ... I spoke with ... Pierre about the problems I was having with Francine. Then he spoke about the frustrations that were due to sexual sublimation and things like that. I found that [his explanation] really made a lot of good sense because, in effect, there was an enormous amount of tension. ... I think that his mother had accepted in a certain way the idea that we would stay together our whole life or something like that.

I inquired, "Did you say to her that you were going to marry her?"

He replied,

No, not at all. I had even said that there was never any question that I would marry anyway. But I think that she kept up a certain hope despite [what I said]. She hoped to convince me sometime. That's it. I started to talk with Francine's mother that things were going poorly with Francine. Then she naturally found that hard to take. ... We slept together. Her parents knew it. They were in the house. We ate together with her parents. It lasted a year more. After that it was over. We were almost like an old couple of 50 years of age. It was terrible. That was one of the reasons ... among others that Francine ... met other guys and ... wanted to know other men. I think that we could have stayed together, but then I would have had difficulty accepting that she probably had been with other men. Just like ... she would have had difficulty accepting my being with other women. ... Her mother took it very hard. Another surprising thing was that it was her father who took it the best. ... In a certain way I accepted our separation very well. ... But emotionally, anyway, it shook me hard because from one day to the next it was an affective relation which was really, really fun with Francine. ... I think that Pierre too had acted as a catalyst. He helped me accept it emotionally. ... I had hung around with him since around eleven years of age. ... His family is almost my second family. ... He took me home with him from time to time. And he came to our place often. We went out together. We went hunting, for example. ... We went out for a beer. ... I was twenty then. ... That year he studied film. He asked me to participate in his films.

Although Jean-Claude does not make the connection himself, his feeling of being a manipulator of people is tied to his having sexual relations with his best friend's sister, his neighbors' daughter. But from his story he is being manipulated every bit as much by his best friend's mother, and even to some extent by his best friend, both of whom like him very much and literally have left him with the feeling that this is his "second family." Indeed, his best friend's mother appears to tolerate the semi-open sexual relation between Jean-Claude and her daughter because on a fantasy level she imagines that they are and will be husband and wife. Moreover, his "openness" about their sexual relation is a quasi-openness, for we are left to infer that either he did not directly bring his and Francine's sleeping together out in the open to all the members of the family, and the result of this situation was a complicated, ambiguous "knowing but pretending not to know" state of affairs that led to the feeling of "an implicit morality at their home."

He and Francine seem to be playing a game with one another to the tune of a modern, cultural role-play drama, perhaps, more stereotypical of the lower-middle-class and upper-working class milieu in which it is enacted in this case. In the first act he claims that he'll never marry anyone. In mid-adolescence she, knowing this, still wants to sleep with him with the semi-knowledge of her family who double-binds her by implicitly letting her know that her ploy is both right and wrong. The wrongfulness is suggested by their relationship not being discussed openly with all in the house and the lack of an attempt to erect a barrier to the brother's room to provide for the privacy they felt they needed for their relationship. When their relationship does not lead to marriage, her anxiously cheering audience, her own family, breaks into different reactions. Her father's unexpectedly "taking it well" may have more to do with his not believing in the traditional expectation that the role of father requires him to censure sexual access to his daughter. Mr. DuBois may also be aware that contemporary society permits a period of premarital sexual experimentation, even though the status of his daughter as a potential mate would be lowered among certain conservative sectors of society. Her mother's "taking it so hard" results from her losing the set-up marriage she had hoped to successfully facilitate and from her being ill-at-ease with the new morality, her half accepting it, and her inability to fully accept, think about, and understand premarital teen-age sexual relations or return to the traditional Catholic values either. Her angst is that of the neither-one-nor-the-other constellation. Jean-Claude's friend, Pierre, the brother, rationalizes the split-up between his sister and his best friend on the basis of the sublimated sexuality and the tension that it had bred. He himself lives in a similar normative order to that of Jean-Claude's. Neither he nor Jean-Claude deals with the issue that such break-ups are inherent in their own narcissistic sexual pattern. Jean-Claude's remark that toward the end he and Francine felt like an old couple who had been together 50 years is related with a bitterness underlain by boredom. Yet a few minutes later he informs us that "emotionally ... it shook me hard because from one day to the next it was an affective relation which was really, really fun with Francine. It wasn't bad at all." I interpret this comment to mean that he found the depth of his relation with Francine very satisfying but found the confining aspects of a close relation impinging on his freedom and imposing obligations to deal with frustrating feelings and emotions. The new sexuality removes him from believing that limitation of sexual access to one's intimate tends to promote feelings of reliability and security, and it implies that communication and personal growth tend to be attained by maximizing contact with the variety of humankind. It recognizes no barriers to the potential communication between human beings. In the new narcissism, pain may be faced by flight. The cost is that one does not have to figure out the reasons for flight unless one be crippled emotionally by the relationship, at which point a professional may be consulted. The other limitation of their new sexual constellation that Jean-Paul and Pierre do not recognize is its leading to isolation and atomization. When they don't have to explore the depths of their most intimate relationships, and, instead, turn to new ones in their place, secrets and sharing of past must be shared partially with new relations, or if one can afford it with a therapist. In Jean-Claude's case, his life-style has led to his need to seek professional help.

Although the psycho-social significance of these two families could be explored in more detail, the information presented thus far is sufficient to compare and contrast them along an interpretative dichotomy bearing on the relationship of friendship to the family.[55] These complex families are good examples because they are filled with "shades of gray" like most families, which defy any pure classification.

If my student's family tends to be satisfying and warm, it also tends to be demanding and restrictive at the same time. We can see this observation in his nervous joke about his early socialization, "Man hath no greater fear than the strap," quickly modified to explain that his mother constantly set and changed rules based on her perceptions of her sons growing up. His pattern led to the balanced development of emotional and cognitive abilities because demands were made on the cognitive level and satisfactions were provided on the emotional level.[56] His and his brothers' taking serious learning activities in school, at home, and in their social lives and their being permitted and encouraged to develop very different personalities, their father's taking them around Montreal when he was at home, all indicate that cognitive and emotional growth took place in and was encouraged within limits in this family-- despite the virtual physical absence of the father for long periods of time.

The second family, somewhat less well off than the first, appears to have created a type of unsatisfying and hostile atmosphere among most of its members. Despite some demands and restrictiveness as to pushing their children to stay in school, not permitting open discussions of sexuality or letting their teen-age children bring home their sexual partners, this family is generally depicted as undemanding and rather permissive to the extent that the parents abrogate their parental role and let it be assumed by neighbor-friends. Their children rationalize their parents' fear and suspicion of the outer world as having developed as a defense mechanism in reaction to the hard times, yet it is seen to be reinforced by cultural forces such as a press expressing lower class values. This family's pattern has built the deviance which Dreitzel's classificatory framework would predict--one of its daughters has spent many years in a mental institution and one of its sons, the interviewee, is in therapy with a professional psychologist at the time of the interview. Yet, part of this family's disorganization, taking place with the physical presence of both parents, must be interpreted as a reaction to rapid cultural change as well. The parents' values are challenged by the changes occurring in Quebec. Their children have been taught in their modern education that openly expressing sexuality in word and deed is a good. But to their parents it is a taboo outside of marriage. The parents are said to feel as though things in the outer world are going too fast for them. In their excessive dysfunctional reaction to deprivation, the parents have become incapable of "perceiving and interpreting, rejecting and recreating the goals and norms of their society in reciprocity" to their grown children.[57] They cannot identify with their children's world, which leads to their inability to take on the perspective of their children. In short, they have helped to create a family scene where friendship could not develop except in the most rudimentary form between two of the children, my interviewee and his sister, who share an apartment, partly in opposition against their parents.

In this discussion it has been my goal to outline a psycho-social analysis of these families to understand the forces that promote and hinder family friendships. Let me stress that these examples do not reflect patterns typical of English and French Canadian families. As we have seen, the rest of my data, unlike the examples, indicate that French Canadian families display more close family friendships than English Canadian families.

The style of the best-friend neighbor was found often among married people with children [14/26 = 53.9 percent and 14/50 = 28 percent of all in-depth interviewees] and single people who had never been married [10/26 = 38.5 percent and 10/50 = 20 percent of all in-depth interviewees]. This style was infrequent among married people who did not have any children [1/26 = 3.9 percent or 1/50 = 2 percent of all in-depth interviewees] and people who were divorced [1/26 = 3. 9 percent]. It was equally prevalent among males and females. People who displayed the best-friend neighbor style of friendship were in largest part between 31 and 60 years of age [13/26 = 50 percent] and in next largest part between 15 and 30 [10/26 = 38.5 percent]. Only about 11.5 percent

[3/26] were older than sixty. It was most common among professionals [12/26 = 46. 2 percent], then white collar workers [8/26 = 30.8 percent], followed by blue collar workers [6/26 = 23 percent]. French Canadians [14/26 = 53.9 percent] enacted this style of friendship somewhat more frequently than English Canadians [12/26 = 46.2 percent].

Conclusion

Montrealers' language, thought, and emotion of friendship and kinship encompass many of the same components--communication, the inhibitors of status and age differences, sympathetic interaction signified by certain gestures and acts, and the circumstantial nature of the relationship. Most of Montrealers family friends are chosen first from mothers or fathers, then from sisters or brothers, then from daughters or sons.

When the whole family is characterized by a warm, open, understanding, accepting, trustful, loving, helping reliable, sharing, enjoyable atmosphere with varying degrees of high similarity in values, beliefs, and attitudes, I have recognized a style of "family-oriented friendship." In the family friendship among the children I have identified a characteristic style, that of the "sibling friendship." Very few husbands and wives considered each other as their closest friend, although confessing love or obligation to one another, they conceived of their spouse as a husband or wife *per se*. Affinal relations such as in-laws were picked as close friends much less frequently than expected, and "near" relatives such as uncles, aunts, grandparents, and first cousins were the least often picked as close friends by the people in my urban sample. Nevertheless, such relationships of affinal friendship point to a style of friendship worth identifying. To this style I have given the label of "Non-nuclear Family Friendship." Some of the ancients suggested that this gradual potential for friendship going from father and mother to distant relatives followed the principles of nature. Other of the classical writers, like contemporary sociologists, emphasized the importance of thinking alike in fostering friendship among family members. Plato plays up the developmental issue that parents show friendship toward their children the more that their offspring prove themselves competent. This competence is seen by Plato as the quality that evokes friendship universally. And Aristotle stresses that friendship in the family is brought on by its members treating one another equally. For Aristotle, like many contemporary exchange theorists, friendship is produced by a quantitative, strict equality in which strict equality comes first and equality proportionate to merit comes second.

Extensive quotations from interviews, essays, and observations suggest that some former studies may have exaggerated the degree to which primary relationships were depicted as being kin-oriented at the more underprivileged end and more friend-oriented at the more privileged end of the social scale because they minimized their informants' accounts.

The Freudian and exchange frameworks offer opposing interpretations of family life. The Freudian emphasis is on the covert, hidden, and unconscious, while the exchange model's stress is on the overt, recordable, and weightable. In the Freudian view friendship may be promoted by proper identification with another member of the family. In the exchange model such identification may take place because various psycho-social forces (common interests, thoughts, power, etc.) are in balance, while in the Freudian view such balance may result from proper identification having occurred.

The psycho-social identification that leads to friendship in the family is linked to stages of human development. The overt signs of these stages are manifested in changes in the civil status of a person. Everyone is born single; some get married; some have children and some do not; some get divorced; some live in alternative lifestyles; and all die. And each of these life events affects friendships within and outside the family. It is to them we now turn.

Notes

1. Oliker, Stacey J., *Best Friends and Marriage: Exchange among Women* (Berkeley: University of California Press, 1989).

2. Skolnick, Arlene, *The Intimate Environment. Exploring Marriage and the Family* (New York: Little, 1973), 125.

3. Gurdin, Joseph Barry, "*Amitié /* Friendship: The Socio-cultural Construction of Friendship in Contemporary Montreal." Ph.D. diss., Department of Sociology, Université de Montréal, 1978, 552-553.

4. Gurdin, J. Barry, "Book review of Robert Bell's *Worlds of Friendship*," *Qualitative Sociology* 6 (Winter 1983b): 365-369.

5.

Interviewees' and Respondents' Real and Claimed Friends by Socio-Economic Class

Count Column %	Without Friends in the Family		With Friends in the Family		Total	
	Claimed	Real	Claimed	Real	Claimed	Real
Blue Collar Workers						
None or a few friends outside the family (0,1,2)	5 12%	7 9%	15 11%	6 6%	20 12%	13 8%
Several friends outside the family (3 and more)	6 15%	15 20%	20 15%	18 19%	26 15%	33 19%
Totals (0,1,2,3, and more friends outside the family)	11 27%	22 29%	35 27%	24 25%	46 27%	46 27%
White Collar Workers						
None or a few friends outside the family (0,1,2)	7 17%	11 14%	14 11%	5 5%	21 12%	16 9%
Several friends outside the family (3 or more)	11 27%	23 30%	34 26%	27 21%	45 26%	50 29%
Totals (0,1,2,3, and more friends outside the family)	18 44%	34 44%	48 36%	32 33%	66 38%	66 38%
Professionals						
None or a few friends outside the family (0,1,2)	4 10%	6 8%	14 11%	5 5%	18 10%	11 6%
Several friends outside the family (3 or more)	8 20%	15 20%	35 27%	35 37%	43 25%	50 29%
Totals (0,1,2,3, and more friends outside the family)	12 29%	21 27%	49 37%	40 42%	61 35%	61 35%
Grand Total	41 24%	77 45%	132 76%	96 56%	173 100%	173 100%

6. Fraisse, Jean-Claude, *Philia: La notion d'amitié dans la philosophie antique: Essai sur un problème perdu et retrouvé* (Paris: Philosophique J. Vrin, 1974), 72-74.

7. Ibid., 58-59.

8. Oliker, Stacey J., *Best Friends and Marriage*, 90.

9. Ibid., 123.

10. Rocher, Guy, "Benchmarks of a Changing Society," in *Forces: 1967-1992: Twenty-Five Years of Evolution in Québec: Education-Health-Economy-Culture-Society-Information-International Relations and Perspectives on the Future. Numéro 100, Hiver 1992-1993*, 22-25 (Montréal: la Société d'édition de la revue Forces), 25.

11. Ibid., 25.

12. See Sévigny, Robert, *Le Québec en héritage: La vie de trois familles montréalaises* (Laval, Québec: Éditions coopératives Albert Saint-Martin, 1979), 6-10.

13. Fraisse, Jean-Claude, *Philia*, 129.

14. Aristotle, "7. Friendship between Unequals." Chap. 7 in *Nicomachean Ethics*, Book VIII, trans. Martin Ostwald (Indianapolis: The Bobbs Merrill Company, Inc., 1962), 227-228.

15. Ibid., 228.

16.

The Nature of Relative Friends: The Relationship between the Categories of Kin-Friends and the Socio-economic Status of the Interviewees and Respondents

Categories of Kin-Friends	Blue Collar Workers	White Collar Workers	Profes-sionals	Total Count and Percentage
Immediately Near:				
Father	7	1 1	1 6	34 (19.5%)
Mother	8	1 7	1 2	37 (21.3%)
Brother	5	4	4	13 (7.5%)
Sister	8	4	1 2	24 (13.8%)
Son	1	2	4	7 (4.0%)
Daughter	9	1	2	12 (6.9%)
Wife	1	1	4	6 (3.4%)
Husband	1	1	5	7 (4.0%)
Subtotal of All Nuclear Family Relationships				140 (80.4%)
Near:				
Uncle	1	2	0	3 (1.7%)
Aunt	0	0	4	4 (2.3%)
First Cousin	0	0	2	2 (1.2%)
Grandparents	2	1	1	4 (2.3%)
Subtotal of "Near" Relationships				13 (7.5%)
Distant Cousins and Relatives	0	1	3	4 (2.3%)
Affinal Relatives:				
Father-in-law	0	0	0	0 (0%)
Mother-in-law	0	0	0	0 (0%)
Brother-in-law	3	1	2	6 (3.4%)
Sister-in-law	3	3	2	8 (4.6%)
Son-in-law	2	0	0	2 (1.2%)
Daughter-in-law	0	0	1	1 (.6%)
Subtotal for Distant Cousins and Relatives and Affinal Relationships				21 (12.1%)
Total of Friends in the Family:				174 (100%)

17. Fischer, Claude S., *To Dwell among Friends. Personal Networks in Town and City* (Chicago: The University of Chicago Press, 1982), 79-88;368-374.

18. Firth, Raymond William and Judith Djamour, "Kinship in South Borough," in *Two Studies of Kinship in London,* ed. Raymond Firth (University of London: The Athlone Press, 1956), 33-63.

19. Piddington, R., "A Study of French Canadian Kinship," in *Readings in Kinship in Urban Society*, ed. C. C. Harris (Toronto: Pergamon Press, 1970), 87.

20. Cicero, Marcus Tullius, *Essay on Friendship. Laelius De Amicitia,* trans. from the Latin with notes by Alexander J. Inglis (New York: The Platt & Peck Co., 1908), 15.

21. Xenophon, *Memorabilia and Oeconomicus,* trans. by E. C. Marchant 4 (Cambridge, Massachusetts: Harvard University Press, 1979), 115.

22. Plato, *Works*, trans. George Burges, 4 (New York: G. Bell & Sons, 1897), 354.

23. Laliberté, Robert, "Étude comparative des parents et des enfants de différentes classes sociales." Chap. 4 in *Aliénation et idéologie dans la vie quotidienne des Montréalais francophones*, eds. Yves Lamarche, Marcel Rioux, et Robert Sévigny, Vol. 1 (Montréal: Les Presses de l'université de Montréal, 1973), 246-247.

24. Bonin, Jacques, "La Socialisation." Chap. 9 in *Aliénation et idéologie dans la vie quotidienne des Montréalais francophones*, 712-716.

25. Laliberté, Robert, *Aliénation et ideologie dans la vie quotidienne des Montréalais francophones*, 244-5.

26.

The Relationship between the Gender of the Interviewees and Respondents and the Gender of Their Relative-Friend

Count Column %	The Interviewees' and Respondents' Gender		
The Gender of Their Relative-Friend	Male	Female	Row Total
Male	29.00 47.50%	30.00 44.10%	59.00 45.70%
Female	32.00 52.50%	38.00 55.90%	70.00 54.30%
Column Total Column %	61.00 47.30%	68.00 52.70%	129.00 100%

Corrected χ^2 = .04523 with 1 degree of freedom; Significance = .8316

27. Gurdin, Joseph Barry, "*Amitié*/Friendship: The Socio-cultural Construction of Friendship in Contemporary Montreal." Ph.D. diss., Department of Sociology, Université de Montréal, 1978, 544.

28. a

The Relationship between Claimed Friends Who Are Kin and Claimed Friends Who Are Not Kin among Blue Collar Workers for Interviewees and Respondents

Count Column %	Claimed Friends among Relatives		Row Total
Claimed Friends Who Are Not Kin	No Claimed Friends among Relatives	Some Claimed Friends among Relatives	
None, One, or Two Non-Kin Friends	5.00 45.50%	15.00 42.90%	20 43.5%
Three or More Non-Kin Friends	6.00 54.50%	20.00 57.10%	26 56.5%
Column Total Column %	11.00 23.90%	35.00 76.10%	46 100.00%

Corrected χ^2 = .03883 with 1 d. f.; Significance = .8438

28. b
The Relationship between Really-Reported Friends Who Are Kin and Really-Reported Friends Who Are Not Kin among Blue Collar Workers for Interviewees and Respondents

Count Column %	Really-Reported Friends among Kin		Row Total
Really-Reported Friends Who Are Not Kin	No Really Reported Friends among Kin	Some Really Reported Friends among Kin	
None, One, or Two Non-Kin Friends	7.00 31.80%	6.00 25.00%	13.00 28.30%
Three or More Non-Kin Friends	15.00 68.20%	18.00 75.00%	33.00 71.70%
Column Total Column %	22.00 47.80%	24.00 52.20%	46.00 100%

Corrected $\chi2$ = .03432 with 1 d. f.; Significance = .8530

29. Gurdin, Joseph Barry, "*Amitié*/Friendship: The Socio-cultural Construction of Friendship in Contemporary Montreal," 1978, 569.

30. Ibid., 559-560.

31.
The Relationship between Real Friends inside and outside the Family and the Ethnicity of the Interviewees and Respondents

Count Column %	Ethnicity of the Interviewees and Respondents		
Friends	French Canadian	English Canadian	Row Total
Outside the Family	11 22.0%	59 47.2%	70 40.0%
Inside and outside the Family	35 70.0%	55 44.0%	90 51.4%
Inside the Family	2 4.0%	6 4.8%	8 4.6%
No Friends	2 4.0%	5 4.0%	7 4.0%
Column Total Column %	50 28.6%	125 71.4%	175 100%

Raw $\chi2$ = 10.41444 with 3 d. f.; Significance = .0154

32.
The Relationship between the Real Numbers of Friends outside the
Family and the Real Numbers of Friends inside the Family for
Questionnaire Respondents

Count Column %	Number of Friends inside the Family			
Number of Friends outside the Family	No Friends in Family	1 or 2 Friends	3 or More Friends	Row Total
No Friends	5 7.8%	2 4.2%	3 23.1%	10 8.0%
1 to 4 Friends	38 59.4%	24 50.0%	3 23.1%	65 52.0%
5 or More Friends	21 32.8%	22 45.8%	7 53.8%	50 40.0%
Column Total Column Percentage	64 51.2%	48 38.4%	13 10.4%	125 100%

Raw $\chi2$ = 9.23401 with 4 d. f.; Significance = .0555

33. Bonin, Jacques, in *Aliénation et idéologie dans la vie quotidienne des Montréalais francophones*, 645.

34. Ibid., 704.

35. Ibid., 647.

36. Bonin, Jacques, in *Aliénation et idéologie dans la vie quotidienne des Montréalais francophones*, 650.

37. Ibid., 651.

38. Lamarche, Yves, Marcel Rioux, et Robert Sévigny, eds., *Aliénation et ideologie dans la vie quotidienne des Montréalais Francophones*, Vol. 1 (Montréal: Les Presses de l'université de Montréal, 1973), 266.

39. Ibid., 257.

40. Garigue, Phillipe, *Famille et humanisme* (Ottawa: Leméac, 1973).

41. Enriquez, Eugène, *De la horde à l'état: Essai de psychanalyse du lien social* (Mayenne: Éditions Gallimard, 1986), 119.

42. Ibid., 121.

43. Kardiner, Abraham, *My Analysis with Freud: Reminiscences* (New York: W.W. Norton, 1977).

44. Fraisse, Jean-Claude, *Philia*, 293.

45. Dreitzel, Hans Peter, *Childhood and Socialization* 5 (New York: Macmillan Publishing Co., Inc., 1973), 16-17.

46. In reviewing the social psychological research on standards of fair treatment, Steve Duck contrasted three kinds: parity, Marxist justice, and equity, and notes that people are happiest when they feel their rewards are equitable. Under parity, everyone gets the same amount of reward. With Marxist justice, the person with the greatest need will get the most, and the person who was already well-off will get the least. Under equity, the person who worked the hardest will get the most, and the person who worked the least will get the least. Interestingly enough, Duck does not note any class variation with this standard. See: Duck, Steve, *Friends, for Life: The Psychology of Close Relationships* (New York: St. Martin's Press, 1983), 108-109.

47. Hutter, Horst, *Politics as Friendship* (Waterloo, Ontario: Wilfrid Laurier University Press, 1978), 178.

48. Skolnick, Arlene, *The Intimate Environment*, 51.

49. Scanzoni, Letha and John Scanzoni, *Men, Women, and Change: A Sociology of Marriage and Family* (New York: McGraw Hill Book Company, 1976), 201-153.

50. Freud, Sigmund, *Group Psychology and the Analysis of the Ego*, trans. and ed. by James Strachey (New York: W. W. Norton and Company, 1959), 2.

51. Ibid., 37.

52. Ibid., 38.

53. Ibid., 39-40.

54. Lindsey, Karen, *Friends as Family* (Boston: Beacon Press, 1981).

55. Dreitzel, Hans Peter, *Childhood and Socialization* 5 (New York: Macmillan Publishing Co., Inc., 1973), 16-17.

56. Ibid., 17.

57. Ibid., 18.

Chapter Six

Friendship over the Years

"Paul and Lise have such a bourgeois life style--children, the family, you know," Roland said looking earnestly but nervously at me, as though he didn't want to relate to me why he had not become friends of people of whom he knew I was fond. I nodded, "Yes, it's quite a different way of life."

Roland, a good-looking male professional in his late twenties had attracted perhaps the fairest young maiden of this town by his cosmopolitan intensity and intellectual curiosity. But why couldn't he become friends with Paul and Lise who were in his same or similar line of work, who had helped secure him a job, and who had also shown such enthusiasm in matters of learning and serious discussion. Granted Paul and Lise were more sedate in personality, more introverted, less willing to offer an opinion unless asked or probed. But Roland and they saw eye to eye on most political matters, which were central to their values. Living so close, how was it that they hadn't become close friends? Should I take Paul's explanation at face value?

The little vignette that I gathered during two summers of field work in a Quebec town illustrates the first area of concern of this chapter, the effect of civil status on friendship. Civil status is a term that sounds awkward or legalistic in contemporary American English. We would generally ask about a person's marital status. Are you single, married, or divorced? How many children do you have? More extensive than the notion of civil status, the French concept of *état civil* also refers to birth, death, and adoption. And, of course, like all lexical items in language, these terms are in flux to reflect changes in our customs. For instance, it is considered increasingly inappropriate to include marital status on resumes because such information has been used in the past to discriminate against potential employees for a variety of reasons.

When I lived in Quebec in the 1970s and did field work there in the summers of 1980 and 1981, there was a great interest in alternative life styles, particularly among anyone who had been to at least junior college, which meant around 27% of the college age-cohort by then. Friedrich Engels's book on the family was widely read and discussed in colleges and universities.[1] R. D. Laing and David Cooper were popular. The bourgeois family, variously taken to mean either the small nuclear or extended family, had been a major institution characteristic of traditional, quite familialistic, Canadian life. All of a sudden it was seen to be an important cause for selfish capitalism and especially its expansionist form of imperialistic war.

Naturally the extent to which these ideas had diffused from Montreal into the hinterland was restrained, but television and radio broadcasts positively depicting the alternatives of being single or living in communes were seen all over the Province, and newspaper articles had reports about the growing numbers of unrelated people sharing apartments in cities and towns in their human interest or lifestyle columns.

Following the times, sociologists began to publish heavier, less widely read tomes such as Jacques Lazure's *The Young, Un-married Couple: A New Form of Sexual Revolution*.[2] And the composite film of the best of Michel Tremblay's theater, *Il était une fois dans l'Est* (*Once upon a Time in the East End*), portraying homosexual life in the poor parts of Montreal, was shown widely all around Quebec. Neither was the Moynihan view of single motherhood held in regard nor was single-parenthood depicted as a major cause of poverty, as in the U.S. press and some social science, nor was it a broad subject of discussion or debate among Quebec social scientists.[3] To the contrary, investigations concerning the provision of day care and other social supports for the working poor were given prominence.

In this atmosphere these issues filtered down in various ways and to different degrees into the lives of real people. Just as the young professional, Roland, obliquely griped about Paul's and Lise's being married and having children--facts which were accompanied in Roland's mind by an equally important series of ideological corollaries--so did Paul and Lise let it be known to me, in a softer and more discreet tone, that Roland's flaunting his conquests, his excesses, albeit off the job, in drink and smoke, were linked to his singleness. In a related issue, Paul had, after all, let Lise know that he felt uncomfortable around her artistic, home-town, good male friend who had let his homosexuality be known openly, and Lise, to accommodate her husband's feelings, left her association with this fellow to a fond memory.

From this sketch of the strong, sentimental reactions to the different kinds of civil statuses in our contemporary society, we can see that society still reinforces its structure of civil statuses by strong positive and negative reactions to it. Today among enlightened Quebecers, sanctions seem to be expressed more by personal avoidance and ambiguous, often unexpressed feelings. This system of civil statuses is still tied to and based upon the biological life span of the human being. Yet, culture has produced enormous variation in the ways in which the aging process is encoded into the social structure. The life cycle of urban Canadians has been related to their family relationships:

> Marital status, age, and the ages of one's dependents are the main criteria in distinguishing the various stages in the life cycle which may be defined as: childhood, adolescence, single living away from the parental home, early married life, child-bearing, old age and widowhood. Other modes of family and living arrangements also exist but the typical individual passes through these stages in this order. Although the association between a person's age and his stage in the life cycle is not perfect--childrearing may be disrupted by middle age, and the normal course of events may be disrupted by death, divorce, or separation--a

person's age is the single best indicator of his stage in the
life cycle.[4]

These authors go on to operationalize four family age groups
indicative of the four stages of the family life cycle:

> 1. the young family, ages 0-4 and 25-34 years; 2. the middle
> stage family, ages 5-14 and 35-44 years; 3. the mature
> family, ages 15-19 and 45-54 years; 4. the older
> households, ages 55+ years.

Moreover, they observe that:

> Since persons aged 20 to 24 years are found at such a
> range of stages in the family cycle including being children
> living with their parents, young singles who have left home,
> newly weds or young parents, they have been considered to
> be a transitional stage.

The life cycle is reflected in the ecology of all the urban areas in
Canada. Montreal, like the other Canadian cities, is characterized by an
imperfect, concentric zonal pattern. This is typical for cities with a
rapidly growing, mobile population. People who are beginning to bear and
rear children live in the outer ring. In this view, the inner suburbs:

> tend to have a somewhat older age profile which
> approximates that of the city as a whole; the inner city
> areas are less family oriented and have a disproportionate
> share of the city's elderly population, young singles who
> have left their parental home, and childless couples.[5]

The changes that I have suggested in my vignettes are reflected in
the writings of demographers, although they are careful to stress that
the demographic changes in Quebec are the case for most of the
developed countries. The demography of the 1970s has been described
as undergoing quite a lot of movement, which included dramatic changes
in the age structure, an end to the lowering of fecundity, the
disappearance of the high level of fecundity, the extension of abortion

and of sterilization, the fall in infant mortality, the lowering of the number of single persons' getting married, a rise in divorce and zero growth due to a deterioration in the balance of exchanges in migration.[6] Yet it is important to remember that marriage is alive and well in Quebec. Young Quebecers marry more and younger than their elders. Instead of indicating a decline in marriage, the higher divorce rate is accompanied by remarriage.[7] Americans and Canadians of the other provinces marry and divorce more frequently and at a younger age than Quebecers.[8]

The Development of Friendship

Friendship appears to gradually develop as early as the first two years of life.[9] Moreover, its development has been empirically discovered to progress at progressively complex levels that roughly correspond to the Piagetian stages, and to be differentiated for girls and boys.[10] As my study is about late adolescent and adult friendship, I will not review this growing body of literature on friendship in childhood in detail.[11] I will be concerned with childhood friendship only in so far as close friends of the late-adolescents and adults in my sample were made in childhood and adolescence and only in so far as general theories of the influence of age on friendship cover these earlier periods.

The process of human development is elaborated by social and cultural meanings underlain by biological realities such as age and sex. Age and gender are primitive classificatory devices with referents in the physical world. All human societies have organized work around them. With greater degrees of societal differentiation, these social selectors exert somewhat less force in recruitment to scarce positions, even though they continue to operate at a relatively high level, in complex societies.

The functions and structures of age grading in pre-literate and peasant societies have been documented and distinctive age levels with their significance have been categorized.[12] In this vein, Beth Hess used a functionalist role theory to explain:

> ... how the ages of people can have important bearing on
> their friendships, affecting whom one has as a friend, the
> kinds of relationships likely to develop between friends at
> various ages, and the conditions under which friendships
> are formed, maintained or dissolved.[13]

In much more down-to-earth language, Letty Cottin Pogrebin sketches plausible friendship scenarios which differ along the following groupings of the human life cycle:

> Infants and Toddlers: Precursors of Adult Friendship; Age 3
> to 10: Solidifying the Social Self; Age 11 to 17: Balancing
> Belonging and Independence; Age 18 to 39: Balancing
> Friendship and Everything Else: Competing Interests; Age
> 40 to 64: Consolidating Gains, Cutting Losses; Age 65 Plus:
> Realities and Surprises of the Later Years; Balancing Old
> Friends and New Friends.[14]

Age Constraints on Making Friends, with a Focus on Adolescence

In childhood and adolescence small age differentials are perceived as major blocks to friendship because individuals of different ages typically share very different activities, hold different attitudes and act in typically different ways. A single, English Canadian, male student in his late teens brought this observation to our attention:

> There are certain points in time where age makes a
> difference. When you are a teenager and you are, let's say,
> 17 or 18, you will find it very hard to make friends with
> people who are 12 or 13, but once you reach a certain age,
> let's say 18 or 19, you'll find that you can be friends with
> almost anybody of any age group. You may find it harder to
> relate to people who are a lot older and a lot younger.

In urban, English Canadian youth culture adolescent boys' best friends play the most significant role in their decisions about joining clubs.[15] This pattern has been interpreted by explaining that younger, middle-class boys are unsure of their roles and lack the means ("cars, money, the latest style") required for taking part in older boys' activities in which dating is more frequent.[16]

Robert Sévigny and Pierre Guimond have observed that the prominence of friendship in French Canadian youth culture depends upon whether the environment is rural or urban. They point out that young French-speaking Quebecers rank friendship in either first or second place in the various sectors of their life as it relates to others. There are youth values (friends, sexual life, and leisure activities) and adult values (family, occupation, religion), which vary in importance of personal satisfaction according to the city or country background.[17]

In examining the conflict of generations in a working-class (Saint-Sauveur) and middle-class (Saint-Foy) urban locality, Camille Délude-Clift and Edouard Champoux noted that in both of these classes friendship is reported to be more important than kinship and is experienced outside of it.[18]

For rural, young Quebec francophones, family, occupation, and religion play a more important part in one's self actualization than in an urban milieu.[19] However, there may be a subcultural contrast in this matter, for this pattern is not clear for the rural communities of single industry in English Canada, where friendship has been described as playing a great role, especially in relation to information on migration, mutual help, and ties in school.[20]

Adolescence has been described as the period of life when friends "come fully to center stage, transcending all other relationships in immediate importance."[21] One of my interviewees--a single woman, twenty-two years of age, who is a receptionist in a medical clinic and a university student, and whose father works for the federal government--described in French which ideas she and her friend held in common:

> ... you know, the ideas that we have at 15 or 16 years of age, which is to say, "Oh, I'm going to get married at 25" ... "We are going to travel a great deal." We wanted to be independent, but at the same time married, you know ... "I want to do this, make a lot of money," but all that has

> changed. That's clear. Let's say today she has done that,
> while I haven't done that at all. We don't have any things in
> common anymore, for example, she paints, makes pottery,
> macramé, and all that ... I telephone her.

The similarity in age of her close friends is related to the fact that certain activities are typical of certain age grades. For example, people of a certain age attend university or go on to the world of work, even though they do not take the same attitudes toward those experiences and issues. In describing her second friend, she describes different reactions to a stage of life very clearly in the following passage:

> I got to know her at university. She leads the same type of
> life, [has] the same kind of ideas apparently. ... She is a girl
> who is very politicized. ... I never was. She has a very
> critical sense of people. She is sociable. ... She is a girl who
> is very free, sexually speaking. There isn't anything that
> can stop her in what she is going to do. She is very
> impulsive too. ... [I met her] at the University of Quebec.
> We met in the same course. We both had an interest [in
> the same subject about which] we spoke between us. ... At
> that time we had no [boy-]friend, steady, so we went out
> together. She came from a country background.

Is there something special about these periods of life that make them particularly conducive to forming close friendships? We can explore this issue by determining at which period of life a person's closest friendships were made. When I replicated Jean Maisonneuve on this question, Montrealers told me and my interviewers that their close friendships began at every period of their lives, even though people from all socio-economic groupings formed significantly more of their friendships exclusively during their childhood or adolescence or during both of these life periods.[22] In contrast to Maisonneuve's data from France, 23% fewer Montrealers (34% in Montreal in comparison to 57% in France) report their close friendships beginning exclusively in adulthood.[23] In comparison to the USA, this aspect of the acquisitive style of friendship is quite pronounced in Montreal, although it is not possible to quantitatively compare my results to the American data, for

Sarah H. Matthews neglects to report the number of her interviewees' friendships which were classified as acquisitive.[24] In Montreal there was a trend for blue collar workers to be more open to new friends as they age in comparison to white collar workers and professionals' making close friends at all periods of their lives after their childhood and/or adolescence.

The psychological basis of friendship, as portrayed by an analysis of the items of the La Gaipa instrument, reveals that age produces statistically significant differences. Generally younger people have a more glowing view of their friend and friendship than do older people.

Cultural Change, Reflected in Language, Rooted in a Historical Period, Affecting Certain Age Groups, Influences Friendship

Having noted this tendency for childhood and adolescence to provide fruitful grounds for the friendship encounter, I must stress the particular historical setting that nourishes the social conditions that bring about this phenomenon.

Attitudes towards age, often seen in linguistic markers, can hinder the formation of friendships by not permitting persons of different ages to be treated with similar degrees of equality. Societal attitudes toward age are intricately tied up with cultural attitudes, which, in turn, make up the distinguishing features of a historical period. Authority and respect were traditionally shown to older people through linguistic markers such as "*Madame, Monsieur, vous*, Sir, Mrs.," and the tension or uncertainty reported in some of my interviews suggests a lingering of this practice that is disclaimed by some observer-proponents of egalitarianism. Others have demonstrated the use of *tu* and *vous* in showing social respect and distance through non-reciprocal address and intimacy and informality through reciprocal address forms.[25] Listen to a French Canadian woman in her mid-to-late twenties, married with two children. With ten years of formal education, she is a housewife. At the time of the interview she had been undergoing psychological therapy and anticipated going through marital therapy.

> ... before ... when I was a little girl, a teacher was something on a pedestal, and he lorded over us. We were the pupils then, you know. Well, now, at my age, teachers are no more than 30 years old. There are even some of them who are 25, 26, 27, who are around my age. And so the trouble that I had when I started this school ... I always ... used the second person plural form of respect, "*vous*," when speaking to people. Then everyone used the informal second person singular [when speaking to others]. I had a lot of difficulty in getting used to it, to call people *tu*. And then now I do it without thinking about it. And so with a *vous*, My Lord, it seems to me to cut off any relationships. The relationships are only superficial, are not in depth. ... The professors, ... My Lord, it was *vous*, and you didn't have the right to tell them that "you made a mistake" because they were insulted. Today, My Lord, it is taken with a laugh. It's a joke, really yes. I am absent-minded, you know ... They're people like anyone else. Whew, before I made a big difference between the authority, you know, the authority was, My Lord, something that you had to respect. It was stronger than we. ... Whew, it's not because he is Prime Minister that he is better ... maybe I don't have the same knowledge as he, but in certain areas, perhaps, I'm worth more than he, you know. People are impressed by that ... You go into the office of the director and you're there, you're all nervous, you know. And the guy lets himself be impressed. Today it seems to me that I see it differently. To begin with ... the 13th of May, My Lord, I felt all helpless, like a little girl who returns to school after a long sickness. It took me maybe a month to feel my way around again, and today I got off to a good start. ... it's going better than before because you were uptight when they made you say something. It was the authority, My Lord. It wasn't a joke. I don't see [things] in the same way any more. Also we live really better. We feel less uptight.

When a younger person says *vous* to an older person and the older person does not reply with a term denoting similar degrees of respect, authority, and seniority, this salutation is non-reciprocal. The existence or non-existence of a morpheme or a response marker for the personal name is cultural in that it is shared by a collectivity and is learned and passed on in groups. It is equally social in that the rights and privileges accorded these words demonstrate stratified spheres of action in the division of labor.

The Similarity in Age among Close Friends

At each of these periods of the human life cycle, there are new developmental experiences, set in particular socio-cultural contexts, which people of a similar age must face. How does passing through these various periods of our human lives affect our choice of friends? It would not be unreasonable to expect that because people confront these similar life issues that they would seek out people of similar ages with whom they could share these fundamentally common realities. On the other hand, there are also opportunities to meet people of different generations from one's own from which friends may be chosen. In the western classics, friendship with people of different ages was often explained by a younger person's charm, comeliness, energy, etc., and an older person's wisdom, insight, experience, etc., complementing each other. Marcus Tullius Cicero summarized the influence of age on friendship in these words:

> It was with such affection that in the days of my youth I loved those older men, Lucius Paulus, Marcus Cato, Gallus, Publius Nasica, and Tiberius Gracchus, the father-in-law of my friend Scipio. But with even greater splendor does this affection gleam when found between those of equal age, as between myself and Scipio, Lucius Furius, Publius Rupilius, and Spurius Mummius. And again in the repose of old age I take pleasure in the affection of young men, as with you and Quintus Tubero, and I find delight also in the attachment of very young men like Publius Rutilius and Aulus Verginius. And since the course of our life and nature is so arranged that a new generation is ever taking the place of a former one, it should indeed be your hope, that you may be able, as the saying is, to reach the goal with those of your own age with whom, so to speak, you started life. But since man holds all his possessions by a very precarious and uncertain tenure, we should always seek out some friends whom we may love and by whom we may

be loved. For if affection and kindness be taken away, all
the joy of living is lost.[26]

These classical qualitative observations on how age bears on close
friendship may be pinned down by a survey question. Jean Maisonneuve
had already operationalized such an inquiry to determine if the
interviewee's friends were approximately of the same generation.[27] So I
repeated his formal entry on my questionnaire:

> 3. Which of these friends are: a) of the same generation as
> yours? b) clearly older (at least ten years older than you)?
> c) clearly younger (at least 10 years younger)?

In composing this question, Maisonneuve explained that it seems
contrived to determine age grades as well as the significant differences
between the age of an interviewee and that of his or her friends.
Moreover, he noted that he picked a range of ten years because it
seemed to correspond to the threshold of the most probable differences
in status and of social weighting of the people whom he interviewed
whose mean age was held constant as much as possible around thirty
years of age.[28] I will refer to each of these categories of Maisonneuve's
as an "age-generation." In my in-depth, recorded interview, I asked
about a similar issue in an open-ended way. In addition to directly asking
about age and friendship, I gathered a variety of cultural artifacts that
shed light on their mutual effects.

The largest part, 62.71%, of my interviewees' friends were of the
same age-generation as their own. A considerable part, 21.61%, of my
interviewees' friends were of an older age-generation. And a noticeable
sub-group, 15.68%, of my interviewees had friends who were of a
younger age-generation. While age homophily characterized a large
proportion of the Montrealers whom I studied, there were still important
numbers of people in my sample who had first older and then younger
close friends. These data suggest that--regardless of their class,
ethnicity, gender, or age--all age groupings first choose persons of around
their same age, then older persons, and last younger persons. However,

single persons show the greatest tendency to have close friends of the same age-generation.[29]

The Changing Meanings of Age and Civil Status Differences in Friendship

By the time I began to analyze my data, it became apparent to me that determining the cutting points for my age categories was not a simple matter. First of all, there were great cultural changes happening in Montreal that altered the definition of what was acceptable behavior for people of younger and older age grades. One of the most striking examples of these upheavals was the effect that quitting the priesthood and various religious orders had on the psycho-socio-cultural lives of real individuals. Quebec had once been widely derisively labeled the "priest-ridden" province. During and after the Quiet Revolution, many priests and nuns left the religious life for a secular one. In gossip, commentary, and satire, it was not infrequently observed that some of these former members of religious orders, now in their forties and fifties, could often be seen frequenting the same leisure spots popular with people from their late teens through early thirties. Furthermore, in the liberating atmosphere of the late 1960s and early 1970s, there were both direct and indirect attacks on age stereotypes. An illustration of these new role models was a national report on the Canadian Broadcasting Company about teaching cross-country skiing to people euphemistically called senior citizens or golden agers. In addition to these news items, there were a variety of public festivities such as Saint Jean Baptiste Day [the Quebec patron saint and "national" day] and various large demonstrations that began to bring out a wide cross-section of people, including people of many different ages, into a community event. The new Montreal architecture of huge malls and underground passage-ways, connected to a relatively inexpensive subway, also permitted any well-bodied person, regardless of age, to sit and watch passersby, sometimes for nothing on a clean, attractive public bench, or sometimes for the price of a coffee and doughnut to sit at an open-air bar. While you could see that some places were more or less popular with different age grades, in all of these places people of vastly different ages mixed on a daily basis.

Regardless of their civil status or gender, similarity of age, or age homophily, characterizes the greater part of Montrealers' close friends. Yet, it was equally true that Montrealers also had close friends who were both older and younger than themselves.[30]

When I asked Montrealers if they had cultivated a real friendship with a person having political opinions deeply opposed to their own, it turned out that married people, in general, but particularly those without children, were more tolerant of political diversity in their close friends' opinions than interviewees and respondents who were single. Single people were considerably less apt to be close friends with others who disagreed with them on political issues. Men were also significantly more likely to have close friends with different political views than were women. To some degree, this influence of civil status on political differences among close friends can be explained by aging. 53.7% of the older in comparison to 43.3% of the younger Montrealers in my sample had close friends whose political views were really different from their own, even though age per se did not produce a statistically significant difference in this regard.

In the political climate of the 1970s in Quebec, the "age" or "generation" gap was widely put forward as an explanation of a more militant stance on the part of the younger versus the older generation. As the Collective in Urban Sociology of the University of Montreal and other commentators had noted, this journalistic impression did not properly distinguish the French-speaking youths' greater emphasis on countercultural values in contrast to their parents' greater emphasis on institutional changes. It would seem that single people, who tended to also be younger, demanded more ideological consistency among their close friends. Such a depiction corresponds to the sketch of youth as idealistic.[31] The other side of this idealism is that it may not be tolerant of differences too close to the self. In a similar manner being single provides a person with somewhat more free time to intensely engage in the great political debates of the day. Even though children often adopt the political party of their parents, that does not mean that parents and children see eye to eye on issues of drugs, rock concerts, premarital sex and freedom, which may, indeed, become salient political issues of a period.

Married people who are either voluntarily without children or who plan to have children in the future had the greatest degree of divergence of political opinion among their close friends. Their having somewhat more "free time" at their disposal than married people with children permits them more time to participate in job and non-work related activities where they would have a greater chance to become close friends of people who do not hold their same political outlook. People who devote long hours to their profession, and ski, theater, film, and concert buffs may run into and subsequently become good friends of people who do not see eye to eye on matters of domestic or foreign policy.

Unless they are shielded by strong social supports provided by great wealth or community, married people with children become tied up with the tasks of childrearing and keeping up a household that may change the great questions of the day into whose turn it is to change the baby, take the children to school, or clear or fix the house or apartment. Such constraints give them greater chances of meeting up with other parents whose political world view is really opposed to their own, even though they may like the way they raise their children or keep up their living quarters. In meeting on a playground or play group with one's children or in school-related activities, couples or single parents with children have a chance of meeting people with different political and other beliefs from their own while sharing the lifecycle reality of parenting.[32]

While both English and French Canadian married people with children chose friends mainly from their own age-generation, English Canadians do moreso than French Canadians.[33] Also, this subgroup of English Canadians chose a somewhat larger proportion of friends who were older than the corresponding subgroup of French Canadians. This pattern may result from their choosing older people, often non-kin met at work, whose social skills and general knowledge they admire.[34]

In my data family solidarity was somewhat greater among French than English Canadians. Among other indicators, French Canadians tolerated greater differences in political opinions among their close friends compared to English Canadians. This observation can be explained by greater family solidarity. In my interviewees' accounts, kin, such as younger brothers and sisters did, in serving as babysitters, consolers in times of divorce, or a set of arms in moving, form the basis of a close family friendship, regardless of their political beliefs.

Although the younger and older people in my study manifested their closest friendships in remarkably similar ways, there are a few statistically significant differences. Compared to "older" people, younger ones evidence somewhat greater activity in their friendships by more frequently going to their friends' homes as well as "going out" with them to cafes, etc. As they age, people also tend to become more wrapped up in their families and careers. Particularly, parents with young children need the convenience of meeting in "child-oriented" places such as parks with play equipment or "child-proof" houses.[35]

Friendship while Single

In the Montreal of the 1970s it was rather common for single young adults to travel together or share an apartment or a house with others of their same age-generation during the period before they entered marriage, into a steady non-married couple arrangement, or into living on one's own as a single person. The West Island, middle-class teacher in her thirties, whom we have met in earlier chapters, vividly describes this experience which had occurred a decade earlier in her life:

> I ... think about these two girls that I knew many years ago. ... My first and deepest friend now lives [in the Caribbean], and she was a girl my own age, with whom I went to a young people's church group in Toronto, and so we had a lot of social activities together. I guess we were friends because we both had the same type of intelligence. She didn't continue school like I was ... . She went to night school, and I've also admired her for being a very intelligent girl. My second best friend was a kind of flippy person, and we fitted together because she was the kind of person that

would make enormous spaghetti dinners and invite the whole crowd in so I would enjoy her friends vicariously, let us say, and then they'd go flying off to some night spot, and then I would end up doing the dishes. But that was the way we'd live together. We shared an apartment, and, let's say, she was the big organizer, but it was myself and the third girl who kind of did the dirty work. Ho. Ha. That's how we all got along. Ha. And at that age--we were in our early twenties--... this particular girl and I hitchhiked around Great Britain together, but she seemed to be very easy-going, and I'm more meticulous, and so, perhaps, her easy-going qualities relaxed me, and my tidiness and my organization kind of picked her up, and, in the end, she was interested, she knew the young man I married, and I knew the young man she married, and we both went through this pre-marital time together, sort of accompanying each other, getting to know young men to see whom we could marry.

In this school teacher's and mother's account, we learn that her circle of young, single women had multifaceted and complementary relationships of emotional and service support in accordance with their different personalities during their years between their families of orientation and procreation. In Beth Hess' notion, their friendships would be best classified as those of substitution, for these single women began to fulfill different needs for one another formerly provided by members of their families of orientation. A key aspect of this emotional support is hashing out serious life problems about who you are, about the nature of your relationships with significant others, and about your philosophy of life. These "rap" sessions have been depicted in humorous and endearing dramas on television, in the movies, novels, and life-style sections of the newspapers which came into the fore in the 1970s. My interviewees found friends better at this type of communication than their own family members, who could be otherwise relied on more for material support. The results of my twelfth question concerning the discussion of serious problems with friends, which is related later in this chapter, show that single people discuss their difficulties with close friends more frequently than do married people. The close friend fills this need for unmarried individuals more readily and remains a possible release for backstage information which may be shared with both significant others.

The subtle quest, revealed in my intervieweee's story, covered her and her apartment-mate's apparent major social thrust of attempting to find the appropriate man with whom to bind themselves in marriage. In other terms, an important part of their being single included shedding their status of young, single women for that of married ones. Being unmarried afforded them more freedom to explore other relationships. At the same time, being single has greater risks of making a person a loner; yet, as we call tell in this woman's account, this possibility is willfully alleviated by seeking out friends and exploring a greater number of friendships. The La Gaipa instrument reveals twelve statistically significant differences which support the notion that single people have higher expectations and hold a purer view of their closest friends and friendship than do married people.

From mid-to-late adolescence being young and single takes on different meanings as the human being confronts sexuality and the social and cultural roles appropriate to an emerging adult. Most of the research on sexuality in Quebec done in the Sociology Department at the University of Montreal in the early 1970s portrayed a strong norm in favor or premarital virginity, and the majority of Jacques Bonin's informants condemned sexual liberty and premarital relations, particularly for girls, although this was much more strongly so among those at the underprivileged end of the social scale.[35] Yet, this same literature suggests French-speaking Montrealers' awareness of a much more permissive sexuality emerging among the youth. And my own inquiry into this matter, reported on in the next chapter, reveals more extensive real sexual behavior by the mid-1970s than the strongly restrictive norm of premarital chastity recorded by these other researchers. In part, owing to these norms prescribing premarital chastity for especially the unmarried woman and motherly fecundity for the mother, and another force favoring status homophily, we would expect some degree of males' choosing other males and females choosing other females as close friends.[36] This expectation was confirmed at a significant level. Moreover, my male interviewees chose single men more frequently than single women as close friends. In part, this pattern came about because women reinforce the norm of premarital chastity by avoiding close friendship with single men to a certain extent. Indeed, my female interviewees chose married women more frequently than did male interviewees. Despite these significant differences, the interviewees, on the whole, had about the same number of friends in each civil and gender category.[37]

According to Ira Reiss between 1920 and 1965:

> young people increasingly came to see the selection of a sexual code and sexual behavior itself as a private choice similar to that made in politics and religion.[38]

Such appeared to be the case for single people in Quebec after the Quiet Revolution. Thus, in examining the style of the boyfriend, girlfriend/*petit(e) ami(e)* in Appendix D, we note that almost 78 percent of the interviewees displaying this style were "single, never married" [7/9 = 77.8 percent which constituted 7/50 = 14 percent of all in-depth interviewees]. Only one married person with children displayed this style [1/9 = 11.1 percent, which constituted 1/50 = 2 percent of all in-depth interviewees].

Friendship during Marriage

Marital status had a little influence on where and through whom friends meet. Around 9.6% of my interviewees met their adult friends through their wife or husband. Thus spouses served as sources for meeting friends much less than did neighbors, co-workers, or having shared a similar off-the-job activity, although somewhat better than the military.[39]

Different social and cultural rights and obligations for men and women entering into a marriage help produce this relatively small number of adult close friendships made through a person's spouse. When a woman enters into a legal marriage, there are social constraints on her to enter her husband's social circle of friends, but the depths of these bonds depend on their authenticity, as the female teacher of English in her thirties, whom we have met before, told me in French:

> You take on a few of our husband's friends, heh? It's rather normal, so ... they are the people who clearly let me drop after my separation. ... I tested a few of them. I telephoned and asked about the news, and, then, how they were doing, just to say hello to them. ... So I felt a kind of coldness on the telephone which made me never call them back. Moreover, judging by their response, that indicated, that meant "it's better that you don't call back." ... That changed my life rather a lot because it made me open my eyes. It was at that moment that I began to count my friends on my fingers, and I realized that I have only two. ... My husband was in business. They were people with whom he had to deal with and all that, and so I knew the wives of those people. [I got to know them] first in those things, through invitations, at congresses, like that, so afterwards we began to visit, and then began to telephone one another regularly. ... I began to understand quickly that, after I had been married five years, when I left my husband, it was smoke, it wasn't built on anything, wasn't true ... People have the impression that if they continue to speak to us that they are going to be seen in the wrong light.

If a married person becomes a friend of his of her spouse's friend, the chances of secret information getting back to one's spouse is increased. This factor certainly contributes to the small number of friends made through spouses in my sample. On the other hand, non-shared close friends may, indeed, enhance the quality of a marriage by providing a supportive human being to sympathize with and comfort the stresses and strains that build up out of different emotional, cognitive, and instrumental needs of each marital partner. Although I found few (7.4%) of the Montrealers in my sample thought of their spouses as close friends, I learned that this classification did not imply a lack of deep communication between spouses.

The style of the family-oriented friendship implies a more diffuse type of positive interaction among the members of the family. As seen in Appendix D, this style was much more frequent among people who were married and who had children [16/20 = 80% with this style or 32% of all in-depth interviewees] as compared to people who were single and never married [3/20 = 15% with this style or 3/50 = 6% of all in-depth interviewees] or divorced [1/20 = 5% who displayed this family-oriented friendship style or 1/50 = 2% of all in-depth interviewees].

In his lectures on love and friendship, delivered at Boston University in the summer of 1977, Hans Peter Dreitzel contended that a couple can maximize communication if it is not interrupted by communication with other loved ones, like children, who demand so much personal and financial responsibility. Empirically, Dreitzel's hypothesis held for Montrealers who were single, but Montrealers' without children so infrequently communicating intimate thoughts and feelings to their close friends disconfirms the generality of his proposition.

Among the Montrealers in my sample, one subgroup of single people discussed their serious problems with their friends most frequently while two other smaller subgroups rarely or never did. While one subgroup of married people with children was the next most frequent civil status category to discuss their serious problems often with their close friends, there were even larger subgroups who never did or did so rarely. However, two subgroups of married people without children tended to rarely or never discuss their problems with friends, while a small subgroup did so. Childless couples may discuss their most serious problems with their spouses more often than with their friends.[40]

Besides being expected to take on the friends of their husband's, married women's access to people of other marital statuses is impeded by tradition. Particularly, they are not supposed to be overly friendly with unmarried males because of an extra risk of breaking the norm of marital fidelity with a category of male who does not have a fidelity norm to maintain. Even though this traditional norm becomes modified in various subcultures to permit or encourage the spouses' opening up to others of different marital statuses, another norm, especially among newlyweds, has it that intimacy must be shared primarily with one's spouse. Among working class American households, wives have been described as almost predictably trying to get their husbands to break their attachment to their high school peer group.[41]

In my own interviews this phenomenon was not that frequent or specific in that the new wife occasionally wanted her husband to break with an old friend, even though the break had nothing in particular to do with any specific age-grade, gender, or place-specific peers such as high school cronies. Moreover, in a few instances, working class husbands in my study felt threatened by their wives' new associates and friends. Let us hear an example of this first type of constraint which a new wife attempted to place upon her husband's close friendship with a woman of an older generation and that older woman's husband. My principal French-language interviewer, Ms. Michèle Verrette, recorded this story while interviewing a woman who had been married between 26 and 30 years and who had had six children. This middle class, French Canadian had been a housewife, translator, teacher, and administrator, and her husband has been a farmer and business man. They live on the north-central part of Montreal island. Speaking in French of her friendship with one of her closest friends, she told Michèle:

> The second friendship is [with] a couple younger than I. It's a long story that goes way back. At that time we were living on a farm. ... One day a young man ... who had $2 left in his pockets ... was looking for a job. And so he looked sympathetic to me. O.K., like any weak woman, we always have a certain influence. My husband said that "you are too young; there's nothing I can do." Fine, well I said, "you can always try him." So afterward he confided to us that he didn't have any more money and that he really wouldn't have known what to do if we had told him "well, you are too young; we absolutely can't take care of you." And, he came from a rather high social level--his father was very strict; he went off on study trips and so he placed his sons on farms to make their own way ... but all the same we had a lot of things in common in the sense that he loved music, songs. The songs make me think that he used to play records every morning before beginning to go to work. And I was a lot older than he, certainly. ... but we had tastes in common. I listened to records. And then, as he loved nature a lot, he talked with my husband about farm things, and with me he spoke of my music. He spoke about the works

of his father's organization. [His dad] had quite a bit of public exposure then, and we got to know the family. A family like them ... [was] not well-off at that time. Those who devote their time for the public good, I assure you, don't have a great deal left for themselves. But they were extremely nice people. ... He is a very dynamic man. I would say it's because he has gotten older and has a lot of business sense, ... perhaps, we could judge him to be in excellent health. ... They got married rather young. Both of them were around 22 or 23 years of age, but as far as the young woman goes, the friendship was very slow in coming. And because women are very intuitive, she quickly found out that her husband was very attached to me, and so I don't exactly know why, but it displeased her at the beginning; it was difficult. But a quality of his personality that I didn't tell about this friend is that he is very diplomatic. He knew that it was a question of time. And so we grew apart for a rather long time. And he had a meeting maybe one or two times a year. ... And so the young wife realized that this friendship that we had for her husband was deeper than all his other friendships that were often only for business. And so she started to confide in us. She is a very happy person, and since then, let's say, it took seven or eight years, but now it works really well. ... There's still about thirteen years difference in our ages.

By including a friend who is single, widowed, or divorced in a relationship with a married couple, another social arrangement is displayed whether it is verbally, consciously, or unconsciously taken into account. In this way, the social status of one friend can act as a model of persuasion on another. Even if it is not discussed, the alternative civil status and its life implications are visible for both parties. The reaction to this difference may lead a friend or a friend's spouse to impose limits on their relationship, or, to the contrary, it may be accepted for its variety. In the following case of a thirty-two year old, male, English Canadian police officer, who has been married between six and ten years and who lives on Montreal's "West Island," we can see how changes in civil status contributed to his and his friend's developing friendship:

The one I might consider as number one friend is a fellow who is ten years my senior. He's 42 years of age, and he has always been, for the past 15 or 16 years, anyway, my best friend. ... He really doesn't have that much education. He was born and brought up on a farm. He is involved in a company that makes [ornaments]. He isn't as well off as other friends that I have, but he really hits home as being a good friend because at any time I've needed him, he has been there. He is the kind of fellow that I could talk to and relate my experiences and my problems to and, by the same token, he has done the same to me. He's a man who's been divorced. He's had ... teen-age children. With his second wife he doesn't have any children at all, but I'm sure he'd like to have some though. But he's not an exceptional person, but he is a very warm person. If you have a problem, he makes you feel like he's really interested and genuinely wants to do something to help you. Part of the baseball team got interested in bowling. I went bowling and met this fellow, and well, he just happened to be around when I was there, or, at any function I was, he happened to be there, and we'd recognize each other and just talk. Eventually we just struck it off a little bit better, and we got interested in one another. And later on I got married and used to invite him to my home, and then he got married and ... he used to invite us to his home, and now we still, as couples, play bridge together, and it's a lasting thing. ... We still see each other and go bowling occasionally. We play bridge once a week. Whenever I am bored, I give my friend a call, or my buddy a call, or best friend a call--whatever you want to call it. We decide to do something together, and we usually involve our wives in what we're doing. ...

In Lillian B. Rubin's interpretation:

we eagarly seek out others who share our social role and circumstance because they help to affirm that part of our self and our life, to validate our connection to our new roles as wife and husband. Soon after, however, we begin to look also for people who see the individual in us, who encourage the appearance of a self-in-the-world who lives beyond the boundaries of the self-in-the-role.[42]

The Remaining Family-Friendship after the Break-up of the Family

If the friendship formed with a spouse's friend is meaningful enough, it may outlast a divorce. In the following episode, a male friend of her husband's remains the friend of the female, French Canadian high school teacher of English in her thirties, whom we have already encountered. Even though this friend of her husband's had discouraged her from getting a divorce, this friendship lasted after the break-up of their marriage.

> ... He knew my husband, so he knew the type of work my husband did. Moreover, he knew the style of life I led with my husband. I knew his wife very well. She is a friend of mine, but, not, let's say, in the sense that I am intending; let's say, a good *camarade*, a good *copine*. So he's the only man, the only person, who advised me against the divorce. And I said I didn't agree with him because he told me, "You know, you live in a grand manner. You are highly thought of and all that. What do you lack? What more do you want? You have a car. ... You have a pretty apartment. Fine, you can travel." I said, "yes," to all this, "but I am always all alone. I didn't get married to be alone." He said, "yes." I have other reasons for living. I have a job. I have friends. ... "You have that, but, in addition, you have financial security." I said, "For me, that isn't a valid reason." About that we didn't agree. To the contrary, I left my husband anyway, and then, I didn't know what he would have to ... say to me. I telephoned him. I had to find out about something, and so he made me laugh on the telephone. "Heh, I was sure that you would call me." I said that I was very well. And he wanted to know exactly all about my news and how it was going.

Human Development's Legacy to Friendship

Throughout this chapter, I have tried to emphasize that the influence of human development on friendship roughly produced gradual, though discrete, changes associated with advancing chronological age, which acts on and is acted upon by changes in civil status and culture in particular historical contexts. Despite these complex, interacting factors, a general psycho-social pattern emerges. As the Montrealers in my sample passed through their life cycle, they appear to become more selective about friends, and to let the requirements of other relationships have precedence over the demands of friendship. I derive this generalization on the basis of statistically significant differences among different age and civil status groups' answers to several of my questions regarding several issues.

First of all, although all Montrealers confide in their most intimate of their close friends to a much greater extent than in the least intimate, those who were married and had children and those people of working class backgrounds more readily ranked their closest friends. As both of these groups bear particular constraints on their time and relatively limited material resources, their more clearly ranking their close friends may reflect the realities of their "budgeting" their lives among significant others.

The West-Island, English Canadian elementary school teacher in her thirties, whom we have met before, enumerated some typical criteria by which close friends are differentiated:

> Yes, I am closer to some of my friends than others. Perhaps, closeness is a time thing. If you have a need such as a place you would like to go and visit, and somebody you know very well lives by, suddenly they become your very close friends because you want to go and stay at their place or they want to come and stay at your place. You are at that moment close friends. I think this is a very hard thing to rank. I think the time factor and the need factor go into this. ... People cannot always be really, really deep with each other. Between close friends there is a great deal of superficiality, just to have a chat, not to be involved, but I agree, I think the difference between being a good friend ... would be the fact that you're non-competitive with a genuine friend and, whereas, you might be possibly competitive or on guard with a business acquaintance or a professional. ...

Even though they did not like being asked to do so, Montrealers ranked their closest friends from most to least intimate.[43] This finding indicates that even closest friends are distinguished by degrees of closeness. That this phenomenon is particularly noticeable among married people who have children as well as among working class people reflects that the pressures of holding down a job and raising children force individuals and couples into being very selective among the people with whom they choose to spend their scarce time. As Letty C. Pogrebin so aptly summarized it: "As life becomes crowded with family, work, and community interests, where does friendship fit it?"[44]

I found that the order in which Montrealers reported their friends from first to last was highly correlated with the rank of each of their closest friends from most to least intimate.[45] Although people expressed a lot of displeasure in being asked to rank their friends, the fact that they do rank them is evidence that they discriminated among their closest friends on how close they felt about them.

Another sign of becoming more choosy in close friendship as a person passes through the stages of the life cycle is an increasing awareness that the demands of family life may lead to conflict with close friends, whereby the friends will be left off in order to avoid conflict with a person's family's different values, tastes, orientations, etc. Although a majority, 62.4%, of both older and younger Montrealers in my sample said they would not give into such family pressure, there is a trend for more Montrealers 31 years of age and older to claim that they had or would sacrifice friend relations for serious reasons of a family nature in comparison to those between 15 and 30 years of age.[46]

Another indicator of this developmental process of cutting down on the proportion of psycho-social energy devoted to close friendships as compared to other social relationships affects the depth of friendship. Although we learned earlier that married Montrealers, particularly those with children, discuss their most intimate thoughts and problems with friends to some degree, so too must it be noted that older Montrealers reveal these same inward depths to their closest friends to a significantly lesser extent than do younger Montrealers.[47]

Friendship Patterns among My Oldest Interviewees

Gerontological studies support the view that old friends display different patterns of friendship instead of having friendships of inferior quality or of a lesser degree compared to friendships of people at younger ages.[48]

There is much disagreement in many of these authoritative versions of what it means to be "up in years." In my treatment of the subject, I will weigh these generalizations about the effect of aging on friendship in chronologically advanced years against the evidence in my data.

Just beginning with the simple indicator of the real number of close friends that an interviewee describes, I found that the older Montrealers in my sample did not have significantly fewer friends than younger Montrealers, and this finding held when I calculated the average number of friends for three age categories, younger (15-30) [mean=4.0], middle (31-59) [mean=3.4], and older (60+) [mean=3.7], based on the questionnaire data, which yielded a mean of 3.8 friends per interviewee for all age groups. When I subsequently collapsed the age categories into just younger (15-30) and older (31+) people for the bulk of the analysis, this finding remained true. Although younger and older Montrealers reported similar numbers of real friends, there are significant differences in distribution of the number of friends reported by these two age groups. In my sample, older Montrealers more frequently told us about having none, one or two, as well as eight, nine, ten or more close friends, in contrast to younger Montrealers who more often described three, five, six, or seven close friends.[49]

This outcome--together with many qualitative observations from my friendship development groups led among older people--would question how many people are accurately depicted by Simone de Beauvoir's statement about the one-up-manship among old friends.[50]

Only a few (15/175=8.57%) of my interviewees were between 61 and 75 years of age. The majority of these (9/15=60%) were still married and had children; three (3/15=20%) were still married but had no children; two were widowed (2/15=13.3%); and one was (1/15=6.7%) divorced. These people tended to stick close to their long-standing friends, while, nonetheless, enjoying new contacts through enjoying new social services that recent progressive provincial and federal policies had opened up to their age peers. An almost 60-year-old, white-haired, rather tall, sociable, talkative, and hospitable French Canadian woman provided us with information on this subject. A wife of twenty-eight years, mother of four children, with nine years of formal education, who had worked as a seamstress for eleven years and as a saleswoman for seven, she explained her friendships as a "Golden Ager":

> We can have many *camarades*, Like me, for example, I am a member of the Golden Agers. We are *copains*, together, you know. It's a circle of friendship, as we say. It's pleasant ... also I'll be a little bit inhibited in speaking only with one or two intimate friends that I can have among my women friends. For example, you know, we'll confide in one another ... Sometimes we can give advice, ... , but that's one thing that you cannot do with just anybody. You can have a lot of friends, but intimately ... to be able to confide in one another, you don't have many people. ... Well, as we belong to the Golden Age Group, there are certain trips that they make, certain benefits that don't cost us too much, that let us see the country, like we will visit factories. It's very interesting to see what goes on in those things. ... So we went to visit a type of company. ... They took us around the factory. ... So you see from the beginning to the end how it is done. ... We ... saw [where] toilet tissues, Kleenex, ... material, ... and cosmetics [were made]. .... Besides there are instructive trips. We went to the Parliament of Ottawa, ... of Quebec. you know, that gives us about the only entertainment we have besides the parties for the Golden Age Group. ... Sometimes there are evening dance parties. You know ... as we celebrate Christmas dinner. All that ... gets us together. ... And so we can't gripe a lot because we have family. But there are many in the group who are alone, and so ... I find that since they organized that, it's a good thing for people because there are a lot of them who would be surrounded all alone by four walls all year.

Particularly noticeable among the highly geographically mobile and/or older people, some expressions of the friend-in-mind are characterized by very pleasant memories of past encounters with friends which are renewed intermittently over the years. My upper-class, English-speaking interviewee, 67 years of age, mother of seven children, spoke of close friends-in-mind:

> And I'll remember the friendship of each of them that I don't see that often, and I still feel ... whenever we have a

chance to meet, we can take up from where we left off ... .
They're people like that that I can pick up with and carry
on. And it's foolish, silly conversation, but I think they
know what I'm talking about, and I admire so many of the
things they're talking about, and I feel I know what they're
talking about, and I admire so many of the things that they
stand for. You know, this is what friendship is in spite of the
fact that they might do things; oh, jeez, they can loose their
temper, and I don't mean dishonorable things ... you know, I
mean with all their weakness, ...

Before delineating what she meant by this kind of friendship in
general, she told me and Ms. Verrette about a particular case of a friend-
in-mind:

> ... Now one was in Montreal recently I hadn't seen for ten
> years, and I didn't see her when she was in Montreal. She
> went back to [The Third World] without seeing me. I was a
> bit hurt and tried to understand it, but she didn't see other
> close friends. ... And then I realized, well, there must be
> some good reason for this. You know, ... she's terribly ill.
> And so, shortly after I'd heard she'd gone back,--she's been
> a missionary nun, she's a fabulous person, you know,--so I
> wrote to her. And I thought, "Well, she's my friend, heh. I
> can write her this." I thought a long time before I wrote it,
> but I wrote and said ... "I'd looked forward so much to
> having heard you were coming and then I realized that you
> weren't particularly well--this is what I heard from a
> mutual friend--and that you had promised that you were
> going to get in touch with some of us." And then I said, "The
> next time,"--I was teasing a bit, but I meant it too--"I won't
> respect your privacy so much." ... What I should have done
> was to 'phone her and make an appointment and say, "I
> must see you, Maureen." You know, but I don't do things
> like that. And she wrote back, "I got the letter yesterday,"--
> and then, there was more to the letter than that--and I
> said, "I'd just like you to know, Maureen, Maureen dear, I
> don't think you realize what an influence you have and
> what your presence means as an inspiration." Because
> friends are inspiring, you know. They give you something of
> their spirit and that you share with them if you are close to
> them. And I regret that not having this chance to share
> that with them. But she wrote back to me and said things
> since she had been here--it'll be ten years in November--
> and she found the changes so tremendous. And she used

the simple term, a simple symbol really, of a lot of things. She said, "Even the faucets, I didn't know how to work them." ... And she said, "I spent a lot of time alone taking streetcar-, bus-rides around the city and what not, ... " But she was going home now ... back to her ... sisters [of a different race] and, you know, the people she has been working with all these years. And she felt alien here. ...

The style of the friend-in-mind is prevalent among the elderly because of the realities of death and retirement.[51] During the interview, this graceful woman, who carried herself with great dignity and composure, cried at several points. In her own words:

You see, the people that I would have confided in or talked out problems [with], they're both dead now, heh. Two female women, heh, both dead so ... one has been dead fifteen years and the other one five and a half ... They were terrific.

Although this lady provides us with much informative detail about these friendships, the point that is relevant here is that for her, these friendships are very much alive in her mind, occupy vivid memories that influence her current thoughts and decisions, and the shining or dim traits of her deceased friends are both part of her consciousness of these relationships. These healthful, intricately woven memories can be likened to a temporal, spatial, cognitive, and affective quilt which warmly covers the style of the "friend-in-mind."

The style of "friend-in-mind" is useful in understanding that the living memory of a close friendship may provide significant psycho-social support despite the attenuation of a friendship due to death or moving in retirement, and this style seems equally important for men and women. The friend-in-mind style is most frequent among people who are married with children, as seen in Appendix D [5/8 = 62.5 percent or 5/50 = 10 percent of all in-depth interviewees]. Of the interviewees who displayed the friend-in-mind style only few were "single, never married" [2/8 = 25 percent or 2/50 = 4 percent of all in-depth interviewees] or divorced [1/8

= 12.5 percent or 1/50 = 2 percent of all in-depth interviewees]. Robert T. Bell has observed that:

> friends serve a somewhat different function for older women than for older men. These men were not likely to have intimate friends for social and emotional support in late life except when they experienced the loss of other resources.[52]

In the following account, it, indeed, appears that although the one close friendship this man has had throughout his life was not characterized by great overt emotional sharing, this friend stands out socio-emotively in this man's psycho-social existence. The depth seems to have come through sharing the knowledge that after enjoying each other's company in youth and young manhood, each friend went on to live a proper life of hard-work, family life, and home which were deeply shared through occasional communication and get-togethers through married life and old age.

Initially, a moderately religious Protestant from a main-line denomination, this man became non-observant in his forties through indifference to practice. He has lived in Verdun, a working-class neighborhood, for 60 of his 69 years. Married for 44 years, this fellow had two daughters. With eight years of formal education, he had worked himself up to a managerial position in a technical department of a national Canadian firm. Speaking of his friendship, he told me:

> ... the close friends that I did have when I was younger, like myself, they grew up and grew older. Some of them moved away. Some of them passed on. Right now I'm not close to any of them. Well, one, his name is Andrew. He is the same age as I. I'd say he'd be 69 now. But as I say, when we were younger, before we were married, we were very close, he and I. Oh, shucks, it's such a long time ago, I don't know exactly how we came to get together. Because I'm going back between 45, 55 years ago now. ... I was married first; I was 26. ... We used to get around together, and we used to snowshoe ... We saw each other occasionally in the summertime. I had a boat ... and he had one too. But mind you, in the summer, we didn't get together too much. He

went his way, and I went mine. ... We were about 14. ... Well we married. I had to stay home a little more, of course. Very often Sundays I didn't get out socially anymore, and so on. And eventually he got married, and he moved up in Ontario, and now he lives in the States. ... Oh, he was probably in his early thirties when he got married, which was later. [We visited him] about four times I guess. ... We haven't gone down to [the South] to see him yet. He came up here once, about two years ago. And he dropped in, ... Yes, he had three daughters. ... He's one of those types who's extremely intelligent. ... He'd go into something, and before he'd complete it, he'd tire of it and start something something else. For example, I remember one time he had learned to speak and write Latin, just from reading the book. That's the type he was. And then he gave that up and decided to become a civil engineer, and he took a correspondence lesson and sailed through that until the last lesson and said, "I'm going to try something else." And that's the way he spent his life. Well, he worked in stockbrokers offices; he wound up working for a [big firm]. ... But if he had stuck with just one thing he would have been very successful. ... He came from Ontario ... most of his schooling was there. He was English Canadian. ... Economically he's all right today. He's retired. He bought his own home, quite a nice place by the way he describes it. ... I usually write him about once a year. We keep each other up to date on the news and let each other know that the other still's alive. ... Well, heh, he was about the only closest friend I had really. Yeah, the others I got to know after I was married, of course. We had quite a few friends. ... When you're not married, it's a pretty free life, heh? You can go and come when you feel like it. There's no strings attached. But, ah, he moved away, and I got married and had a family. All the friends that we knew then were in the same position as we.

When I inquired whether or not he ever talked about religion or politics with Andrew, he answered me:

No, not really. At one time, I don't know if you'd remember ... the C.C.F. Party. Yeah, the beginning of that, he, during the Depression, he didn't work too much, and he got in with this outfit, and he thought this was a good system. And, ah, I never argued with him about it, really. ... But he was quite interested in that, but the question passed, and he got a job and did pretty well, so that was forgotten. ... As I say, we both had our lives. What he did didn't affect me and vice versa. We never tried to impose, no, never. ... I never discuss [religion] with anyone.

After telling me that his and Andrew's greeting consisted of saying "hello" and arranging to do something, never shaking hands or touching, he went on to relate to me how aging had affected his social life:

... You'll have the same experience when you grow older. As you grow older, you have less inclination to have parties and get around, you know. You're more content to stay at home. You have your interests with your family and your wife and so on. And other people stay away, so you sort of drift apart. ... It's kind of hard to explain the aging process to a young person. Actually you've got to live through it to understand what I might mean. ... So you really have to have the experience to *fully* understand. But as you grow older, you'll find that the spirit is willing, but you also realize that you're not physically able to do the things that you did before, as much as you'd like to do them. ... At one time I'd think nothing of going around the river here all day long, no problem at all. I still feel that I'd like to do it, but I know that I couldn't last much more than half an hour.

Conclusion: Do Age and Civil Status Create Role Constellations that Shape Friendship?

In what she qualified as "this necessarily speculative essay," Beth Hess identified four role constellations, typically occurring at particular periods of life, which bear on friendship.[53] Receiving varying degrees of emphasis over an individual's life course, these roles connect friendship to other ones. She refers to these as 1) fusion, 2) substitution, 3) complementarity, and 4) competition. *Fusion* refers to a person's being a friend and other more central relationships at the same time. For example, parents whose children are friends may become close friends too. "Fused friendships attach to the principal spheres of adult activity: family, work, community."[54] *Substitution* is typified when an individual cannot seek certain goals through certain means at a life period and chooses to replace the original goals and means in friendship by others.

And substitute friendships take place when individuals do not live in kinship units or are prevented from performing customary aspects of kinship roles. A new, single younger immigrant, college and other youthful migrant from home, a person in the military service, mental hospital, prison, or home for the aged may form substitute friendships at any time in his or her life cycle. In Beth Hess's schema, *complementarity* occurs when an individual has close friendship along with other relationships in such a manner that the adequacy and performance of one depends upon the opportunity to perform the other role at a particular age. It can happen in childhood, adolescence, adulthood, or old age, but, she writes:

> Competition among close friendships is especially marked among mature adults of the middle years where friendships are likely to be differentiated and compartmentalized. Competition is found also in adolescent peer groups especially where an individualistic achievement oriented school and diffusely loyal, mutually supportive peers have opposing values. Older persons are the least likely to be subject to competition among friendships because they are comparatively less involved in major role obligations. Their established friendships imply greater opportunity for resolving conflicts over time allocation and value allegiance.[55]

It will be recalled that in my Montreal data childhood and/or adolescence proved to be the most fertile periods of a person's life for forming close friendships. This finding lends credence to Hess's notion that role competition may be more marked among mature adults of the middle years. That older people more readily admit that they have sacrificed or would sacrifice friend relationships for reasons of a family nature, if the question were raised, also shows that competition with family roles becomes more noticeable as a person ages. Likewise, that single people more readily discuss their most intimate problems and thoughts with friends in comparison to married people lends some support to Hess's claim that role competition in the middle years competes with friendship in a central area, intimate communication. In addition, my finding that single people have the greatest tendency to have friends of their same age-generation can be accounted for by their having to seek out similar aged friends with role obligations more compatible with their own. Likewise, that younger people have friendships which manifest themselves somewhat more frequently outside the home and that older people meet their friends somewhat more at work suggest that younger people have less competitive friendship roles compared to older people, who are engaged in a wider variety of roles derivative from their greater centrality to the sphere of work.

Even on the basis of her own discussion, complementarity and fused friendship definitely are described as occurring at most periods of the human life cycle, as does substitution, when individuals are not wrapped up with kin. In essence, only her category of competition permits one to distinguish friendship during the middle years and among adolescent peers from other life periods. In brief, even in her own elaboration, Hess's role constellations, while suggesting differential role patterns for the different periods of human development, do not adequately differentiate the friendship roles for each stage of the life cycle. When I attempted to apply her categories as a conceptual framework to analyze my in-depth interviews, these concepts did not seem to sort out the main thrust of the social action in friendship at various stages of the life cycle. In only sixteen of my in-depth interviews did the concept of fusion relate the central role constellation of a person's friendships to his or her age. Complementarity and substitution were evident in only five cases, and competition in four. Indeed the factor of spatial proximity or propinquity, operating in four of my in-depth interviews, is related to fusion in that being a neighbor fuses with being a friend. Yet, propinquity puts more emphasis on the basis of meeting than on simultaneously playing different roles typical of a developmental stage. Even though these role constellations did not shed much light on the interpretation of each of my in-depth interviews, the notion of competition provides a plausible explanation for some of the aggregate differentials in my data.

Another problem with Hess's idea of developmental role constellations for friendship is its ahistoricity. As one woman tells us in this chapter, the liberalization and laicization of education in the Quebec Catholic schools carried over into the structure and content of language. Such an event might be clarified by the notion of complementarity in that her adequacy and performance of being a student was dependent on a democratized educational milieu. This environment was reflected in the egalitarian language of address and attitudes which relaxed her enough psychologically that her ability to learn was enhanced. In turn, this less stressful milieu created the possibility for her to become friends with her teachers and fellow pupils. To take this phenomenon out of its historical context robs it of its most meaningful aspect.

Shifting economic forces could very well shift the empowerment of age-grades. It could very well be that if elderly people must become politically and socially mobilized to maximize their social position, their friendships would once again face the competition derivative of roles more central to a society's economic life.

Notes

1. Engels, Friedrich, *The Origin of the Family, Private Property, and the State*, with an introduction and notes by Eleanor Burke Leacock. 1st Edition (New York: International Publishers, 1972).

2. See Lazure, Jacques, *Le jeune couple non-marié: une nouvelle forme de revolution sexuelle* (Montréal: Presses de l'université du Québec, 1975).

3. See "Single Parent Families by Marital Status and Sex of the Head, 1971," (Gauthier, Hervé, 1977, 119) [*Evolution démographique du Québec*, Office de planification et de développement du Québec]. Sources: OPDQ's estimation from Statistics Canada, Characteristics of Families by Marital Status, Age, and Sex of the Head, *Census of Canada, 1971*, 2.2-6, 93-718, table 51.

4. Ray, D. Michael, ed., *Canadian Urban Trends*. 3 vol. 1 (Toronto: Copp Clark Publishing, 1976), 207.

5. Hill, Frederick I., *Canadian Urban Trends*. 3 vol. 2 (Toronto: Copp Clark Publishing, 1976), 31.

6. Duchesne, Louis, *Annuaire du Québec 1979-1980*, Gouvernement du Québec. Ministère de l'Industrie et du Commerce. Bureau de la statistique du Québec (Québec: L'Éditeur officiel du Québec, 1980), 180.

7. According to the *Historical Statistics of Canada, Second Edition*,

> The number of decrees absolute granted in Canada has risen sharply as a result of the 1968 changes in divorce legislation. Divorces rose to over 57,155 in 1978 compared to an average of about 11,000 divorces per year over the period 1966-68. British Columbia's divorce rate was 326.7 per 100,000 population, and Alberta 310.4, the highest rates among the provinces. By comparison, Newfoundland and Prince Edward Island had the lowest rates, 75.0 and 110.7. ... Estimates based on divorce rates in 1971 indicate that about one-fifth of those persons who married between 15 and 25 (born during 1946-56) may obtain a divorce by the time they are 45. ... [It should be noted that] almost twice as many divorces were granted in 1977 to female petitioners as to males. See Leacy, F. H. *Historical Statistics of Canada: Second Edition*. Ottawa: Statistics Canada, 1981), 124.

8. For the cross-classification of marital status by age and sex groups for Quebec in 1971, see: de Grandmont, Pierre (publié sous la direction de). *Annuaire du Québec 1977/1978*. Gouvernement du Québec. Ministère de l'Industrie et du Commerce. Bureau de la statistique du Québec (Québec: L'Éditeur officiel du Québec, 1979), 352; 357.

9. See: Rubin, Zick, *Children's Friendships* (Cambridge, Massachusetts: Harvard University Press, 1980), 27.

10. Selman, Robert L., "The Child as a Friendship Philosopher," Chap. 9 in *The Development of Children's Friendships*, ed. Steven R. Asher and John M. Gottman (Cambridge: Cambridge University Press, 1981, 242-272); see: Bigelow, Brian J. and J. J. La Gaipa. "Children's Written Description of Friendship: a Multidimensional Analysis." *Developmental Psychology*, II, (1975) 857-858. Bigelow, Brian. J.,

"Children's Friendship Expectations: A Cognitive-developmental Study," in *Child Development*, 18 (1977).

11. See: Butkowski, Bill, *The Company They Keep: Friendship in Childhood and Adolescence* (Cambridge University Press: in press); Corsaro, William A., *Friendship and Peer Culture in the Early Years* Norwood (New Jersey: Ablex Publishing Co., 1985); Field, Tiffany, Jaipaul L. Roopnarine, and Marilyn Segal, eds., *Friendships in Normal and Handicapped Children* (Norwood, New Jersey: Ablex Publishing Corporation, 1984); Pogrebin, Letty Cottin, *Among Friends: Who We Like, Why We Like Them, and What We Do with Them* (New York: McGraw-Hill Book Company, 1987), 341-349.

12. Varagnac, A. in Maisonneuve, Jean, *Psycho-sociologie des affinités* (Paris: Presses universitaires de France, 1966), 104-105.

13. Hess, Beth. "Friendship," in eds. Matilda White Riley, M. Johnson, & A. Foner, *Aging and Society: A Sociology of Age Stratification* 3 (New York: Russell Sage), 1972, 389.

14. Pogrebin, Letty Cottin, *Among Friends,* xii; 341-367.

15. Vaz, E. W. "Middle-Class Adolescents' Self-Reported Delinquency and Youth Culture Activities," *The Canadian Review of Sociology and Anthropology/La revue canadienne de sociologie et d'anthropologie*, 2: February, 1965, 55.

16. Ibid., 56-57.

17. Sévigny, Robert and Pierre Guimond. "Psycho-sociologie de l'actualisation de soi. Quelques problèmes de validation," in *Sociologie et sociétés* 1-2 (Montréal: Les Presses de l'université de Montréal, 1969-70), 262.

18. Délude-Clift, C. and E. Champoux, "Le conflict des générations," in *Recherches sociographiques* 14, 1973, 164;168.

19. Sévigny, Robert and Pierre Guimond, "Psycho-sociologie de l'actualisation de soi. Quelques problèmes de validation," in *Sociologie et sociétés* 1-2 (Montréal: Les Presses de l'université de Montréal. 1969-70), 258.

20. Lucas, R. A., *Minetown, Milltown, Railtown. Life in Canadian Communities of Single Industry* (Toronto: University of Toronto Press, 1971), 184;185;215; 258;290;350;374-5.

21. Rubin, Lillian B., *Just Friends: The Role of Friendship in Our Lives* (New York: Harper & Row Publishers), 1985, 110.

22. Gurdin, Joseph Barry, "*Amitié*/Friendship: The Socio-cultural Construction of Friendship in Contemporary Montreal." Ph.D. diss., Department of Sociology, Université de Montréal, 1978, 340-347.

23. Maisonneuve, Jean, *Psycho-sociologie des affinités* (Paris: Presses universitaires de France, 1966), 208.

24. Matthews, Sarah H., *Friendship through the Life Course: Oral Biographies in Old Age* (Newbury Park: Sage Publications, 1986), 52-58.

25. Lambert, Wallace E., in eds. David Koulack and Daniel Perlman, *Readings in Social Psychology. Focus on Canada* (Toronto: Wiley Publishers of Canada Ltd., 1973), 33, 34-48.

26. Cicero, Marcus Tullius, *Essay on Friendship. Laelius De Amicitia*, trans. from the Latin with notes by Alexander J. Inglis (New York: The Platt & Peck Co., 1908), 65-66.

27. Maisonneuve, Jean, *Psycho-sociologie des affinités*, 107-111;513.

28. Ibid., 107.

29. *The Relationship between the Interviewees' and Respondents' Civil Status and Their Friends' Age-Generation Controlling for the Socio-Economic Status of the Interviewees and Respondents*

Friends' Age-Generation	Socio-Economic Class	Civil Status (Counts)			Total (Counts)	Total (%)
		Single	Married without Children	Married with Children		
Same Age	Blue Collar	19	6	18	43	18.22%
	White Collar	31	5	17	53	22.46%
	Professional	27	5	20	52	22.03%
	Subtotal Column %	77 70.6%	16 50.0%	55 57.9%	148	62.71%
Older Age	Blue Collar	5	4	3	12	5.08%
	White Collar	9	3	10	22	9.32%
	Professional	10	2	5	17	7.20%
	Subtotal Column %	24 22.0%	9 28.1%	18 19.0%	51	21.61%
Younger Age	Blue Collar	3	3	8	14	5.93%
	White Collar	3	2	7	12	5.08%
	Professional	2	2	7	11	4.66%
	Subtotal Column %	8 7.3%	7 21.9%	22 32.2%	37	15.68%
	Grand Total Column %	109 46.2%	32 13.6%	95 40.3%	236	100.00%

30. *The Relationship between the Interviewees' and Respondents' Civil Status and Their Friends' Age-Generation Controlling for the Gender of the Interviewees and Respondents*

Count Column %	Civil Status						Row Total
Friends' Age	Single		Married without Children		Married with Children		
	Male	Female	Male	Female	Male	Female	
Same	45 72.6%	33 68.8%	7 58.3%	9 45%	24 61.5%	32 54.2%	150 62.5%
Older	11 17.7%	13 27.1%	3 25%	6 30%	8 20.5%	11 18.6%	52 21.6%
Younger	6 9.7%	2 4.2%	2 16.7%	5 25%	7 17.9%	16 27.1%	38 15.8%
Column Total	62 25.8%	48 20%	12 5%	20 8.3%	39 16.3%	59 24.6%	240 100%

31. Délude-Clift, C. and E. Champoux, "Le conflict des générations," in *Recherches sociographiques* 14, 1973, 164;168.

32. *Question #19 "Have You Cultivated a Real Friendship with a Person Having Political Opinions Deeply Opposed to Your Own? A. Yes B. No." The Relationship between the Interviewees' and Respondents' Civil Status and Their Friends' Political Opinions*

Count Column %	Civil Status			Row Total
Friends' Political Opinions Different from Yours?	Single	Married with Children	Married without Children	
Yes	33 41.3%	12 70.6%	30 50%	75 47.8%
No	47 58.7%	5 29.4%	30 50%	82 52.2%
Column Total	80 51%	17 10.8%	60 38.2%	157 100%

Raw χ^2 = 5.03025 with 2 d. f.; Significance = .0809;

Number of Missing Observations = 18

33.

The Relationship between the Ethnicity of the Interviewees and Respondents Who Are Married with Children and Their Friends' Age-Generation

Count Column %	Ethnicity		
Friends' Age	French Canadian	English Canadian	Row Total
Same Age	18 49%	38 62%	56 57%
Older Age	5 14%	14 23%	19 19%
Younger Age	14 38%	9 15%	23 24%
Column Total Column %	37 38%	61 62%	98 100%

Raw $\chi2$= 0.7805; Significance = .001 with 2 d. f.

34. Question #10, "How Do Your Friendships Manifest Themselves Most Often?" The Relationship between the Interviewees' and the Respondents' Age-Generation and Their Manifestations of Friendship with Their Six Closest Friends

Count / Column %	Interviewees' and Respondents' Ages		
Manifestations of Friendship	Younger Age	Older Age	Row Total
By Invitations and Mutual Visits at Each Other's Home	251 26.1%	228 22.4%	479 24.2%
Through Conversations and Meetings outside Your Home, e.g., in the Street, a Cafe, etc.	215 22.3%	203 20%	418 21.1%
In Activities and Communal Get-Togethers away from the Job: Political or Social Activities	178 18.5%	190 18.7%	368 18.6%
Artistic or Sports Activities	167 17.3%	175 17.2%	342 17.3%
At Work[*]	38 3.9%	57 5.6%	95 4.8%
Others (Please Specify:)	114 11.8%	164 16.1%	278 14%
Column Total Column %	963 48.6%	1017 51.4%	1980 100%

Raw $\chi2$ = 13.35733 with 5 d. f.; Significance = .0203;
Number of Missing Observations = 25

[*]As the possible choice of "manifesting friendship at work" was accidentally left off the English-language questionnaire, the results must be read with caution. Despite this error, there is some evidence from question #9 that 19.8% of friendships began at work, the second most important locus of beginning close friendships, which did not vary significantly for those background variables studied. Yet, ethnicity did produce some variation in the results of question #7, for which many more English than French Canadians reported close friends in their same occupation.

35. Ishwaran, Karigoudar, ed., *The Canadian Family: A Book of Readings* (Toronto: Holt, Rinehart & Winston of Canada Ltd., 1971), 128. Also see: Bonin, Jacques. "La Socialisation," Chap. 9 in *Aliénation et idéologie dans la vie quotidienne des Montréalais francophones*, Vol. 2, eds. Yves Lamarche, Marcel Rioux, et Robert Sévigny, (Montréal: Les Presses de l'université de Montréal, 1973), 712-714.

36. Moreux, Colette, *Fin d'une religion? Monographie d'une paroisse canadienne-française* (Montréal: Presses de l'université de Montréal, 1969), 128.

37. Gurdin, J. Barry, "*Amitié*/Friendship: The Socio-cultural Construction of Friendship in Contemporary Montreal," 498-503.

38. Reiss, Ira L. "The role of sexuality in the study of family and fertility." Paper read at the conference on "Family and Fertility," sponsored by the Center for Population Research and the National Institute for Child Health and Human Development, June 13-16, Belmont, Elkridge, Maryland. Mimeographed, 1973.

39. *The Relationship between Where the Interviewees' and Respondents' Friends Were Met and Their Civil Status. Questionnaire: "#9. These Adult Friendships Came About through: ..." & Interview: "#4. Could You Tell Us How These Friendships Got Started and about How Old You Were When They Got Started?"*

Count Column %	Civil Status			
Adult Friendships Came about due to:	Single	Married with Children	Married without Children	Row Total
Being a Neighbor	40 26.5%	11 25.6%	30 25.2%	81 25.9%
In Military Service, in War, or in Captivity	5 3.3%	1 2.3%	8 6.7%	14 4.5%
Working or Coming into Contact on the Job Together	36 23.8%	8 18.6%	18 15.1%	62 19.8%
Having Similar Pastimes or off the Job Activities	15 9.9%	7 16.3%	13 10.9%	35 11.2%
Having Met through Your Wife (or Husband)	5 3.3%	6 14%	19 16%	30 9.6%
Having Met through a Common Friend	31 20.5%	7 16.3%	20 16.8%	58 18.5%
Chance (Indicate the Circumstances:)	19 12.6%	3 7%	11 9.2%	33 10.5%
Column Total Column %	151 48.2%	43 13.7%	119 38%	313 100%

Raw χ2 = 20.14635 with 12 Degrees of Freedom.
Significance = .0644; Number of Missing Observations = 31

40.

#12. Do You Discuss Your Most Intimate Problems and Thoughts with Your Friends? [Indicate Which One of the Following Three Descriptions Best Fits Each of the Friends:] A. Often B. Rarely C. Never." The Relationship between the Frequency of Interviewees' and Respondents' Discussion of Intimate Problems and Thoughts with Close Friends and the Civil Status of the Interviewees and Respondents

Count Column %	Frequency of Discussion of Intimate Problems and Thoughts with Friends				Row Total
Civil Status	Often	Rarely	Never	*A Tie	
Single	44 62%	13 39.4%	14 43.8%	3 60%	74 52.5%
Married without Children	3 4.2%	8 24.2%	3 9.4%	0 0%	14 9.9%
Married with Children	24 33.8%	12 36.4%	15 46.9%	2 40%	53 37.6%
Column Total	71 50.4%	33 23.4%	32 22.7%	5 3.5%	141 100%

Number of Missing Observations = 34; Raw $\chi 2$= 13.48166 with 6 d. f.; Significance = .0360

41. Bell, Robert R., *Worlds of Friendship* (Beverly Hills, California: Sage Publications, Inc., 1981), 135.

42. Rubin, Lillian B., *Just Friends: The Role of Friendship in Our Lives* (New York: Harper & Row Publishers, 1985), 147-148.

43. Gurdin, Joseph Barry, "*Amitié*/Friendship: The Socio-cultural Construction of Friendship in Contemporary Montreal," 1978, 604-615.

44. Pogrebin, Letty Cottin, *Among Friends,* 351.

45. Gurdin, Joseph Barry, "*Amitié*/Friendship: The Socio-cultural Construction of Friendship in Contemporary Montreal," 1978, 604-615.

46."#15. *Have You Sacrificed or Would You Sacrifice Your Friend Relationships for Serious Reasons of a Family Nature if the Question Were Raised? A. Yes B. No." The Relationship between the Attitude of Being Willing or Not to Sacrifice a Friend Due to Family and the Interviewees' and Respondents' Age*

Count Column %	Interviewees' and Respondents' Age		Row Total
Would You Drop a Friend for Serious Family Reasons?	Younger	Older	
Yes	28 31.1%	36 45%	64 37.6%
No	62 68.9%	44 55%	106 62.4%
Column Total	90 52.9%	80 47.1%	170 100%

Corrected $\chi2$ = 2.91389 with 1 d. f.; Number of Missing Observations = 5; Significance = .0878

47. "#12. *Do You Discuss Your Most Intimate Problems and Thoughts with Your Friends? [Indicate Which One of The Following Three Descriptions Best Fits Each of The Friends:] A. Often B. Rarely C. Never." The Relationship between the Age of Interviewees and Respondents and Their Discussing Intimate Thoughts and Problems with Friends*

Count Column %	Age of Interviewees and Respondents		Row Total
Frequency of Discussion of Intimate Problems and Thoughts with Friends	Younger	Older	
Never	16 18.6%	16 22.5%	32 20.4%
Rarely	14 16.3%	28 39.4%	42 26.8%
Often	52 60.5%	25 35.2%	77 49.1%
*A Tie	4 4.7%	2 2.8%	6 3.8%
Column Total	86 54.8%	71 45.2%	157 100%

$\chi2$ = 13.503 with 3 d. f.; Number of Missing Observations = 18; Significance = .01

48. See: Adams, Rebecca G. and Rosemary Blieszner, eds., *Older Adult Friendship: Structure and Process* (Newbury Park, CA: 1989); Kaufman, Sharon R., *The Ageless Self: Sources of Meaning in Late Life* (Madison: University of Wisconsin Press, 1987); Matthews, Sarah H., *Friendship through the Life Course: Oral Biographies in Old Age* (Newbury Park: Sage Publications, 1986). Here it should be noted that although I am underscoring the psycho-social importance of the style of "Friend-in-Mind" for the oldest of my interviewees, this style was actually most frequent among my interviewees between the ages of 31 and 60 [5/8 = 62.5 percent of those characterized by this style]; then among those between 15 and 30 [2/8 = 25 percent]; and least frequent among those between 61 and 76 [1/8 = 12.5 percent]. The style of the "Friend-in-Mind" was more often seen among professionals [4/8 = 50 percent] as compared to blue collar [2/8 = 25 percent] and white collar [2/8 = 25 percent] workers. It was observed more frequently among male [6/8 = 75 percent] as compared to female [2/8 = 25 percent] in-depth interviewees. Ethnicity did not create distinctions for this style, which was equally frequent among English Canadians [4/8 = 50% percent] and French Canadians [4/8 = 50%].

49.

The Relationship between the Number of Close Friends and the
Interviewees' and Respondents' Age

Count Column %	Interviewees' and Respondents' Age		Row Total
Number of Close Friends	Younger	Older	
0 Friends	2 2.2%	5 6.2%	7 4%
1 Friend	1 1.1%	6 7.4%	7 4%
2 Friends	8 8.7%	9 11.1%	17 9.8%
3 Friends	15 16.3%	9 11.1%	24 13.9%
4 Friends	11 12%	11 13.6%	22 12.7%
5 Friends	16 17.4%	11 13.6%	27 15.6%
6 Friends	19 20.7%	7 8.6%	26 15%
7 Friends	13 14.1%	6 7.4%	19 11%
8 Friends	1 1.1%	6 7.4%	7 4%
9 Friends	2 2.2%	4 4.9%	6 3.5%
10 or More Friends	4 4.3%	7 8.6%	11 6.4%
Column Total	92 53.2%	81 46.8%	173 100%

Raw $\chi2$ = 19.89660 with 10 d. f.; Significance = .0302; Number of Missing Observations = 2

50. Beauvoir, Simone de, *La vieillesse: essai* (Paris: Gallimard, (1970) 1972), 472-473.

51. Bell, Robert R., *Worlds of Friendship* (Beverly Hills, California: Sage Publications, Inc., 1981), 178.

52. Ibid., 183.

53. Hess, Beth. "Friendship," in *Aging and Society: A Sociology of Age Stratification* 3 (New York: Russell Sage), 1972, 389.

54. Ibid., 362.

55. Ibid., 369; 370; In this respect, it is significant that my in-depth interviewees and questionnaire respondents reported overwhelmingly putting aside some time for their friends at any cost, even if their jobs were most time and energy consuming. Their ethnicity, gender, age, and civil status made no difference in this regard. However, there was a very slight trend for blue collar workers to admit not putting aside time for their friends more than people of other socio-economic statuses, as can be seen in the following table, which replicates Jean Maisonneuve's question #14:

"Even If Your Work Is Most Time and Energy Consuming, Do You Try to Put Some Time Aside for Your Friends at Any Cost? A. Yes B. No." The Relationship between the Interviewees' and Respondents' Socio-economic Status and Allocation of Some Time for Their Friends

Count Column %	Socio-economic Status [SES]			Row Total
Do You Set Some Time Aside for Your Friends at Any Cost?	Blue Collar Worker	White Collar Worker	Professionals	
Yes	37 84.1%	62 93.9%	57 95%	156 91.8%
No	7 15.9%	4 6.1%	3 5%	14 8.2%
Column Total	44 25.9%	66 38.8%	60 35.3%	170 100%

Raw $\chi 2$ = 4.67269 with 2 d. f.; Significance = .0967;

Number of Missing Observations = 5

Chapter Seven

Men, Women, and Close Friendship

The Debate

Today an acrimonious debate is raging as to whether women or men make better friends and whether their differences in friendship are brought about primarily by biology, culture, society, or psyche. This debate is not new. In his own time, Cicero summarized the contrasting views of the Greek philosophers regarding this matter in the following passage:

> Others are said to hold a view even more unworthy of man ... that it is for self-protection and aid that friendships are to be sought, not for any feeling of kindness or affection. And so they say that the less self-confidence and strength a man possesses, the more likely he is to desire friends. Hence it is that women, being as they are but frail creatures, more eagerly seek the protection of friends than men, the poor more eagerly than the rich, and those who have suffered some reverse of fortune more than those who are considered fortunate. O wondrous wisdom! For those who rob life of friendship, the best and sweetest gift of the gods, must be considered as robbing the universe of the sun. For what is that freedom from care of which they prate?[1]

Contrasting to Cicero's view, many classical and modern poets, writers, philosophers, ethnographers, and sociologists would share Georg Simmel's early sociological claims, in the quote below, on the greater propensity under simpler social conditions for men, compared to women, to make and maintain close friendships.[2] Indeed they often enunciate these differentials even more sharply.[3]

> Women are the less individuated sex, variation of individual women from the general class type is less great than is true, in general, of men. This explains the very widespread opinion that, ordinarily, women are less susceptible to friendship than men. For friendship is a relationship entirely based on the individualities of its elements, more so perhaps even than marriage; because of its traditional forms, its social rules, its real interests, marriage contains many super-individual elements that are independent of the specific personalities involved. The fundamental differentiation on which marriage is based, as over against friendship, is in itself not an individual but a species differentiation. It is therefore understandable that real and lasting friendships are rare at the stage of low personality development; and that, on the other hand, the modern highly differentiated woman shows a strikingly increased capacity and an inclination toward it, both with men and with women.

Let me emphasize that there is no unanimity among the classics in sociology about this matter. Differing from Simmel, Tönnies sees the lesser differentiation of simpler social forms as more conducive to friendship, as he makes clear in the following passage:

> The common people are similar to women and children in that to them family life, along with neighboring and friendship, both of which are closely related to family life, is life in and of itself ... For women, the home and not the market, their own or friend's dwelling and not the street, is the natural seat of their activity.[4]

Unlike Tönnies' but similar in outcome to Simmel's position, although different in the biological basis of its explanation, is Lionel Tiger's thesis. He argues that males form stronger and more stable bonds, which are based on biological and social substrata. But Tiger's critics point out that women's friendships were not praised or studied on account of males' domination of societies. In modern times, if women had no need to bond, their voluntary organizations would fall apart.[5]

In his essay on the psychoanalysis of the social bond, the French psycho-sociologist, Eugène Enriquez, goes so far as to assert that women have a tendency to mistrust friendship, affection, and tenderness when these feelings aim to avoid meeting with the body. "Woman will suspect, therefore, all feelings with an inhibited goal."[6]

In feminist literature, women are depicted as being more capable of friendship because of their long socialization to the role of expressiveness. Neo-Freudian feminists trace the origins of this expressiveness to little girls' not having to abruptly break away from their mothers in the manner that the Oedipal drama forces little boys to do. A version of this position was put forward in an article that appeared in a popular Canadian periodical: "Anywhere you find women you will find them more committed to their friends and associates, more able to spend time and energy on them, more likely to stay in contact."[7]

In a similar vein, Lillian B. Rubin argues:

> Women have more friendships (as distinct from collegial relationships or workmates) than men, and the difference in the content and quality of their friendships is marked and unmistakable.[8]

About the superior quality of women's friendship, Rubin and MacDonald concur.[9]

Feminists observe that the process of socialization in Western cultures inculcates different friendship patterns for the two different genders. MacDonald clearly makes this case:

> Differences in friendship making patterns between males and females begin to be noticeable soon after the neighborhood sandbox set breaks up and little girls and little boys emerge. ... For little boys, these years are a direct continuation of the sandbox years, the fort-building years, the chemistry-set years.
> Their social life is haphazard, always connected with action and doing: organized hockey, football, baseball, boys scouts, the YMCA, and just plain hanging around some guy's basement or street corners ...

As long as a guy could do something with another guy, even if it was just kicking a can around a street lamp or shooting pool, nobody really analyzed or criticized. You changed companions when your interests changed and you rarely questioned that you would have companions when you wanted them. You didn't think about being popular with the guys, you thought about competing with them, trying to stand out in the crowd somewhat as an individual.

In contrast, the little girls would suddenly tighten up under constant scrutiny. She went to school, she helped around the house. Even if she played basketball for an hour after school, worked on the class yearbook, spent three hours on Saturday afternoon window shopping, there was hardly a moment not accounted for. Girls simply were not allowed to "hang around," and come in and say "Oh, I was just out with the girls".[10]

While MacDonald loosely sketches the difference in boys and girls socialization that accounts for differences in their adult friendships, Lillian B. Rubin identifies a psychological process that produces them. In her explanation:

... This split between the emotional and the erotic components of attachment in childhood has deep and lasting significance for the ways in which we respond to relationships--sexual and otherwise--in adulthood. For it means that, for men, the erotic aspect of any relationship remains forever the most compelling, while, for women, the emotional component will always be the more salient. It's here that we come to understand the depth of women's emotional connection to each other--the reasons why non-sexual friendships between women remain so central in their lives, so important to their sense of themselves and to their well-being. And it's here that we can see why nonsexual relationships hold such little emotional charge for men.[11]

Rubin's scenario makes for good reading, but other empirical studies would deny the great difference between the young sexes which she has portrayed. Thus, two male social psychologists found that the number of friendship dimensions used by male and female children is not significantly different.[12] Likewise, in the Quebec context of this study, two other male psycho-sociologists recorded that "being able to count on others"--one of the major components of friendship--is observed more frequently among boys than girls in the country and Montreal regions in Quebec. So too, in an urbanized context, girls have a greater feeling of being left to themselves or have less knowledge of how their society and milieu can, in need, come to their aid.[13]

In addition, marketing research has found French Canadian women:

> ... to be far more skeptical and mistrusting of individuals and business. ... In a way the mistrust of the French Canadian has some justification in fact. For the francophone, *La Survivance* has been a part of life since 1760. So it is not surprising that she approaches the world with more than the average amount of skepticism.[14]

Despite these ethnic differences, a meta-analysis of 172 studies of socialization suggests that only in the area of parental encouragement of sex-typed activities--out of 19 areas studied--do parents make systematic differences in their rearing of boys and girls.[15]

The Feminist Case for Gender Differences in Friendship --and Its Critiques

Lillian B. Rubin outlines a feminist psychoanalytic explanation for the differences in the friendships of men and women. Basing her interpretation on the fact "that mother, a woman, is almost always the primary caregiver in infancy," she argues that:

> When, as a small child, a boy must separate himself from his mother, it is the anatomical differences between them that can give some reality to the need, that make reasonable this demand that otherwise feels so *un*reasonable.
> To protect against the pain wrought by this radical shift in his internal world, the child builds a set of defenses that will serve him, for good or for ill, for the rest of his life. This is the beginning of the development of the kind of ego

boundaries so characteristic of men--boundaries that are fixed and firm, that rigidly separate self from other, that circumscribe not only his relationships with others but his connection to his inner emotional life as well.

For a girl, the formation of a gender identity requires no such wrenching breaks with the past. Since she need not displace the internalized representation of mother, there's no need to build defenses against feeling and attachment, therefore no need for the kind of rigid boundaries a man develops as a means of protecting and maintaining those defenses. This means that, as a women, she'll develop ego boundaries that are more permeable than a man's--a fact of paramount importance in the management of both her internal life and her external one.

It is in this part of the developmental scenario that we see the birth of the empathic and relational capacities for which women are so well known, and which serve them so well in their friendships. Since she and her mother are the same gender, a girl never has to separate herself as completely and irrevocably as a boy must. As a result, her sense of herself is never as separate as his; she experiences herself always as more continuous with another; and the maintenance of close personal connections will continue to be one of life's essential themes for her. Consequently, she'll preserve the capacity, born in the early union with mother, for participating in another's inner life, for sensing another's emotional states almost as if they were her own--the capacity that, in an adult, we call empathy.[16]

Drawing on Rubin's and other feminist writers, Letty Cottin Pogrebin--a founding member of *MS.* magazine--devotes several chapters of her book to the differences between the friendships of men and women and the possibility for friendships between them.[17] Her description is similar to Lillian B. Rubin's and Luise Eichenbaum's and Susie Orbach's.[18] More sociologically nuanced is the work of Rebecca G. Adams and her psychologist co-author, Rosemary Blieszner, and the English sociologist, Pat O'Connor.[19] Some male writers such as psychiatrist, Terry A. Kupers, agree with the feminist view that men's friendships are lacking in comparison to women's.[20]

Davidson and Duberman found that while men had higher levels of trust for their best friends than women, they took fewer risks and were more impersonal in their conversations with them. They also interpreted their data as meaning that men interacted superficially with and put little into the personal and interactional bases of their friendships. Having observed these sociologists' scornful attitude toward men at a conference, I am left wondering how objective their classification of their data really is. When men talk with their close friends about their jobs or sports or a social issue, they frequently reveal personal information and emotions. Such exchanges, combined with their everyday knowledge of how their friends have acted in past situations, solidify men's feelings of trust in their friends.[21]

Other biased descriptions have interpreted men's friendships as morally inferior. For example, Stacey Oliker writes:

> The women I interviewed do practice another form of discretion, however. They scrupulously distinguish arenas of individual liberty from those of communal responsibility, and they deliberately practice reserve in the former. Now it may be that men practice this form of discretion as well. The women I spoke to, however, believed that their husbands, and men in general, do not develop many nonkin ties that would elicit the same degree of communal responsibility. And however close or attached their friendships may be, if men practice more concealment-- more discretion, in Simmel's sense of the term--they have a narrower terrain of moral exchange and fewer opportunities for commitment and constraint.[22]

I feel sure that Quebec's male architects of the Quiet Revolution and much progressive legislation that resulted from that period would be offended at Oliker's suggestion they did not develop nonkin ties that elicited the same degree of communal responsibility as women. Moreover, I believe that most fair-minded women would also acknowledge the intellectual and legislative accomplishments of such men. Although I have not interviewed such greater and lesser civic lights for this study, the men whom I did interview manifested equal moral exchange and no more concealment within their friendships than women. Moreover, after interviewing many men--particularly older ones-

-James Maas reached almost diametrically opposed conclusions to these feminist writers. He concluded:

> There is as much variation and intensity in men's friendships as there is in women's ... One result of those conversations, however, was that I set aside my questions about *men's* friendships. My main interest now is the way *each man* relates to his own friends. If I've derived anything from the interviews, it's not that men have more or fewer friends than women, it is that men relate to their friends in their own ways.[23]

Basing my analysis on many different quantitative and qualitative pieces of evidence in the following pages, my conclusions regarding gender differences in friends are much closer to those of Maas than those of Eichenbaum and Orbach, Pogrebin, Rubin, or Oliker. However, Maas's recorded conversations with men evidenced a much greater difficulty in men's forming and maintaining close friendships compared to my interviewees. Relevant to this contrast is that the depth and importance of friendship in his interviewee who was a French immigrant to the United States evoked resonances of the older French-speaking Canadian males in my sample. In this vein, it is significant that Lillian Rubin rejects an explanation based on biological origins for the differences between the friendship patterns of men and women. Her argument for the strong differentials in the friendship patterns of the genders is based on socially structured differences in learning. My comparative data from Montreal suggest that part of the variance Rubin and Pogrebin attribute to gender can be better explained by ethnicity in Montreal. Furthermore, it is noteworthy that in his original Italian-language book and in its French translation, Francesco Alberoni analyzes friendships between men and between a man and a woman in history and literature. These friendships included Hamilton's in Henry Miller's *Tropic of Capricorn*, Marx's and Engel's, Rudolf von Jhering's and Carl Friedrich von Gerber's, Frederic Dannay's and Manfred B. Lee's and others'.[24]

Basing herself on studies of Bowlbyan attachment theory, Pat O'Connor reasons that male children would be more likely to be provided with a "secure base" because interaction with male children is more responsive and extensive, as they are more highly valued. This contention, largely built on one study published in 1972, is refuted by a 1991 meta-analysis of 172 studies of parents' differential socialization of boys and girls. Hugh Lytton and David M. Romney, Professors at the University of Calgary, Alberta, Canada, found that, in North American studies, the only one area of socialization out of nineteen "to display a significant effect for both parents is encouragement of sex-typed activities. In other Western countries, physical punishment is applied significantly more to boys. Fathers tend to differentiate more than mothers between boys and girls."

Pat O'Connor ignores the possibility that boys as a group may have a stronger predisposition for exploration (in the sense of roaming from a secure base, not necessarily being more interested or anxious). From Bowlby's attachment theory, no prediction can be made as to whether or not the attractiveness of the child will be increased by a mental concept held by the adult caregiver, such as knowing the child is male. Even though the differences were nonsignificant in most socialization areas, Lytton and Romney acknowledge that "the direction of these differences (e.g., more prohibition of aggression for girls, more warmth for girls) were in the expected direction, and indicate some slight differential treatment that may amplify children's existing behavioral tendencies. Such differential treatment may indeed result in greater inhibition of aggression or greater nurturance in girls."[25] It is a matter for further empirical research to discover whether adult interactions with male or female infants is affected significantly by their mental concept of the child's sex or by the infant's set of particular behaviors (regardless of the infant's sex), such as activity level, amount of eye-to-eye contact, and reaction to being touched or held.

Even when sensitive to the importance of childhood socialization, sociologists have generally insisted that social structure and culture, that are constantly in flux, explain major features of on-going human interaction. In sociological literature, the peer group has been seen to play a powerful role in socializing the human being from childhood through adolescence. Moreover, in cross-cultural studies, girls' more nuturant behavior and greater interaction with adults and children have been interpreted as derivative of the greater household and childcare roles ascribed to them rather than their continuing to engage in attachment behaviors because they are less attached to a secure base, as suggested by O'Connor's hypothesis.

When considering Pat O'Conner's contention, it behooves us to consider 1990 census data from Statistics Canada to take notice of striking social and cultural changes. These data show that women have seen their salaries increase more rapidly (3.2%) than their male counterparts (1.3%) in Quebec in the last five years studied. Moreover women make up 20% of the best paid workers in 1990 compared to 14% in 1985. In terms of upper level managerial positions, women have gone up 44%, even though their average salary of $48,609 remains considerably less than males at $79,463 in these kinds of positions.[26] Would a society that so devalued little girls be willing to make such dramatic changes in such a short period of time? A more plausible argument would be that Quebec has been less generous toward children of both genders, even though the governments of Quebec and Canada have been more generous than their southern neighbor, the United States. Even if the income of Quebec single parent families has gone up 11% in five years, 47% of poor families have a single female head of household. If childrearing were considered an equally valuable occupation to computer programming and compensated accordingly, these figures on single parents and their children living in poverty would, no doubt, be reduced dramatically.

The Quebec Context

The particularities of Quebec history most certainly contributed to special patterns of friendship in Quebec. The Catholic world-view prescribed the role of *la guardienne du foyer* to the woman. In this position, a woman would have to form most of her friendships in the family circle. But being limited to family does not necessarily imply a lack of close friends.[27]

Some authors have accorded a special importance in the interaction between mothers and daughters in Quebec literature. Like the daughter, Canada, "though ... initially overcome by hostility ... can never fully abandon her very strong feelings of attachment and continuity with the mother."[28] Moreover, in Canadian literature the man has been described as more "gentle and retiring" than in American literature.[29]

With the advent of urbanization and industrialization, the traditional patterns of English- and French-speaking Montrealers have changed. Some of the older configurations surely linger on. Yet, friendships became open to more voluntaristic, more diffuse, less institutionalized and less ritually defined content as the church and rural society lost their grips on the population. To what extent do these forces still exist and how do they operate? Let us examine my study of contemporary Montreal friendships for these answers.

How Gender Bore on Friendship in Montreal of the 1970s

If contemporary women are so much better at communicative behavior than men and if they feel a need to communicate much more than men, then one would expect that they would turn to women much more often as close friends. In the same fashion, if men have had to suppress their emotional selves and at most have action-oriented friendships, then a researcher would not expect males to report very many close friends or to describe communication as an important part of their close friendships. Moreover, stated in Terry A. Kupers even more extreme version,

> Discussions of men's friendships traditionally begin with the way men have learned to distance each other and keep their cards close to their chests as they climb up the hierarchy in a dog-eat-dog world. Then there is the issue of homophobia. And, of course, it's all true.[30]

Contrary to what one would expect if Rubin and Kupers had identified a universal law predictive of gender differentials in friendship, in Montreal both women and men reported that they had more close friends of both genders than only all female, all male, or no friends.[31] Similarly, according to writers such as Rubin and Kupers, both men and women should prefer women friends because they are better listeners, more supportive, and more tender. Thus one would expect women and men to have many more women friends in order to fill a need to have someone better at communicating. Asked in one way, people answered that complete gender homophily characterized around one-fourth of the male and one-fifth of the female friendships. Contrary to what we would have expected on the basis of Rubin's theory, males showed a slightly greater degree of all-male-friends than do females all-female-friends. A few more females than males said that they had no friends. My finding that both males and females had around 65% of their close friends of both sexes supports Simmel's contention that the highly differentiated, modern person has a "strikingly increased capacity and inclination toward close friendship."

Friendship between members of the opposite sex is a subject of popular interest and folk wisdom.[32] Traditionally, it has been held that male-female relationships can have only sexuality as their ultimate object. In modern times popular articles, talk shows, and personal conversations continued to be intrigued by this issue. The fact that more Montrealers have at least one friend of the opposite sex is a good behavioral indicator that men and women in the real world of an urban, industrial society deal with each other not only as sexual objects. Furthermore, some interviewees said that they were conscious of the gender of their friend only on occasions. This is not to say that sexuality is absent from the relationship of friendship between members of the opposite sex. Rather, holding the double statuses of man-friend and woman-friend toward each other, they learn to negotiate the place of sexuality in their developing relationship.

Even though most persons have at least one close friend of the opposite sex, a larger number of their close friends are of their same sex. This state of affairs is evidence that the principle of homophily is at work. Males choose males more frequently than females for close friends. In like fashion, females have females more often as close friends. This explanation of like-attracting-like remains a more economical explanation for social actors' choosing others of their same gender more often as close friends than some of the entertaining, recent psychological accounts.

In trying to comprehend the psycho-social forces working in favor of gender homophily among close friends, Jean Maisonneuve framed two questions which I repeated to Montrealers. These items, #17 and #18, inquired,

> Have you developed at a given moment of your life relations of strict friendship with a person of the other sex? a. yes b. no. Even if this has not happened to you, do you think that a true friendship is: a. possible between a man and a woman? b) is impossible between a man and a woman?[33]

More of my interviewees and respondents replied that it is possible to have a friend of the opposite sex than actually had an opposite-sex friend at the time they answered the question or in the past. Around a third of my respondents had one or more friends of the opposite sex at the time of the interview or had had a relationship of strict friendship with a person of the other sex during the course of their lives. There were no significant differences between younger or older males or females of English or French Canadian ethnicity or of blue or white collar working or professional socio-economic groupings in this regard. This outcome is particularly captivating because the literature portrays working class women as having a more conservative sex role ideology, which would lead them to construe male-female friendships as romantic relationships.[34] My empirical finding that class does not make a difference in persons' conceiving of or of actually having close friendship across the sexes is consistent with Simmel's theory in that further differentiation in society would lead to greater similarity in the friendship patterns of women and men because the egalitarianism in friendship choice spreads to all classes.[35]

Gender similarity in the choice of the majority of a person's friends is the case in both Quebec and the rest of North America. People are aware that each gender has more close friends of the same gender, but they do not find this state of affairs to be irregular or something to be overcome.

Feminist ideology has had a considerable influence in urban Montreal. In the 1970s feminism may have been somewhat relatively less salient in comparison to some aspects of women's liberated thinking in the largest North American megalopolis. By this observation I mean that the Montreal of the 1970s turned out some excellent guides to birth control by health care workers, had small activist groups of the various currents of feminist thought, showed some advances of women into politics and the professions, and the like; however, the extent of membership and variety of these movements seem to have been less widespread than in the largest cities of the United States of America, although it may have been comparable to cities of similar size in the United States. It is informative to recall that women in Quebec did not get the right to vote until 1940. Although section 15(1) on Equality Rights of the *Canadian Charter of Rights and Freedoms* forbids discrimination on the basis of sex, the discussion of this dramatic change in the press or electronic media in Quebec was rather moderate until it was signed in 1981. However, by the 1990s, Seymour Martin Lipset recalls that Canadian women now participate in higher education and the labor force more than Americans and express greater liberalism in sexual behavior, which has resulted in a lower birth rate, especially in Quebec. He explains these differences on the basis of the lesser strength of traditional religious values about gender in Canada as compared to the United States. On the other hand, Quebec feminists have argued that the "Yvettes Phenomenon," the political impact of more traditional women, has displayed real political muscle in recent elections.[36]

If solidly lower-middle class women were going out for their "night with the girls" in the mid-1970s, they did not fall into this sample, or if they did, it did not strike them as an important element to discuss when dialoguing on their closest friends. In seven years of residence in Montreal, I noted somewhat increasing numbers of lower-middle and working class women going out together to restaurants, parks, discos, Man and His World, etc., but in comparison to Boston, Detroit, Philadelphia, or San Diego, this segment of the population seems somewhat smaller. And my qualitative observations are supported by a comprehensive analysis completed in the mid-1970s that found that Canadian culture's greater conservatism, respect for authority, and ascription contributed to family and gender behavior being "more traditionalistic ... than in the United States." Consistent with these values were data which showed that Canadian women in all categories represented a much smaller percentage of the labor force in comparison to the United States.[37]

This modal, matter-of fact experience of the bearing of gender on friendship is well-established in several accounts of women in my data. In contrast to Americans, very few of the interviewees in Montreal used the language of interpersonal relations to clarify why gender homophily and friendships across the sexes occur. Montrealers told about concrete circumstances in which the gender differential between themselves and their close friends was present. Listen to this eighteen year of age, female, English Canadian, CEGEP (junior college) student, whose father is a manager for a large company and whose mother is a housewife:

> I'd say that Wayne is my closest friend; he's closer than Audrey is, mainly because he's a guy. I'm much more at ease with a male than I am a female because in high school--like I say--I had a few bad run-ins with girls, and it sort of leaves you weary of other females; so naturally I find that I was a lot closer to Wayne than Audrey, like I was open with both of them, but more so with Wayne, and I'd turn to him before I'd turn to Audrey. ... When I first met them I knew Wayne before I met Audrey, and I remember the first day when she walked in and saw Wayne with his arm around me like a big brother, you know? Like I could

see the jealousy in her eyes, but it turned out that she is just like that naturally. But after that, we got to know each other, and we grew a lot closer, and we found we could talk openly with each other--freely. We used to depend on each other. And our good times--like we used to work on different committees; like they used to work on the newspapers, and I used to work on the radio. We used to play games with each other--football games for the two organizations and, ah, we'd go to a lot of parties together, and we'd just go horseback riding or something like this, you know, we were together quite constantly. We used to play bridge in this coffee shop like most university students do and cut classes ... .

The subject of the relationship of gender to close friendship has been explored in various media. Director Don Owen and Producer Julian Biggs recount a friendship between two working class, English Canadian women in their late teens and early twenties. Their film is called *Notes for a Film about Donna and Gail*. When they come to Montreal, the somewhat older of the of the young women is more concerned with the day-to-day practicalities of earning a living and keeping up her room. The younger and more physically attractive adolescent is dependent and temperamental. The older friend is not very pretty, but is supportive, if not motherly, to her sometimes almost childlike friend. Eventually, they get employment as seamstresses in a clothing manufacturer. They enjoy spending most of their time just hanging around town being together, going swinging in the park, fixing their hair, or decorating a room which they eventually take together near the inner city. When the older friend takes an interest in a young man and displays her greater sexual permissiveness, her younger friend feels hurt. She takes out her pain in absenteeism and finally in a desperate destruction of the decorations and order of the room they share. That scene terminates their relationship.

From a sociological perspective the film throws light onto the spontaneous liking which grows that happens in some friendships. It depicts how the objective similarity in gender did not become subjectively experienced until one of the young women did not wish to place as much time, interest, or energy as her friend in going out with young men. Even if the older woman was enacting the social role of "finding a man" that is traditionally expected of young women, the disagreement which arises in this friendship had more to do with the choice of one friend to share her affection with another person. Likewise, the choice of the younger woman to favor maintaining their dyadic close friendship over imitating her friend's behavior in undertaking an intimate relationship with a man can be viewed as a different preference rather than a childlike, inwardly directed activity associated with some of her other immature idiosyncrasies such as still sleeping with a stuffed animal. But the relationship's end indicates that their friendship was built on some incompatible conduct. One of the young women is overly dependent on her friend, while her older friend does not examine that her quest for a partner of the opposite sex need not necessitate her dropping her female friend. These problems could have been pointed out to these friends and reframed to prevent the break up of this close friendship.

Although this movie dramatizes the pathos of friends' breaking up, its images convey the message that these single working class women have fewer close friends because they hold more traditional sex role stereotypes. In this regard, my study found no significant class differences in having a close friend of the opposite sex. Thus, the film's hint that working class women may eschew friendships in order to find a marital partner is probably truer of the past than of the present Montreal configurations of friendship. Among the interviewees of each socio-economic class, the proportions of male and female friends were extremely close.[38]

More important than class is age, for older persons have fewer friends of both genders and more frequently have no friends.[39] Despite these facts, neither older women nor men had significantly fewer close friends of the opposite sex or believed that friendship across the sexes was less possible compared to younger people in Montreal, although Rubin claims that "cross-sex friendships are likely to be most common in a younger population."[40] In brief, the major impact of age on friendship appears to be on its attenuating the number of close friends, and in so doing, the number of close friends of the opposite sex grows smaller.[41]

Almost 65 percent of my interviews and respondents chose closest friends of both genders rather than limiting themselves exclusively to men or women friends or abstaining from close friends. Approximately 15 percent had only male friends; 12 percent had only female friends; and approximately nine percent had no friends.[42]

English Canadians had more close friends who were males and French Canadians more close friends who were females.[43] These differences can be accounted for in several ways. In the sociological literature of the period when I gathered my data, the French Canadian father was portrayed as playing a rather authoritarian role.[44] Greater degrees of instrumentalism on his part may lead to greater degrees of prestating expressive behavior with the mother, which, in turn, would subsequently lead to the association of the father's instrumental behavior with males and the mother's socio-emotive behavior with females. It would follow, then, that greater degrees of friendship would be manifested as expressive behavior towards females among French Canadians. On the other hand, I clipped an article of "pop-sociology" that suggests that men communicate more easily with women and women more easily with men. In my English translation, Langevin confides:

> ... I communicate more easily with women and I prefer their company (even Platonic) to that of men. The great majority of persons whom I consider as my friends are women. I confide more easily in them than men and most of them avowed to me that the converse was true. I consider them more fun, less uptight, more energetic, more natural, more courageous, and more honest too regarding themselves. (Here again, the women that I know say they prefer the company of men for similar reasons).
>
> Finally I note that contact for me is easier with women, and especially it is enriching, because the "bullshit" that goes on among men (business, the rat-race, competition), and which often impedes all intimate communication, rarely goes on between a man and a woman. Still I hear three of my friends tell me that they have enough of

competition between women that too often blocks them from having other than superficial relations with persons of their sex and that they can count on the fingers of their right hand the women who know them as several men know them.

I was going to say it: the men who really know me (and whom I know) can be counted too on the fingers of my (left) hand, while the women that I see again more than three times know me well. Also I believe (finally I hope) that it is mutual.[45]

Recall the previously reviewed market research describing French Canadian women as being more mistrusting? Two different methods of analysis I used led me to different conclusions. I found no significant differences between them and others regarding Maisonneuve's category of fidelity, which includes trust.[46] However, when I analyzed these same data by protothematic analysis, there were a few significant differences, including one about trust, which came to light. The second protothematic division, comprising items such as "depending on, loyalty, counting on, relying on, sticking by, etc.," characterized English Canadian women's definitions significantly more than French Canadian women's. In addition, the tenth prototheme reveals a very strong tendency for English Canadian women's definitions of friendship to emphasize "love, affection, etc.," more so than French Canadian women's. Compared to French Canadian males, English Canadian males' definitions underscored that friendship was "something that should last a long time" and that a friend was a "person you are with a lot of the time," my sixteenth prototheme. The theme of understanding and acceptance, my third prototheme, is significantly more important among English Canadian females than males, but there are no significant differences in this area among French Canadians of the different genders. There is also a strong tendency for English Canadian males, compared to English Canadian females, to emphasize "helping out in time of trouble," the concern of my seventh prototheme. No such differences were noted between the genders for French Canadians. Finally, French Canadian males stress the physical side of friendship, prototheme nineteen, to a significantly greater extent than French Canadian females.[47] Although not crossvalidated by content analysis, protothematic analysis points to ethnicity's constructing many of the differences in the cognition of friendship concerning dependability, love, fidelity, understanding, helping out, and physicality. Gender produced six statistically significant chi-squares out of the 35 items on the La Gaipa instrument dealing with the psychological underpinnings of friendship. Women found the following traits of friendship to be more important than men: "Concerned with my welfare and helps promote it"; "Considerate of my feelings"; "Thinks my ideas are important"; "Stands by me through anything"; "Advice given when asked for"; "Feels that I am an important and interesting person." However, as the results of these different methods produced inconsistent results, I may not reliably attribute any significant differences to either gender or ethnicity in the construction of these varying written definitions of friendship.

In short, if the newspaper report of the market research suggesting that French Canadian women are more mistrusting of others has any truth in it, it could be that this initial lack of trust is limited to the marketplace or initial interpersonal encounters.

It has been claimed in feminist writings and some social science that expressive behavior leads women to ponder their interpersonal relationships more than men. If this difference is true, women should report asking themselves the various questions on Maisonneuve's questionnaire more often than men. However, using question #24 as an indicator, I discovered more men than women said that they often asked themselves such questions, while more women than men said that they sometimes think about these matters. Slightly fewer women than men never wondered to themselves about their own close friendships.[48]

The Fear of Homosexuality Impeding Close Friendship

In much social scientific, liberationist, and popular writing about close friendship, the fear that such closeness between two persons of the same sex may be a sign of a homosexual relationship has been a recurrent theme.[49] Generalizing on this topic in the U.S.A. of the 1950s, Talcott Parsons related this structuring of affect in friendship to its economic base.[50]

Close friendship may be perceived as having a sexual element to it regardless of the gender of the friend. When close friends are of the same sex, society may express its resentment of being shut off from the relationship, especially if the close friends possess some attribute that is marginal to the group such as being outstanding in success or ability. If close friends are also marginal to a group, the group may apply strong pressure against them. For instance, the socio-cultural constraint on homosexuality may be indirectly maintained by insinuating that two close friends of the same sex are homosexual even though this is not the case. The young man who illustrated the style of neighbor friend told me in French:

> ... It was in secondary school that we began to get to know one another quite well, given that, not because we had a common enemy, but it was almost the case, that there was another guy we knew whom we didn't like, and who didn't like us ... But he, the other guy, had the chance of having the gang on his side, you know. That meant that he had strength in the final analysis ... At that time he called, he had found a killer of a word in the dictionary then ... that really got around. He found the word, "eunuch." ... Then he broke something of mine, a thermos ... We didn't really know the meaning of the thing, which made us look it up in the dictionary. ... So it was really funny, you know, because the fact that I constantly hung around with Jean-Paul, that he was all the time with me, you know, we were squarely taken for homosexuals in the strongest sense of the term. ...

In the case of two close friends of the opposite sex, society looks at the friendship as a mask of a love relationship or a heterosexual encounter. In referring to friends of the opposite sex, Jean Maisonneuve brought to our attention the model of skepticism or suspicion evident in history and custom for the times when gallantry or marriage were the only alternatives for friendships between men and women. But Max Weber's review of the writing on friendship among the early Protestant theologians makes it amply clear that such suspicion also applies to close friendship between men. The eminent sociologist wrote:

> ... Combined with the harsh doctrines of the absolute transcendentality of God and the corruption of everything pertaining to the flesh, this inner isolation of the individual contains, on the one hand, the reason for the entirely negative attitude of Puritanism to all the sensuous and emotional elements in culture and in religion, because they are of no use toward salvation and promote sentimental illusions and idolatrous superstitions. ...
>
> It comes out for instance in the strikingly frequent repetition, especially in the English Puritan literature, of warnings against any trust in the aid of friendship of men. Even the amiable Baxter counsels deep distrust of even one's closest friend, ... Only God should be your confidant.
>
> ... Every purely emotional, that is not rationally motivated, personal relation of man to man easily fell in the Puritan as in every ascetic ethic, under the suspicion of idolatry of the flesh. In addition to what has already been said, this is clearly enough shown for the case of friendship by the following warning: "it is an irrational act and not fit for a rational creature to love any one farther than reason will allow us... It very often taketh up men's minds so as to hinder their love of God" (Baxter, *Christian Directory*, iv, p. 253). We shall meet such arguments again and again.[51]

Besides this suspicion against close male friendship in Catholicism among the Jansenists, who had an important influence on the Church in Quebec, a much earlier rule against friendship in the medieval monasteries prompted Aelred of Rievaulx to write *Spiritual Friendship* to defend and promote its innocence and purity.

Writing again in the 1960s of the relationship between opposite sex friends, Jean Maisonneuve believed that there was a more permissive model evolving through mixing members of the opposite sex at all levels of daily life.[52]

By the 1970s, when I undertook my study of friendship, there was empirical evidence being amassed that supported my qualitative observations that sexual norms were in a period of great flux.[53] The normative standard of that new sexual morality promoted an ethic according to which friendship could be built on sexual attraction and activity as well as its other traditional expectations and behaviors. The code of the 1970s encouraged hetero-, homo-, and bi-sexuals to eroticize the society to maximize collective happiness.

In Michel Tremblay's play, Luc, a now successful actor, puts his finger on this new ethic in speaking to his former homosexual lover, Jean-Marc, "I fuck left and right, [but deep down inside], I come to make a difference between my feelings and desires. That's it."[54] In so doing, he had the deepest conviction that he had not been unloyal to his friend and lover. Despite the hype given to this new morality, a tension existed between the different sexualities and seemed to function well only among those who maintained a pluralist vision of mutual respect and live-and-let-live. The eroticization of close friendship placed a new unit of meaning on the older definition of the relationship and redefined the sexuality of its members.

A good example of these trends may be gleaned from Montreal's newspapers of the period. The local homosexual press, influenced by various liberationist ideologies, ran columns entitled "Friends" and "*Le Club des Amis pour Tous.*" The friends referred to in these papers were persons advertising their own physical appearance and personalities, hobbies, professions, interests, sexual tastes, characteristics they desired in another person and an address to contact them. These entries took on the format of newspaper advertisements and varied in content from persons seeking sexual encounters to lasting love relationships. In some respects this usage of the word, "friend," resembled the billing of beer, clothing, and other consumer items as "friends" which I recorded during the field observations, and in format was quite like ads for relationships, usually heterosexual, found in *The Montreal Star, Le Coureur d'Aubaines*, and *Le Jour*, but not in *Le Devoir* or *La Presse*. They were discreetly announced in *Le Montréal Matin* and *Le Journal de Montréal*. During this period *The Gazette* ran listings of organizations for homosexuals but no ads for individual "friends" were noted. Even though these popular cultural changes were very real, it behooves us to keep them in proper perspective.

This sexualized version of friendship starkly contrasted to two other contemporary consumer-directed friendship media found in the Montreal of the 1970s. *The Friendship Book* has no passage in its allegoric, pietistic style which gives the slightest idea of how the sex of a person might relate to friendship.[55] Likewise, the more philosophical, thoughtful gift-book, *To Be a Friend: Sayings and Verses Celebrating the Beauty of Friendship* has no reference to gender's contributing to friendship.[56] These two works represent the Aristotelian type of friendship in contrast to a modernized Platonic version propagated by the folkways of the Age of Narcissism.

To inquire into this matter, I adopted a double-tracked strategy. I designed one set of "objective" or "close ended" items for the respondents to my written questionnaire and one set of "subjective" or "open ended" questions. In this analysis--which I omitted from my doctoral thesis for reasons of space and discretion--I will "triangulate" or "crossvalidate" the information from these two sources, and refer to other related surveys. In the in-depth-interview I asked,

> Does sexuality enter or has sexuality in all of its various forms come into play in each of your various close friendships? What is and what ought to be the role of sexuality in intimate friendship?

And, in the course of our open-ended conversation, my interviewers and I asked specifically about the role of touch (tactility) in the interviewees' close friendships.

On the written questionnaire I sought the following responses for *each one of the respondent's closest friends up to a maximum of ten*, although to be brief here I will list only the form of the question for the first friend:

4-8. Circle the Following Responses That Correspond to Your Experiences: 1 = yes, often; 5 = no, never:

FRIEND 1

4. My friend and I hold hands.	1 2 3 4 5
5. My friend and I embrace each other.	1 2 3 4 5
6. My friend and I kiss each other.	1 2 3 4 5
7. My friend and I make love without orgasm.	1 2 3 4 5
8. My friend and I make love with orgasm.	1 2 3 4 5

Tactile behavior characterizes between and third and a fourth of the friendships observed, while there is a sexual component to approximately fifteen to twenty percent of the friendships studied. Both sexuality and tactility decrease as friends become less close.[57]

No background variable produced any significant differences in these tables. Thus, several widely held beliefs are disputed by these results, but here I will take up only the one relevant to the present discussion of the influence of gender on closest friendship. If women display greater expressive behavior, this trait should also carry over into friendship. At the least it would be expected that women would hold hands, embrace, and kiss their closest friends more than men. Yet, my female and male respondents displayed remarkably similar tactile behavior.[58]

It will be surprising to many that a notable minority of my interviewees would reveal that they had frequently made love with or without orgasm with their closest friends. However, a deeper analysis reveals that such behavior was most likely with the closest friend. As I will shortly corroborate with qualitative data, I interpret this outcome to be evidence of the "boy friend/girl friend, *petit(e) ami(e)*," style of friendship. Yet, this pattern provides evidence that sexual mores were changing to permit such interaction at least with the closest heterosexual friend among my interviewees.

How do I know these figures do not point to a greater permissiveness of homosexuality among close friends in Montreal? First of all, although I and my other interviewers sensed some degree of tension in the interviewees' responses to this question, to our great surprise both men and women of all ages were unusually frank in their answers. Hear what a few of them had to say about this matter. You will recall the elementary school teacher and mother in her thirties, of English Canadian background, who resides on Montreal's "West Island." She replied:

> Before I married sexuality entered into all my friendships with young men [Ha. Ha. Ha.] but not with young women. This never interested me, but I was always interested in the fellows with whom I went out. But true to the traditional form, when I met the young man who was to become my husband, this became a completely singular attraction and has remained so for thirteen to fourteen years. In knowing both men and women, I find very little sexual thoughts enter into my knowledge of either sex. I will say that on occasion some man who is a very good-looking man in my eyes, I see this as a sexual attraction in a fantasy world because I'm, perhaps, old enough and experienced enough to know that the realities are not nearly as glamorous as our dreams, so quite often I'll come home and kind of ponder somebody I have met and think, "My, why do I like that person, and do I have physical feelings towards that person?" Many times when it is a husband, the reason I like that husband is because of the attitude I see him portraying towards his own wife which makes me think of him as a husbandly, masculine person within that context, and were I to be involved with him, he would be a different person ... This doesn't happen very often. ... My husband and I usually have a laugh over it.

The English Canadian, male, police officer in his thirties, whom we have also met before, was described by his interviewer as "a very sensitive person." His interviewer described him in the following words,

> He is a policeman who believes he should get to know people better, so he takes courses in human relations and humanities. He also thinks his fellow policemen should. He is a policeman, a human being, a friend to people, and a buddy, and not classified as a pig. ... All I can say is that it is too bad that we don't have more policemen like him serving us.

In answering this particular question, this officer was more inhibited than the school teacher above; he replied:

> Well, a fellow would need a quart of booze to drink before answering that one. Sexuality is quite the thing today. Take, for example, James and his wife and myself and my wife. When we get together, there certainly isn't any sexuality discussed. We don't look on each other's wives to the point we think we could make them or anything of that nature. We just respect each other, and we just never talk about the problem of sexuality. The only time that it will come up is probably when we have a good joke to tell, but even then, it's vulgarity more than sexuality.

One of my oldest interviewees, in her late sixties, the mother and wife who recounted how she thought of her grown children as friends, notices an evolution in custom in this regard, "Well, I'll often touch a person, heh." I interjected, "I noticed you kissed your girl-friend good-bye."
She responded,

> Well, every time I see her I don't do that. She's just come back from abroad. She's been away for six weeks. She just dropped in tonight.

I inquired, "Is there an English, Scottish, Irish difference?"
She answered,

> No, ... I think it's an individual thing because I'll kiss her good-bye, or I'll touch John Doe next door. He's quite ill at present, and I'll go in and see him and bring him eggnog. When I leave ... , I'll often touch him like this. "Bye, John. I'll see you tomorrow." ... Well, I do this to children; when we greet friends that I haven't seen for a long time--I mean male or female.

Remembering her description of one of her closest friends, I inquired, "Was Jenny cool?"
She responded,

> I didn't kiss her good-night when I'd leave her. I'd say, "Good-bye, Jenny." ... I mean I would if I hadn't seen her for

a while. No, I mean I smile or pat, or I mean I would if somebody feels a bit distressed, I'll lean over and pat their hand. I do it unconsciously just like you do with a child.

I pushed, "Could this develop into a love relationship?"

She retorted,

> Oh, Dear God, No! Because you settle those things mentally a long time before. ... It isn't exciting or anything like that in the sense when, but I greeted Henry last night, I and my husband was with me, I kissed him good-bye, ... -- and we don't see each other that often. There's much more of it in recent years than there used to be years ago. ... Well, I noticed it in my parents friends. I never saw, perhaps, I wasn't looking for it either, when the male, you know, husband and wife came into greet my father and mother, I never noticed the husband kissing my mother. ... whereas now ... .

Quite to my surprise, the stereotypes of the very cold English Canadian and the very warm French Canadian did not seem to be supported in these qualitative accounts anymore than they were in the quantitative data. Equally surprising was the honesty and openness with which people spoke of the sexual element in close friendship. The unemployed, young, French Canadian male who had worked at a variety of jobs told me in French that there are few sexual or "sexed" elements in his friendships, but he is aware that it is repressed.

> There is little contact between us. We hug; we have wrapped our arms around [one another]. We do not kiss ... more and more, I don't know, but anyway it seems to me that it is lacking, you know.

One of his close male friends, of European background, he hugs occasionally, and he regards him as being warm. Indeed, this friend has touched him a lot, although he does not respond in kind. But with his close female friend, they experience the gamut of tactile and sexual experience:

> With [her] it has an enormous importance. I think that it
> has a very big place, just the contact. We hug one another
> very, very tenderly. It's practically stroking. It's very, very
> sensual. It's funny because whether or not we make love,
> [we stroke one another].

With his other close male friend whom he has known for years and
with whose sister he has had a sexual relationship, he relates:

> We wrap our arms around [one another] a lot. We talk a
> lot. ... Once it was summer ... we went out dancing. Then
> [while] I was shooting the bull with him, I held his hand or
> just grasped our hands tightly. It was really fun. It was
> funny, anyway, we expressed tenderness and affection
> toward one another.

Another twenty-two year old, married, French Canadian woman who
has a junior college (CEGEP) diploma in theater and who has held a
variety of odd jobs from being a waitress to a researcher was quite open
with Michèle. She said that she is aware of the sexual attraction that
exists between her and her same sex friend but has never engaged in
any sexual activity with her. Speaking in French, she put it this way:

> I'll answer right away. It's really spontaneous. You can say
> it ought to be this or that way for everyone to act like she
> wants. I remember sometimes when I saw my chum,
> Ginette, come. We liked one another so much that she told
> me, "Damned, if I were a lesbian." I said to Ginette, "We
> ought to try it." She was afraid she would feel badly
> afterwards. That's it. We both had the urge, you know. I
> was curious to [do] it. I am still curious, but I have never
> done it. Among other things I remember when I hadn't seen
> Ginette for a long time I was more attracted to Carol. Yes,
> ... when I saw Ginette I lunged at her; then I said to her
> that I would have liked to make love I was so happy to see
> her. It was not just the desire. It has surely never
> happened, and then I think that she would have reacted
> badly. I do not know if I am a latent lesbian. In any case, I
> know that I have this desire no matter what.

Speaking of one of her male friends who is not her husband, she reported,

> My chum, Richard, he is the only chum with whom I have already slept. That has absolutely not disturbed our relationships; it has even strengthened them. Yes, once, I said, "Richard, it stops there. It's as simple as that."

Although the variety in this experience of tactility and sexuality in close friendship is tremendously rich, I will conclude with one example of a very low degree of these behaviors. The interview is with a man in his mid-forties, a French Canadian husband and father of three children, who has been for ten years a representative of a company that installs machines. Conversing in French, Ms. Verrette inquired if, on his birthday, his close friends would give him a kiss. He curtly replied, "No." Not stopping with his answer, she asked, "Or embrace you?" At this point he spelled out what he meant.

> No, that's pretty much the European style. ... A good handshake, heh, when it has been a long time you haven't seen each other, a good friend whom you respect, you give him a good handshake. For women it's the same. You give a little peck, but among men, I believe it's pretty much the European mentality.

Exploring how this style affected his other relationships, Ms. Verrette asked about what he does with his children.

> Heh, the two youngest, I hug them, yes, before going to bed in the evening. They'll come hug me, but the oldest who's 14, he's started to give me his hand. He's a little inhibited. ... When I come home from work, then I see him. It's not that I don't see him. It's not that he doesn't want to, but he's inhibited. I'm not inhibited. ... I hug him or shake hands. He feels ... that he's becoming a little man.

Gay men and lesbians may mention people of their own sexual orientation more frequently as friends, but this relationship may not be sexual.[59] The one openly gay man in my sample, a fellow in his mid-thirties and a manager in financial affairs, put it this way:

> Sexuality is only one thing in a day. It's not much. Because if one makes friends only for these things, it's not good. It's certain that everyone needs sex, but if the goal of making friends [were that it wouldn't be worth it]. I hug Norma. When I see Henry, "Hi, little guy. How are you?"

Because people in general were open to talk about sexuality and tactility per se in their close friendships--with great concern on my and my other interviewers' parts for the utmost confidentiality--I believe they would have been willing to discuss homosexuality had it played a role in their close friendships. Indeed, I was amazed at the openness of some very influential men who fell in my random sample to report having found their close friends physically attractive, but drawing the line with their close friends in not entertaining sexual relations with them. Here I may note that I had to sign one legal document concerning the confidentiality of my interview over and beyond my ethical, sociological statement. On the other hand, the fact that up to ten close friends are characterized by at least substantially low rates of making love with or without orgasm with their close friends may indeed point to at least infrequent homosexual contacts among the respondents to my written questionnaire.[60] When I designed my instrument, I felt that it would have unnecessarily blocked communication in the rest of the interview if I had directly asked for the gender of the friend with whom a sexual relation was shared. However, to go beyond my present inferences would require such probing.

Here I should note that in his posthumous book, Allan Bloom examines the place of erotic attraction in close friendship.[61] In Bloom's review of the deep friendship between the French philosopher of friendship, Michel de Montaigne, and the French Renaissance humanist, Étienne de La Boétie, he observes that erotic attractions competed with their friendship, but that friendship came first for them.[62] According to Bloom, their friendship was about philosophy, their two souls dedicated to a mutual search for the truth. In contrast, in discussing Shakespeare's literary characters, Hal and Falstaff, it is Bloom's opinion that they:

> are soul mates, and without any touch of solemnity, they prove the possibility of a purely spiritual association, based upon mutual admiration of intellectual gifts, without necessary admixture of anything bodily, or of money, or of power. Those things are present, but they are not the core of the experience. It is, really, an erotic relationship, the attraction based on the potential for shared insight.[63]

The Girl-Friend/Boy-Friend, or *Petit(e) Ami(e)* [Style D]

A not uncommon tale that is typical of tactile and sexual behavior reveals another style of friendship, that of "the girl-friend/boy-friend, *petit(e) ami(e)."* In this style, we can identify the role of the sexual component in close friendship that was reported at least at low levels among around a quarter of the respondents to my in-depth interview. This young, single male is nineteen years of age, of English Canadian Protestant background, with fifteen years of formal education. At the time of the interview he was a student at McGill University. His father is the director of a large corporation and his mother a housewife. All of his three closest friends are near his age. Sam is 20, Claire is 18, and Susan is 19, but there is a little diversity in their socio-economic backgrounds. Claire and Susan are upper-middle class as is my interviewee, although Claire is less well educated, and Sam comes from a middle-middle class family. Claire is Catholic; Susan is Protestant; and Sam is Jewish. Even though the two young women do not know one another, Sam knows both of them. In answering my questions about how each of his best friendships fills certain psychological needs, Martin shared the following thoughts:

> Well, a combination of Sam, Susie, and Claire fills my physical, emotional and mental needs; Susie and Sam through being school friends. I can talk about things at an academic level, and a higher education level. Having sex

with Claire fills my physical needs, and an emotional
friendship between both Susan and Claire fills the female
side of an emotional relationship, and as far as a male
emotional relationship, Sam and I are very close.

To my question on the role of sexuality in intimate friendships,
Martin replied:

> ... I have had a few intimate friendships in which sexuality
> does not enter into it at all, such as friendships with males
> and with some females whom I wasn't sexually attracted
> to at all. It has come into play with others.

My interviewer probed, "Do you have sex with Susan and Claire?"

Jokingly, Martin added,

> And Sam? I had sex with Susan a year and a half ago until
> we broke up and after that we had stopped having sex, but
> I don't think it really affected our friendship. We are still as
> close ever; the only thing which could affect our friendship
> is us being a little far away right now. With Claire, I am
> having sex with her right now, and, I think, if anything, it is
> enhancing our relationship."

In speaking of his women friends, he says that Claire "is a little
warmer than Susan would be" and the way Susan acts on things "is
based on knowledge she has gained through an academic sort of sense.
But she is a very good-natured person, very easy going, sympathetic,
understanding." Sam has "a good sense of humor, and he is a fun loving
person, loves a good laugh."

Martin's friendship with a sexual component was disturbed to some
extent by his use of illicit substances, although he felt it important to
underscore that his intake of drugs had had both a negative, and, by
inference, a positive influence on two of these closest friendships. Martin
continues,

> Well, there was a point at one time where I was getting
> very, very nervous from smoking too much hashish, and, I
> think, that this was affecting my relationship with a few

friends, but what I did was I quit smoking for a month, and it sort of cleared out my head quite a bit, and this solved a lot of problems. ... I wasn't seeing Susan very often at the time I had this problem, and I'm actually, I'm never ... stoned or buzzed or high of whatever you want to call it when I see Susan because Susan doesn't smoke, and I would like to be on the same level as she is. Sam and I have been getting high together for quite sometime, so we are quite used to each other, so that wasn't any problem either. But with Claire there was a slight problem in that I was very nervous and a little bit insecure from smoking too much around her, and this was creating what we could call "bad vibes" between us, so I decided to quit for a month, and it really helped things quite a bit.

Although the names I have assigned to this style of friendship are evidently sexist, they are nevertheless the frequent glosses people in Montreal used to refer to this style of relationship in the mid-1970s. Moreover, they reflect the meshing of philia and eros characteristic of this style of friendship. Readers will also note that these words denote youth, even though they are glosses used by people of all ages. As we can see in the case of Martin, sexuality and communication of various kinds stood out differently in each of his closest three friendships. His former sexual bond with Susan did not preclude their maintaining and even further developing an exchange of ideas and understanding once their physical bond had ended. She, who had been his "girl friend," is now his close friend. Such a style of relationship may account for most of the frequency of the low levels of "making love with and without orgasm with friends" reported in the tables earlier in this chapter. Likewise, Claire is currently his girl friend--that is, he is involved in a relationship of intense sexual experience accompanied by having good times at parties and sports. She even gives him more material things than he would like. His male friend, Sam, shares some of his most intense psycho-physical moments in their common indulgence in hashish. The researcher is left to infer that the physiological base of this drug experience may represent a symbolic and real medium of psychic and physical communion that are also characteristic of profound sexual experience.

Indeed, the drug behavior may be a subculturally normatively appropriate way to express such closeness among males. Likewise, humor, the outcome of which is laughing, lights up the mind while it shakes the body--thus providing a channel for these male friends to fulfill such a psycho-physical need.

The boy friend/girl friend style is not limited to late adolescents or young adults. Although other labels such as "my woman friend" or "my male friend" and the like may be less sexist replacements for these other nomers, the greatest numbers of single, divorced, and widowed people of all ages continue to employ these words. When *eros* and *philia* are combined in the same relationship, these two constituents tend to exert forces that tug the relationship between these two poles.

Conclusion

Maisonneuve explains the social process of same sex bonding on the basis of identification which causes the members of one sex to consider those of their same sex as like themselves, and those of the opposite sex as unlike themselves. The culture reinforces this bond of sexual community through separating the kind of world boys and girls experience in their everyday life. In the first seven years, there is little sexual separation. This is also seen in girls' and boys' not displaying a significantly different number of friendship dimensions. After the seventh year, when goals, groups, and leaders appear, sexual segregation begins, and objective physiological differences become an obstacle to exchange of common goals and feelings. Adults' inculcation of boy-girl differences contributes to this splitting of the sexes. Then, in adolescence, individual friend and love choice becomes the rule. Some individuals experience no erotic tensions; others are confused over them; and other dissociate spiritual love and sexual attraction. At this stage intersex friendship steps up, even if the adolescents are still feeling pressure to reduce the ease and warmth of intersexual relations. "In this fashion the adolescent often begins to feel as rather 'normal' a sexuality without love, and the experience of amorous friendships as almost marginal."64

Since Maisonneuve's work, the general public has become more exposed to a model of sexuality without love, but, at the same time to a model of love-friendships. In the Montreal of the 1970s changes toward eroticizing friendship took place only among small segments of the population. What is more common is a style of friendship--that of the boy friend/girl friend, *le / la petit(e) ami(e)*. In this style sexuality typically accompanies communication and helping out each other. It is evolving along with new glosses for it from a typically pre-marital cross-sex intimate relationship into one that can take place among predominantly singles of all ages.

Notes

1. Cicero, Marcus Tullius, *Essay on Friendship. Laelius De Amicitia*, trans. from the Latin with notes by Alexander J. Inglis (New York: The Platt & Peck Co., 1908), 33.

2. Simmel, Georg, *The Sociology of Georg Simmel*, trans. and ed. Kurt Wolff (New York: Free Press, [1908] 1964), 138.

3. See: Brenton, Myron, *Friendship* (New York: Stein and Day Publishers, 1974 (1975)), 142-143.

4. Tönnies, Ferdinand, *Community and Society*, trans. Charles Loomis (East Lansing: Michigan State University Press, [1887] 1957), 168; 62.

5. Brenton, Myron, *Friendship*, 144-145.

6. Enriquez, Eugène, *De la horde à l'état: Essai de psychanalyse du lien social* (Mayenne: Éditions Gallimard, 1986), 120.

7. MacDonald, D., "Sex and Social Participation." in *Chatelaine*, 47 (March 1974): 24-26.

8. Rubin, Lillian B., *Just Friends: The Role of Friendship in Our Lives* (New York: Harper & Row Publishers, (1983) 1985), 129.

9. MacDonald, D., "Sex and Social Participation." 24-26.

10. Ibid.

11. Rubin, Lillian B., *Just Friends*, 102-103.

12. Bigelow, B. J. and J. J. La Gaipa, 1972.

13. Sévigny, Robert and Pierre Guimond. "Psycho-sociologie de l'actualisation de soi. Quelques problèmes de validation," in *Sociologie et sociétés* 1-2 (Montréal: Les Presses de l'université de Montréal. 1969-70), 259.

14. Sheldon, Michael, "Francophone Women Are Different," *The Montreal Star*, 25 September 1976:H-I.

15. Lytton, Hugh and David M. Romney, "Parents' Differential Socialization of Boys and Girls: A Meta-Analysis," in 109 *Psychological Bulletin* (1991):267-291.

16. Rubin, Lillian B., *Just Friends*, 91; 95-96.

17. Pogrebin, Letty Cottin, *Among Friends: Who We Like, Why We Like Them, and What We Do with Them* (New York: McGraw-Hill Book Company, 1987, 251-340).

18. Eichenbaum, Luise and Susie Orbach, *Between Friends: Love, Envy, and Competition in Women's Friendships* (New York: Viking, 1988).

19. Adams, Rebecca G. and Rosemary Blieszner, eds., *Older Adult Friendship: Structure and Process* (Newbury Park, CA: Sage Publications, 1989); Blieszner, Rosemary and Rebecca G. Adams, *Adult Friendship* (Newbury Park, CA: Sage Publications, 1992); also see: O'Connor, Pat, *Friendships between Women: A Critical Review* (New York: The Guilford Press, 1992).

20. Kupers, Terry A., "Menfriends: Others Shy away from and Define as 'Too Needy' the Man Who Wants to Build Close Male Friendships," *Tikkun: A BiMonthly Jewish Critique of Politics, Culture and Society*, March/April 1993, 54.

21. My first experience of this ideological rejection occurred when I attended Lynne R. Davidson's and Lucile Duberman's paper read at a session on His and Her Perspectives on Intimacy at the American Sociological Association. While their paper, "Same Sex Friendships: A Gender Comparison of Dyads," was interesting and well presented, they claimed that there was a dearth of research on friendships by and about

men. When I pointed out that, contrary to their claims, a large body of such sociological literature on friendship existed--including my then new Ph.D. thesis--some of which came to different conclusions from their work--they appeared to be angry and defensive toward me. Their subsequent published paper also does not seem to hear what the men they studied had said other than on a superficial level.

22. Oliker, Stacey J., *Best Friends and Marriage: Exchange among Women* (Berkeley: University of California Press, 1989), 120. Although I had published on friendship in journals and had presented at conferences of American sociology before her book (See: Gurdin, J. Barry, 1979a,b; 1982; 1983; 1984; 1986; 1988), Stacey J. Oliker does not cite any of my work. Similarly, I had informed Professor Lillian Rubin at her Northwestern University talk about my work well before she published her book on friendship, but she does not address any of the issues that I had raised or Professor Jean Maisonneuve had raised before me. Likewise, another sociologist, Rebecca Adams, expressed interest in my work and corresponded with me but fails to cite any of my work. In a fairer vein, the popular feminist authors, Letty Pogrebin, and sociologist and writer, J. L. Barkas, do cite my work. At several annual meetings of the American Sociological Association during the 1980s papers were given that dealt with friendship and their authors claimed that hardly any research had been done on friendship in sociology, even though they failed to cite many pieces of research available in J. L. Barkas' excellent, published bibliography and other sources. Nor does the English sociologist, Pat O'Connor, cite S. N. Eisenstadt and L. Roniger's 1984 book, even though it was published by Cambridge University Press. A male sociologist sympathetic to the feminist perspective, Peter M. Nardi, came up to me after I had given my talk on styles of friendship at the American Sociological Association in 1989, and requested a paper for his book. I mailed him a proposed article. When I did not hear from him for some time, I wrote him, and he returned to me my material. When his book appeared, no mention of any of my published or unpublished work was acknowledged. Despite these trends, when a scholar knows of published work in her or his field that

presents countervailing evidence to some of her or his arguments, it can be considered bias or poor scholarship when this other work is ignored. One cannot read the current feminist writings on friendship without being aware of such gender-polarized discourse and its derivative social action. In my own writing and research I attempt to address all sociological research on friendship as well as major books in related fields regardless of the gender of its author.

23. Maas, James, *Speaking of Friends: The Variety of Man-to-Man Friendships* (Berkeley, CA: Shameless Hussy Press, 1985), 135.

24. Alberoni, Francesco, *L'amicizia* (Milan: Garzanti Editore s.p.a., 1984), 22; 152-154; 154-157; 158-159. Alberoni, Francesco, *L'amitié*, trans. Nelly Drusi (Paris: G. P. Ramsay, 1987).

25. Ibid., 32. Also see: Lytton, Hugh and David M. Romney, "Parents' Differential Socialization of Boys and Girls: A Meta-Analysis," in 109 *Psychological Bulletin* (1991):267-291;287.

26. See: Whiting and Edwards (1975), cited in ibid., 287; Also see: Paré, Isabelle, "Montréal, capitale de la pauvreté: 22% des Montréalais vivent sous le seuil de la pauvreté; plus qu'à Saint-Jean, Terre-Neuve," *Le Devoir*, 14 avril 1993, A-1, A-8.

27. Gurdin, Joseph Barry, "*Amitié*/Friendship: The Socio-cultural Construction of Friendship in Contemporary Montreal," Ph.D. diss., Department of Sociology, Université de Montréal, 1978, 506-550.

28. Seymour Martin Lipset, *Continental Divide: The Values and Institutions of the United States and Canada* (New York: Routledge, 1990), 63. Also see: Mary Jean Green, "Writing in a Motherland," (French Department, Dartmouth College, Hannover, N.H., 1984). I questioned the well-known writer of short stories about Montreal, Mavis Gallant, about Mary Jean Green's metaphor on Michael Krasny's call-in talk-show on KQED (National Public Radio) in San Francisco on October 7, 1993. She found that the notion was an interesting, academic one, but had not really given it much thought.

29. Seymour Martin Lipset, *Continental Divide*, 64. Also see: McGregor, Gaile, *The Wacousta Syndrome: Explorations in the Canadian Landscape* (Toronto: University of Toronto Press, 1985), 137, 143-147.

30. Kupers, Terry A., "Menfriends," 54.

31. *The Relationship between the Gender of the Interviewees and Respondents and the Gender of the Interviewees' and Respondents' Closest Friends*

Count Column %	Gender of the Interviewees and Respondents		Row Total
Friends' Gender	Male	Female	
Male and Female Friends	58 66.7%	55 62.5%	113 64.6%
Only Male Friends	21 24.1%	5 5.7%	26 14.9%
Only Female Friends	3 3.4%	18 20.5%	21 12%
No Friends	5 5.7%	10 11.4%	15 8.6%
Column Total	87 49.7	88 50.3	175 100%

Raw χ^2 = 22.30177 with 3 d.f.; Significance = .0001

32. Gurdin, Joseph Barry, "*Amitié*/Friendship," 1978, 63.

33. Maisonneuve, Jean, *Psycho-sociologie des affinités* (Paris: Presses universitaires de France, 1966), 514.

34. Gaskell, Jane S. "The Sex-role Ideology of Working-class Girls," in *The Canadian Review of Sociology and Anthropology*, 12, 4, 1975, 460.

35. Gurdin, Joseph Barry, "*Amitié*/Friendship," 1978, 425-426.

36. Seymour Martin Lipset, *Continental Divide*, 191. Also see: Jean, Michèle, Jacqueline Lamothe, Marie J. Lavigne , and Jennifer Stoddart, "Nationalism and Feminism in Quebec: The 'Yvettes' Phenomenon," in *The Politics of Diversity*, eds. Roberta Hamilton and Michèle Barrett (London: Verso, 1986).

37. See: Brenton, Myron, *Friendship* (New York: Stein and Day Publishers, 1974), 146. Also see: Seymour Martin Lipset, *Continental Divide*, 189.

38. Gurdin, Joseph Barry, "*Amitié*/Friendship," 1978, 405.

39. Ibid., 383.

40. Rubin, Lillian B., *Just Friends*, 209.41.

41. *The Relationship between the Age of the Interviewees and Respondents and Their Beliefs and Realities of Having Opposite-Sex Friends, Controlling for the Gender of the Interviewees and Respondents*

Count Column % Ideas and Realities of Having Friends of the Opposite Sex	Female		Row Total
	Age of the Interviewees and Respondents		
	Younger	Older	
Having One or More Friends of the Opposite Sex	33 29.7%	26 28.6%	59 29.2%
Having Developed at Least One Strict Friendship with a Person of the Opposite Sex during One's Life	35 31.5%	30 33%	65 32.2%
Believing That a True Friendship Is Possible between a Man and a Woman	43 38.7%	35 38.5%	78 38.6%
Column Total	111	91	202
Column %	55%	45%	100%

Number of Missing Observations=3; Raw $\chi2$=.05599 with 2 d. f. Significance=.9724

Count Column % Ideas and Realities of Having Friends of the Opposite Sex	Male		Row Total
	Age of the Interviewees and Respondents		
	Younger	Older	
Having One or More Friends of the Opposite Sex	37 33%	24 28.9%	61 31.3%
Having Developed at Least One Strict Friendship with a Person of the Opposite Sex during One's Life	33 29.5%	21 25.3%	54 27.7%
Believing That a True Friendship Is Possible between a Man and a Woman	42 37.5%	38 45.8%	80 41%
Column Total	112	82	195
Column %	57.4%	42.6%	100%

Raw $\chi2$ = 1.35429 with 2 d. f. ; Significance = .5081

42. Gurdin, Joseph Barry, "*Amitié* / Friendship: The Socio-cultural Construction of Friendship in Contemporary Montreal," 1978, 378.

43. *The Relationship between the Gender of the Interviewees' and Respondents' Closest Friends and the Ethnicity of the Interviewees and Respondents*

Count Column %	Interviewees' and Respondents' Friends' Gender		Row Total
Ethnicity of the Interviewees and Respondents	Male	Female	
French Canadian	91 25.3%	111 33.8%	202 29.4%
English Canadian	269 74.7%	217 66.2%	486 70.6%
Column Total	360 52.3%	328 47.7%	688 100%

Corrected $\chi2$ =5.662862 with 1 d.f. ; Significance=.0173

44. Garigue, Phillipe, *La vie familiale des Canadiens français* (Montreal: Les Presses de l'université de Montréal, 1962).

45. Langevin, Serge. "L'amitié homme-femme, ça se peut!" 4, 9 *Nous* (Montréal: Nous Magazine Limitée, 1977), 72.

46. Gurdin, Joseph Barry, "*Amitié* / Friendship: The Socio-cultural Construction of Friendship in Contemporary Montreal," 1978, 227, 228, 235.

47. Ibid., 266-286.

48. *Question #24. "Has It Truly Occurred to You to Ask Yourself Such Questions (or at Least Some) about Your Friends? a. Often b. Sometimes c. Never." The Relationship between the Gender of the Respondent and the Frequency of the Inquiry*

Count Column %	Gender of the Respondents		Row Total
Frequency of Inquiry	Male	Female	
Often	14 25%	5 7.9%	19 16%
Sometimes	22 39.3%	37 58.7%	59 49.6%
Never	20 35.7%	21 33.3%	41 34.5%
Column Total Column %	56 47.1%	63 52.9%	119 100%

Raw χ^2 = 7.71604 with 2 d. f.; Significance = .0211; Number of Missing Observations = 6

49. Miller, Stuart, *Men and Friendship* (Boston: Houghton Mifflin Company, 1983), 129-142.

50. Parsons, Talcott, *Essays in Sociological Theory Pure and Applied* (Glencoe, Illinois: Free Press, 1954), 198.

51. Weber, Max, *The Protestant Ethic and the Spirit of Capitalism.* Translated by Talcott Parsons (New York: Charles Scribner's Sons, 1958), 105; 106; 222-224.

52. Maisonneuve, Jean, *Psycho-sociologie des affinités*, 116-117.

53. See: Scanzoni, Letha and John Scanzoni, *Men, Women, and Change: A Sociology of Marriage and Family* (New York: McGraw Hill Book Company, 1976), 78-79. Also see Lipset, Seymour Martin, *Continental Divide*, 86-87; 113-115; 191-192.

54. Tremblay, Michel, *Les anciennes odeurs* (Leméac, collection Théater Leméac, numéro 106, 1981), 17.

55. Gay, Francis, *The Friendship Book* (London: D.C. Thomson & Co., Ltd., 1975).

56. Lewis, Edward and Robert Myers, eds., *To Be a Friend* (Kansas City, Missouri: Hallmark Cards, Inc., 1967).

57. When I undertook the analysis of these data, log-linear and other multivariate techniques were not available to me, so I used simple conditional tables. Some sociologists loosely call the process of working with these "partialing out." In this analysis I controlled for the closeness of the friend as well as sexual status, ethnicity, age, socio-economic class, and marital status. Although a gamma coefficient (γ) is not very appropriate for a 3 by 3 or larger table where one or both of the variables is nominal, cell analysis can be of help in interpreting the differences in large contingency tables. By not too great a jump in logic, my variables of "tactile and sexual behavior among close friends'" going from "holding hands through making love with orgasm" can indeed be conceived of as ordinal, as can the "incidence of tactility and sexuality among close friends'" going from high to absent. For these reasons I will report gammas (γ) for these data.

When the results for all the friends are summed up for each of the respondents, we may witness the reported global incidence of tactility and sexuality among the Montrealers and their close friends in my study in the following table:

The Incidence of Tactility and Sexuality among the 10 Closest Friends in This Study of Urban Montreal in the Mid-1970s

Count Col %	The Incidence of Tactility and Sexuality among Close Friends in This Study of Urban Montreal in the Mid-1970s				Row Total
Tactile and Sexual Behavior among Close Friends	High	Medium	Low	Absent (0)	
My Friend and I Hold Hands.	49 29%	67 32.4%	138 15.7%	996 19.9%	1250 20%
My Friend and I Embrace Each Other	43 25.4%	48 23.2%	164 18.6%	995 19.9%	1250 20%
My Friend and I Kiss Each Other	42 24.9%	63 30.4%	148 16.8%	997 20%	1250 20%
My Friend and I Make Love without Orgasm	9 5.3%	16 7.7%	223 25.3%	1002 20.1%	1250 20%
My Friend and I Make Love with Orgasm	26 15.4%	13 6.3%	207 23.5%	1004 20.1%	1250 20%
Column Total Column %	169 2.7%	207 3.3%	880 14.1%	4994 79.9%	6250 100%

Kendall's Tau B = .01596; Significance = .0745; γ = .03058;
Somer's D (Asymmetric) = .02448 with Item Dependent. = .01040 with Degree
Dependent; Somer's D (Symmetric) = .01460

58. The Incidence of Tactility and Sexuality among up to One's 10 Closest Friends in This Study of Urban Montreal in the Mid-1970s Controlling for Gender

Count Column%	The Incidence of Tactility and Sexuality among Close Friends in This Study of Urban Montreal in the Mid-1970s							
Tactile and Sexual Behavior among Close Friends:	**Females**				**Males**			
	High	Medium	Low	Absent	High	Medium	Low	Absent
My Friend and I Hold Hands	29 29.9%	37 33.6%	76 15.5%	528 19.9%	20 27.8%	30 30.9%	62 15.9%	468 20%
My Friend and I Embrace Each Other	27 27.8%	25 22.7%	90 18.3%	528 19.9%	16 22.2%	23 23.7%	74 19%	467 19.9%
My Friend and I Kiss Each Other	24 24.7%	44 40%	73 14.9%	529 19.9%	18 25%	19 19.6%	75 19.3%	468 20%
My Friend and I Make Love without Orgasm.	4 4.1%	3 2.7%	131 26.7%	532 20.1%	5 6.9%	13 13.4%	92 23.7%	470 20.1%
My Friend and I Make Love with Orgasm.	13 13.4%	1 .9%	121 24.6%	535 20.2%	13 18.1%	12 12.4%	86 22.1%	469 20%
Column Total Column %	97 2.9%	110 3.3%	491 14.7%	2652 79.2%	72 2.5%	97 3.3%	389 13.4%	2342 80.8%

Summary Gammas (γ) for "Degree of Tactility and Sexuality among Respondents and Their Close Friends in Montreal of the Mid-1970s by Gender": Zero-Order γ = .03058; First-Order Partial γ = .03599

59. Boldt, Edward D., Neil E. Lindquist, and G. Anne Percival, "The Significance of Significant Others," *The Canadian Review of Sociology and Anthropology / La Revue canadienne de sociologie et d'anthropologie* 13(3)(1976): 345-351. Also see: Nardi, Peter M., "Sex, Friendship, and Gender Roles Among Gay Men," in *Men's Friendship*, (Newbury Park, CA: Sage Publications, Inc., 1992), 173-152. A 1993 study in the United States of America done by the National Opinion Research Center at the

University of Chicago found in the General Social Survey of 1,400 people that "2.2 percent of men have had homosexual sex in the last 12 months, and 3.1 percent report having sex with a man within the last five years. (The figure is controversial because many gay rights activists cite a figure from the 1948 Kinsey study, which found 10 percent of Americans are gay.)" See: Cass, Connie, "Most U.S. spouses are faithful, study finds," *San Francisco Examiner*, 19 October 1993.

60. Please note that I calculated the results for these data for each friend, one through ten. These tables are presented in Chapter Nine, Note 62, pages 385-392.

61. See: Bloom, Allan, *Love and Friendship* (New York: Simon & Schuster, 1993), 423-424.

62. Ibid., 417.

63. Ibid., 409.

64. Maisonneuve, Jean, *Psycho-sociologie des affinités* (Paris: Presses universitaires de France, 1966), 129-131.

Chapter Eight

A Clinical Sociology of Friendship

I became gradually aware that my research on friendship brought about an emotional response in the people whom I studied.[1] This reaction surprised me because Jean Maisonneuve had neglected discussing it, although Horst Hutter, Janet Reohr, and I observed that many other scholars reacted to investigating friendship with a strong emotionality, usually negative, in contrast to my interviewees and respondents, who typically found the friendship interview a positive experience.[2] To many of the people in my sample, particularly in in-depth, audio-recorded sessions, the interview was varyingly moving, refreshing, tender, relieving, creative, sad, happy, productive, and/or growthful. The history of research on friendship done after the Second World War reveals major similarities and differences between therapists and friends and the therapeutic implications of friendship.[3] In brief, the literature indicates that for those who are friendless and suffer from this state, there is solid evidence that an intervention aimed at promoting friendship can relieve psycho-social stress and enhance mental and physical health.[4]

Influenced by a profoundly emotionally changing experience in a Gestalt group led by Hans Peter Dreitzel while attending his lectures on love and friendship in the summer of 1977, I designed my own group to promote the understanding and development of friendship.[5] The experience with Dreitzel marked a great change in my approach to group dynamics, for before I had been extremely cautious and critical of the group movement without appreciating its healing potential.[6] Until then, I had approached the topic only through the eyes of the distanced psycho-sociologist.

Besides my experiences in Hans Peter Dreitzel's group and as a group facilitator myself, I was inspired by the exercises in the main textbook I chose for my undergraduate courses on small group dynamics.[7] Drawing upon these sources and Jean Maisonneuve, I came up with the following discussion group exercise which I adapted to each particular group I led or organized:

Videotaped Exercise in a Discussion Group on Close Friendship

The exercise: This group is to try to find out what cultural, social, and personality forces help build close friendship. Each group member is to contribute specific facts based on her or his own life experiences. After each and every group member tells about the details of his or her closest friendships, or lack of close friendships, throughout his or her life, the group will draw up a list of the social, cultural, and personality forces that are the bases for closest friendship. The group must explain this list by developing a theory of closest friendship. Finally a group definition of friendship should be spelled out.

Specifications: For each friend that you talk about and for each group member telling about a friendship, describe the age, sex, socio-economic class (education, occupation, and income), ethnicity, race, propinquity (nearness in space), residence, and marital status (single, married, divorced, with or without children) of each person brought up. If a friend discussed happens be a relative, indicate the relationship of this person to you.

Questions to be considered:

1. What is a friend? What is or what are, in your opinion, the sign or the signs of a true friendship?

2. What word or words do you use to refer to a close friend? Do you use close friend, best friend, good friend, buddy, chum, pal, or other expressions? Please define the words that you use and explain the differences in their meaning.

3. With how many persons are you presently linked in an active friendship? Excluding the members of your family; including the members of your family?

4. Specify when each close friendship that you discuss here began and how long it has lasted (or lasted in the past).

5. Where were these friendships begun? (as a neighbor, at work, off the job activities, through your husband, wife or common friend, or by chance?)

6. What do you do with each of your closest friends?

7. Do you discuss your most intimate concerns with your closest friends often, sometimes, or never?

8. Try to rank each of your closest friends from most to least intimate.

9. Even if your work is most time consuming, do you try to save time for your friends at any cost?

10. For serious reasons of a family nature, have you sacrificed or would you sacrifice a close friend, if the question were raised?

11. Have you nourished at some point in your life relations of strict friendship with a person of the opposite sex?

12. Even if it hasn't happened to you, do you think that true friendship is possible or impossible between a man and a woman?

13. Have you ever had a real friendship with someone having political opinions deeply opposed to your own?

14. Do you feel certain pullings among your different friendships?

15. Do you try to get several of your friends together as often as possible or do you prefer to meet them separately?

16. In what circumstances during your life have certain friendships broken (e.g., due to moving, change of job, shift of position on the same

job, a change in private life such as marriage and divorce, a change in your opinions, ideas, beliefs, mutual letting it fall by the wayside, a real fight, for no particular reason)?

17. To what do you especially attribute the force of a friendship from the least to the most important? (For example: being able to get together easily and often, having the same tastes, having the same ideas and opinions, belonging to the same social milieu, to a really unexplainable attraction.)

18. Do you often, sometimes, or never happen to ask yourself at least some of these questions concerning your friends?

19. Are you linked in an active friendship different from the usual feelings of affection between relatives with certain persons in your family? If so, tell us their gender and their relationship to you. Are these persons or one of them your best friend?

Although you may think about and take notes on these questions before the videotaping, no notes are to be brought to the videotaped session.

In a companion paper to my review of the literature and commentary on the therapy of friendship, I summarized my empirical findings, which were based on eight self-led friendship development groups with 65 participants at a quite traditional Catholic college in Chicago. These groups included women and men, blacks and whites, from their late teens through middle age, single, married, and divorced people with and without children, many of whom work many hours outside class.

In analyzing these groups, it was found that the subject matter of the course established the underlying emphasis in their content. They peaked when discussing the possibility for men and women to become friends. Much of the analysts' commentaries on these groups centered around "side conditions," especially the amount of time they had met prior to engaging in these friendship development sessions.

I empirically verified several therapeutic qualities of these groups. They have been documented: (1) to help overcome the fear of talking about and analyzing a deep relationship in subcultural milieu where this is not sanctioned behavior; (2) to relieve communication snags by teaching active listening and other skills; (3) to aid understanding of deep feelings; (4) to develop participants' abilities to be more flexible and tolerant of other participants' types of friendship styles; (5) to promote participants' comprehension of the difficulties in their own friendships in an environment supportive of feedback; (6) to provide a place for analyzing and evaluating one's own friendships; (7) and to help participants see options for conducting their own close friendships in alternative ways.

The folk theories of friendship developed in these groups were seen to display a variety of contradictory platitudes and facts which most often were not perceived by participants. Moreover, these groups provided occasions for affirming religious and national rituals and symbols referencing normative, though not often real, intragroup characteristics.

Friends may be good therapists, especially with supplemental training in communicative skills, for treating socio-emotive dysfunctions; this is especially true in terms of dealing with the alienation of large numbers of people affected by socio-emotive disorders who may not otherwise receive human encounter during times of institutional retrenchment. On the other hand, professional therapists possess particular skills and training that may alleviate distress and promote growth for many individuals whose signs of distress may remain unnoticed even by close friends. Lastly, I have documented that the clinical sociologist, by employing many different social scientific perspectives, may shed light on the psycho-social dynamics of any given friendship from which he or she may derive a strategy for repairing or enhancing friendships at risk.

Friendship Development Groups

Up to this point I have reviewed the dynamics of nine self-led friendship development groups that took place at a college in Chicago. When led by a trained leader over longer or shorter periods of time in different socio-economic and cultural milieus, these groups take on some notably different features. To highlight some of the potentialities and limitations of friendships development groups, I will compare and contrast a group to certain aspects of the self-led ones at the college.

In this section, I will focus on one group I led once a week over two months for slightly more than one hour per session in the late mornings of July and August 1983 in a convalescent center in one of Chicago's poorest neighborhoods. The people in this group were "mainstreamed" adult men and women, which is to say that a variety of poor, elderly, substance-abusing, handicapped, mentally ill, or learning-impaired people found themselves placed or chose to live in this quasi-state supported institution. Critics of "mainstreaming" often refer to this practice as "dumping." I compare and contrast this disadvantaged group to one I facilitated among educated and talented people in Northern California.

A salient commonality of all the groups was that they were free to their participants. While this practice is more democratic and Socratic in that it places the leader on a more equal footing with the participants, it reduces the amount of effective command the facilitator may use to deepen exploration of relationships. This outcome results from the participants' feeling that they stand to lose little monetary investment if they withdraw either completely or only in face from the on-going interaction. In short, to promote understanding of friendship a facilitator must chose between democratic and Socratic values, on the one hand, and the potentiality of greater involvement by the participants when they pay, on the other.

A shared trait of the college groups and the one at the convalescent center is that the general social setting with its pattern of statuses and roles explained the most salient contours of interaction within the friendship development groups. Among the educated and talented group, the hierarchy within the group quickly reasserted itself, although there were two exceptional lapses on the part of new members whose statuses in the group had not yet coalesced. Both revealed extensively high degrees of their inner-selves, with fervent levels of socio-emotive intensity. In contrast, with one exception, members high in the external status hierarchy refused to undergo self-disclosure by the possible revelation of backstage information that could jeopardize their position in the external status hierarchy. Such a problem can be minimized--as I have done in other groups--by negotiating a formal written contract in which all members agree to share with one another significant aspects of their friendships. As with the college students, in the convalescent center the external status hierarchy constantly reasserted itself within the friendship development group by deflecting the interaction about friendship towards a mystified restatement of the images and assumptions about group participants when they were not in the group. Two examples of this phenomenon are instructive for facilitators who might have to deal with similar situations where a highly pluralistic population is lodged in close quarters.

In one of the groups, a participant was identified by the staff as being very learning impaired. This middle-aged woman of southern Caucasian background was proud of her liaison with a man many years her senior. At occasional unprovoked instances, she would lash out in the harshest deprecations at a very polite, but rather passive, woman of African American ancestry, who was similar in age, and an alcoholic. It was clear in my mind that the first woman was an embittered racist. In the group, I pushed her to explore the nature and origin of her feelings toward blacks and to get black people to respond to how it felt to hear such vicious calls. To some extent this modulated her opinions and behavior. Watching the interaction in other parts of this institution, however, it became clear to me that the great majority of people in intermediate positions of authority over the white woman were black. Like many aides of other racial backgrounds in many other institutions, several manifested an attitude of impersonality, stern directivity, and a lack of care for the institution's denizens. In short, it seemed to me that, in part, the black woman was being used as a scapegoat for the white woman's anger at her attendants--i.e. people in the external hierarchy. Another example is the treatment of a man in his thirties by some of the socio-emotive stars in "The Friendship Club"--the name which some of the members gave to this group. This fellow had been labeled as either "mentally retarded" or schizophrenic to me by various institutional agents and group members. Rather frail, unshaven, and with acne, this man would usually initiate a response to my questions to the group on friendship, but he would quickly digress into a long story of how his teachers in a religiously-run high school had harmed him. He trembled and shook as he incessantly repeated this tale. I was able to bring him back into the friendship discussion by interrupting his monologues and asking others what they thought he had meant about this or that point he had made. This man seemed to exude warmth which he needed reciprocated. I tried to get a large, older woman who seemed to listen to his tale to agree to work on a friendship with him, but she and others would revert to their pre-established labels for him in the convalescent center's hierarchy. To them he was a "nice boy" who had a great command of the local baseball scene. But they wouldn't be friends with someone "crazy."

So much for the difficulties. There are common features of success to report. Profound sharing of the deepest friendships by some of the participants led other participants to reexamine their own friendships and the general potential for friendship to enrich their lives on cognitive and socio-emotive levels. Besides my own observations and formal documents, this conclusion has been relayed to me by the most therapeutically well-trained and experienced professionals who have viewed this intervention. Secondly, even though it was not experienced by everyone nor cathected to the same extent, the peak experience of this exercise afforded, through particular insight gathered through self-disclosure or group feedback, a temporary high of tenderness, cherishing, and transcendental relatedness that likewise characterizes the summits occasionally shared by close friends.

Without the intervention, people usually sat around the public waiting room staring into space, often with washed-out faces in a background of Muzak, infrequently interrupted by blurted out announcements on the public address system. The lack of trust among the residents was depicted by their carrying their valuables with them-- for some toted in a bag. And the harshness of human communication was seen in the inattention of guards to their clients and the "commanding" style of attendants. In this atmosphere the best that can be expected of a person is what it takes to be called nice, namely, in the words of one resident, "He never bothers nobody." In such a world of idealized avoidance, unless their present situation is changed, they think that friendship is a thing of the past. It is into this scene that the facilitator of friendship may bring people to appreciate what a friendship means, what role it has played up to now, and how it can continue to be a significant part of their lives. Such reawakening toward the value of intimate human relationships would not have been possible unless someone had worked on something akin to a friendship development group. In the world of social service cutbacks, society seems to provide the residents of such institutions with minimal contact to come to grips with the human relatedness part of their lives.

Weekly or biweekly visits by clergypeople performing religious rites offer them their one chance at transcendental escape, and the clergy people who provide such services are usually minimally paid, often harassed by the church hierarchy, which is jealous of their small but, nevertheless, independent source of funding. Not unexpectedly, the volunteers foreseen by the conservative and right wing ideologues of social welfare are "few and far between" in such a milieu.

There appears to be a host of serendipitous effects of these friendship development groups which stimulate relating to fellow residents. For some for whom intimate encounter may have been thought to be buried, the possibility may have been subsequently revived. Thus, one hardened alcoholic, who participated in a few sessions and then dropped out calling them "Looney Tunes," and another regular participant not long after wanted to get married. Two other severely physically-disabled individuals, a woman and a man in their thirties from very different backgrounds, touched one another's hands and exchanged states of enthralled mutual understanding and caring that overcame an initial shyness of meeting someone else who was a paraplegic. One elderly man, who thought that he could be friends only with "The Holy Mother of God," began to realize that his calling one of his sons a bum and another a thief may have had something to do with their not coming to visit him despite his desperate wish that they and their families would spend time with him. Moreover, by my leading an interested elderly female participant to visit him on her walker, they began to speak and share sentimentally valuable possessions. Finally, some participants-- highly deviant in their ability to speak or desist from perpetual movements of great anxiety such as rocking back and forth and rubbing their arms up and down--could eventually communicate limited sentences and signs of being at ease with others. For the more core members, basic problems of everyday existence came to the fore--of dealing with others or intolerable institutional policies. In addition, through this formal context they were able to share with others whom they deal with daily feelings of positive regard and hope for deepening their relationship. In one case, claiming to have had a lobotomy because of his violent behavior, an older man bestowed respectful and sentimental compliments on his male and female closest friends.

Having looked at the therapeutic quality of friendship development groups for clinically promoting friendship, we must recall the real world factors that destroy close friendships and propose a clinical strategy for dealing with such forces.

Maintaining and Breaking up with Close Friends

To consider how people maintain their closest friendship is to look at the forces which bind friends together; to investigate the break-up of close friendship is to study the failure, dysfunctions, historical, and personal changes in the forces that keep friends close.

Maisonneuve identified a scale of attitudes that constitute a progression from minimum to maximum friendship. These items include the following nine entries on his and my questionnaire: putting some time aside for your friends at any cost even if your work is most time and energy consuming (Question 14); thinking that one must *not* leave off certain friendships sometimes for reasons of social responsibility or on account of new occupations (Question 16); cultivating a real friendship with a person having political opinions deeply opposed to your own (Question 19); having it truly occur to you often or sometimes to ask yourself such questions (or at least some) about your friends (Question 24); often discussing your most intimate problems and thoughts with your friends (Question 12); not having sacrificed one's friend relationships for serious reasons of a family nature if the question were raised (Question 15); having at least one friend of the opposite sex (Question 2); giving a ranking of 1, i.e. a first place position, to attributing the strength and firmness of a friendship to "a really unexplainable attraction" (Question 23); and having at least one friend of a different trade or occupation from your own (Question 7).[9]

Maisonneuve came up with the term "friendliness [*amicalité*]" to designate "precisely and singularly the unequal propensity to value friendship either through an attitude of non-exclusive openness or by the affirmation of its priority over any consideration of an affective, social, or pragmatic nature."[10] Maisonneuve had found six degrees of friendliness [*amicalité*] in France which varied from: I. maxima--five + responses on questions 14, 16, 24, 15, & 2; II. forte--four + responses; III. average--three + responses; IV. less than average--two + responses; V. weak--1 + response; VI. minimal--0 + responses.[11]

In trying to replicate Maisonneuve's scale of friendliness [*amicalité*] in Montreal, I carried out six runs on the combined in-depth interview and questionnaire data for the various combinations of questions (= Q) 14, 16, 19, 24, 12, 15, 2, 23, and 7. Using all of these questions yielded a coefficient of reproducibility of .7376 and a coefficient of scalability of .1441.[12]

For the combined questionnaire and indepth interview data, the best results were obtained using five questions, #23, #19, #15, #2, and #14, which yielded a coefficient of reproducibility of .8466 and a coefficient of scalability of .4104.[13]

None of the runs produced valid Guttman scales using the generally accepted guidelines that the coefficient of reproducibility has to be higher than .9 to be considered valid. Nor did any of my calculations result in a coefficient of scalability well above the value of .6 required for concluding that a scale is truly unidimensional and cumulative. Thus in Montreal, Maisonneuve's six degrees of "friendliness [*amicalité*]" were not replicated.

While Robert B. Hays' research based on college students might suggest that if close friendship were to be maintained, the friends would have to engage in a wide range of activities and share intimately while engaging in those activities, my own results based on a sample much more widely reflective of the entire population points out that social forces in the real world may operate to disestablish close friendship regardless of the level of intimacy or range of activities.[14]

The fact that close friendships can come to an end contradicts a main theme of friendship, namely that it is long-lasting, constant, and loyal.[15] However, from ancient to modern times, thinkers have noted that close friendships do break up on occasion, and they have sought to explain why close friendships can come to an end.[16]

To find out how and for what reasons close friendships draw to a close in our times, I asked Montrealers Jean Maisonneuve's question about the circumstances in a person's life where his or her friendships had, if ever, been broken.[17]

As the results for this question were reported in a table in my chapter on "Some of My Best Friends Are ... ," here I will refer only to the magnitude of the percentage of answers falling in each category of response. Globally most close friendships were broken because of moving (28.2%). Secondly, changes in private life such as marriage and divorce were found as the next most frequent force terminating friendship (18.7%). Thirdly, changes in occupation were found to bring about the end of close friendship (13.9%). Fourthly, changes in one's ideas, opinions, and beliefs break up friendship (11.4%). Fifthly, growing tired of one another's company and a real fight are about equally disruptive of close friendship (8.8%). The sixth most destructive influence in friendship is attributed to no particular reason (6.2%).

Finally the least important cause for friends' falling apart was a change of position on the same job (3.7%).

While some psycho-social forces undermine friendship, others maintain or even strengthen friendship. Understanding both of these phenomena provides the clinical sociologist with the knowledge of what builds or ruins intimate friendship. Let us begin by asking what people themselves perceived as the forces that maintain and/or strengthen their friendships.[18]

In contrast to Maisonneuve's data from France, Montrealers rank "having the opportunity to be together quite often and easily" as the primary, not secondary, attribute of friendship.[19] "Having the same tastes" comes close behind but, nevertheless, occupies a secondary, not a primary, position in Montreal. Item #4, "belonging to the same social milieu," falls in third place most probably because response #3, "having the same ideas and opinions"--accidentally omitted from the coding sheets for the interview data--is found in third place in the questionnaire's results and augments the "other" category in the in-depth interviews' outcome. Very close to the latter, response #5, "a really unexplainable attraction," comes in fourth place. Other bases for friendship scored in last place on all sets of data.[20] These generalizations apply to all the major demographic variables in my study.

Throughout this book I have stressed that each period of history constructed a relatively different relationship of friendship. Just as each historical division developed a characteristic way of thinking about friends and friendship and acting with friends, so do these differing friendships imply thinking and acting in certain ways if friendship is to be maintained. Greek theorizing on the breaking of friendship derives from two different periods of thought. During the period of the Homeric poems of the fourth century B.C., social life seems to be considered as a natural fact of which the rules could be determined. The Greeks saw friendship as a cure for injustices; the capability for friendship was made synonymous with virtuousness. For them, a person had to reform himself and withdraw from political preoccupations.[21] To not do so would preclude friendship or set the grounds for its destruction.

In the second period from around the fifth century, man was seen to have an original place in the universe. From this position, it follows that man should look at himself to find out what explains and justifies social life. As the world of states was threatened and problematical, private *philia* (friendship) was set up as a model. This required thinkers to find out the rules that enable *philia* to remain stable and to reconcile agreement and usefulness.[22] When these rules broke down or did not work well, friendship would be predicted to end.

Throughout classical philosophy, thinkers give advice on what to do and what not to do in friendship. If you did not follow their suggestions, the implication was that friendship risked a break up. Hesiod warns us to be prudent in cultivating friendship and to maintain it with constancy and sincerity.[23] In the sentence of Solon, the public is warned, "Don't be prompt in acquiring friends, nor prompt, when you shall have acquired them to reject them as unworthy."[24] A series of concepts such as the Pythagorean *dikè*, "part due," *kairos*, "treating one on the same footing as oneself," *harmonia*, and *philanthropia* provided the dynamics behind keeping friendship intact or from splitting up.[25]

Each age of philosophy and social science recognized generative forces that built up or tore apart friendship.[26] For instance consider what Marcus Tullius Cicero admonishes his readers through the voice of Laelius to do in the following passage:

> Listen then, best of men, to the points which were frequently mentioned in the discussions which Scipio and I used to have on the subject of friendship. On many questions we did not agree. For he used to say that nothing was more difficult than for friendship to endure up to the last day of life. For, he said it often happens that interests alter or the friends disagree on political questions; that men's dispositions change, sometimes through adversity and sometimes with the growing burden of years. And as an illustration of this he would cite an example from boyhood, because the great affection which boys sometimes have for each other is frequently laid aside at the same time that they discard the garb of boyhood. If it

does not persist until early manhood, still, he said, it is sometimes destroyed by rivalry for marriage or in the struggle for some other advantage which both cannot obtain. For if any continue longer to be friends, still friendship is ruined if they chance to become rivals for some public office. For nothing is more destructive to friendship than the desire for wealth in most men and the rivalry for honor and fame in all our best men; since from this, great enmity often arises between the best of friends. Even violent separations, generally justifiable, spring up when something is wrong is asked of a friend; for instance the gratification of lust, or assistance in a crime. For if he refuse, though he do so for honor's sake, still he will be charged with betraying his friendship by him with whose desires he is unwilling to comply. Moreover, those who would venture to ask anything from a friend, by that very demand show that they would be willing to do everything and anything for a friend, and by the continual complaining of such men not only are friendships frequently destroyed but even eternal enmity is often engendered. Thus there are many vicissitudes which threaten friendships that Scipio said that he believed that the escape from them depended not merely on wisdom but also on good luck.[27]

In the modern period, social scientists have identified different factors which support, prevent, or break down friendship, as I will show in the next chapter on the meanings of friendship.[28]

According to these varying accounts, the negativity of Self, collusion, connivance, and destructive interpersonal rhetoric are the basic forces which kill friendship.[29] These phenomena operate in addition to or underlie the social forces such as moving, breaking up in a private relationship, a change of ideas, and the like which end close friendship. These processes which are destructive of friendship may be focused on and modulated in the context of a friendship development group.

As I reported in the chapter on ethnicity, even in the relatively geographically stable Quebec of the 1970s, the great horizontal mobility afforded the populations of an urban, industrial society accounted for the largest number of broken close friendships. The other side of this same phenomenon is that people saw having the opportunity to get together quite often and easily as the primary force maintaining their close friendships.

Likewise, the greater freedom regarding intimate relations characteristic of a highly differentiated society, but particularly expanded by culture in the late 1960s and 1970s, permitting more open and more easily dissoluble bonds in marriage, was related to the second most disruptive factor in close friendship. In addition, a notable number of break-ups of close friendships resulted from changes in occupation, which are derivative of the structure of the complex division of labor of today's industrial and post-industrial societies.

Looked at from the positive side, people attributed belonging to the same social milieu as an important factor in bonding friends. In short, important factors in the break-up of close friendships are brought on by the features of the larger social organization, although other factors such as debilitating, incurable disease may break some and build other friendships.[30]

The Buddy-*Copain-Copine*-Phenomenon [Style C2]

One of the variants of the "similar-interest" close friend is the "buddy-*copain-copine* phenomenon" in my chapter on styles of friendship. As the coming tale relates, two middle-aged French Canadian, male white collar workers share the pastime of hunting--definitely the central action in their friendship. As the interviewee is the first cousin of his friend's wife, their friendship also displays aspects of the non-nuclear family style. However, besides this activity, the family tie, and similar demographic characteristics, their friendship is on the rocks to a large extent because they are unable to share much else, particularly any feelings or understanding of critical life issues. At the time of the interview, this fellow was 43 years of age and married with three children. He had seven years of formal education, and seems proud that he is a trainer for an international company for which he has worked approximately ten years. This man and his family live in a southeasterly section on the Island of Montreal.

Translating from my and Ms. Verrette's interview at his family home, we were told,

> For me, a friend is a person you can trust, let's say, in whom you can confide. ... [whereas "a chum" is] ... a type you'll meet, heh, once here and there, while a friend you like [is] a person you'll try to go out of your way for, heh, to meet more often and to party with. ... like me, I love sports, and I'll go hunting and. fishing [with a friend], while I wouldn't do that with a chum ... .

When Michèle inquired if he could really confide in a friend, he avoids the question by replying indirectly,

> yes, ... , in my line of work it's hard. Before, I had several friends, but today it's difficult to ... I travel so much ... [yet] ... We can speak together, no problem. We do sports together.

He tells us that he is three years older than his friend whom he met about a decade ago at a family gathering. His friend is better off financially than the interviewee, as he is a director in a business. He is somewhat better educated, too. In telling us how they met, he informed us,

> My first cousin and [my family] saw one another like that; we visited as neighbors. We weren't really friends, not until we started to do sports together did we become true *copains* [which took] ... two years ... because we didn't see each other very often. He was rather busy with his work and me too, and the only time we met was at family get-togethers, Saturday nights. We took a dance course together ... .

In describing his friend's personality, he calls him:

> a decent sort (*un chic type*). He is almost always agreeable, but he's not a softy (*mitaine*). If there's something needs talking about, we'll discuss it. ... He's the type who thinks before responding. In my opinion, he's a very intelligent person. ... What do we discuss? Why two lovers of sport! ... a little about our work too.

Around ten years before they had changed jobs about the same time, they talked it over quite a bit, but he doesn't think his friend's change of jobs influenced him. He says that his greatest fear was his limited knowledge of English, of which his friend had a better command. In describing his own personality, he informs us that he's a very patient person, but when he's had it, he can be rather violent. He's not afraid of work, but he likes to relax a lot from time to time. His weakest point is his pride.

It is not until the latter part of this long interview that this service representative breaks the story of his ruptured close friendship, and he lets us know about his difficult situation, not in response to the question about broken friendships, but in response to the question about congruence, about whether what the interviewee thinks about his friends corresponds to what he does with him. He tells us,

> ... when you go on these organized hunting parties ... there is a guide who is sent to us from the government. And so, heh, the guide was taking care only of him, ..., and so, I let it be known that I was conscious of it, and so [my friend] ... said that it wasn't his concern. ... [My buddy] said, "But the guide knew that you killed an elk last year; so he said he was trying to hunt only with me so that I could kill an elk this year." ... I agreed. ... He was conscious of that, but at least he could have heard me out, given that the two of us paid the same amount; ... "he was trying to hunt only with you to give you a chance ...; he didn't even look at me."

I inquired, "And what was your friend's response?"

Our interviewee replied,

> ... that I wasn't at all right. [My buddy said,] "I find that he did a good job ..."; he tried his best so that we could have our elk." And then I said, "No, ... I don't agree with you because for him it was not a question of being a friend or a relation; it's work that there's to do, and he ought to give as much to one as to the other. Maybe I, at that time could have said, "No, heh, go with him to give him a chance to hunt." That's what I would have done. But I made him aware of the situation of what had happened; ... he didn't agree.

I asked, "And how did you feel afterwards?"

He replied, "Very bad; yes, still ..."
I didn't let the matter drop and asked, "How much did it cost you?"

He answered,

Oh, it's not a question of money' it's a question of principle;
it's not the money. The trip cost us each about, let's say,
altogether, maybe $300. No, it's not a question of money.

"Did you get an elk?" I wondered.

And this fellow replied, " 'Missed 'em."

Wanting to get to the heart of the matter, I asked,"Both of you?"

We missed two elks the first evening; we wounded them,
then lost them. That's what heated us up again; let's say,
in coming back, I said what I thought.

"Did he remain your intimate friend?" Michèle wanted to clarify.

"No, but I would say that it's not like before."

I asked, "Do you think that it will start up again eventually?"

He was frank: "I do not know. It depends pretty much on him."

I asked, "And your differences, about how long has it been?"

"In September, beginning October [of last year].":

He confided,

... I feel that when we meet, it's not the same friendship; I
even feel there is a coldness because he was insulted that I
spoke to him like that.

I kept playing the role of the other, "How did you speak to him?"

He explained,

Well, I spoke to him the last day. When we spoke,
everything was over, and I said to him, "If you haven't
killed an elk, heh, it's not because the guide didn't try to get
you to kill it." He said, "What do you mean?" Well, I said,
"You always hunted with him. He never asked or even had

the idea of saying, 'Good, today, come with me; we'll hunt together.' Never, never."

To fill in I urged him, "Could you go a little into this story with some other details that enter into this affair?" He responded,

Yes, we have a truck; we bought a truck together, my friend and I. So we bought it equally and have separately all the expenses and repairs, ... On the trip in question, the first day we saw two elk, he was driving ... By the time he stopped the truck, I had the time to get out and start to shoot, but he did it a little late; so the next day, to make a joke, I said, "if you had stopped the truck more quickly," ... "Well, yes," he said, "the truck ... doesn't stop any more quickly than that." And I said, "I'm going to show you that it stops more quickly." It was me who was driving. We were on the open road. I started to apply the breaks, but the truck didn't stop. There was a brake system line that broke; so we were stuck in the Laurentian Park in the north with a line of brakes broken. It was easy to find. When we went to the garage and tried to repair it, and the more he fiddled around with it, the more it got broken; so we had to send to Quebec City for a piece by bus, and, anyway, it cost $44. Then there's no one who knows ... I said that because even my wife doesn't know it.

I interjected, "It was your idea to buy this particular truck? ... I mean the kind of truck that you ..."

He underscored, "It was our idea, our idea."

He picked up my thought in the middle,

It is because I had the chance to buy; so I spoke to him about it, and so I was certain. "Yes, yes,"--... he who doesn't know about mechanics--he said to me, "if you hadn't applied the brakes, so strong, you wouldn't have broken the oil line." I said, "Let's see, would you have liked it less if we came next to Beaver Hall in Montreal and ran into three or four cars and may have hurt or killed someone? Heh, ... , we are lucky in one sense that it happened out on the highway. It's normal to apply the brakes a little hard once in a while to test them." But he doesn't know anything about mechanics. "No, if you hadn't done that, the brakes

wouldn't have broken. It's an old truck; the line was rotten."
It's over. What luck, really, that we had that there!

Michèle got back to a point of communication,

Did you speak about that and your friendship at last? So,
say, you were angry because you hadn't shared cost of the
repairs?

He replied:

We didn't talk about it. We didn't discuss it. Nothing
because I still have nothing and so we took out an
insurance policy for this truck. There's one that's coming.
How can I put it. It's not money. We must agree on that.
It's a question of principle. I say he doesn't want to pay me
for the brakes, and it's not right.

Trying to get the facts straight and explore possible compromises,
Michèle asked,

Do you think that he thinks that he must pay for half or
that he thinks [he must pay for] nothing at all?

"Oh, he knows it. He thinks, but he says that he has nothing to do
with it because it's not his fault."

I still wasn't satisfied with the discrepancy between his claiming
that he wasn't bothered by the monetary aspect and still complaining
about it, "Do you know why you paid for it? ... ."

I repeat what I said. It's not a question of money. It's a
question of principle because ... he thinks that I'm not right.

Still trying to play the role of the other to get out his feelings, I put
forth a scenario,

Did you think that, let's say, he could ... think it's not the
amount that you paid but that, let's say, that you're
responsible for it. In a certain manner he counted on your
knowledge of mechanics and finally the merchandise you
bought ...

He responded:

No, no, no. He knew it was an old truck that belonged to an
iron store here. It was still very good, but others wanted to
exchange it for a new one. Oh no, it's really a bargain, you
could say. It wasn't expensive. Oh no! There is no question
of money in it.

Coming up with a possible resolution, Michèle interjected, "Let's
say now ... each of you understands that he is going to telephone first."

He responds quickly, "Oh, no, ..., we have seen one another since
that time. We've seen each other, but it's not like ... ."

Attempting to touch his emotions, I implored, "But how does it
feel?" Then Michèle elaborated on what I meant, "Each of you has a
feeling of being, of being abused or of having ..."

He answers,

I believe that he believes that he's right to think in that
way. Then I think it's not right. It's stupid, that's it. I don't
want to lose a friend for something so simple as that.

Finally relevant to his discussion of this breaking friendship are
his earlier remarks on how income and other social factors come into
play in the choice of one's friends. He said,

If I am a friend with someone ... and we decide to go
someplace; if he decides he can't afford it, well
automatically without wishing for it, he would not become a
friend because he couldn't tag along, because he doesn't
have a big salary. But only there are those who make less
because they have big families and so the budget is just
about right and who can't afford things that I could. I'm
speaking about trips, vacations; heh, we go spend two
weeks in the south, a hunting trip; it sounds funny to say,
but a hunting trip isn't cheap. If the guy doesn't have a
couple hundred bucks for his hunting trip, automatically he
can't become your friend; why I have neighbors who are
nice guys (*chic types*)--they are friends, but heh, that's not
the same thing as the one I am speaking about.

Interpreting This Tale of Breaking the Style of Friendship of "The Buddy - *Copain - Copine*"

This interview can be understood clinically by various modes of interpretation. If it is examined in terms of statuses, roles, and sentiments, which are attached to them, this tale becomes almost stereotypical of the image of the tough male chauvinist who is so bound by socialization to a lack of communication of feeling that the only thing he knows to share is competition with other men. But an adequate explanation lies more deeply. It is true that hunting as the center of shared activity of this friendship is a traditionally male sphere. Yet, the interviewee feels closer to this friend than other friends or chums. And he is quite frank about being hurt that these events have come to pass. He feels ambivalent about whether or not this friendship can get back to its former high. Their communication is not at a totally inconsequential level, for they discussed together the most serious job change of their careers, even though this service representative consciously denies that his friend's change of job influenced him. In the central focus of this conflict, our interviewee was angered that his friend did not recognize that the hunting guide was spending all the time with his friend, and says that he probably would have gone along with this arrangement had he been asked first.

Although our interviewee consistently maintains that he is not concerned about not getting his money's worth out of his guide and that he is mad about the principle--which he never clearly states--the fact that he comes back to the monetary aspect often is an indicator that this indeed troubles him. On the surface, we must conclude that the principle of the matter to him was that he was not asked to relinquish his equal access to the guide. If his friend had indeed formally requested greater use of the guide because the interviewee had killed an elk the previous year, it would have been a formal recognition of the interviewee's rights to the guide. But the moral claim for such a request would have had to be based on the fact that our interviewee had already killed an elk the year before. It seems to me that the interviewee is asking his friend to acknowledge the interviewee's first place position as a symbol of male prowess, being a recognized master of the hunt--a request to which his friend refuses to accede.

This interpretation is reinforced by the second critical scene related to us--that of the failure of their mutually-owned truck's brakes far north in Laurentian Park. Here again he disparages his friend's knowledge of a stereotypically masculine skill in modern culture, i.e. automotive mechanics, and claims that there is nothing usual about jamming down on a truck's brakes to test them at high speeds. At the same time, the whole incident was carried out to prove that his friend could have stopped the truck quickly enough to kill an elk. Again, he wants to be in first place in the world of the male role vis-à-vis his friend--but this time he doubly fails; the truck doesn't stop; the brakes fail; and they are stuck in the park waiting for a $44 part to arrive from Quebec City. His friend feels that our interviewee's behavior was juvenile and led to an unnecessary expense and loss of vacation time, not to mention twice having his masculinity threatened by his friend. So could this story be analyzed from the point of view of the sociology of gender roles. A sociologist of the family might chuckle and explain these events as typical vacation or trip behavior where intimates spending so much time together get on one another's nerves by inevitably stepping on one another's sacred beliefs or usual ways of going about doing things.

There is still another, much deeper, phenomenologically inspired interpretation of this same material. In the case of my interviewee and his buddy, the conscious basis of their friendship lay in their common interest in hunting, which brought them to go out into the "wilds" together. In Jean Maisonneuve's thinking, such an interest in hunting shared by friends is a sector of "a contingent content of their personal ideal." The ego seeks to express and reserve for itself such "vectors and sectors of the person's ideal."[31] Like other friendships based on common interests, my interviewee's and his friend's relationship displayed elements of their ideal values. They enjoyed getting away into the parks to express themselves as men ought to according to their cultural values. Here I can note that the macho image seems much less a part of Canadian culture, in general, and less so in French Canadian culture, in particular.[32] Nevertheless, there exist important historically valued symbols of the tough French Canadian male *voyageur*, trapper, woodsman, through the hardy men who opened the roads of northern Quebec and the hockey players of Montreal's *Les Canadiens* to the modern, collective variety who built the James Bay Project. Such images have been captivated in several French-language films, such as the comedy, *Les Mâles*.

My interviewee's and his friend's relationship, like other friendships of interests, embodies unconscious and conscious expectations that the two friends could share their mutual liking of hunting in the great outdoors. Such an expectation involved creating "an external mediation by the promotion of a common place where each can communicate and associate" with "a certain sharing and exchange" but where "they relate less to the category of being together" and "to being with" than to that of "being next to and of being like me" or "like him."[33]

However, the difficulties that they are experiencing in their friendship can be understood as arising from differing unconscious expectations in the narcissistic component of their choice of one another as friends. If Freud is correct that every attraction is partially narcissistic and that every affinity implies a certain collusion (*connivance*) of the two narcissisms (narcissistic and anaclitic), then these friends' relationship can be enlightened by understanding the interplay of their narcissistic component.[34] It is obvious that in my interviewee's ego feeling and his conscious understanding, he is the better hunter, driver, and mechanic. The narcissistic component in his friendship leads him to expect deference on the part of his friend in the second critical scene related to us--that of the failure of their mutually owned truck's brakes far north in Laurentian Park.

In an oblique way, i.e. a matter-of-fact statement, he acknowledges his friend's superiority in the world outside his friendship, i.e. in terms of his friend's greater education and income, to us, the outside interviewers; however, there is no evidence that he communicates this admiration to his friend. What counts is that their friendship is in jeopardy because of the events surrounding their hunting together, the crux of their friendship. His *copain* only tacitly acknowledges our interviewee's superiority in hunting--by using it as a legitimate claim to get to use most of the guide's time. Yet, perhaps, some of our interviewee's hurt results from his own knowledge that he needs the services of the guide to kill an elk. Subconsciously, such a recognition would undermine his narcissistic desire to be admired by his friend as the better hunter. To make matters worse, his friend's dismissal of his driving prowess as being foolish in the incident involving the brakes may disturb him particularly because it belies his narcissistic claim for admiration as being the better driver, mechanic, and hunter. As Maisonneuve's psychoanalytically influenced phenomenology informs us,

> concerns of accomplishment come into play all the way up to a conscious level which simultaneously confers upon these friendships dynamism and, in large part, experienced meaning.[35]

Looking at his tale of friendship prompts me to take a position in a debate about friendships based on common interest. A case has been made for making room for the relationship of companions in the bonds of cooperation founded on an community of tasks and interests.[36] In opposition to Suttie, Max Scheler does not place them in the realm of sympathy and love.[37] I side with Scheler in this regard, for such a style as that of the "buddy-*copain-copine*" is subject to rather easy strain and termination.

Offering different clinical interpretations emphasizes that I regard these as perspectives or frameworks with which to view human reality, not absolute keys to truth. All these views converge to conclude that the relationship between these two men is very superficial, unstranded, not broad, and emotionally shallow. This style of friendship is found among women as well as men.

Although it was not my and Ms. Verrette's goal in interviewing, exploring this man's conflict with his buddy, in part by playing the role of the other and in part by sensitive listening, provided him with some psycho-social catharsis and better cognitive understanding of what had gone wrong in his buddy style of friendship. Some would call this therapy. By no means was this either complete or intentional. This interviewee was not one who called back to engage in further exploration. However, had he chosen to engage in a friendship development group, it would behoove the facilitator and/or other participants to suggest supportively similar kinds of interpretation I have offered here. Besides this interpretation, a therapeutic group would have pointed out to him how what he regarded as jokes and honest statements of fact served as destructive interpersonal rhetoric. Explaining the motivation of such speech and supportively outlining alternatives for it in groups involving him and his friend could have helped their relationship and freed them from socio-culturally influenced asocial behavior.

The Tradition of Psychoanalysis in the Clinical Sociology of Friendship

In the tradition of much French psycho-sociology, Maisonneuve's interpretations of friendship show a Freudian input. With this impact in mind, it is instructive to recall that Freud's great friendships,

> follow the same rhythm: intense friendship for several years, then complete break, usually to the point of hatred. This was the fate of his friendship with Breuer, Fliess, Jung, Adler, Rank, and even Ferenczi, the loyal pupil who never dreamed of separating himself from Freud and his movement ... Freud tended to depend on people, and, at the same time, he was ashamed of and hated his dependency.[38]

In Lillian B. Rubin's psychoanalytically influenced sociology of the gender differences in friendship, she would interpret such break-ups as Freud's being importantly influenced by male-ego boundaries being firmer and fixed in contrast to women's, which are more permeable. In Rubin's interpretation, in heterosexual men, the erotic component is built up and the emotional played down, whereas the opposite is true for women. Yet, interpreting Freud's friendships à la Lillian B. Rubin may have less explanatory power if Jeffrey Masson is correct in his evidence that Freud's friendship with Fliess displayed a homoerotic element.

The French male sociologist, Eugène Enriquez, published a psychoanalytic interpretation of friendship in 1983 sharply at odds with the interpretation of friendship published by the American female sociologist, Lillian B. Rubin, in 1985, which I reviewed in Chapter Seven. Rejecting Claude-Lévi-Strauss's interpretation that the acts depicted in Freud's *Totem and Taboo* are symbolic and have never been committed, Eugène Enriquez insists that the murder of the father by his sons in the Oedipal scene occurred and that incest had to happen in order for it to be so radically forbidden. He equally stresses that this was not an isolated act but rather a theory of acts which show in a repetitive way that murder is not only a cherished specter but also a noteworthy event which makes sense: the murder of the father, certainly, but also murder of fathers.[39]

On the basis of this assumption, Enriquez finds that women intuitively mistrust friendship and affection when the goal of these sentiments aims to avoid contact with the body. In his thinking, a woman will suspect all sentiments with an "inhibited goal." She knows that this is not love in the sense of accepting otherness and reciprocal desires. In Enriquez's view, for women, friendship is either a loving fascination of an hypnotic type or of bonds of solidarity, which is to say, of reciprocal identifications which entail the formation of uniform and non-differentiated egos. Such bonds introduce individuals to the construction of collective behaviors, and not to specific and inventive conduct such as loving relationships. The woman knows that the group, which is held together only by the libidinal bond, is in reality the grave-digger of real love, which is nourished by differences, hesitations, remorse, and creativity. Enriquez notes that Freud had already stressed the homosexual character of the human group.[40]

In his view, Freud gives woman the role of the guardian of erotic values and thus of life, whereas man is always given to accept a world of doubles, of those like himself in the strongest sense of the term or a world where he can still feel himself to be an infant before an all powerful and benevolent father. In Enriquez's view, woman will always tend to appear as an intruder who will upset the tranquillity of the homosexual relationship, of which one of the possible outcomes is its articulation with the death drive.

Eugène Enriquez believes that woman recalls that incest is always possible. He reminds us that incest is the consequence of a crime committed in common. For him, incest is the result of a pack of brothers, of their first homosexual oath, and of their first and simultaneously their most serious attempt at a bond of love. To be born, civilization must proclaim community, exogamy, and the choice of new objects. It must proclaim the forbidden, "You will not have sexual relations (therefore you do not have the right to have sexual relations) with the object that you, however, love the most." For Enriquez, civilization leads thereby to a first dissociation between bodily love and affection and between blood ties and bonds of alliance. Civilization emerges from the repression of the first love.[41]

While Eugène Enriquez and Lillian B. Rubin agree that little boys separate from their mothers, they give different reasons for this separation. For Rubin, the anatomical differences between a small boy and his mother make reasonable the separation which otherwise feels so unreasonable, but for Enriquez, as the repressed always returns, civilization will attempt to use the desires which have been repressed to weave community bonds. It will try to constitute groups solidly bound by love of the Mother Goddess or of God the Father--by figures whose beings preserve always the nostalgia and cannot accept the definitive separation.[42]

At this point in their scenarios of human development, these two sociologists also differ radically. For Enriquez, the prohibition of sleeping with one's mother is completed by infantile sexuality in its manifestations and is translated into a requirement of an identical sexual life for all. Here Rubin sees two very different kinds of development for boys and girls. In her view, a boy copes with the pain of this shift by building a set of defenses that will serve him for better or worse for the rest of his life. At this point, the boy begins to develop the fixed and firm ego boundaries that rigidly separate himself from others and that circumscribe his relationships with others and his connection to his own inner emotional life. In Lillian B. Rubin's view, the girl's gender identity does not require such a wrenching break with the past because she does not need to displace the internalized representation of the mother. From her perspective, the girl does not need to build defenses against feeling and attachment and thus does not need to develop rigid ego boundaries to protect her defenses. For Rubin, the girl's more permeable ego boundaries constitute a paramount fact in the management of her internal and external life.

While for Enriquez men are better at community bonding because they had to bind together to kill their father, Rubin sees a woman's self as more continuous with the other which allows her to maintain close personal connection and empathy with others.[43] In contrast, it is clear from Enriquez's citations that Freud thought that women had fewer social interests than men and a lesser ability to sublimate their instincts. Freud explained that this lesser social interest was due to the asocial character of all sexual relations. For Freud, lovers suffice unto themselves. Likewise, the family puts an obstacle in the way of abandoning a narrower circle for a larger one.

For Enriquez, woman speaks the truth about love. The truth is that direct sexual bonds are the place of mutual recognition and thus of the dangers tied to this recognition--perception of the castrated body of the woman and of the castration of the man. These sexual bonds are the space where the stake of paternity and maternity is played out--accepting the child of, wanting to be the father and mother of, entering into bonds of filiation. Direct sexual bonds are the motor of the desire of knowing and of an activity of pleasure of thought. They are the only place where pleasure of the body and of the soul cannot be dissociated. The sexual bond is invading, exclusive, and sometimes terrifying.

Enriquez poses the question, "Why is it up to the woman to speak the truth about love?" He replies that it is by her speech and her deeds that man is recognized as possessing strength and giving pleasure. Enriquez states that man can give pleasure to almost any woman and that is why he can rape alone or in a group. Engène Enriquez believes that a woman can revel only with some men who are able to make her body speak.[44]

Even though both Lillian B. Rubin's and Eugène Enriquez's differing, neo-psychoanalytic accounts of the genesis of friendship are intriguing scenarios, they both suffer from being excessively armchair hypotheses. While media attention makes the reality of incest common knowledge today, Enriquez's implication that the tale of Oedipus is a historical reality in some generic sense for all humanity is refuted by contemporary science, and even Kardiner reported that Freud thought of it as a "just so" story. Likewise, Rubin's claim that all women are better at empathy and human connectedness than men because they did not have to separate radically from their mothers does not take into account the wide variety of forms of socialization cross-culturally nor does it explain why various male religious functionaries, therapists, political leaders, musicians, and others have been described in history, literature, art, and social science as being empathetic and able to inspire and forge strong links to other human beings. Nor does Rubin's notion of the derivative permeability of women's ego boundaries enabling friendship explain the wide variability I found in the friendships of the women reported in this study. In brief, Lillian B. Rubin's interpretation of the origin of male-female differences in friendship suffers from a strong feminist ideological bias.

On the other hand, both Freud's and Enriquez's claim that women are mistrustful of friendship is refuted by much evidence from history and sociology presented throughout this book. Besides overemphasizing the woman's role as a sexual being, Freud and Enriquez lose sight of the connectedness and empathy Rubin discovers but exaggerates in women's friendships. Conversely, by raising a working hypothesis of brothers getting together to kill their father to the level of objective reality and characterizing that reality as homosexual, Enriquez exaggerates the male ability to form social bonds and undervalues the possibility for social ties to positively transform human beings despite the existence of crime.

I believe that my application of Jean Maisonneuve's social phenomenology in the preceding section confers a meaning upon friendship more usable by agents of social change than do the psychoanalytic views of friendship offered by either Lillian B. Rubin or Eugène Enriquez. Still, their sociological and psychoanalytic interpretations that arrive at opposing meanings of friendship are important and need to be addressed.

Notes

1. Gurdin, J. Barry, "The Therapy of Friendship," *Small Group Behavior* 17 (1986): 444-457.

2. See: Hutter, Horst, *Politics as Friendship* (Waterloo, Ontario: Wilfrid Laurier University Press, 1978); Reohr, Janet, "The Place of Reciprocity in Friendship." Ph.D. diss., Boston University, School of Education, 1978. Some of this negative feeling towards friendship research resulted from the rising influence of structuralism. Structure was prestigiously separated from sentiment, and friendship had been considered something sentimental from the earliest consideration of it by social scientists. Secondly, the anti-social psychologism of structuralism and the anti-personality position of a majority of orthodox Marxists associated friendship studies with neo-behaviorism, empiricism, and neo-conservatism. While these points of view created a generally hostile climate for friendship studies, other schools of thought primarily interested in ethology, symbolic interactionism, ethnomethodology, humanistic Marxism, continuing structural functionalism, social psychology, and elite analysis, nevertheless, pursued studies of friendship from many perspectives.

3. See: Gurdin, J. Barry, "The Therapy of Friendship," *Small Group Behavior* 17 (1986): 444-457. Also see: O'Connor, Pat,

Friendships between Women: A Critical Review (New York: The Guilford Press, 1992), 2.

4. See: Duck, Steve, *Friends, For Life: The Psychology of Close Relationships* (New York: St. Martin's Press, 1983), 166.

5. See: Gurdin, J. Barry, "Groups for the Development of Friendship," *Small Group Behavior* 19 (1988).

6. See: Lasch, Christopher, *The Culture of Narcissism: American Life in an Age of Diminishing Expectations* (New York: Norton, 1978). Schur, Edwin M., *The Awareness Trap: Self-absorption instead of Social Change* (New York: Quadrangle Books, 1976).

7. See: Johnson, David W. and Frank P. Johnson, *Joining Together: Group Theory and Group Skills* (Englewood Cliffs, New Jersey: Prentice Hall, 1975). See: Maisonneuve, Jean, *Psycho-sociologie des affinités* (Paris: Presses Universitaires de France, 1966). One group that I facilitated contrasted dramatically with the one in the convalescent center and those at the college discussed in the main text. The people who participated in this very different group were poets, artists, and social activists in San Francisco. On Saturday, February 27, 1988, this group was filmed by Artists Embassy International for showing on Cable Channel 25. In the later group, the emphasis on external social hierarchy was muted, perhaps because in their subculture a greater range of sensitive personal information was permitted--which had less impact on long-term job and career possibilities for them.

8. Gurdin, J. Barry. "Groups for the Development of Friendship," *Small Group Behavior* 19, (1988).

9. Maisonneuve, Jean, *Psycho-sociologie des affinités,* 251.

10. Ibid, 250.

11. Ibid., 255.

12. The correlation coefficients for all of these questions resulted in the following matrix:

Questions	Q16	Q19	Q24	Q12	Q15	Q2	Q23	Q7
Q14 (Time)	.2143	.5543	-.3241	.3973	.6706	.4750	-.0714	-.4560
Q16 (Responsibility)	1.0000	-.4008	-.5513	-.0855	.1892	-.1075	-.3859	.0943
Q19 (Political)		1.0000	-.0820	-.0323	.1077	.5448	.2403	.2150
Q24 (Ask Yourself)			1.0000	.1905	-.5328	-.1075	-.3859	-.1290
Q12 (Discuss)				1.0000	.3611	.0233	.3714	-.2866
Q15 (Sacrifice)					1.0000	.3538	.2599	-.0189
Q2 (Opposite Sex Friend)						1.0000	.0619	-.0154
Q23 (Unexplainable)							1.0000	-.2281
Q 7 (Different Occupation)								1.0000
Scale Item	-.1968	.1527	-.3107	.1377	.2277	.2344	-.0396	-.1027

13. Gurdin, Joseph Barry, "*Amitié*/Friendship: The Socio-cultural Construction of Friendship in Contemporary Montreal." Ph.D. diss., Department of Sociology, Université de Montréal, 1978, 659-668.

14. Hayes, Robert B., "The Development and Maintenance of Friendship." 1 *Journal of Social and Personal Relationships* (London: Sage Publications Ltd.), 1984, 75;77.

15. Gurdin, Joseph Barry, "*Amitié*/Friendship: The Socio-cultural Construction of Friendship in Contemporary Montreal," 1978, 235-236;264-312.

16. Ibid., 2-161.

17. Maisonneuve, Jean, *Psycho-sociologie des affinités*, 515.

18. Such a question was posed by Maisonneuve, and I repeated it on my questionnaire:

23. To what do you attribute the strength and firmness of a friendship? (Classify the answers from 1 to 5, noting 1 as the motive which you judge to be the most important, down to 5 as the least important):
_____due to the fact of having the opportunity to be
      together quite often and easily [#1];
_____due to the fact of having the same tastes [#2];
_____due to the fact of having the same ideas and opinions [#3];
_____due to the fact of belonging to the same social milieu [#4];
_____due to a really unexplainable attraction [#5];
_____other, please specify [#6]:

Two mistakes were accidentally made which throw off these answers to some extent. When data analysis was begun, it was discovered that the response, "other, please specify," had been left off the French version of the written questionnaire, and that the response, "due to the fact of having the same ideas and opinions," had been left off the coding sheets for the in-depth recorded interview data forms. Despite these accidental omissions, responses #1, #2, #4, and #5 are correct on all forms and their results are unhampered by the aforementioned flaws.

19. Maisonneuve, Jean, *Psycho-sociologie des affinités,* 246-8.

20. *Question #23, "To what do you attribute the strength and the firmness of a friendship? (Classify the answers from 1 to 5 noting as 1 the motive which you judge to be the most important down to 5 as the least important)." Note that it was necessary to add a sixth rank due to actual responses.*

The Relationship between the Responses regarding the Strength of a Friendship and Their Rank from Most (1) to Least Important (6)

Count Column %	Rank of Response						Row Total
Responses regarding the Strength of a Friendship	1	2	3	4	5	6	
Having the Opportunity to Be Together Quite Often and Easily	57 31.1%	40 24.8%	30 19.7%	15 10.5%	19 11.7%	1 10%	162 20%
Having the Same Tastes	35 19.1%	36 22.4%	47 30.9%	28 19.6%	13 8%	2 20%	161 19.9%
Having the Same Ideas and Opinions	24 13.1%	28 17.4%	22 14.5%	22 15.4%	16 9.9%	0 0%	112 13.8%
Belonging to the Same Social Milieu	22 12%	31 19.3%	25 16.4%	33 23.1%	44 27.2%	4 40%	159 19.6%
Due to a Really Unexplainable Attraction	24 13.1%	22 13.7%	22 14.5%	39 27.3%	45 27.8%	3 30%	155 19.1%
Other, Please Specify	21 11.5%	4 2.5%	6 3.9%	6 4.2%	25 15.4%	0 0%	62 7.6%
Column Total Column %	183 22.6%	161 19.9%	152 18.7%	143 17.6%	162 20%	10 1.2%	811 100%

Somers's D (Asymmetric) = .20199; with Responses Dependent = .19771; Somers's D (Symmetric) = .19982

21. Fraisse, Jean-Claude, *Philia: La notion d'amitié dans la philosophie antique: Essai sur un problème perdu et retrouvé* (Paris: Philosophique J. Vrin, 1974), 33.

22. Ibid., 32.

23. Ibid., 47-48.

24. Ibid., 150.

25. Fraisse, Jean-Claude, *Philia: La notion d'amitié dans la philosophie antique: Essai sur un problème perdu et retrouvé* , 55-64.

26. Ibid., 11-116.

27. Cicero, Marcus Tullius, *Essay on Friendship. Laelius De Amicitia*, trans. from the Latin with notes by Alexander J. Inglis (New York: The Platt & Peck Co., 1908), 1908, 25-26.

28. Gurdin, Joseph Barry, "*Amitié*/Friendship: The Socio-cultural Construction of Friendship in Contemporary Montreal," 1978, 684-765.

29. See: Hutter, Horst, *Politics as Friendship* (Waterloo, Ontario: Wilfrid Laurier University Press, 1978); My notes are from the course of Hans Peter Dreitzel on "Love and Friendship" at Boston University, Summer 1977; Maisonneuve, Jean, *Psycho-sociologie des affinités,* 439; Metzger, Nancy J. and Gerald M. Phillips, *Intimate Communication* (Boston: Allyn and Bacon, 1976).

30. The friendships to which I refer are those of a man of English Canadian origin who was happily married with two children and who was in perfect health enjoying a successful career when he suddenly learned his body would wither to total incapacitation within a short time, and only his mind and sexual organs would be left with normal functioning. After he lived beyond the time he expected, his wife withdrew from any communication with him except delivering his children to the hospital, but his closest male friend from before his illness remained loyal. Besides this friendship he formed one of *philia* with one of his nurses and one of *eros* with another. All these friendships were of the utmost importance in granting him the psycho-social strength to live. See: Gurdin, J. Barry, "Friendship between Nurses and Their Patients--An Atypical Case Study." Paper delivered as part of the session on "Bridging the Gap from Hospital to Home. Fifth Annual Conference ARN/RNI (Association of Rehabilitation Nurses), Chicago, Illinois, 1979b.

31. Maisonneuve, Jean, *Psycho-sociologie des affinités,* 443.

32. Reviewing literary critiques and film, Seymour Martin Lipset comes to a similar conclusion. Quoting Gaile McGregor, he notes that "The Canadian man is more 'gentle and retiring.' " See: Seymour Martin

Lipset, *Continental Divide: The Values and Institutions of the United States and Canada* (New York: Routledge, 1990), 64, 188.

33. Maisonneuve, Jean, *Psycho-sociologie des affinités,* 443.

34. Ibid., 434-435.

35. Ibid., 433-434.

36. Suttie, Ian D., *The Origin of Love and Hate* with a Preface by Dr. J. A. Hadfield (London: Kegan Paul, Trench Trubner and Company, Ltd., [1935] 1939).

37. Maisonneuve, *Psycho-sociologie des affinités,* 37.

38. Fromm, Erich, *Sigmund Freud's Mission: An Analysis of His Personality and Influence* (New York: Harper & Bros. Publishers, 1959), 38, 40.

39. Enriquez, Eugène, *De la horde à l'état: Essai de psychanalyse du lien social* (Paris: Éditions Gallimard, 1983), 48-49. In this passage and the following text referred to through footnote 42, I have done an abridged translation, paraphrasing and editing of Eugène Enriquez's text. I have thus omitted parts of his sentences that added details to his main thought but which created overly dense and almost incomprehensible English sentences. Likewise, I have stuck as closely as possible to Lillian B. Rubin's words and thoughts but not put them in direct quotations in this section, for I selected them only for contrastive purposes in comparing them to Enriquez or to Fromm's interpretation of Freud's friendships.

40. Ibid., 120-121.

41. Ibid., 121.

42. Ibid., 122.

43. See: Gurdin, J. Barry, *Amitié / Friendship: An Investigation into Cross-cultural Styles in Canada and the United States,* 272-273.

44. Enriquez, Eugène, *De la horde à l'état,* 120.

Chapter Nine

The Meanings of Friendship

[(Friend)/(ship)] has meanings which different social agents construct differently in varying settings. This meaning is spoken about, enacted, observed, and reduced from various disciplinary perspectives.

The major components of the notion of friendship are trust, communication, help, reliability, likeness, durability, sharing, affection, understanding, enjoyment, sincerity, corporeality, signs, company, conflict, respect, materiality, concern, spirituality, unexplainability and specifics. These specifics point to development, toleration, degrees, good, equality, rarity, relationship, intelligence, wanting, agreement, kinship, and particulars.

Friendship is culturally encoded within a cognitive field which distinguishes it from other social relationships. It refers to a voluntary act. Being friends means forming a bond with persons who tend to be like oneself in terms of many criteria, or, to the contrary, with persons who possess the qualities one lacks. Doing friendship means having a relationship which usually lasts a long period of time during at least one cycle of life frequently because of proximity in residence or work. Friendship is characterized by degrees of relationship between a small number of intimate persons who sometimes feel being pulled in different ways among themselves. Friends are concerned with spending time with each other and not giving up their bond for social mobility. Friendship allows for differences of opinions among friends who sometimes break off their association, usually because they change their place of residence or undergo a major change in private life such as marriage or divorce. Friends think about friendship sometimes.

In reality, friendship means a possible additional bond within the kinship system. In fact, friends can sketch their closest friends' personalities, which they usually esteem or at least respect and support. Emotionality and affectivity exude from friends who also understand, advise, talk, and gesticulate non-verbally to each other with some degree of feedback. Friendship includes acts of helping out friends and feelings of being able to depend on friends generally for psycho-social, rather than, substantive material kinds of exchange.

Without too much doubt, it is often assumed that these components of friendship systematically relate to one another. However, their interplay has been interpreted differently by various folk, social scientific, and philosophical explanations.

In using phenomenology to understand friendship, one methodological stumbling block has been the phenomenologist's ultimate claim of truth as "I see it that way."[1] This position has lead to inconsistent interpretations of the relations among these elements of friendship. Given this situation, some of these divergent viewpoints in social scientific studies of friendship need to be reviewed, compared, and contrasted to sort out the most precise description. In covering this territory, I will review some diverse facets of friendship; referents of the friendship experience; friendship from within the relationship; the roles of fantasy, imagination, and the unconscious in friendship; and the relationships between friendship and society.

Some Differing Facets of Friendship

Phenomenologists or other humanists should not be overly disturbed if their accounts of the same object differ, for an object of inquiry such as friendship may be viewed from several horizons. The expectation that all treatments of human relations should produce the same conclusions is derived from the natural science paradigm of the social sciences. Unlike material objects, human beings are sentient, thinking, and intentional creatures.

Inspired by Erving Goffman's version of symbolic interactionism, Robert Paine summed up the Western, middle-class type of friendship by three ideal characteristics, "autonomy, unpredictability and terminality."[2]

Jean Maisonneuve's cross-class, statistically grounded, social phenomenology picks out three main groups of sentiments which constitute friendship. These are "the sense of confirmation, the sense[s] of mutual accomplishment and personal enrichment, and the sense of communion."[3]

Horst Hutter criticized Parsonian sociology's characterization of friendship as "particularistic, affective, diffuse, and other-oriented" because such a characterization does not move beyond the level of taxonomies and does not distinguish friendships clearly enough from other relationships defined by these traits. Hutter goes on to stress that structural functionalism fails to penetrate the subjectively felt meaning of friendship.[4]

These three perspectives on the essential features of friendship stress diverging aspects of the friend experience. In contrast to the emphasis on freedom in the writings of these three scholars, the Anglo-American social psychological tradition depicts friendship as a graduated process of intimacy. Thus, Murray S. Davis identifies a

> major force that transforms isolated intimates--the routinization of their cycle of coming togethers and going aparts. Intimates increase the binding power of this force insofar as they intersect, or even overlap their customary routines of movement and insofar as they puncture the pellicle of privacy that causes the unacquainted and, to a lesser extent, the merely acquainted to bounce off each other whenever they run into each other by chance.[5]

Even when George McCall refers to this element of freedom in friendship, it is with emphasis placed on its structural limitations. He considers that social control is

> peculiarly up to each member to accomplish. ... Because there is only one other member, one cannot 'blow the whistle' on another, calling attention of other members to the offender.[6]

Within this same intellectual tradition, Irwin Altman and Dalmas A. Taylor write:

> Thus as people continue to interact and maintain a relationship, they gradually move toward deeper and deeper areas of their mutual personalities through the use of words, bodily behavior, and environmental behavior.[7]

The Referents of the Friendship Experience

Similar referents to the friendship experience are grouped under different components by these authors, and they disagree about the nature of some of the same referents.

Paine's concept of friendship as a "personal and private relationship" emphasizes that "a personal relationship is between particular persons" and that "it is personal in that a man defines his relationship with another on the basis of the experience he has had with him." By privacy he means,

> that the relationship may be established and maintained independent of reference to the various group derived statuses of the individuals. It also means that particular individuals may choose whether or not they will communicate to others the content and norms of the relations between them.[8]

It is difficult to accept that middle class friendship, even in today's Newfoundland, in more urban parts of Canada, or in the United States, is so free from the control of the larger society, for macro-societal forces did enter into most Montrealers' closest friendships in my own and other studies.[9] Beyond the institutional role constraints noted by Hutter, in Montreal, I documented how the traditional elements of the division of labor and the historical character of groups influenced the interaction between friends or inhibited formation of friendship between males and females, youngers and olders, English and French Canadians, blue collar and white collar workers and professionals, singles and married persons with and without children. In addition, I gathered extensive data on Montrealers' descriptions of their close friends' personalities and of my and my interviewers' descriptions of the interviewees' and respondents' personalities.[10]

That these factors are active in close friendships is linked to friendship's being a personal relationship, for being of a particular sex, age, ethnic, class, and civil status are characteristics inherent in the persona of the friend. Because friendship is a relationship which encourages the preservation of its interactants' whole selves rather than their merging into a new dyadic self, toleration, respect, and appreciation of these ascribed and achieved statuses are the modes of recognition of these differences in true friendship. Likewise, for Max Weber friendship is a communal relationship because

> the orientation is based on subjective feeling of the parties, whether affectual or traditional, that they belong together.[11]

While Paine is in agreement on the affective nature of friendship and its demands on intimacy and confidence, he claims that this line of reasoning will present the researcher only with a number of questions about affective relationships. To the contrary, what for Maisonneuve is most essential about this affectivity is its personality:

> Thus we go from a centripetal to a centrifugal perspective hardly without noticing it, where I am "strengthened" and "strengthening" in turn, but the dominant axis remains in terms of "I"; it aims at what I receive or what I give; in all

cases I feel valued from this first confirmation of being "recognized" by another to being "cause" for him."[12]

The affectivity in friendship is handled very differently by other social scientists' writings on friendship.[13] About this matter, Robert Paine says,

> I mean that the basic 'motive' or rather affective meaning and value of friendship is the *sense of worth* ... it imparts to the person enjoying it. If I dared spell this out further, I would say that what is 'special' about the affective aspect of friendship is that the friend is one who understands one, who can explain one to oneself; alternatively a person is able to see himself in his friend.[14]

Jean Maisonneuve does indeed dare to spell out the affective content of friendship. Maisonneuve's notion of "the sense of confirmation" overlaps with Paine's idea of the "sense of worth," and has other sources besides mutual understanding and the mirror image of the self.

> It covers a group of feelings of gratifying and reassuring tonality, notably:--the pleasure of feeling that you exist, that you count for someone;--that of feeling preferred, chosen as a friend;--the feeling of a kind of vulnerability due to the sole fact of being together;--the pride of feeling capable of bringing something to another and also more specifically of being for him a source of joy.[15]

For Maisonneuve "a sense of mutual accomplishment and enrichment" can be disentangled from another group of feelings of "an expansive tonality which evokes a transformation of the person and his perception of the world thanks to the friendship exchange." Other feelings he identifies in friendship include the following:

> 1) The impression of acceding to a more intense and authentic mode of existence, by distilling and maturing: the environment is stripped of everyday confusion to reveal meanings unnoticed heretofore. 2) The correlated feeling of personal growth, while before the friendly encounter I

vegetated in some respect. From then on I am able to express myself with vigor and fervor. Eventually [I will be able] to create. 3) The feeling that it is a relation of exchange, of mutual benefit, for I aroused the same latent resources in my friend. ... This latent message of each partner to the Other in friendship as in love [is]: "Thou becomest what thou art."[16]

Finally Maisonneuve takes up

a set of feelings which are harder to sort out than the preceding because they are nearly always experienced outside or beyond language in the sequence of contemplation, creation, or exultation. ... of being together, of profound intimacy, and of a "we" where the I and the Thou are no longer truly discernible.[17]

He found non-exclusive modalities of this communal intimacy:

The peaceful intimate ("being together"): Here we touch upon what D. Ochanine, in his thesis on *Sympathy*, named the state of "repose for two," in describing it as an immediate, silent, agreement requiring no operative interaction and stripped of intentionality, but supposing a partner before whom we are free not to carry our mask, [and] whom we have no need or no longer a need to conquer.[18]

Maisonneuve's "fruitful intimacy" and doing-together have less to do with the affective side of friendship than "lyrical intimacy" by which he contrasts the more sober character of jubilation in friendship to the exaltation of love. Sometimes lyrical intimacy appears in some quiet phases of friendship or in bursts of cooperation and search for creativity. He describes these experiences in the following passage:

We are here at the height of communion in friendship when the "we" takes on full consciousness of its reality and tends more or less to verbalize what it lives as to get nearer one's friend and to concretize it even more through speech. ... These experiences imply a mixture of surprise and certitude: surprise because they are experienced as a sort of grace, of chance and of revelation exceeding all expectation; certitude because they are there in their striking evidence and not to be rejected to the point of giving the sense of a predestination to the encounter and to the affective bond.

They introduce the friends together in a spatio-temporal milieu which cannot be reduced to banal distances and hours. There one touches on a kind of existential property of whatever kind of intimacy. In this respect, there always appears a difference, if not of nature, then at least of degree and amplitude between the intimacy of friendship and of love. While love can totally transform ordinary experience and invade the whole existential field, friendship has a more partial effect and remains compatible with other modes and affective bonds. Friendship breaks the bothersome time and boredom of the everyday and arouses a quality of fullness which fills the inner-time and suspends it in some way ... for a very brief period. ... Friendship time appears calmer and more homogeneous. Even if it contains moments of emotive intensity (during certain exchanges of secrets, discoveries or the success of some common undertakings), it does not introduce any ruptures as radical as love in the everyday run of things.[19]

Concerned with the preconditions for affectivity to function in friendship, Hutter finds that the organic solidarity of modern society, which is built on complementary differentiation of social roles and subgroups, thwarts individuals in the search for friendship. Modern individuals end up relating to each other with only parts of their personalities because this complementariness of roles fragments bonds into many specific parts and prevents diffuse and total relationships.[20]

Much earlier, Émile Durkheim explained the determination of friendship relations by an "apportionment of functions," which led to "a feeling of solidarity." He wrote:

Everybody knows that we like those who resemble us, those who think and feel as we do. But the opposite is no less true. It very often happens that we feel kindly towards those who do not resemble us, precisely because of this lack of resemblance. These facts are apparently so contradictory that moralists have always vacillated concerning the true nature of friendship and have derived it sometimes from the former, sometimes from the latter. The Greeks had long ago posed this problem. "Friendship," says Aristotle, "causes much discussion. According to some people, it consists in a certain resemblance, and we like those who resemble us: whence the proverbs 'birds of a feather flock together' and 'like seeks like,' and other such phrases. Others, on the contrary, say that all who are alike are opposed to one another. Again, some men push their inquiries on these points higher and reason from a consideration of nature. So Euripides says,

> The earth by drought consumed doth love the rain,
> And the great heaven overcharged with rain,
> Doth love to fall in showers upon the earth.

Heraclitus, again, maintains the 'contrariety is expedient, and that the best agreement arises from things differing, and that all things come into being in the way of the principle of antagonism.' "

These opposing doctrines prove that both types are necessary to natural friendship. Difference, as likeness, can be a cause of mutual attraction. However, certain differences do not produce this effect. We do not find any pleasure in those completely different from us. Spendthrifts do not seek the company of misers, nor moral and honest people that of hypocrites and pretenders; sweet and gentle spirits have no taste for sour and malevolent temperaments. Only certain kinds of differences attract each other. They are those which, instead of opposing and excluding, complement each other. As Bain says, there is a type of difference which repels, another which attracts, one which leads to rivalry, another which leads to friendship. If one of two people has what the other has not, but desires, in that fact lies the point of departure for a positive attraction. Thus it is that a theorist, a subtle and reasoning individual, often has a very special sympathy for practical men, with their quick sense and rapid intuitions; the timid for the firm and resolute, the weak for the strong, and conversely. As richly endowed as we may be, we always lack something, and the best of us realize our own insufficiency. That is why we seek in our friends the qualities that we lack, since in joining with them, we participate in some measure in their nature and thus feel less incomplete. So it is that small friendly associations are formed wherein each one plays a role conformable to his character, where there is a true exchange of services. One urges on, another consoles; this one advises, that one follows the advice, and it is this apportionment of functions or, to use the usual expression, this division of labor, which determines the relations of friendship.[21]

In relation to the issue of affectivity in friendship, Hutter takes historical note that when ancient Greek society was not able to meet the universal human needs of self confirmation through intimacy and self-revelation between the sexes, friendship became an intra-sexual relationship.[22] Those contrasting patterns of friendship were articulated in the different views of friendship espoused by Plato, on the one hand, and Aristotle (together with the Stoics and Epicureans) on the other.

Friendship from within the Relationship

A central point of disagreement in the literature centers around Paine's concept of "rules of relevancy of friendship." They refer

> principally to the internal arrangement of the relationship rather than to rules of impression management for the outside world; and within the relationship the rules refer less to content and more to conduct. Above all else, the rules of relevancy in friendship relate to the fact that friends are closely concerned with the evaluation each places on the other.[23]

So too would Gerald D. Suttles and C. S. Lewis agree in their emphasis on the personal code of the friendship dyad--even to the extent of its defying the surrounding society's norms. Yet, Maisonneuve might ask Paine why, if a friend is so concerned with the other's evaluation, does the partner tend to "ignore or to hide from the other and himself the secret joys which their relationship gives him."[24] And Dreitzel would argue that friend may not want to enter into a collusive relationship with his or her friend but unconscious drives may bring on such collusive acts.

Hutter's work on ancient Greece and my work in contemporary Montreal show how social and cultural typified actions operate within close friendship so as to prevent close friendship from arising. These "typified actions" or "styles" may be conscious or unconscious, but they are derived from real friendships where the external world puts pressure on the internal arrangement to conform to the established patterns.

Another area in which these studies of friendship reach varying interpretations is in regard to the measure of personal autonomy afforded a person in handling a relationship and in making or breaking a close friendship. Although similar to Suttles's later analysis, Paine's description of this aspect of friendship is the most idealistic of all the accounts:

> Privacy in a personal relationship, then, means that the relationship may be established and maintained independent of reference to the various group-derived statuses of the individuals. It also means that particular individuals may choose whether or not they will communicate to others the content and norms of conduct of the relations between them. In short, the hallmark of a personal/private relationship is the measure of autonomy afforded to a person, both in the way he handles the relationship and in his original decision to make the relationship and in any decision to break it.[25]

Although such privacy might be a perfect state of friendship, and even though individuals do escape social controls to a large extent when they work at it in their friendships, Maisonneuve's and my investigations link this personal/private aspect to the socio-cultural determinants we found in real friendships.

In Hutter's description, the personal/private realm in friendship is a product of the character of the Self. This consideration raises an issue which is passed over in Paine's criterial typology in that it implies that the character of the ego, which is essentially psychological, sets the tune for the role base of the friend, which is explicitly denied by Paine.[26] Hutter stresses that a friend must fulfill his or her friend's needs or the relationship risks termination.[27]

In my study of Montreal friendships there was a nearly universal recognition among the interviewees that they generally felt differently with a close friend than with a contact on the job, a business client, a teacher or a priest, and that the difference consisted in their feeling relaxed, at ease, and non-competitive with their close friends. Even so, they perceived a continuum which varied in different circumstances. If they were in a bad mood or had a hard day at work or at school, these products of the impersonal and public world carried over into their get-togethers with their close friends. In short, the distinction between these two realms was highly blurred in everyday life.

These considerations certainly call into question Paine's notion of a terminal relationship and Suttles's emphasis that friends' basic assumption goes "beyond a mere presentation of self in compliance with 'social dictates,' " for only among the most socially graceful for whom friendship is a central relationship might it be true that

> ... where it is the will of the friends, the content or conduct of a friendship may not be carried into social interaction with other persons; it stays inside of the relationship which generated it. ... In summary, the making and breaking of friendships in our society is largely a matter of personal choice that is beyond social control.[28]

Paine seems to be confusing norms with socio-cultural reality. The fact is that contemporary society exerts control over friendship. For example, in earlier chapters we observed that modern society, in providing mobility for its citizens, ruptures friendship through moving, which is a by-product of greater horizontal and vertical mobility. Similarly, in offering people more supple legal forms of terminating marriages, there was an unanticipated social consequence of greater chances of breaking with close friends when divorce occurs.

Fantasy, Imagination, and the Unconscious in Friendship

Another area in which quite different shades of meaning have been attributed to friendship is in the importance accorded to fantasy, the imagination, the unconscious, and the phenomena of collusion and connivance.

Maisonneuve reviews the studies that underscore that friendship is full of ideal values.[29] This relationship organizes the friends' needs to attain these goals to the best of their ability so much so that any eventual change in their ideal could be considered as a transformation in their system of needs, thereby bringing about a disturbance in their established relationships. In this context, he reminds us that Freud was concerned with the influence of the ego ideal in determining the object of choice and in the meaning of the process of idealization of this object. In his interpretation, the Freudian ego ideal could be considered as the inheritor or substitute for narcissism or the self love that the child initially nourishes towards itself. Freud posited this as normal and spontaneous and defined it as the libidinal complement of egoism. Thus, narcissism manifests itself in the experience and choice of the friend, including the desire and pleasure of being loved or inversely the fear, pain, and shame of not being paid back. On this Freudian base, Maisonneuve proposed that:

> Every affinity is founded in large part on narcissistic connivance ... To the extent ... that every choice carries with it a narcissistic component, every affinal encounter takes on at least the form of a connivance where the narcissism of each can and ought to find its use.[30]

Empirically there is evidence for this narcissism in replicating Maisonneuve's point of view of the definitions of friendship. In Montreal I found in classifying my respondents' definitions within Maisonneuve's five categories, that ego-centered definitions were the most frequently occurring among both English (48% [of the definitions]) and French Canadians (40%).[31]

Examining the role of imagination in friendship, Maisonneuve noted that friends can concoct extremely rich images from their surroundings, particularly those which they desire but do not have. Through friends, persons may confer reality on some of their dominant fantasies. When two people enact some of their core fantasies, Jean Maisonneuve would speak of a true affinity between them.[32] But he is quick to point out that such narcissistic connivance does not explain all bonds of friendship.[33]

Independent of Maisonneuve's influence, Hans Peter Dreitzel spelled out an even more extensive Freudian role interpretation of collusion within close friendship, love relations, and marriage in his lectures at Boston University in the summer of 1977. Dreitzel sketches basic modes of dyadic relationships. For Dreitzel, human beings tend to regress to childhood, and this process becomes pathological only if it is a permanent regression. According to him, mature, self-supporting adults form complementary relationships between progression and regression. Dreitzel defines collusion as an unconscious play interaction between two persons on the basis of a similar unresolved personality conflict. It is expressed in different roles. These persons do not share the same conflicts; rather they have different conflicts. This conceptualization refers to polarization of the same constant which produces overcompensation in one partner and regressive behavior in the other. Both partners perceive the interaction as self-therapeutic within a dyadic relationship. According to Dreitzel, the partners' collusive attempts in self-therapy will fail owing to Freud's "return of the repressed." They reappear in totally different spheres of relevance. A working relationship does not rely on what the case is but rather the image of what it is.

Although I did not intend to gather evidence of collusion in my study of Montreal friendships, some striking examples turned up, especially in relation to the question on how, if ever, the interviewee's close friendships were broken. If one interprets aspects of the dialogues as fantasy or projection of possible circumstances of imagination, again ample documentation for these phenomena is evident in my material.

Like Dreitzel and Maisonneuve, Gerald M. Phillips and Nancy J. Metzger accentuate the collusive aspects of friendship; however, for them collusion is best located through a rhetorical approach to interpersonal relations.[34] Like Dreitzel, these scholars have dealt with real human communicational problems through social psychological techniques, but, unlike Dreitzel and Maisonneuve, they do not translate this experience into a Freudian explanatory model. Their eclectic theory borrows heavily on exchange theory. Like Paine they emphasize the importance of the public/private distinction in a contrast between interaction, which

> refers to relationships conducted under the prevailing norms of a large society [and transaction which] refers to the private and voluntary exchanges made as two people seek to go beyond what is permissible in the main society toward the negotiation of the constitution of a private and intimate relationship.[35]

Like Dreitzel, they believe that

> both parties exert influence on each other. There must be a psychological connection before it can be assumed that rhetoric is taking place [but in the exchange that occurs they think that each party] has the same responsibility to use rhetoric in the transmission of offers of exchange and to use rhetoric in analyzing such offers once they have been made.[36]

Drastically different from Dreitzel and Maisonneuve, they assume an essentially rational basis for human relationships. Like Dreitzel, they acknowledge that roles and norms that get built into the intimate relationship restrict the choices of people. Unlike Dreitzel, they see the conflicts arising from any particular source rather than a basic personality conflict. From Hutter's phenomenological perspective, Phillips's and Metzger's approach would seemingly lead to the establishment of inauthentic relationships because they neglect particular values and essential relations within friendships. Moreover, because they do not posit a persisting ego to which another intimate friend could relate, interaction with the Other becomes a series of self-interested manipulations aimed at a desired rhetorical result. For these two authors claim that:

> In short, rhetorical strategy in the interpersonal situation must be seen as role. Role is a complicated process of projecting various selves to others for approval and ratification. We select different roles to get different effects. The thrust of rhetorical invention in the interpersonal situation is toward the selection of the proper role to select to achieve the desired result.[37]

In "The Psychodynamics of Greek Friendship," Horst Hutter takes up the problems of collusion and connivance as products of the particular Greek pattern of friendship and as general properties of enmity. Similar to Suttles's point that "not all disclosures of self are attended by the good fortune of friendship," Hutter spots the potential for collusion in the nature of the friend relationship.[38] He writes:

> The paradox of power in friendship and enmity is, however, that no power is as total as the power one has over friends. There is no one who is as vulnerable to the actions of Self as a friend. ... The moment Other is thought to take advantage of Self's openness, Self will react with defensiveness. ... Defensiveness and hostility by Self call forth the same in Other. ... The reaction tendency to fear by Self is an assertion of its own power either over Self or Other. If Self, however, attempts to assert his power over Other, Other will react similarly.[39]

Furthermore, in the following passage Hutter depicts the psychological forces which lay the groundwork for collusion, which he later traces to adults' attempts to recapture their first love and its "substitute for the loss":

> The problem of Self relating to Other in openness about its positivity and negativity would be simple, if it were only a matter of intellectual cognition, but Self is also related to itself affectively. It loves itself in its positive image and hates itself in its negative image. Likewise, it loves that in Other which confirms its own positivity and hates that in Other which confirms its negativity. Hence, Self is initially related to Other both in love and hate. It is both enemy and friend of itself and of Other.[40]

Because this state of affairs characterizes real world friendships, Horst Hutter observes:

> The identification by Self and Other with each others' negativity must be critical in the case of friendship. ... Self overcoming, that is, overcoming of the negativity of Self takes place in terms of a set of values, a vision of the good. ... [which] must be shared by friends.[41]

Having observed that,

> In the Platonic system love is seen as the motive force of friendship, as the soil from which the flower of friendship springs. Holding that without passion there would be no friendship, Plato sees both love and friendship as a unified human drive which is the creative power responsible for the productions of man.[42]

In contrast to Plato, Horst Hutter stresses reason's underlying Aristotle's notions of friendship:

> Aristotle solves this problem by defining *philia* as a state of character. The virtuous man, governed by the rational elements in his soul, has a general disposition of philia. .... His harmonious character and his sense of justice enable him to both form deep and lasting friendships with a few like-minded individuals and to approach everyone else ... with kindness and fairness.[43]

Hutter notes that when the Greeks stressed same-sex *philia* and *eros*, they attenuated friendship and love between men and women. In Hutter's view, the institution of *hetaeries* and the practice of *paidikon eros* were costly to the family and other groupings in which men and women were related to one another. And in his perspective,

> a psychological predisposition cannot be made to account for the rise and persistence of a social structure. ... Behind the sexual antagonism there is the larger pattern of sex segregation with its ultimate roots in the economic and military division of labour.[44]

Secondly, Horst Hutter implies that the social structure forced the man's friend and love partner to become his competitor and enemy in the struggle for dominance and excellence. Thus, while the Greeks of the classics praised friendship, they also had created a system in which friendship was fleeting and untrustworthy.[45]

Finally, Hutter points out that *paidikon eros* was practiced by the upper classes and was economically costly. Moreover, as experienced by Socrates, homosexual desire needed to be sublimated to result in peace and harmony. At the time of the Peloponnesian War, *paidikon eros* came to be viewed as a Spartan practice, and Athenian aristocrats who practiced it were suspected as being Spartan sympathizers. To the middle and lower classes, who were the main advocates of democracy, *paidikon eros* appeared treasonable and unconstitutional.[46]

Friendship and Society

Hutter reminds us that:

> ... Yet, experience teaches us that certain societies, as well as certain times, are more favorable to the full development and cultivation of friendship than others. There have been long periods in Western history in which the ideals of friendship were nearly forgotten.[47]

My written questionnaires, recorded in-depth interviews, and secondary material all lend support to the observation that friendship was alive in Montreal in the 1970s. In brief, most (96%) of my interviewees described in detail a human relationship which they called and lived as close friendship. Their notions and experiences touched on all the classical criteria for friendship, although the present experience in Montreal gives a particular coloring to particular elements of the classical experience. Very few persons (4%) claimed that they had no friends or were unable to describe any close friendships. Despite these proofs for the existence of friendship, many barriers to forming or maintaining close friendships in contemporary Montreal were found to be social and cultural in character.

According to Shmuel Eisenstadt and Luis Roniger, the analysis of the place of trust (solidarity) and of meaning in the construction of the social order took on a new direction with the emerging predominance of the functional school in anthropology and especially of the structural-functional school in sociology.[48] The structural-functional approach focused on how the dimension of solidarity (trust), meaning, and--to a smaller degree--power is institutionalized in the construction of the social order. These dimensions of social life were defined as needs which every social system (and in a different way personalities and cultures) must meet. In probably the best known version of this school, the need for solidarity (integration) can be see as equivalent to trust. The social system's other needs included: pattern maintenance (meaning); the need for maintaining instrumental orientations (closely related to, but not entirely identical with power); and the need for adaptation to the respective system's environment. Shills stressed the crucial importance of primary relations and of solidarity and trust as basic components of any social interaction or social system.[49]

In Eisenstadt's and Roniger's analysis only in human beings beyond the toddler stage does attachment become combined in the search for meaning. This quest is closely connected to the vicissitudes of the institutionalization of trust. Only at this time is this search endowed with the special symbols of pure dialogue between man and man and man and God, the "I and Thou." To express this quest most clearly, they quote Martin Buber:

> in every sphere, in every relational act, through everything that becomes present to us, we gaze toward the train of the eternal You; in each we perceive a breath of it; in every You we address the eternal You; in every sphere according to its manner. All spheres are included in it, while it is included in none ... When the perfect encounter is to occur, the gates are unified into the one gate of actual life, and you no longer know through which one you have entered.[50]

Having identified this juncture, Einsenstadt and Roniger are able to situate trust and intimacy within the larger social system:

> The search for such pure pristine trust and intimacy and for equal participation in pristine meaning, for the pure dialogue, becomes most fully articulated in situations in which the potential for breakdown of the extension of trust develops, and in situations of transition from one institutional realm to another. In turn, as has been indicated in sociological studies of friendship and in the comparative study of age groups and youth movements, this potentiality develops especially when such realms are structured according to different principles and entail dissimilar ways of interweaving of trust, meaning and instrumental and power relations.[51]

Within this social system's orientation, Cora DuBois identified a matrix of cross-cultural dimensions and categories.[52] The Montreal styles of friendship may be classified into DuBois' framework, as follows:

	Exclusive	Close	Casual
Expressive-Instrumental	Primarily Expressive D, E	Expressive-Instrumental A1, A2, A3, A4, B1, B2, C1	Largely Instrumental C2
Dyadic-Polyadic	Dyadic/Exclusive A1, A2, A3, A4, B1, B2, D, E	Multiple Dyads A1, A2, A3, A4, B1, B2, C1, D	Polyadic C2
Intimacy (confidence, responsibility)	Inclusive D, E	Selective A1, A2, A3, A4, B1, B2, C1, D	Incidental A3, A4, C2
Mutability	Assumed Permanent A1, E, D	Hoped Durable A2, A3, A4, B1, B2, C1, D, E	Not Stressed C1, C2

A1 Family-oriented Friendship; **A2** Friendship after the Break-up of the Family; **A3** The Sibling Friendship; **A4** The Non-nuclear Family Friendship
B1 The Neighbor-friend; **B2** Best-friend Proximity;
C1 The Similar-interest Close Friend; **C2** The Buddy-Copain-Copine Phenomenon;
D The Girl-friend/Boy-friend, *Petit/e Ami/e;* **E** The Friend-in-Mind

When attempting to classifiy the styles of friendship in Montreal within DuBois's dimensions and categories, I find her categories to be not mutually exclusive. While I induced the styles of friendships to account for the main ways Montrealers experienced their friendships, DuBois's categories overlap with the attributes of the styles I identified. In all fairness, it should be emphasized that DuBois was working within a structural-functionalist perspective while I was employing a social phenomenological framework. Even though Eisenstadt and Roniger's reformed structural-functionalist description of the place of friendship in the social system reviews DuBois's above matrix, it places more emphasis on essential qualities of a very deep friendship in contrast to DuBois's. While DuBois's model attempts to derive cross-culturally invariant features of friendship, she admits that such friendship goals as expressiveness and instrumentalities "might be seen as poles of a continuum rather than as mutually exclusive concepts."[53]

Religious World View and Friendship

I would like to suggest that the need for pattern maintenance (meaning) with regard to friendship in the Quebec in the 1970s was broadly framed within the contours of Canada's religious heritage, where church (Anglican and Catholic) and ecumenical (United Church) traditions have been depicted as the major institutional agents. In contrast to American religious groups, these major Canadian religious groupings have not emphasized "moralism." Rather they have assumed the "sense of the permanent imperfection of man, of Original Sin."[54] The Kettering-Gallup survey of 1975 found that 20 percent fewer Canadians held that their religious beliefs were important to them as compared to Americans (56% to 36%). For some time around ten percent fewer Canadians than Americans report that they are believers (86 to 87% to 95 to 96%). Compared to Americans, 15 percent fewer Canadians believe in "life after death" (69 to 54%). On a wide variety of indicators of religious belief and practices, Canadians varied between being ten to twenty percent less traditionally religious than Americans.[55]

Derivative of their religious beliefs and practices, the Center for Applied Research in the Apostolate (CARA)-Gallup data done in the early 1980s suggest that:

> the sectarian Americans are more puritanical than the more ecumenically Protestant Anglo-Canadians, and the predominately Catholic Francophones are the most tolerant of all. In reaction to the statement, "Marriage is an outdated institution," 19 percent of French Canadians agreed, as did 11 percent of English Canadians and 7 percent of Americans. Francophone Canadians (24 percent) were also more likely than Anglophone Canadians and Americans (18 percent) to believe that "individuals should have a chance to enjoy complete sexual freedom without being restricted." Reacting to the statement, "a woman wants to have a child as a single parent but she doesn't want to have a stable relationship with a man," 58 percent of Americans voiced disapproval, compared to 53 percent of Anglo-Canadians and 34 percent of Francophones.
>
> A similar pattern was reflected in replies to "[S]omeone says that sexual activity cannot entirely be left up to individual choice, there have to be moral rules to which everyone adheres." Fifty-one percent of Americans agreed, as did 49 percent of English Canadians but only 34 percent of French Canadians.
>
> In the late 1960s and early 1970s, Americans were more likely than Canadians to believe that "it is wrong for people to have sex relations before marriage." In 1969, 68 percent of Americans agreed, whereas the percentage for Canadians for 1970 was 57 percent. By 1973, the American figure had dropped to 48 percent while the Canadian had fallen to 36 percent.[56]

In Lipset's view, much of organized Christendom has changed its orientation to the secular world in the postwar decades. The traditionally established churches have become the foremost exponents of liberation theology and of values close to those of socialism. Lipset writes that both Roman Catholicism and important parts of Anglicanism as well, have always viewed capitalism and the bourgeoisie with suspicion. Like the aristocracy and gentry, the churches disliked the logic of bourgeois society and regarded the business class as materialistic, rationalist, liberal, and frequently anti-clerical. Before World War II, the churches in Europe, Latin America, and Canada were allied to right-wing forces, but usually to their corporatist and antibourgeois elements.

Seymour M. Lipset notes that the destruction of fascism during World War II helped to deligitimate such politics. Since then, in much of the developed and Latin American worlds, many in the churches have turned toward a left-wing, anticapitalist, and communitarian position. In this current, Lipset observes that the United Church of Canada endorsed a 1988 statement by Canada's Catholic bishops that has much in common with socialism. He also reports that the United Church:

> has become a major force in the last 30 years in pressing for increased spending on social welfare programs and for the rights of prisoners, workers, and Canada's native peoples.[57]

Jeremy Boissevain's description of Catholic and Protestant differences in the Netherlands of the 1970s sounds similar to differences I reviewed in the third chapter of this book. In his view, Catholics are more open, optimistic, and vivacious, whereas Protestants are more sober, somber, and reserved.[58] Here, I must note that he was writing about Calvinists, whereas in Montreal the Anglo-Canadians' religious beliefs, practices, and related behavior were rooted in Anglican and United Church traditions, which had evolved in a way much closer to Canadian Catholicism.

Nevertheless, some definite distinctions remain and Boissevain's explanations for these differences are worth considering:

> Briefly, the Catholic needs to make use of other persons in order to obtain salvation. He is dependent upon the clergy for the performance of the many important rituals of his religion: baptism, confirmation, marriage and even the last rites on his death bed. Moreover, there are other rituals, such as confession, Mass, Communion, and the celebration of obligatory religious feasts, which he can perform only

> with the help of intermediaries. Not only does he require the
> assistance of others to practice his religion, he also
> approaches God through the saints who, because they are
> closer to God, and were once human, can be appeased and
> influenced to intercede on his behalf. There are striking
> similarities between the use of intermediaries in the
> religious field and the brokerage and patron-client relations
> which are particularly strong in Catholic countries. ...
> Contact with other persons is not as important for the
> Protestant. He can obtain salvation by faith alone.[59]

As is evident in the data reviewed by Lipset and in the Quebec
sociological studies I reviewed in the earlier chapters of this work, by the
1970s both the Catholic and Protestant subcultures in Montreal had
undergone enormous secularization. In this setting, the Catholic and
Protestant *Weltanschauung* translated into new dichotomies in the
relatively secularized city.[60] I think it is reasonable to speak of a
pattern of "the steadfast friend" as being a Protestant ideal type and the
"friend as confidant" as a Catholic ideal type. This contrast summarizes
the various statistically significant differences I reported in
subcategories of my cognitive data, underlies various statistically
significant differences between English and French Canadians in many
behavioral indicators of friendship, and explains some of the
qualitatively varying in-depth and clinical accounts reported in this
book. However, I wish to emphasize the softness of this contrast
because, in particular for the definitions of friendship, these significant
differences were not crossvalidated by differing techniques. Offering an
explanation of these differences, Francesco Alberoni has argued that
Kant's ethic of impartiality has served as the basis of the modern
state's organization in Protestant countries, in contrast to Catholic
countries, where an ethic of feelings has perpetuated privilege.[61]

As we have seen in the review of the impact of religious traditions
and values, an ethic of sexuality is derivative of religious belief.
Moreover, we have seen that the place of sexuality in friendship
assumed an important place in the classical discussions of the subject,
and that there had been enormous change in English and French

Canadians' attitudes and behavior regarding sexuality during the period I gathered my data. At the time I presented my dissertation, I did not present the data I had gathered on sexuality in friendship, in large part because my dissertation was already too long. However, by not including this information, I underemphasized the erotic element present to some degree in Montrealers' friendships. It is precisely this erotic element that is at the center of the controversy about the structure of trust in society in the 1990s. Before we summarize this controversy and take a position in the debate, let us consider the empirical evidence my Montreal respondents reported for the role of sexuality with each of their ten closest friends.[62]

At a very abstract level of sociological theorizing, Shmuel N. Eisenstadt identifies friendship's core attributes beyond the primordial, sacred, and civil types with their strong tendency for institutionalization. In Eisenstadt's view,

> friendship embodies the purely personal values; not just "psychological" attributes or "primary" relations, but the combination of these with spiritual and moral qualities which can be embodied fully only in individuals in their personal capacity as moral beings.[63]

Eisenstadt relates these characteristics to friendship's combining deep meaning and potential brittleness. These qualities are linked to the ambivalent relation of friendship to the institutional order. Citing Elliott Leyton, Eisenstadt notes that in many societies friendship is potentially subversive of institutionalized relationships or membership in collectivities. He concludes that friendship tends to create trust by assuring that the struggle between the groups or networks to which the friends belong will not exceed certain limits and will not become anarchic or chaotic.[64]

But does the infusion of sexuality into friendship cause it to exceed certain limits and become anarchic or chaotic? Here we meet two opposing views. One of the perspectives basically views sexuality in friendship as a mattter-of-fact reality that has empirically led to a deepening of friendship in certain subcultural groups. Thus, Peter Nardi found that gay men are sexually attracted and involved in the early stages of their friendship, and they may later get to know someone and cease sexual involvement as an "incest taboo" emerges among the family of friends.[65]

In contrast, while open to loving sexuality, gay or straight, Michael Lerner cautions that, "The decline of rigid sexual standards has mixed results." He notes that,

> Through an endless and all-consuming quest for new social alliances and sexual conquests, the emotionally battered worker seeks to forget about the daily assaults on his/her dignity and worth at work. Whether it be through illicit affairs, nightly partying in search of Mr. or Ms. Right, the worker experiences a pseudo liberation that would be more real if a deep emotional contact with other human beings could be made.

Lerner concludes:

> While the sexual crusaders are right, I believe, in arguing that divorcing sexuality from love and commitment and a sense of the sanctity of other people is a destructive path, they could actually change things if they joined with forces that seek to democratize and humanize the world of work.[66]

In other parts of his writings and talks, Michael Lerner has pointed out that the New Leftists of the 1960s ended up going through many intimate relationships by holding themselves and their intimates to impossibly high standards. In Lerner's view, his generation of progressives eventually self-destructed by turning their anger on their loved ones and, finally, themselves when they could not live up to their own standards that failed to take into account the limitations of human beings. This history has led to a lack of trust among many of the developed world's activists of Lerner's cohort, which has had a terrible impact on movements for social change in our time. Lerner's historically specific observation would be predictable by Shmuel Eisenstadt's comparative, transhistorically identified observation that there is a brittleness in friendship because it is closely linked to a pristine discourse for truth.

With a different take on the same matters, Francesco Alberoni devotes an entire chapter to contrasting friendship and erotic relationships. Alberoni observes that,

> an erotically interesting person could have no other quality or virtue. It is not necessary that the person be intelligent, honest, or courageous. The erotic attraction has nothing to do with moral judgment. ... Eroticism ... sees only the erotic quality and does not seek the person him- (her-)self but the experience.[67]

More in line with Alberoni's position, Allan Bloom, nevertheless, recognizes the erotic in Socrates' relationship with Alcibiades. However, Bloom underscores that "Socrates talks of his good friends. Nietzsche of his best enemies. Friendship is that relation constituted by *logos* and is logocentric."[68] In comparison to love, Allan Bloom insists that "friendship is gentler, soberer, without frenzy. It, unlike love, is necessarily reciprocal."[69] Bloom stresses that friendship "is beyond mere bodily need and can be thought to be more distinctively human."[70]

The styles of friendship I identified in this book were as close to those experienced by Montrealers in the mid-1970s as I could accurately summarize from the varied sources of my data. The embedment of four of my styles of friendship in the family was constructed by the complicated cognitive and behavioral processes discussed in my chapter on friendship and the family. Likewise, the importance of the styles of the neighbor-friend, best-friend-proximity, and similar-interest-close-friend show that the kinds of friendship patterns existing in the Montreal of the mid-1970s were attached to the larger macro-sociological structures. At the same time, these styles of friendship constituted a variety of learning experiences which could themselves grow into deeper friendship or provide a stepping-stone toward a more pristine relationship, the social traits of which were identified by DuBois, Eisenstadt, Maisonneuve, Paine, Hutter, and Roniger. However, the pristine ideal-type of friendship to which other styles and patterns were compared was very rare in the Montreal of the mid-1970s.

Montrealers divulged an erotic component to their friendships with around one-fifth of their six closest friends at minimally a low level. Even if an erotic component manifested itself primarily within the boy-friend/girl-friend, *petit(e) ami(e)* style of friendship, it may have been related to the notion of the "body-politic" or to a type of sexuality without commitment prevalent during the 1970s. This style of friendship may have contributed to a cycle of feeling perpetually unfulfilled sexual desire discussed by Lerner, which, in turn, may have led to feelings of lack of societal trust in forming caring, long-term, intimate relationships. Such a pattern could have contributed to an exaggerated identification with one's larger ethnic or national group as a compensation for the intimacy that one sought, but did not find, in the boyfriend, girlfriend, *petit(e) ami(e)* style of friendship. This psycho-social dynamic could very well be a factor in the demographic decline which many French Canadian intellectuals and media personalities have bemoaned, regretted, and feared. However, I offer this interpretation quite hesitantly, as Hutter, in identifying a similar syndrome to Lerner's, does not depict it as so historically specific. Rather, Horst Hutter sees such thwarted searches for friendship linked to the complementary differentiation of roles and subgroups that typify modern industrial society.[71]

The Social Basis of Friendship

Having verified the widespread existence of friendship, its social functions may be considered. In my Montreal material, society and culture produced precise subjective and/or objective chance differences in some different social and cultural groups' aspects of friendship. Therefore, I would revise somewhat Albert's and Brigant's description of the role of the social system in friendship to read,

Thus the social structure gives its members differential chances to enter into friendships with certain characteristics with other members with certain attributes.[72]

With regard to the role of such attributes as vicinity and similarities, I concur with Maisonneuve that rather than operating in a mechanical fashion, they acquire a more or less conscious value for the partners through an experience.[73]

Yehudi A. Cohen's and Robert Brain's work would indicate that friendship has existed in band, tribe, chiefdom, and state political levels of organization. It has been found at hunting and gathering, horticultural, agricultural, early and late urban, pre-industrial, and post-industrial levels of economic organization.[74]

Writers have found friendship under capitalism, socialism, and communism. Yet friendship develops better under certain social conditions than others. The trouble is that authors' ideologies and pessimistic or optimistic outlooks have so tainted the correlations between society and friendship that these associations should be viewed most cautiously. I would agree with the age-old notion that the fear and terror of dictatorial regimes and hierarchical organization militate against friendship, although friendship has not completely died out under them, probably because they have not been able to completely totalize in the real world. On the other hand, a moderate level of bureaucratization, in part derivative of the social welfare state policies of the Canadian, Quebec, and Montreal governments, has eased the extent to which friends and other intimates have had to depend on each other in extreme situations brought on by poor health, natural, or economic disaster. Such policies helped to secure an individual from the economic ravages of ill health, unemployment, and urban blight. Planned public transportation and urban design, incorporating art into the world of commerce, opened up access to a greater extent the urban space available for friends to enjoy together and, thereby, reduced the rigidity of the class barriers from which friends could be drawn.

A Brief Description of Montreal Friendships in Classical Terms

By far the largest part of the Montrealers studied displayed the Aristotelian useful or pleasant forms of friendship. Very few Montrealers reported a friendship that tended toward Aristotle's criteria for a "perfect" form of friendship. The Aristotelian acknowledgment of truth over loyalty to a friend did not empirically pose a threat to Montrealers' friendships in the mid-1970s. As only 11.4% of the friendships broken in my sample were due to a change of an idea or opinion, it can be inferred that my interviewees and respondents did not often fight over differing truths which would bring them to question their loyalty to friends.

A significant subgroup of Montrealers engaged in the boy- or girl-friend/ *petit(e) ami(e)* style of friendship which embodied elements of *eros*, Plato's motive force for friendship. However, as I have suggested, some of the Montrealers of the 1970s who enacted this style of friendship may have lacked a rule of commitment, which led them to feeling unfulfilled in their intimate relationships. This emptiness may have been, in part, satisfied by intensified quests for feelings of union within ethnic and/or national collective identities.

However, sharing and communicating one's inner life take on extraordinary importance in Montrealers' attitudes and actions with their closest friends, and for this reason they bypass the place given them by Aristotle. In Montreal, close friends give primary importance to talking over problems or just chatting about what their friends think about current events in the public or private world. Montrealers also wanted to feel that their closest friends understood their feelings and that they understood their friends' feelings about these happenings. Here an ambiguity arises. Plato claims that this is possible only for the just man because his love of wisdom and philosophic way of life preserve harmony in his soul and, thereby, make him evoke the trust of other men. Aristotle would say that this is possible because friends are equal in virtue.[75] And Maisonneuve explains the possibility of attaining communal intimacy by friends' sharing a same dominant stylistics as much on the level of meaning as on the level of sign.[76] In my opinion Aristotle's criterion of an equality of virtue is an essential prerequisite to the state of communal intimacy both in theoretical and empirical terms, for, in the words of Cicero, concord can exist between men of different virtue but friendship cannot.

An Epicurean note in the Montreal experience of this relationship is the emphasis on friendship as being indispensable to the happy life. Montrealers spoke about wanting friendship in good and hard times and had abundant anecdotes to back up their memories. In the local newspapers politicians were extolled for their having good friends as a sign of their happiness and others were pitied for being friendless.

Notes

1. See: Douglas, Jack D., *Understanding Everyday Life. Toward the Reconstruction of Sociological Knowledge* (Chicago: Aldine Publishing Co., 1970), 15-16; Lauer, Quentin "Evidence," in *Phenomenology: The Philosophy of Edmund Husserl and Its Interpretation*, ed. J. L. Kockelmans (Garden City, New York: Doubleday Co., Inc., 1967), 154.

2. Paine, Robert, "In Search of Friendship: An Exploratory Analysis in 'Middle-Class Culture.' " *Man, The British Journal of Social Anthropology*, January, 1969, 519. Robert Paine's article is reprinted as "An Exploratory Analysis in 'Middle-Class' Culture," in *The Compact: Selected Dimensions of Friendship*, ed. Elliott Leyton (Toronto: University of Toronto Press [for Memorial University of Newfoundland], 1974), 117-137.

3. Maisonneuve, Jean, *Psycho-sociologie des affinités* (Paris: Presses universitaires de France, 1966), 469-474.

4. Hutter, Horst, *Politics as Friendship* (Waterloo, Ontario, Canada: Wilfrid Laurier University Press, 1978).

5. Davis, Murray S., *Intimate Relations* (New York: The Free Press, 1973), 55.

6. McCall, George J. "The Social Organization of Relationships," in *Social Relationships*, ed. George J. McCall (Chicago: Aldine, 1970), 27.

7. Altman, Irwin and Dalmas A., Taylor, *Social Penetration: The Development of Interpersonal Relationships* (New York: Irvington Publishers, Inc., 1973), 27.

8. See Paine, Robert, "In Search of Friendship," 1969, 513.

9. Suttles, Gerry D., "Friendship as a Social Institution," in *Social Relationships*, eds. George McCall *et al.* (Chicago: Aldine Publ. Co., 1970), 95-135.

10. See: Gurdin, Joseph Barry, "*Amitié*/Friendship: The Socio-cultural Construction of Friendship in Contemporary Montreal." Ph.D. diss., Department of Sociology, Université de Montréal, 1978, 810-813; 819; 833; 838. The spatial limitations on my thesis and this book do not permit me to report the data I gathered on friends' personalities.

11. Weber, Max, *Economy and Society: An Outline of Interpretive Sociology* eds. Guenther Roth and Claus Wittich (Berkeley, California: University of California Press, 1978), 40-41.

12. Maisonneuve, Jean, *Psycho-sociologie des affinités*, 469.

13. See Kemper, Theodore D., *A Social Interactional Theory of Emotions* (New York: Wiley, 1978); Kemper, Theodore D., "Love and Like and Love and Love," Paper read at the American Sociological Association, 1983.

14. Paine, Robert, "In Search of Friendship," 507.

15. Maisonneuve, Jean, *Psycho-sociologie des affinités*, 469.

16. Ibid., 470.

17. Ibid., 470.

18. Ibid., 470.

19. Ibid., 472-473.

20. Hutter, Horst, *Politics as Friendship*, 1978, 178.

21. Durkheim, Émile, *The Division of Labor in Society* (New York: The Free Press, A Division of Macmillan Publishing Co., Inc., 1933), 54-57.

22. Hutter, Horst, *Politics as Friendship*, 1978, 80.

23. Paine, Robert, "In Search of Friendship," 511.

24. See: Suttles, Gerry D., "Friendship as a Social Institution," in *Social Relationships*, eds. George McCall *et al.* Chicago: Aldine Publ. Co.,

1970), 113; C. S. Lewis cited in Alberoni, Francesco, *L'amicizia* (Milan: Garzanti Editore s.p.a., 1984), 85; Maisonneuve, Jean, *Psycho-sociologie des affinités*, 439.

25. Paine, Robert, "In Search of Friendship," 513.

26. Ibid., 507.

27. Hutter, Horst, *Politics as Friendship*, 1978, 22.

28. Suttles, Gerry D., "Friendship as a Social Institution," 1970, 116; Paine, Robert, "In Search of Friendship," 514.

29. Maisonneuve, Jean, *Psycho-sociologie des affinités*, 431-433.

30. Ibid., 433-441.

31. Gurdin, Joseph Barry, "*Amitié*/Friendship: The Socio-cultural Construction of Friendship in Contemporary Montreal." Ph.D. diss., Department of Sociology, Université de Montréal, 1978, 238-240.

32. Maisonneuve, Jean, *Psycho-sociologie des affinités*, 454-455.

33. Ibid., 457.

34. Metzger, Nancy J. Metzger and Gerald M. Phillips, *Intimate Communication* (Boston: Allyn and Bacon, 1976), 24.

35. Ibid., 59.

36. Ibid., 59.

37. Ibid., 153.

38. Suttles, Gerry D., "Friendship as a Social Institution," 119.

39. Hutter, Horst, *Politics as Friendship*, 12-13.

40. Hutter, Horst, *Politics as Friendship*, 16.

41. Ibid., 17.

42. Hutter, Horst, *Politics as Friendship*, 92.

43. Ibid., 116.

44. Ibid., 60.

45. Ibid., 87.

46. Ibid., 87.

47 Ibid., 176.

48. See: Eisenstadt, S. N. and L. Roniger, *Patrons, Clients and Friends: Interpersonal Relations and the Structure of Trust in Society* (Cambridge: Cambridge University Press, 1984), 21.

49. Ibid., 21-23.

50. Eisenstadt, S. N. and L. Roniger, *Patrons, Clients and Friends*, 40. Their quote is taken from: Martin Buber, *I and Thou* (Edinburgh: T. and T. Clark, 1975 (c.1970)).

51. Ibid., 40.

52. DuBois, Cora, "The Gratuitous Act: Introduction to the Comparative Study of Friendship Patterns," in *The Compact: Selected Dimensions of Friendship Patterns,* ed. Elliot Leyton (Toronto: University of Toronto Press [for Memorial University of Newfoundland], 1974), 16-20.

53. Ibid., 18.

54. These traits are summarized by Lipset, who draws heavily on the writings of Canada's leading sociologist of religion, Reginald Bibby. See: Lipset, Seymour Martin, *Continental Divide: The Values and Institutions of the United States and Canada* (New York: Routledge, 1990), 79-80.

55. Ibid., 84-87.

56. Ibid., 86-87.

57. Ibid., 87-88.

58. Ibid., 79-80.

59. Boissevain, Jeremy, *Friends of Friends: Networks, Manipulators and Coalitions* (Oxford: Basil Blackwell, 1974).

60. Meilaender, Gilbert C., *Friendship: A Study in Theological Ethics* (Notre Dame, Indiana: University of Notre Dame Press, 1981).

61. Alberoni, Francesco, *L'amicizia* (Milan: Garzanti Editore s.p.a., 1984), 44-47.

62.

The Incidence of Tactility and Sexuality among the 10 Closest Friends in This Study of Urban Montreal in the Mid-1970s

Friend 1

Count Column %	The Incidence of Tactility and Sexuality among Close Friends in This Study of Urban Montreal in the Mid-1970s			
Tactile and Sexual Behavior among Close Friends	High	Medium	Low	Absent (0)
My Friend and I Hold Hands	20 23.3%	22 25.3%	52 17.9%	31 19.3%
My Friend and I Embrace Each Other	23 26.7%	23 26.4%	49 16.8%	30 18.6%
My Friend and I Kiss Each Other	22 25.6%	23 26.4%	49 16.8%	31 19.3%
My Friend and I Make Love without Orgasm	6 7%	9 10.3%	76 26.1%	34 21.1%
My Friend and I Make Love with Orgasm	15 17.4%	10 11.5%	65 22.3%	35 21.7%
Column Total Column %	86 13.8%	87 13.9%	291 46.6%	161 25.8%

The Incidence of Tactility and Sexuality among the 10 Closest Friends in This Study of Urban Montreal in the Mid-1970s

Friend 2

Count Column %	The Incidence of Tactility and Sexuality among Close Friends in This Study of Urban Montreal in the Mid-1970s			
Tactile and Sexual Behavior among Close Friends	High	Medium	Low	Absent (0)
My Friend and I Hold Hands	10 40%	11 33.3%	24 14.8%	80 19.8%
My Friend and I Embrace Each Other	5 20%	9 27.3%	31 19.1%	80 19.8%
My Friend and I Kiss Each Other	5 20%	9 27.3%	30 18.5%	81 20%
My Friend and I Make Love without Orgasm	1 4%	3 9.1%	39 24.1%	82 20.2%
My Friend and I Make Love with Orgasm	4 16%	1 3%	38 23.5%	82 20.2%
Column Total Column %	25 4%	33 5.3%	162 25.9%	405 64.8%

The Incidence of Tactility and Sexuality among the 10 Closest Friends in This Study of Urban Montreal in the Mid-1970s

Friend 3

Count Column %	The Incidence of Tactility and Sexuality among Close Friends in This Study of Urban Montreal in the Mid-1970s			
Tactile and Sexual Behavior among Close Friends	High	Medium	Low	Absent (0)
My Friend and I Hold Hands	8 33.3%	10 38.5%	21 14.7%	86 19.9%
My Friend and I Embrace Each Other	6 25%	5 19.2%	28 19.6%	86 19.9%
My Friend and I Kiss Each Other	7 29.2%	9 34.6%	23 16.1%	86 19.9%
My Friend and I Make Love without Orgasm	1 4.2%	1 3.8%	36 25.2%	87 20.1%
My Friend and I Make Love with Orgasm	2 8.3%.	1 3.8%	35 24.5%	87 20.1%
Column Total Column %	24 3.8%	26 4.2%	143 22.9%	432 69.1%

The Incidence of Tactility and Sexuality among the 10 Closest Friends in This Study of Urban Montreal in the Mid-1970s

Friend 4

Count Column %	The Incidence of Tactility and Sexuality among Close Friends in This Study of Urban Montreal in the Mid-1970s			
Tactile and Sexual Behavior among Close Friends	High	Medium	Low	Absent (0)
My Friend and I Hold Hands	5 41.7%	7 35%	18 15.4%	95 20%
My Friend and I Embrace Each Other	3 25%	4 20%	23 19.7%	95 20%
My Friend and I Kiss Each Other	3 25%	8 40%	19 16.2%	95 20%
My Friend and I Make Love without Orgasm	0 0%	0 0%	29 24.8%	96 20.2%
My Friend and I Make Love with Orgasm	1 8.3%	1 5%	28 23.9%	95 20%
Column Total Column %	12 1.9%	20 3.2%	117 18.7%	476 76.2%

The Incidence of Tactility and Sexuality among the 10 Closest Friends in This Study of Urban Montreal in the Mid-1970s

Friend 5

Count Column%	The Incidence of Tactility and Sexuality among Close Friends in This Study of Urban Montreal in the Mid-1970s			
Tactile and Sexual Behavior among Close Friends	High	Medium	Low	Absent (0)
My Friend and I Hold Hands	5 29.4%	9 42.9%	12 13%	99 20%
My Friend and I Embrace Each Other	4 23.5%	3 14.3%	19 20.7%	99 20%
My Friend and I Kiss Each Other	4 23.5%	7 33.3%	15 16.3%	99 20%
My Friend and I Make Love without Orgasm	1 5.9%	2 9.5%	23 25%	99 20%
My Friend and I Make Love with Orgasm	3 17.6%	0 0%	23 25%	99 20%
Column Total	17 2.7%	21 3.4%	92 14.7%	495 79.2%

The Incidence of Tactility and Sexuality among the 10 Closest Friends in This Study of Urban Montreal in the Mid-1970s

Friend 6

Count Column %	The Incidence of Tactility and Sexuality among Close Friends in This Study of Urban Montreal in the Mid-1970s			
Tactile and Sexual Behavior among Close Friends	High	Medium	Low	Absent (0)
My Friend and I Hold Hands	1 20%	8 40%	11 14.7%	105 20%
My Friend and I Embrace Each Other	2 40%	4 20%	14 18.7%	105 20%
My Friend and I Kiss Each Other	1 20%	7 35%	12 16%	105 20%
My Friend and I Make Love without Orgasm	0 0%	1 5%	20 26.7%	104 19.8%
My Friend and I Make Love with Orgasm	1 20%	0 0%	18 24%	106 20.2%
Column Total	5 0.8%	20 3.2%	75 12%	525 84%

The Incidence of Tactility and Sexuality among the 10 Closest Friends in This Study of Urban Montreal in the Mid-1970s

Friends 7, 8, 9, And 10

Count Column %	The Incidence of Tactility and Sexuality among Close Friends in This Study of Urban Montreal in the Mid-1970s				Row Total
Tactile and Sexual Behavior among Close Friends	High	Medium	Low	Absent (0)	
My Friend and I Hold Hands	0 0%	0 0%	0 0%	500 20%	1250 20%
My Friend and I Embrace Each Other	0 0%	0 0%	0 0%	500 20%	1250 20%
My Friend and I Kiss Each Other	0 0%	0 0%	0 0%	500 20%	1250 20%
My Friend and I Make Love without Orgasm	0 0%	0 0%	0 0%	500 20%	1250 20%
My Friend and I Make Love with Orgasm	0 0%	0 0%	0 0%	500 20%	1250 20%
Column Total	0 0%	0 0%	0 0%	500 2500	6250 100%

Summary Gammas (γ) "The Incidence of Tactility and Sexuality among the 10 Closest Friends in This Study of Urban Montreal in the Mid-1970s":

Zero-Order $\gamma = .03058$

First-Order Partial $\gamma = .06443$

These results from my purposive sample should be compared to the random, representative sample of University of Manitoba students done a few years before my data were gathered. See Perlman, Daniel, "The Sexual Standards of Canadian University Students," in *Readings in Social Psychology: Focus on Canada*, eds. Koulack, David and Daniel Perlman (Toronto: Wiley Publishers of Canada Limited, 173), 139-160.

63. Eisentadt, S. N., "Friendship and the Structure of Trust and Solidarity in Society," in *The Compact: Selected Dimensions of Friendship*, ed. Elliott Leyton (Toronto: University of Toronto Press [for Memorial University of Newfoundland], 1974), 141. Also see: Leyton, Elliott, "Irish Friends and 'Friends': The Nexus of Friendship, Kinship, and Class in Aughnaboy," in ibid., 93-104.

64. Ibid., 141-143.

65. See: Nardi, Peter, "Friendship among Gay Men," in *Men's Friendships* (Newbury Park, CA: Sage Publications, 1992), 182.

66. Lerner, Michael, *Surplus Powerlessness: The Psychodynamics of Everyday Life ... and the Psychology of Individual and Social Transformation* (Oakland, CA: The Institute for Labor & Mental Health), 78.

67. Alberoni, Francesco, *L'amicizia* (Milan: Garzanti Editore s.p.a., 1984), 106-108.

68. Bloom, Allan, *Love and Friendship* (New York: Simon & Schuster, 1993), 543.

69. Ibid., 547.

70. Ibid., 548.

71. Hutter, Horst, *Politics as Friendship*, 178.

72. Albert, R. S. and T. R. Brigante, "The Psychology of Friendship Relations: Social Factors." *Journal of Social Psychology*, 1962, 33-47.

73. Maisonneuve, Jean, *Psycho-sociologie des affinités* (Paris: Presses Universitaires de France, 1966), 484.

74. Cohen, Yehudi, ed., "Patterns of Friendship," in *Social Structure and Personality: A Casebook* (New York: Holt, Rinehart, and Winston,

1961), 352-354. See: DuBois, Cora, "The Gratuitous Act: Introduction to the Comparative Study of Friendship Patterns," 15. Also see: Brain, Robert, *Friends and Lovers* (New York: Basic Books, Inc., Publishers, 1976). However, I must note that not all social scientists agree with this point.

75. Hutter, Horst, *Politics as Friendship*, 93.

76. Maisonneuve, Jean, *Psycho-sociologie des affinités*, 502.

Chapter Ten

Conclusion

Throughout this work I have sought to heed Jean Maisonneuve's admonition to study friendship at the level of small cultural islands without forgetting to return to the continent of the larger global society.[1] On the waters between these islands and the mainland several recent mariners in the 1980s and 1990s have forded a passage marked by insight into their own as well as others' friendships.[2] Their voyages are attractive but fraught with the danger that the clear patterns they see on the horizon are only their authorial projections. In the course ahead, I will steer between personal revelation and evidence that my many quantitative and qualitative findings point to as social and cultural "facts." Before I embark, let me add that I hold as true Erving Goffman's observation that both social actors and societies require a certain amount of "backstage information," if they are to remain mentally healthy. So I will share with you, my readers, some parts of a few, but not all, elements of all the friendships I have been fortunate enough to experience. In so doing, I have changed all the names of my friends. If these disclosures leave you to seek out more, I have kaleidoscopically embedded other of my friendship tales into *Border of Lilies and Maples,* a novel about my decision to dissent from the United States of America's involvement in the War in Vietnam. But, as you would soon note in pursuing that reference, my ethical decision to oppose the war was influenced by the friendships I formed.

{Communication} in {Head-to-Heart} and {Steadfastness} in {Institutionalized-to-Chosen Similar-Interest Friendship}-- The Orthogonal Facets of Friendship--Take on Their Deepest Meaning in Concrete Scenes of Human Life in Particular Historical Settings

When I arrived in Toronto, Ontario, Canada, in the fall of 1968, I found lodging in a changing inner-city ethnic neighborhood about a twenty minute walk from the campus of the University of Toronto. The neighborhood was lined with three-story, brick houses, which were painted in lively colors by incoming Portuguese immigrants, many from the Azores Islands. On the corner was a Ukrainian cultural center and a few Ukrainian or part-Ukrainian families. My landlady and her husband with their young daughter and infant son were from the Hungarian countryside. The asphalt-covered playground of the elementary school across the street bore the name of one of the recent kings of England. It was set off from the street by a high, chain-linked fence. I rented a gable on the third floor of that house for $11 Canadian dollars a week. On the third floor, ascended to by a narrow staircase on the left, was my room, facing the front of the house, and two rooms, one next to mine, and one behind it. Each was separately inhabited by a native-born, English-speaking Canadian, one from a small city a few hours north of Toronto, and one, I believe, from the Maritime Provinces. The fellow from north of Toronto was a student in his late teens or early twenties and was studying at a local polytechnic institute. The other man in the room next to mine was in his late twenties or early-to-mid thirties. At the time I was 21. We always smiled and were cordial to one another. We exchanged pleasantries such as "Hi; good morning; how're doing?" In a whole year I never recall having one deep conversation with either man. Yet, despite living in such close quarters, we never fought nor said a bad word about one another. No one ever complained to the landlady about his immediate neighbors.

On the second floor there lived three other men, and there was a common kitchen with a shared stove and refrigerator for all the tenants. One of the men was a master's degree student in his late twenties or early-to-mid thirties. He had immigrated to Canada from Hungary as an adult. He was also an observant Catholic. Another of the men on the second floor was from Egypt. Then, in his mid-twenties, was Faleem, a student of engineering from Pakistan. His father was a professor at a top university in his country. Although he was a Muslim by birth, he was non-observant. Faleem's door was always open, and when I arrived, he already had a small circle of friends, a student about his age of Indian background from South Africa, and a non-observant Hindu by religion, and a younger, very tall fellow from East Africa, who was of Gujurati Indian ethnicity. Less frequently, a somewhat older engineer of Tamil Indian background would join us.

Faleem and I became good friends. I was newly arrived from the United States of America with a fresh B.A. and a quarter's work toward an M.A. at UCLA. I was born into an underclass, Reform Jewish family--my father, who after many years of WPA, unemployment, etc., worked in the millinery department of a large store in Minneapolis and died when I was two. Shortly afterwards, my mother became very ill. I was brought up in a southern town, in a middle-class neighborhood, from the age of three to eleven, by a non-observant Jewish father's brother, a shoe salesman, and his Protestant wife, who had worked in sales before marriage and then became a homemaker. In my twelfth year, as my uncle was dying, I was given the choice between a semi-residential Jewish orphanage and a southern, Protestant preparatory school. I chose the latter, paid for primarily from my father's Social Security benefits with additional contributions from other uncles and aunts. In my high school the Jewish students were required to attend the local Methodist Church and be present every morning at chapel, so formally I was educated more in mainstream Protestant beliefs and practices than Jewish ones. However exposed to white, Anglo-Saxon, Protestant upper-middle-to-upper class culture I may have been in high school, my own economic marginality and positive association with liberal Judaism were major factors in my participating in the tail-end (because of my later age-cohort) of the civil rights and the middle-and-end phases of the anti-war movements.[3]

First of all, as struggling students at a highly competitive university, most of our time was occupied by studying, reading, and writing. Second of all, we had hardly any disposable income for things like movies, theater, and dances. That does not mean that our friendships were dull! We would socialize over food, by visiting the many free parks, open air markets, ethnic neighborhoods, and occasional friends' parties. Our conversations covered each other's beliefs, habits, feelings, and opinions about the issues and discoveries of the day. I introduced young women to Faleem and Faleem's "circle." Our one big trip together was when Ativitarama had come back from working in the Canadian west, and we all traveled together to Quebec City during winter vacation. We all also had our individual free-time interests which brought us to spend a considerable amount of our time in other activities. I was active in an American exile anti-war group, then volunteered some time organizing teen-ager and pre-teen activities at the University Settlement House, and finally became active in the movement to stop the extension of the Spadina expressway in favor of expanding the subway. Faleem was not involved in my political work but would ask me questions about it and basically sympathized with the goals for which I was working.

An external observer would certainly underscore the importance of propinquity in initiating our friendship, but, being fellow boarders (neighbors) would not have been a sufficient explanation if we had both not been gregarious young men who were genuinely interested and open to people of other backgrounds. Beth Hess would say we were substituting for other primary relations, for we were constrained as isolated individuals to seek out others at this stage of our lives. Drawing on the work of R. S. Weiss, Pat O'Connor would point out that we were providing each other with social integration and nurture. We helped each other out in complementary, very meaningful ways. Faleem was a good cook of Pakistani food. He would prepare chicken, vegetable, and beef curries, various flour and yogurt dishes and share them with me. Given my meager budget and then ignorance of food preparation, I had become fond of basic old standbys--particularly Canadian sardines, which then sold for 10 cents a tin can. Faleem would joke at my American peanut butter and jelly sandwiches. Occasionally, our Egyptian and Hungarian fellow boarders would join us in the kitchen and introduce us to items of their national cuisines. I helped out Faleem and his circle by introducing them to young women and by keeping them up on the latest controversies in the social sciences and social issues.

During the year Faleem grew to like the young women with whom I had become friendly. One was Deena, a native Canadian of North American Indian background, and another, Karin, was a young woman who had immigrated to Canada from Scandinavia in her teens. The third, Deborah, two years older than I, had grown up in Toronto, but had been born in Eastern Europe of Jewish parents. When I say Faleem liked, I mean we enjoyed being in one another's company, laughing at one another's jokes and tales, talking or walking around this city. Later I became close to two of Deborah's other friends, Nancy, a woman her age who had grown up in Toronto, who was a first generation Canadian of Japanese working class origin, and Rehana, who was a student from Pakistan with family in Canada. Years later Faleem's and Rehana's lives would touch briefly romantically, just before Rehana's tragic death.

The year, 1968, has recently been described as a millennial year.[5] The intensity of personal exchange and the striving to create a more just, egalitarian world filled the air with feelings of brother- and sisterhood. The vibrancy of human contact--particularly with people outside of one's own ethnic and religious heritage--led one to believe that it was possible to overcome any inhibition or taboo preventing absolute unity with another person in the here and now.

At The University of Toronto, I had a separate set of intellectual friends, two women and two men, and toward the end of my year and a half in Toronto, I started growing close to another woman in my graduate program. The first two women friends were quite different in ages. Ursala was of German ethnic background and was around my age. She spoke German well and had lived and studied in her parents' country of origin. Edith was a middle-aged woman, originally from Austria, who had spent many years in the United States. She had a young daughter and was living with her apart from her husband. We were terribly serious about ideas but all felt a need to grasp those ideas through lived experiences. We constantly talked about the relations of the individual to the society and culture, but for all of us that meant our own place in the contemporary world too. I believe it was this more general openness to any and all ideas, with a historical, personal rootedness, with an emphasis on drawing on our own experiences, that gave us a strong emotional attachment to one another and in opposition to the more bookish British and emerging French structuralists, whose paradigm was popular in anthropology at the time.

My friend, Jack, was middle-aged and had returned to graduate school after being a newspaper man for many years. He was married with two sons and lived on the islands off Toronto, which many of the city's artists, writers, and other bohemian types like to frequent. Jack was my closest male, English Canadian, Protestant friend in the decade I spent in Canada. Again, his literary interest and newspaper experience had made him enthusiastic and tolerant toward the variety and wonder of the human experience. He was a political progressive, and we shared similar views on the big questions of the day. But we also discussed the hard facts of making it, of where and how we were going to get the next buck. And we shared with each other the pains and frustrations of family life. He was upset that his teenage son had started to smoke when he had given it up. I would bemoan my estrangement from my extended family to him. We both had strong Fabian and pro-environmental shared visions of a social democracy--but were also engaged in real community reformist action which was frowned upon by some new leftists of the time. We had a sense of pleasure being together and of confiding in and understanding each other. We were frank and sincere with each other and had a community of ideas and tastes. We boosted each other's morale when we were unhappy about serious problems in our lives. In short, we communicated very well along the dimensions Maisonneuve had identified.

My other friend, John, was much shier. He had grown up in an English Canadian Ontarian environment, but had a French Canadian surname. He was just a few years my senior and lived in much more conventional housing than Jack's. We would discuss the lives of the other graduate students and the different courses we were taking. He had a much greater grasp of the realities of life in Ontario--particularly socio-economic class--than I, and laid them out to me in plain, unadorned English. I helped introduce him to another shy English Canadian woman graduate student in whom he expressed an interest in dating. He would share with me his dreams of living in the tropical south seas, and I would present him with my utopian dreams of a peaceful, more egalitarian world.

When I spent a year in a doctoral program in social anthropology and lectured at the University of Stockholm in 1970, I corresponded with Faleem, Deborah, Rehana, and Karin. Rehana, Deborah, Nancy, and Nancy's sister and cousin came to visit me in Stockholm. I will not delve into my close friendships in Stockholm here, for several of them are sources of the relationships developed in *Border of Lilies and Maples*.

And now we get to Montreal, Quebec, Canada. Before I came back to Canada, I wrote Karin asking her if I could stay at her apartment while looking for a job and my own place. She quickly wrote back that I was welcome. Karin was working at a university library at the time and taking acting lessons. Soon I became active in the American exile community in Montreal and was the resident manager of the American Refugee Service's hostel for draft resisters and deserters in the mid-winter to early-summer of 1971. Karin was dating other men and was very busy with her union participation on her "practical job" and her acting lessons. Besides managing the hostel, I also held down a job teaching English as a second language. Despite our very busy schedules, Karin and I would meet frequently and discuss our different loves to one another. I was still enamored with the woman I had lived with in Sweden, and she with an actor with whom she was performing. Despite the fact that she was a young woman and I a young man, our friendship without *eros* continued to grow stronger. We saw eye to eye in politics and art. We both loved nature. Having grown up in Scandinavia, she was an excellent skier, and we would hitchhike into nature together. We both loved Scandinavian culture, and our shared beliefs in a very equal, activist, pro-environmental social democracy left us with a common, almost religious fervor. She would provide me contacts to help the young men I was aiding while running the hostel. Through two of my students, recent immigrants of Czech origin, I obtained summer employment on a project studying the medical anthropology of a Reserve of one of the Indigenous Peoples of Canada.

At the same time I began to know and grow closer to Margaret and Jean-Paul, close friends of Karin's. Margaret is an English Canadian woman who grew up in the same Ontario town as Karin. She is a widely read person who has traveled with Karin in Europe. Jean-Paul and Margaret had married in their early twenties when marriage was out-of-style among intellectuals. Jean-Paul is a perfectly bilingual, bicultural French Canadian who spent many years in Ontario. When we met, he was studying philosophy at an English-language university in Montreal. Margaret and Jean-Paul always maintained an attractive, homey apartment and an interest in music, literature, the arts, and history. Theirs was always a haven from the turbulent world in which their politically activist friends would come for a beautifully spread-out meal or an evening of chess or Jalna, the television serial of an Ontarian aristocratic family. First Margaret worked when Jean-Paul went to school. Then Jean-Paul got a teaching position and Margaret had two daughters and stayed at home with them, and is now re-emerging into the world of work after over decade of mothering.

During the summer of 1971, Deborah and Nancy realized that Rehana was extremely distraught and had suggested that Rehana seek psychiatric help. She was hospitalized that same summer. When she was released, she wrote me asking if she might come visit me where I was working on a project in a Canadian community of Native People. I agreed but during her visit did my best to persuade her to return to Pakistan to be with her family. Rehana wanted to continue her studies in Montreal. Karin, Margaret, and Jean-Paul felt that Rehana should try

Montreal to see if she would like it. Rehana wanted to share an apartment with Karin, me, and another colleague of Karin's. We knew that Rehana suffered from sleeplessness and told her that we could help her find a place near ours because we both needed our rest. I was going to return to do a Ph.D. in sociology at the University of Montreal, and Karin's acting career was becoming evermore filled. We emphasized that she would be welcome to come over to be with us, although we also stressed that our new tight schedules would make it more difficult for all of us to get together. She found a nice one-room apartment in walking distance from our apartment. My mother stayed in her apartment when she came to visit me when Rehana was visiting her relatives in the United States.

Even though I realized that Rehana came from the upper class of her society and Faleem from the intelligentsia of his country, I felt they might be romantically inclined toward each other. Faleem was still in Toronto. They dated awhile. When all her friends and acquaintances thought she was leading a happy, productive life, Rehana took an overdose of sleeping pills. Karin and I bore the tragedy of finding our friend's beautiful body stained by the drugs which had propelled her to her eternal rest. We had to contact the police, her brother, and help arrange the funeral. Her friends filled the room where her body lay, after the local Islamic burial society had prepared it according to the rights of her heritage. Jean-Paul contacted her university, in which a semester had just begun, to see if they would refund part of her tuition to help pay the cost of her funeral. "No," they said. Nor was Jean-Paul able to get the university to help when one of Rehana's circle recalled the name of the student who had furnished her with sleeping pills. Later when Jean-Paul was having difficulty finding a college teaching position, I cut out and mailed to him an ad from a Quebec paper that eventually led to an interview which he successfully passed. He accepted the job and soon afterwards began working and raising a family in this Quebec town.

In the friendships I have just described, you might identify elements of the styles of "neighbor friend, best friend proximity, and similar interest close friend" which I had outlined more rigorously earlier in my work. You might even note that the various family styles of friendship I found in Montreal were absent among my own friendships: *no* "family-oriented friendship, *no* remaining family friendship after the break up of the family, *no* sibling friendship, *no* non-nuclear family friendship." This observation does not mean that the principle of amity in kinship was absent in relationships with some members of my family. But my family relationships were framed clearly as those of kin. Looking at these friendships described so far, an outsider would observe that they all occurred when I was single, among people aiming for careers in the arts, helping professions, or academia, among people who worked for a living but who were of very modest means. Most of these people were unwed. These friends took an active interest in people of different cultural backgrounds from their own, although there were some social class differences which were not significant because the immediate income of most of these people was not greatly disparate.

As I began to teach part-time while completing my Ph.D. studies, Karin's acting career grew from a hobby to major performances at top theaters. We moved from a $45 a month cold water flat. I went into a shared apartment with a French and a French Canadian male undergraduate student in a middle class neighborhood near my university but continued to shelter two or three other men fleeing the War in Vietnam. By this time, Karin needed to take her own flat close to her place of work downtown. One of the men I was sheltering met another young American who was such a warm and affable person with a budding talent in music that, getting the support of my other two paying apartment mates, they persuaded me to break my hardfast rule of giving a free place to stay only to draft resisters or deserters. Soon afterward, Nate moved in as did a close friend of one of the paying roommates. Nate was from a middle-class African American family from a large American city, and although he had been raised as a Christian, had now converted to Islam, in which he was becoming increasingly devout. Karin came to visit, and she and Nate soon fell in love. Although Karin had been born a Lutheran and had had one short conversion experience in her youth to a fundamentalist Christian sect, most of her adolescence and adult life she had wavered between being a non-observant agnostic or atheist. By all standards of the day, she was a liberated, progressive woman.

By the end of the summer Karin and Nate's romance had reached the stage that she had to make a decision of whether or not to convert and follow Nate's faith or to give up the relationship. Having just completed a graduate course with one of Quebec's top Rogerians, I was very non-directive in our discussion about her important decision. During our long discussion part of Karin's anxiety about what to do was expressed in laughter about her proposed important decision. I stressed the importance of Karin's making her own decision, although I tried to sketch various scenarios that her proposed change of lifestyle would entail. Karin made the decision to marry Nate, who had by then adopted the Muslim name of Ali. I was not invited to the marriage ceremony but was invited to be with her sister and mother when they came to Montreal to be present for the birth of her first child. I was so busy in graduate school, teaching, and politics that the deep discussions, feelings, and experiences Karin and I shared were stored as though they had never been put on hold.

While hitching to the university from my all night job downtown as a hotel receptionist, I got a lift with another Scandinavian at the end of his teens who, though working in the business world at the time, intended to go to the university. On the short ride past the mountain, it turned out that we shared activist political views and he was impressed with my knowledge of Swedish and Scandinavia. Despite the almost ten year difference in our ages, and his higher class background, Lars and I saw quite a lot of each other along with Björn, his same-age apartment mate from his same country. Lars drove me to several of my interviews for my dissertation and I showed him and Björn around Montreal. After his first year in university, Lars switched from business to history and became more involved in various progressive causes. When he and another undergraduate friend of his moved into the old United Farm Workers support apartment, Lars invited me to be the third roommate. I accepted. Besides intensely discussing politics and history, Lars and I retained a supportive discussion of problems in our personal lives. Despite his agnosticism, he would take me to cultural events at his country's church, and, on occasion, he would attend an event at the Sadie Bronfman Center or overhear a group from Hillel meeting in our apartment. Occasionally, we would discuss our love lives with each other, but usually in the joking, playful spirit of the 1970s that encouraged an independent, uncommitted, libertine sexuality as a social good. Alone among my leftist friends, when anti-Zionism had begun to be evoked as a necessary credential for being politically correct, and had begun to become a cause of friction with our other roommate, his friend, he made it explicitly known to me that he saw Israel's reason-for-being as legitimate, even while we both criticized specific policies and acts of that country.

Later that summer, Karin's friend, Ilse, came with her new male friend and several of her crowd of friends from many countries who were living in Toronto to stay at our apartment for the Olympics, which took place in the summer of 1976. Of course, Ilse, Karin's close friend, and I spent a long time discussing Karin's totally new life, so diametrically opposed to her former existence. While not denying the extremity of her reversed existence, she was of the opinion that once a woman married, had children, and became a homemaker much of the routine was strikingly similar anyway. Even though I found Ilse's explanation threw a different light on Karin's new status, I remained concerned at her reply to my question about happiness. I saw Karin and Ali only once again after that meeting. Yet, in my visits to her childhood friend, Margaret, and her husband, Jean-Paul, we always spend considerable time catching up on glimpses into Karin's and Ali's household via news from Karin's brother.

Friendship during the Middle Years of Life

So after this stage of early adulthood while completing our higher education, the character of our friendships began to change as some friends continued in new roles as parents and professionals while others remained committed to alternative life styles.

Permit me a slight digression. My longest and very dear friendship with Alan Solomon began when I was three and he four. We went to the same kindergarten, Sunday school, public elementary school, and junior high school. From the time I was nine to eleven, we lived in the same neighborhood in back of each other. I lived with my paternal uncle and aunt and he with his father, mother, brother, and maternal grandmother. Later his paternal grandmother moved to the same town, and I knew and visited her as well. We grew up together and had similar interests. We enjoyed the time we spent together daily. When my family life began to deteriorate with my uncle's terminal illness, his family provided me with great emotional support. We were both very intellectual as were two of our other close childhood friends. From as early as I remember, we were both very liberal. Yet, we enjoyed riding bikes, playing catch, and camp as much as board games and music. When I was sent to live elsewhere, we kept up through letters describing our changing major interests, beliefs, feelings, and activities.

Our first disagreement was over the War in Vietnam. Alan Solomon served in the Air Force, was a Humphrey supporter, and I chose to go to Canada and Sweden. Yet, we continued to correspond at least once a year and discussed our lives, families, and the issues of the day. I have never much cared for shopping; yet I recall spending almost a day selecting Alan's and his wife's, Jenny's, wedding present. When I came back to the United States, I flew back to the south to visit Alan and meet his wife, Jenny, for the first time in person. She and I hit it off from the beginning and enjoyed singing late sixties songs of love and liberation together. Jenny and Alan soon after had their only child, Noah.

The Reagan-Bush--and, to a lesser extent, Mulroney--years have been a disaster for my cohort of Ph.D.s, especially in the humanities, social sciences, foreign languages, and philosophy. After almost fourteen years of teaching and research in various capacities in universities and colleges, I lost my assistant professorship and subsequently started my own sociological practice, To Love and to Work: An Agency for Change.

Yet, as I was strongly morally opposed to the military build-up and the attack on social welfare and the environment during the Reagan and Bush Administrations, I was determined to spend much time fighting both the reasoning and ends of the neo-conservative coalition. In November 1982, I also married and was blessed with a healthy, handsome son in October 1983.

Although Alan had high degrees in pure mathematics and mathematical education, he also suffered from the cutbacks to higher education and the demographic decline in the traditional university age cohort. During the period when he too intensively looked for work, I regularly sent him job advertisements in the major American press. Besides consulting, counseling, revising the current book, and writing *Border of Lilies and Maples*, I was engaged in primary child care for my son, while my wife was working on a research project. Both Alan and I have had to worry about making ends meet and the financial constraints have severely limited our calling and visiting each other. But this does not limit the importance of Alan in my psychic life, and I suspect that I touch a similar chord in his. Does this behavior not resemble my style of *friend-in-mind*? Alan recently had a paid trip to the Bay Area to attend an intensive convention. His superior in the educational hierarchy was with him so he was only able to squeeze an afternoon and evening to first be with me and then meet my family for the first time. After showing him Berkeley, we met my wife and son in San Francisco. They had met before only through photographs, letters, and very infrequent, long-distance telephone calls. It so happened that Ron, the extremely bright teenage son of my wife's best friend, was in town for a computer convention and to see his grandparents and was to stay with us that evening as well. Alan and Ron talked of their conventions, and Ron and I reminisced about the Latin opera he and his fellow pupils of high school Latin had composed and performed. We all enjoyed the Japanese food, and then we took the public bus to our favorite coffee shop.

After dessert, my wife, son, and Ron hopped the streetcar home, and Alan and I walked over to the Haight, where we talked of the difficulties as well as the pleasant parts of our marriages. We shared the pains and struggles and hurts we had undergone over the last eight years. We spoke of the therapy we had received and of our relaxed versus our wives' similar strictness approaching issues of toilet training our sons. We felt together. We understood. We shook hands when we greeted; although I had a desire to hug my friend, I sensed he felt it inappropriate. Yet, he is so much better at supportive words of praise for my accomplishments than I for his. Surely, his are as worthy as mine. I felt bad about my withholding. We send our children small presents from time to time. I occasionally write his parents and have visited them once with my wife. After Alan's visit, his wife, child, and he came to stay for a vacation at our house during his summer vacation. We delighted in hosting our family friends and showing them the beauty of the Bay Area.

Pat O'Connor would probably say that Alan and I were providing each other with reassurance of each other's worth, a sense of reliable alliance, and attachment. That sense of attachment has grown as Alan has celebrated through interviews in various media being in the same classes and schools as and being a friend of the current President of the United States, Bill Clinton.[7] It was with pride that Alan described to me waiting in line for hours to be greeted by the new President who referred to him as "my friend," and who gave him a big hug.

What has happened to Lars in his thirties and Jean-Paul, Margaret, and I in our forties? Lars calls me a few times a year for an hour or more chat. On the telephone, he told me about keeping my infant son's photograph on display in his apartment. He came to visit me and my wife in Chicago. We gave him a good tour of the city. We had a great time together. We talked about our research--he was then completing his doctorate in history and planed to return to his native land, as he did in the early years of his marriage. He was open about his love life and the inside secrets of social activism on his campus. We swapped references of books we had admired. Following his suggestion I read George Kennan's *Nuclear Delusion*, and I suggested that he check out Jan Elster's works. For the first time, I sensed his concern about the incredibly tight job market in academia and whenever I find a possibility for him, I clip it out and suggest that he apply for it. We reminisced about the time we spent as roommates, and he filled me in on what had happened to the lives of his younger activist friends: one of his good friends had decompensated; another had married and was struggling to make a living. We mutually reaffirmed our similar values by reciting tales of challenge to unjust authority and policy that often result in hardship and pain. He disclosed to me the anguish of his family at his nephew's having fallen victim to a caper that has seemingly incapacitated him. I listened and inquired if they have tried this or that technique to help him. Later he told me about a serious health problem, and I personally requested the leading physician in the world in this area to take him on as a patient. Here Pat O'Connor would note an element of obtaining guidance in our friendship.[8]

He related the lives of his brother and sister and friends whose lives I have followed through reports over the years. When Lars married, I spent much time selecting his and his wife's wedding present, which I had to mail them, as finances did not permit me to accept attending his wedding. His wife and I recently had a long conversation on the telephone, and he and I recently chatted about his actively raising his daughter, his teaching part-time at a university, his health, and regrets at being unable to obtain a full-time position in his field.

Jean-Paul and I corresponded once or twice a year until about four years ago, when my stressful job counseling chemically dependent people, and then analyzing data on them, drained all my energies and spare time, not to mention my reluctance to discuss my downward mobility with friends. He, Margaret, and their daughters planned to come stay with us but were unable to do so--I believe because of the expense of traveling with a whole family from Quebec to California. Jean-Paul's letters are filled with humor and seriousness about his daughters' lively, contrasting personalities and Margaret's traumas in re-entering the job market. I rely on Jean-Paul's descriptions and commentaries of contemporary Quebec as being as insightful as the best I have heard at the University of California, Berkeley. I tend to load my letters to them with photographs and written sketches of our life in San Francisco and Chicago.

When I look for a deeper meaning in my friendships of the 1970s in Canada, I find that they illustrate friendships that, while infused with more Platonic elements than most Montrealers reported on in this book, nevertheless, remained basically Aristotelian. They were Platonic in that they were to a great extent among people in their twenties and thirties who were striving toward attaining "truth" through intellectual efforts or political action or creating "beauty" in the arts and who, in doing so, cultivated themselves through their relationships with their closest friends. This movement transforms the friends' characters to enable them to attain a fuller and richer expression of friendship. Lying along the intersection of the {institutionalized-to-chosen similar-interest friend} and the {head-to-heart} facets, these friendships described here were characterized by *philia*, not *eros*.

On July 13, 1995, I turned 48 years of age, had been married almost ten and a half years, and have been very active as a parent of my son. If I have alluded to how my earlier friendships are changing as we age, I also have tried to emphasize that my own friendships are not very representative of most of the Montrealers I studied. My patterns may reflect some trends of the baby boomers who went on for graduate education or pursued an artistic or activist career, but even among this cohort, one should not generalize from my experience.

Friendships with Chronologically Old Friends

When reviewing my oldest interviewees' and respondents' friendships, we heard accounts of both disengagement and on-going active friendships with the older man's and woman's interviews I cited in detail.

With my oldest friends in the United States of America, we hardly ever discuss issues of sexuality--a subject I and my closest friends in my late teens, twenties, and thirties rarely avoided. But with my friends in their eighties and two in their nineties, I am beginning to discuss issues of aches, pains, and physical limitations more--things that they were much less willing to talk about before they were 85 than now. I find that if they suffer from a stiff neck or back, and if I initiate the offer, they will let me massage the hurting part and get some temporary relief and caring. Or, as when death comes, I was recently honored by being asked to throw the earth on the grave of a friend by my friend's wife, also my good friend.

The three widows and one widower who count as my chronologically oldest friends have been generous toward my son. When he was born, when we visit, and on his birthday or special occasions, they send cards and presents and prepare us special meals when we visit. When we lived in the same apartment building, one of these coupled friends would occasionally baby-sit. We send pictures, write, call, and visit them when time and money permit. Indeed, we often share deep thoughts, sometimes if we visit an art gallery or reminisce about their rich pasts. All of these friends are very bright people who read and appreciate art, music, literature, travel, history, social issues, or foreign languages.

But we are, perhaps, less revealing of personal information that is potentially embarrassing or painful than I am with my closest friends my own age. However, this issue of depth, of knowing the person unto him- or her- self, I am beginning to believe was a myth of the late 1960s, which lingers in growth, feminist, and some other politically activist sub-cultures. No person can be totally transparent to others and survive mentally and socially. Indeed, even in the best friendship, certain traits of a close friend are unacceptable to the Other. For this reason, I agree with S. N. Eisenstadt and L. Roniger, that when the search for attachment and Gregory Bateson's metameaning combine, this search then becomes endowed with the special symbols of true trust and pristine meaning and in the search for the pure dialogue between people and God.[9]

Prejudice Even within Friendship

Now I must touch on, perhaps, the most sensitive issue I have raised in summarizing my close friendships thus far. To avoid it would shirk a moral responsibility and hide a deep insight into my close friendships. The noted American sociologist of friendship, Beth Hess, asked, "Do

American Jews have different friendship patterns than born again Christians? If so, why?"[10] Then Victor J. Seidler described how difficult it was for him to be openly Jewish in his friendships in England.[11] And Seymour Martin Lipset outlines important structural and cultural differences between the Canadian and American Jewish communities.[12]

I would answer Beth Hess by stressing that there is great deal of variation within the American Jewish community. If you come from a lower class family and identify with the left social democratic tradition of an important part of your North American ethnic subcultural heritage, to which you have added an environmentally conscious social activism, as I have, then your friendship patterns will probably be very different from your cousins who were born into higher socio-economic strata and who have entered business, law, or medicine, or from your sister, who, like mine, converted to Catholicism and whose political views have tended to be conservative.

When the solidarity of the New Left began to dissolve in the 1970s, an important element in that dissolution was an anti-Zionism which culminated in the United Nations plank labeling Zionism as racism in 1975. Although this proclamation, through much pressure, has recently been repealed by the United Nations, it was reaffirmed at the Muslim summit in Dakar in 1991. Frequently those Jews, such as I, who had put their lives and careers on the line in progressive forces of the day, and whose espoused feelings of Jewish nationalism were limited to accepting the legitimacy for the existence of the State of Israel and being concerned for its welfare, were attacked as though they subscribed to the political platform of the Israeli right wing. In Canada I experienced this rejection to varying degrees, either through direct or indirect verbal expression or through personal avoidance, on the part of a few of my closest Gentile friends, who had become non-observant, atheists, or agnostics in regards to their own religious upbringing. One of these persons converted to Islam, and another returned to its observance.[13] Although I have participated in the various religious celebrations of both my French Canadian Catholic and English Canadian Protestant friends, and one of my Muslim immigrant friends, with the exception of my Scandinavian male friend, none of my close friends ever attended or expressed an interest in attending even a secular Jewish event. This observation does not deny the existence of French, English, and "Other" Canadians who took an active, sympathetic interest in Jewish religious and cultural life of the 1970s. However, such people were not among my activist close friends, nor among nearly all other social activists I have known or met.

Mason Wade, the noted American historian of French Canada, describes a long history of French-Canadian anti-Semitism.[14] As a reaction to these negative sentiments, great strides toward accepting both Jewish and other minority groups have been made since the 1930s, when Everett C. Hughes described a Quebec that sought a villain.[15] Looking at the English-Canadian side of this prejudice in her excellent history of Canadian sociology, Marlene Shore reviews the quotas limiting the numbers of Jews at McGill University towards the end of the 1920s until during the Second World War, and McGill's, like many other Canadian universities, turning a deaf ear to pleas from German and Italian refugee scholars.[16]

For the Quebec of the period when the data for this book were gathered, the mid-1970s, James E. Curtis and Ronald D. Lambert wrote:

> Perhaps one of the most significant findings for negativity for out-groups is the apparent existence of comparatively high anti-semitic [*sic*] feelings in French-speaking Canada. Nearly one-quarter of the French Catholics expressed negative feelings towards Jews. Comparable figures for English Catholics and English Protestants were lower at 15 per cent and 10 percent respectively. Negroes received similar levels of rejection (7 - 10 per cent) from each subgroup. ... The discrepancy between French Canadians' rejection of Jews (24 per cent) and English Canadians (8 per cent) is pronounced. The *meaning* of Jews for French Canadians is quite unclear--whether, for example, it is in terms of their religious status or their symbolism of the more economically powerful in the English-Canadian community in Quebec.[17]

It is also significant that throughout the 1970s the only mention of Judaeophobia in the official publication of the Department of Sociology at the *Université de Montréal* was in a very few translations of prestigious American Jewish sociologists writing about other countries, primarily Germany and the United States. Not until 1983 did that publication deal extensively with Quebec's minority groups, when Jacques Brazeau briefly summarized the history of Judaeophobia, and Michel Laferrière reviewed the history of the conflict of Jews and Protestants in Montreal's Protestant School Board. Social scientists' writings on Montreal's Jewish community are focused on monographic accounts of subcultures or institutions, ecology and identity, or reactions to the Holocaust.[18]

Other empirically well-researched, in-depth studies of anti-Semitism continue to record high levels of anti-Semitism in Quebec up to the 1990s. Professor H. Taylor Buckner of Concordia University's Department of Sociology and Anthropology reviewed the major findings of 2,000 Canadians' attitudes towards Jews and other minorities surveyed by professional interviewers each September since 1983 by Environics (formerly C.R.O.P.) on the basis of a modified probability sample with an estimated accuracy of plus or minus 2 percent. Other Concordia faculty members, Frank Chalk, Kurt Jonassohn, and Steve Scheinberg, were on the research committee and read early drafts of Buckner's paper. Altogether a total of 14,188 interviews have been conducted. In his summary, H. T. Buckner found that "the percentages of prejudicial answers have risen in 1989 for all the minority groups in our study [Jews, Italians, Poles, Blacks, Chinese, and Pakistanis]."[19]

These general trends determined the context of my friendships and other important relationships. Most of my friends and colleagues during the 1970s were becoming increasingly secular while not deeply examining the religious base of their own social activism. Many lost any sympathy for Israel's legitimacy and became anti-Zionist to varying degrees with scarcely any knowledge of Jewish history or the reasons for which the great majority of Diaspora--and particularly their local-- Jewish communities had become so strongly supportive of Israel. Here it should be noted that Professor Buckner and his collaborators report that:

> Canadians' perceptions of increasing anti-Jewish sentiment are little influenced by the actions of Israel, though people who are pro-Israel seem to fear that they are, and people who are pro-Arab seem to hope that they are.[20]

While these sociologists have surely recorded the attitudes that surfaced, my point for my friendships is that my friends who were social activists, artists, actresses, writers, and intellectuals tended to be trend setters for a society's contours of justice and standards of high culture. Attitudes and behavior toward Jews have often been barometers of how a society treats other ethnic groups and its own working and lower classes. Michael Lerner underscores that the American Left's failure to deal with its own internal anti-Semitism has been an important force blocking social justice in the U.S.A. since the end of the War in Vietnam.[21]

In a 1984 survey of 3,377 Canadians, Professor Robert Brym of the University of Toronto, and Professor Rhonda Lenton of McMaster University in Hamilton, Ontario, found:

> Ten percent of Catholics who spoke only English at home disliked Jews. That is 4 percent below the national figure for all Canadians. In contrast, 24 percent of Catholics who spoke only French at home displayed such attitudes: nearly twice the national figure. The latter figure was identical for Quebec considered alone.[22]

These Canadian sociologists attributed these higher levels of anti-Semitism among French-speaking Catholics to the teachings of the Catholic Church.

Another poll done in 1987 of 3,500 Canadians done by Professor Joseph F. Fletcher of the Department of Political Science of the University of Toronto and York University's Institute for Social Research asked:

> Who are the people who rank relatively highly on anti-
> semitism? and who ranks relatively low?

He found:

> ... women are just about as likely to rank high as are men.
> And the young are just about as likely to rank high on anti-
> semitism as the old. And party affiliation doesn't make
> much of a difference either. What does make a difference is
> *region*. And where the problem is gravest is here in Québec.
> On our index over seventy percent of Québecers fell into
> our highly anti-semitic category--not one-third as one would
> expect on the basis of chance and as occurred in every
> other region. It is over 70% here.[23]

In 1989 I brought up the issue of anti-Semitism in Canada in a published exchange with Abraham J. Arnold over his book review of Michael Brown's *Jew or Juif? Jews, French Canadians and Anglo-Canadians 1759-1914*.[24] Then the well-known Canadian Jewish writer, Mordecai Richler, published the findings of these polls in the September 23, 1991, issue of the *The New Yorker* and caused quite a flurry of angry criticism among both English- and French-language nationalist and other writers, part of which he reports in his book related to his article, *Oh Canada! Oh Quebec!: Requiem for a Divided Country*.[25]

Here I wish to comment on a few pieces he does not discuss. Jean-Hugues Roy rightfully points out that according to the B'nai Brith between 1988 and 1991, the number of incidents of anti-Semitic behavior--varying from a fire bomb at a Vancouver synagogue to turning over tombstones in Jewish cemeteries--has increased over the whole continent of North America. Between 1988 and 1991 the number of such incidents almost tripled from 61 to 171 in Ontario, while it stabilized at 31 in Quebec. In 1992 there were 25 acts of anti-Semitic vandalism in Montreal compared to 97 in Toronto.

Quoting Teboul's *Myths and Images of the Jew in Quebec*, Roy notes:

> The Jew remains a stranger because he is not perceived as
> belonging or of being able to belong, to the collective
> memory and cultural space of Quebec.

Interviewing this junior college professor fifteen years later, Jean-Hugues Roy notes that Victor Teboul thinks that the situation has hardly changed.[26] During the 1980s Teboul founded a review, *Jonathan,* that was aimed at presenting the complex character of the Jewish community to a non-Jewish audience. The magazine folded five years later. Roy also interviewed Jack Jedwab, who is Director of Community Relations at the Canadian Jewish Congress's Quebec Section. Mr. Jedwab was cited as saying:

> The ostracism which the Jewish community lives is all the more trying because we are treated often as New-Quebecers. However, we are an important historical minority which has been present in Quebec for several generations. Our roots are here, but certain persons persist in uprooting us.

Jean-Hugues Roy also asked the opinion of Joseph Gabay, the President of the Sephardi Community of Quebec. He believes that it is possible to reduce the distance between the French-speaking majority and the Jewish community, although he feels:

> It would be utopian to think that one could fill in a definitive manner the distance between the Jewish community and the French-speaking majority, just as it would be utopian to think that one could fill the trench between French Canadians and English Canadians.

Jean-Hugues Roy ends his piece on a positive note. He gives credit to Joseph Rabinovich of the Association of Jewish Schools for directing an exchange program between primary students of the Jewish and French-speaking schools. While he thinks that Francophone Quebecers are more open than they have ever been to know "the others," Mr. Rabinovich notes that the requests for such exchanges come almost entirely from Jewish schools. Roy also observes that the contacts between the French-speaking and Jewish Quebecers have increased through such events as the playwright, Dora Wasserman's, translation of Michel Tremblay's play, *The Sisters-in-Law*, into Yiddish. Jean-Hugues Roy concludes that whereas Richler is not entirely right, perhaps he is not entirely wrong either.

In the same issue of the periodical for which Mr. Roy writes, Éric Parenteau summarizes a brief history anti-Semitism in Quebec from 1807 until 1960.[27]

There have been some heroic efforts to better Catholic and Jewish understanding in Quebec. Under the auspices of *Le Cercle Juif*, the French-speaking arm of the Canadian Jewish Congress, several interfaith dialogues took place in 1970 in the spirit of the Vatican Council's Declaration on the Jews. At the urgings of McGill Professor Pierre Anctil, several Jewish and French Canadian academics, intellectuals, and professionals met with this goal in mind and issued a manifesto stressing the possibility for a shared future which both groups wish to build together out of a sense of mutual respect. A native of Quebec City and a practicing Roman Catholic, Pierre Anctil, helped co-found Dialogue St. Urbain, which organizes cultural events to promote understanding between Jews and French Canadians. Anctil is fluent in Yiddish and has taught courses on Jewish Montreal.[28]

Even taking into consideration some of these positive developments, the Catholic-Jewish dialogue of rapprochement appears to occupy a notably less prominent place in Quebec compared to the United States of America. In part, this has resulted from former social and cultural alternativists's having revolted from their own religious upbringing and having frequently settled into a comfortable consumerism. Such Jews, Protestants, and Catholics, who, in past generations, would have served as bridges among their communities of religious orientation, have let professional elites assume the role in such dialogue. Polite and often tense silence appears to be the outcome of such a cultural and structural pattern. Yet, this outcome might be interpreted as derivative of the greater secularization of all major religious groups in Quebec after the Quiet Revolution and the greater influence of Zionist and socialist currents in Quebec Jewry, in contrast to the greater influence of Reform Judaism and liberalism in the United States. However, other structural features, such as the role of the Canadian Jewish Congress, as the sole representative of Canadian Jewry, may have acted to quell the diversity of views within the Jewish community heard by the French-speaking majority.[29]

Several prominent Catholic and Jewish progressive thinkers have recently identified the underlying social psychology, theology, and politics to the blockages in close personal communication between them that I have just described in my own friendships. The continuing high levels of anti-Semitism among French-speaking Catholics in Quebec need to be addressed by an educational program within Catholic educational institutions, by increased inter-faith dialogues and meetings, and by a media campaign to address the non-observant and nationalists who hold such attitudes.[30]

Although other forces of attraction studied in this work bring Catholics and Jews into close friendships, when a deep level of intimacy is reached, the issues discussed by these writers inevitably arise. In my observations of such close friendships, it seems to me that American Catholics have faced these issues more than French-speaking Canadian, observant or lapsed Catholics.

Here I would like to mention the work of two French-speaking, Quebec women who have attempted to grapple with the problem of anti-Semitism. Esther Delisle, whose revised doctoral dissertation was recently published as *Le Traître et le Juif: Lionel Groulx, Le Devoir, et le Délire du Nationalisme d'Extrême Droite dans la Province du Québec, 1929-1939* [*The Traitor and the Jew: Lionel Groulx, Le Devoir, and the Rage of the Nationalism of the Extreme Right in the Province of Quebec, 1929-1939*], exposes the rabid anti-Semitism and fascist political leanings of the historian, priest, teacher, and pioneer of Quebec nationalism, Lionel Groulx, who remains a positive symbol to many Quebec nationalists even today. A sample of the Abbot's prejudice, and by no means his most extreme, is a letter he wrote in 1954 after the Holocaust. Lionel Groulx described every Jew as having an "innate passion for money, a passion that is often monstrous and that removes all his scruples. He will do anything for money. And so we find him at the bottom of every murky affair." Two of Esther Delisle's doctoral committee's five members voted against her, and, as of August 23, 1993, she was reported as having little hope of securing a teaching position at any Quebec university.[31]

Lise Noël's book, *L'intolérance: Une problématique générale* [*Intolerance: A General Framework*], won the Governor General's Literary Prize of The Canada Council in 1989. Dr. Noël's book outlines the salient features of anti-Semitism in world history and compares the experiences of Jews with other minorities to arrive at generalizations.[32] Beyond her erudition and compassion, I know Ms. Noël to be more open and accepting of Jews than nearly any other member of the French-speaking, Quebec intelligentsia I have met or known.

However, there are aspects of her book that convey a distorted view of contemporary Judaism, which is shared with and derived from some current feminist writings, but which may reflect her primary exposure to Judaism in Canada and France. I will cite just two examples from her text, although I could go into many more. She writes, "Each day, the Jew, moreover, thanks God "to not have been created a woman."[33] While it is true that there is such a prayer in Orthodox Judaism, the noted American Jewish feminist, Pnina Tobin, notes "That prayer has probably been spoken more often by anti-Semitic non-Jews than by Jewish worshipers." In Letty Cottin Pogrebin's June 1982 essay on "Anti-Semitism in the Women's Movement" of *Ms.* magazine, reprinted in her 1991 book, she reminds us that in December 1981 a major focus of attention of Catholic, Jewish, and Protestant Feminists of Faith was "the disconcerting trend toward anti-Semitism in the writings of some Christian feminists."[34] Dr. Noël observes, "However, like Judaism which reserves the study of the Torah to men, the Catholic Church has hardly encouraged the education of women."[35] On the contrary, in the Reform (also known as Liberal or Progressive) branch of Judaism as well as in the Conservative, and Reconstructionist branches of Judaism, women are, in fact, encouraged, and do, indeed, study the Torah and other sacred writings. There are increasing numbers of Jewish women who are rabbis and cantors. These movements comprise around two-thirds of the observant Jewish community in North America today. Ms. Noël's book with many similar interpretations seems to be based on exclusive reference to Orthodox Judaism and even ignores the writings of Orthodox Jewish women who consider themselves to be feminists and who give entirely different interpretations to their roles and rites than does Dr. Noël.[36] I wonder if Lise Noël would recognize as Jews the incredible diversity in age, gender, marital status, sexual orientation, socio-economic class, disability, and race that she would encounter in many contemporary Reform, Conservative, and Reconstructionist temples and synagogues in the large cities of the United States today.

I do agree with Clift and Arnopoulos that in recent years the English-speaking, historically Protestant institutions in Quebec have been much more serious than French-speaking, historically Catholic ones in enacting the ideals of a society where religion, race, ethnicity, gender, and national origin play less a role than personal merit. Here I must suggest lines for further sociological research.[37]

Basing himself on the 1986 census, Charles Shahar found the Jewish population of Montreal at 96,470, "well below the peak of 115,000 during the 1970s." In Montreal, the Canadian Census lists 109,480 Jews by religion and 114,220 by ethnicity in 1971, and 96,710 Jews by religion and 95,825 by ethnicity in 1991. Jews decreased from 1.22 per cent of the Canadian population in 1981 from 1.28 per cent in 1971.[38] In 1993 *The Gazette* cited Montreal's Jewish population at "about 85,000."

A compendium of both qualitative and quantitative information makes it clear that large segments of the Jewish community showed signs of anxiety by the rise of the separatist and nationalist movements in Quebec both politically and economically. A large part of the emigration of Jews from Quebec was a young, college-educated, and bilingual population. The remaining Jewish population has been reported as being the demographically oldest in North America next to Miami's.[39] Is there a relationship between Montreal's 615,000 people living under the poverty line, 203,000 officially listed as unemployed, and Jewish young people's leaving Quebec?[40] Seymour Martin Lipset presents evidence that Canadian Jews have made a major contribution to

Canada's economic development.[41] Thus, one might conclude that Jewish young people's exodus from Quebec in the 1970s may have resulted in fewer businesses being developed in Quebec which led to fewer jobs being available for the unemployed. Comparative evidence from Europe and the United States would also suggest that Jews contribute disproportionately to the arts and academic life, and when they leave a geographic area, there results a greater cultural and academic conformity.

While I commend the efforts of the Canadian sociologists cited above, I would encourage them to do further studies investigating the social psychology of this large out migration. Did these people feel threatened by various manifestations of nationalism, of little possibility of obtaining employment in an economic sector within or dependent upon the state, when only around 3.6% of non-French Canadians benefit from such positions, of discrimination in employment or business loans, etc.? And I would hope economists and others would undertake some analyses of the costs of this out-migration.

With this decline of her community, one might be tempted to sympathize with the use by Ruth R. Wisse, Professor of Yiddish and English literature at McGill University, of part of the moral teaching of the great Jewish sage, Hillel, in the title and content of her new book.[42] Unfortunately, her translation of Hillel to read, "If I am not for myself, who will be for me? And being for myself, what am I? And if not now, when?" emphasizes one's own concerns before others, in a way Hillel did not mean, if the standard Orthodox, Conservative, and Reform prayerbook translations are accurate.[43] The more widely held rendition, which gives an entirely different, more liberal view, is: "If I am not for myself, who will be for me? But if I am only for myself, what am I? And if not now, when?"[44]

On reading her book, I wonder if Ruth R. Wisse ever visited the other side of Mt. Royal where *l'Université de Montréal* is located. When I was a graduate student there in the 1970s, she could have met Jews of Sephardi and Ashkenazi backgrounds who had friendly relations with Arabs, but who at the same time firmly responded to anti-Zionist and anti-Israeli propaganda in the media. Moreover, she could have met Jews with a variety of liberal and social democratic views who engaged in a variety of local social change activities and yet who remained critical of Soviet totalitarianism and anti-Semitism and supportive of Soviet refuseniks. Professor Wisse's attack on Jewish liberals and leftists appears contradicted by her own admission that it was Canada's Progressive Conservative Minister of External Affairs, Joe Clark, who fabricated a story accusing Israel of trying to starve Palestinians by holding back convoys of food before the Canada-Israel Committee on March 10, 1988, thereby obtaining unanimous Arabic support for Canada's bid on the Security Council.[45] Nor does Ruth R. Wisse acknowledge that it was two Jewish men of the left who openly described the negative impact nationalistic policies were having on Montreal's Jewish community in Israel and Canada.[46] Nor does Dr. Wisse discuss their successful court challenge of the editor of Montreal's influential daily, *Le Devoir*, who was more than disparaging of their article.[47] And would it be conceited of me to bring to her attention that my raising the issue of anti-Semitism in Canada was published by *Jewish Currents*, a magazine of the left?[48]

Before leaving this section, it is important to return to Beth Hess's question, "Do American Jews have different friendship patterns than born-again Christians? If so, why?" A recent cultural artifact, a deep and moving film about the friend/enemy relationship between two Jewish men set in Montreal throws light on this question. *The Quarrel* depicts the meeting of two former best friends who have become enemies.[49]

Both are Holocaust survivors who have lost their wives and friends to Nazism, but who have had two diametrically opposed reactions to this tragedy. Chaim Kovler is an Orthodox Jewish rabbi whose father was head of the Yeshiva in Bialystock, where his friend Hersh Rasseyner was the best student. Hersh has become a Yiddish-language novelist and advice columnist who is visiting Montreal from the United States to read from his latest work. When they meet for the first time in fifteen years on Mount Royal, they cannot ignore each other, for they are practically all the "near and dear" they have left in this world. For

Hersh, Hitlerism meant sin in the world, but for Chaim this slaughter of innocents was definitive evidence of God's silence. Yet, Chaim believes in human reason and the goodness of people.

Their old quarrel resurfaces during a rainstorm on Mount Royal, where their American and Canadian Jewish selves' differences are symbolized by Chaim's breaking into a public tool shed to seek cover during a rain storm, and Hersh's law-abidance not being willing to commit such an infraction. For Hersh, being good is passing on the wisdom of the Torah and acts of kindness derivative from its teachings to the next generation. But for Chaim, skepticism and humanism are the new *Bible*.

Even their bodies are as different as their views. Chaim is tall, tastefully dressed, and handsome. Hersh is short, traditionally garbed, and not very physically comely. Their intense arguments, embraces, jokes, and battles let the audience realize that these men know and emote towards each other to the depths of their soul. If Israel refers to the people who wrestle with God, then these two men do so to the depths of their spirits.

To answer Beth Hess, it would seem to me to be unlikely, though not impossible, that a Christian fundamentalist male preacher, say from Memphis or Birmingham, would fight and affectionately and furiously reminisce all afternoon with his best friend from childhood who becomes a moderately well-known writer from New York or San Francisco, and stick together to refight religious versus secular battles for such a length of time. It is unlikely that such friends would have lost most of their families and friends to such ideologically based fanaticism as fascism, which would propel them to see issues in terms of their ultimate life and death consequences. It is unlikely that there would be such an amount of touch in their interchange. The fact that I have not seen or heard of an American producer with this possible scenario may, indeed, point to the culturally patterned contrasts that Hess's question implies.

Finally, it is encouraging to know that some born-again Christians and American Jews are working together on such projects as former President Jimmy and former First Lady Roslyn Carter's Habitat for

Humanity to build housing for needy families. It is highly probable that friendships between individuals from these groups will be made during the course of doing these good deeds, which express both religious heritages' commonly held values.

Now that the reader has a sense of the author as a human being with friends--an experience that must bear on an analysis of friendship-- let us review some of this study's major findings about friendship.

Gender and Friendship

Around 65 percent of Montrealers in my study had both male and female friends, although more of their close friends were of their same gender. Montrealers reported that around one-fourth of men's friendships were only with other men, and one fifth of their women's friendships were only with other women.

In terms of the way men and women in Montreal defined friendship-- their cognitive maps of friendship--I came up with different results depending on the method of analysis and indicators that I used. Hence, I cannot reliably attribute any significant differences to either gender in this regard. With this caution in mind, I did find that some indicators yielded significant differences by some methods. These contrasts throw into question some of the large differences being attributed uniquely to gender in the early 1990s. For example, more men than women in Montreal reported often asking themselves the kinds of Maisonneuvean questions about their friendships that I replicated. Such a finding is inconsistent with the notion of women being better at expressive behavior. By protothematic analysis, English Canadian males, compared to English Canadian females, emphasized "helping out in times of trouble," whereas no such gender differences were found for French Canadians. This finding and others reviewed in Chapter Seven suggest that ethnicity and other variables intervened in the construction of the cognitive map of friendship in the mid-1970s in Montreal. It is true that the similar-interest-close friend style was much more frequent among men interviewed in-depth [22/29=75.86% men] compared to [7/29=24.14%] women. Likewise, the style of boy-/girl-friend/*petit(e) ami(e)* was found much more frequently among male [7/9=78%] compared to female [2/9=22%], single [7/9=78%] compared to divorced [1/9=11%], married without children [1/9=11%], and younger [6/9=67%] compared to older [3/9=33%] in-depth interviewees. However, cell analysis of the quantitative results of my questionnaire respondents does not replicate this difference between males and females in regards to tactility and sexuality within close friendship. From these differences, do we conclude that men's friendships are more "side by side" and women's more "face to face," as has been recently argued?[50]

More exactly, we can see the similarities between my similar-interest-style of friendship and the notion of social companionship. But, since it has been pointed out that such friendships produce feelings of happiness through "spontaneity, playfulness, permissiveness and candor," this style seems to overlap with Aristotle's friendship of pleasure.[51] In Chapter Eight, I recalled that the meaning of friendships based on common interest revives an old debate between Suttie and Scheler, which makes me loath to downgrade their quality generally, while being able to point to the weaknesses in the related style of the buddy-*copain-copine*. Moreover, my data on the incidence of tactility and sexuality in females' as contrasted to males' friendships did not reveal large differences in non-verbal expressions of affection.[52] And my data are consonant with representative samples of attitudinal and behavioral change regarding sexuality in Canada during this period.

The affinities created by negotiation and socialization to clothing, fantasies, play, and the like still give the great majority of women more in common with other women and more men in common with other men. They follow through this commonality in selecting others of the same sex and complementing these experiences with persons of the opposite sex. Meanwhile, women's entry into the work force, talk shows, articles, and a few hot debates help alter this social determination. Maisonneuve explained this social process of same sex bonding on the basis of identification, which causes members of one sex to consider those of their same sex as like themselves, and those of the opposite sex as unlike themselves. Even though there was same sex bonding and even though the style of the boyfriend/girlfriend, *petit(e) ami(e)* characterized a significant per cent of my in-depth interviewees, most Montrealers also had close friends of the opposite gender whom they did not consider as sexual objects. Rather most Montrealers appreciated the differences of their friends' complex personalities in the modern world.

I find Maisonneuve's sociological explanation to be more economical than Enriquez's, O'Connor's, and Rubin's opposing psycho-analytical, attachment, and psycho-dynamic explanations which I have reviewed.

By the 1990s, the debate about the quality of men's and women's friendship has taken on a bitter tone. In its most extreme form, it has been argued that lesbian friendships are the "prototype of true female friendships and the only ones that can bring about change in the distribution of power within society."[53] In stark contrast, from the grave, we are reminded that friendship is "logocentric" and "gentler, soberer, without frenzy. It, unlike love, is necessarily reciprocal" and "is beyond mere bodily need."[54]

In the debate over whether men or women are better suited for close friendship, I conclude that the empirical evidence I have amassed indicates that both genders are equally capable of deep and meaningful friendship, although women may stress somewhat more communication and men steadfastness in their friendships. Such a finding goes against much of classical philosophy, which depicted men as more capable of close friendship and against an important current in contemporary feminist writing that claims that women tend to have more meaningful friendships owing to their expressive roles, learned from early socialization, where women experience no dramatic break with their mothers and men experience sharp boundary differentiation through the resolution of the Oedipal conflict.

Just How Brittle Is Close Friendship?

There is an important point of disagreement in interpreting the extent to which breaking friendships is a natural part of the relationship in a modern society or a historically aberrant outcome of the late 1960s and 1970s which has seriously undermined the possibility for social solidarity as human beings approach the Third Millennium. I reviewed Shmuel N. Eisenstadt's notion that friendship is potentially brittle because it embodies the closest particularistic relations between two persons while selecting the friend on the most universalistic criteria. Later, with Luis Roniger, the great social theorist, S. N. Eisenstadt, explained that only when the search for attachment combines with the search for meaning does the search become endowed with the special symbols of pure trust, pristine meaning, and "I and Thou" dialogue.

In more empirical examinations, the studies evolving out of Steve Duck's work and the *Journal of Social and Personal Relationships* appear to encompass two diametrically opposed answers regarding friendship's brittleness. On the one hand, in the introduction to this work, I quoted Robin Gilmour and Tuvia Melamed's concern that the late 1960s and seventies did, indeed, take a more short-term and disposable view of relationships. Independently, I pointed to the work of the philosopher and psychotherapist, Michael Lerner, who offered empirical and clinical observations supporting this view and added to it the concern that such relationships were undermining trust, and, therefore, the possibility for progressive social change in society. On the other hand, Duck's and Sants's emphasis on the strategies used to intensify and restrict friendship's development document cognitive and behavioral processes by which friendships are ruptured or built. Their work is not dissimilar to a social penetration process that was postulated by Altman's and Taylor's theory and that I criticized on empirical and theoretical grounds in Chapter Two.[55] Indeed, the continental sociologists' work which was referred to throughout much of this book depicts many more unconscious factors at play that undermine friendship in the real world and a less regular process of making friendship, depending on the style of friendship constructed.

Those who see changes throughout the life course bringing a person to find new friends as older ties are broken also depict breaking friendship as a normal feature of the social order of the modern world.[56]

The network theorists also have described how friendships are maintained or broken in terms of properties of networks. Thus, Robert Milardo found that dense networks had a greater chance to be stable and enduring, diverse in content, and more intense than loosely knit networks.[57] And Wellman focused on the fact that married women who work must bear a double load of having a wider range social ties but not feeling that they have the time and energy to form close relationships with them.[58] And Wiseman presents evidence that violating unwritten contracts of friendship leads to their rupture.[59]

My study would agree with Horst Hutter's in that certain ages seem to encourage friendships more than others. Although these periods seem to be characterized by non-institutionalized, specific, diffuse, and combined symmetrical and complementary differentiation, it is difficult to translate reliably these Parsonian attributes to concrete societies and interpersonal relationships.

My work in the tradition of French sociological phenomenology and the network theorists in British and American sociology and social psychology depict breaking up with friends as an observable social phenomenon which can be explained in terms of social, psychological, and developmental factors and which is predictable during the life course in a modern, complex society.

On the one hand, in Chapter One, I presented evidence that the Montrealers of the mid-1970s gave similar importance to their major social cognitions of friendship, including fidelity, when compared to the French of the 1950s. And, in Chapter Two, I reviewed my finding that almost 92 percent of Montrealers said that they tried to put some time aside for their friends, even if their work is most time and energy consuming, and that a little more than 62 percent of my respondents claimed that they either had not sacrificed nor would they sacrifice a friend for serious reasons of a family nature. On the other hand, in Chapter Nine, I reviewed evidence that Montrealers enacted an erotic component with around one-fifth of their six closest friends at minimally a low level. I interpreted this pattern to be evidence that Montrealers may have been enacting a type of sexuality without commitment within the boy-/girl- friend/*petit(e) ami(e)* style of friendship during the 1970s. However, the differences between Montrealers' expectation of fidelity in part of their cognitive map of friendship, combined with at least one style of friendship that may not have been loyal, may have left them with at least an unconscious cognitive dissonance. I hesitantly offered the interpretation that such an experience may have led to feelings of a lack of trust in intimate friends that may be a psycho-social factor in the demographic decline of French Canadians during this period. However, I noted that while two social theorists have general agreement on this trend, Michael Lerner emphasizes its historic specificity, while Horst Hutter explains its being linked to the complementary differentiation of roles and subgroups that typify modern industrial and post-industrial society.

Some philosophical, psychotherapeutic, social scientific, and media warnings regarding a flippant attitude about dissolving friendship should be taken seriously. Indeed, the popular joke that Californians form "flaky" relationships may express culturally encoded anxiety about the most advanced post-industrial state's relationship patterns, including friendship, on the part of an admiring world that loves the state's creativity, ethnic pluralism, natural beauty, and wealth but fears the potential loneliness and lack of social concern of the isolated individualist.

If the accounts in this study document that friendships of different styles were psycho-socially very meaningful to social actors in a modern, urban, industrial city in a more generalized mixed economy during the 1970s, I believe this finding is colored by my willingness to stick closer to my interviewees' accounts than to speculate and be judgmental about the quality of friendship in modern society. Yet, as only 11.4% of the friendships broken in my sample were due to a change of an idea or opinion, it can be inferred that the search for metameaning characteristic of the purist form of friendship was probably rather restrained in the Montreal of the 1970s. Likewise, since most close friendships were dissolved because of moving (28.2%), then changes in private life such as marriage and divorce (18.7%), then changes in occupation (13.9%) , and a few to changes in position on the same job (3.7%), all these sources of strain testify to social factors breaking friendships over and beyond the core values of the relationship. This finding is supported by the fact that Maisonneuve's scale of friendliness, of valuing friendship either through an attitude of non-exclusive openness or by putting friendship before affective, social, or pragmatic considerations, confirmed for his French data from the 1950s, could not be replicated on my data from the Montreal of the mid-1970s.

Since growing tired of a friend's company (9.2%), a real fight with a friend (8.8%), and breaking with a friend for no particular reason (6.2%)-- all process-like variables--were less notable, though still important, in Montrealers' friendship dissolutions, it would appear that major social forces exerted a greater impact on breaking with a friend than forces internal to the relationship. Moreover, my finding that the Montrealers of my sample displayed an erotic component with around one-fifth of their six closest friends at minimally a low level and accounts about the boy- and girl- friend/*petit(e) ami(e)*style of friendship, together with the revelations about my activist circle of friends in this chapter, do lend some credence to Gilmour's, Melamed's, Lerner's, and Bloom's differing but overlapping concerns about the particular brittleness in friendships of the later 1960s and 1970s. Basing himself, in part, on post-World War II ideological changes in all major Canadian religious groups, Seymour Martin Lipset observed that Canadians have greater communitarian values in comparison to Americans. These greater communitarian values may have lessened the decline in societal trust. Depicted as being a psycho-social outcome of the breakdown in close relationships, such diminishing trust has led to less support for collectivist policies among the electorate.

As I have taught an introduction to philosophy in French in a Quebec college as well as sociology and as French sociological phenomenology draws heavily on philosophy, I found it appropriate to cite classical and few modern philosophical references to explain the forces that make and break close friendships.

Friendship and the Family

In my in-depth interviews, I identified four styles of friendship that were found in the family: A1) the family-oriented friendship, A2) friendship after the break-up of the family, A3) the sibling friendship, and A4) the non-nuclear family friendship. Only A1), A3), and A4) occurred frequently.

I emphasized that Montrealers' language, thought, and emotion regarding friendship and kinship encompassed many of the same components: communication and sympathetic interaction signified by certain gestures, acts, and circumstances. Most Montrealers chose family friends from mothers or fathers, then from sisters or brothers, then from daughters or sons. Very few husbands and wives considered each other as their closest friend, although confessing love or obligation to each other, they conceived of their spouse as a husband or wife *per se*. Affinal relations were chosen as close friends much less frequently than expected, and uncles, aunts, grandparents, and first cousins were the least often picked as close friends in my urban sample. Some philosophers explained that this order of choice followed the principles of nature. Other classical writers and modern sociologists stressed the importance of sharing common beliefs as a basis for family friendship, but the sociologists stressed that this possibility was constrained by the reality of class, age, and other social factors as well as cultural change.

Methodologically, I expressed a concern that sociologists who depicted the more underprivileged end of the social scale as being exclusively kin-oriented and the more privileged end as being more friend-oriented had minimized their informants' accounts and maximized their reliance on rigid analytical grids.

I compared the Freudian and exchange frameworks interpretations of family life in their bearing on the question of the possibility for friendship in the family. In the Freudian view, friendship may be promoted by proper identification with another member of the family, while, in the exchange model, such identification may take place because various psycho-social forces are in balance. Finally, I illustrated how these models could be applied to contrastive styles of friendship in two real Montreal families.

Ethnicity and Friendship

Overall, in combining the quantitative and qualitative indicators of friendship in my study, ethnicity explained the greatest amount of variance among all the variables investigated. Most Montrealers to whom I have reported these results react with a "So what's new?" However, many Americans, including professional sociologists and anthropologists, have reacted with either shock or incredulity that this pattern should be the case, as though my results had violated the national code of a pluralist society. At a time when the ideal of the melting pot is giving way to one of multi-culturalism, this reaction suggests to me that the old ideal is still an important value for many Americans. It is significant that I have had a significant number of requests for my published articles on the impact of ethnicity on friendship from Eastern Europe, as though what I have reported reflects a significant aspect of their daily life.

There is a slight trend for respondents to be progressively more open to outgroups among their close friends as one goes from lower through middle to higher occupational groupings. Even though ethnic homophily among closest friends characterized all ethnic groups in Quebec, all groups have a considerable proportion of their close friends from other ethnic groups. I have explained this phenomenon in terms of the contact hypothesis, the principle of similarity, and qualitative documents. Certain subcultures in which ethnic differences are either played down or appreciated for their diversity may promote building close friendships across ethnic boundaries, as do certain ecological features of the city of Montreal.

Let me stress that ethnicity did not play the determinant role in all styles of friendship and did not always predict styles of friendship in the direction that qualitative documents suggested. For example, I found that while English Canadians (5 [56%]) displayed the style of the boy-/girl- friend/*petit(e) ami(e)* somewhat more than French Canadians (4 [44%]), this contrast was not great among my in-depth interviewees. My late and honored teacher's, Marcel Rioux's, portrayal of French Canadians as tending to be more Dionysian and English Canadians as more Apollonian would have predicted a notable and opposite trend from this contrast, for which civil status, sex of the interviewee, and age produced greater differentials.

Class and Friendship

Around 58 percent of the Montrealers in my study reported that the greatest number of their friends came from a milieu like their own in terms of resources and goods possessed. Around 27 percent of my interviewees and respondents had friends who were more prosperous than themselves. and over 15 percent had friends who were less well-off.

Around 48 percent of Montrealers had friends of their same educational level. About 27 percent of Montrealers' friends were better educated, and about 24 percent were less educated than my interviewees and respondents.

Around 52 percent of the people in my sample had friends who were in their same trade or occupation, and about 48 percents of their friends were in different trades or occupations.

When I combined the indicators of Montrealers' friends' wealth, education, and occupation, I found that about 86 percent had closest friends who were characterized by mixed class components. Around 13 percent had friends with strictly the same indicators of socio-economic class, and slightly more than one percent had closest friends with strictly different class indicators.

These trends were illustrated by the psycho-social sentiments that support them. Although the principle of homophily explains these patterns, some important sociological accounts by Quebecers in the 1970s tended to interpret the different class experiences of friendship in rather rigid Marxist analytical grids. While relying on some of their insights, I discussed the limitations of this viewpoint for understanding the impact of class on friendship.

Friendship over the Years

About 63 percent of my interviewees' and respondents' friends were of their same age-generation, about 22 percent were of an older age-generation, and over 15 percent were of a younger age generation. However, single persons showed the greatest tendency to have close friends of their same age-generation.

Married people in general, but particularly those without children, were more tolerant of political diversity in their close friends' opinions during the mid-1970s. It appears that single people, who tended to be younger, demanded more ideological consistency among their close friends, while married people without children formed a wider variety of ties in job and non-work related activities that gave them a greater chance to become close to people who did not hold the same political views.

Only around 10 percent of my interviewees and respondents met their adult friends through their husband or wife, although this figure went up five to six percent for currently married people. Furthermore, married people with children and blue collar workers more readily rank their closest friends from most to least intimate. This trend reflects the pressures of holding down a job and raising children. These constraints tend to force these social groups into being very selective among their friends with whom they choose to spend their scarce time.

In a related matter, although around 62 percent of both older and younger Montrealers said that they would not give into family pressure to drop a friend in order to avoid conflict with a person's family, more Montrealers 31 years of age and older claimed that they had sacrificed or would sacrifice friend relations for serious reasons of a family nature in comparison to younger people. In a similar vein, more younger than older Montrealers discuss their most intimate thoughts and problems with friends to some degree.

Friendship and Mental Health

Throughout this work, I have referred to works rooted in what the French call *psycho-sociologie*, which overlaps in important ways with what the English-speaking, and some of the French-speaking, worlds refer to as clinical sociology. These concerns led me to develop the small group exercise reported in this book to help people better understand and possibly improve their own and others' close friendships. In addition, this orientation led me to do a thorough search of the literature that clearly established that interventions into friendships could help better people's mental well-being.[60] Besides these groups, my data from the in-depth interviews for this book and my student essays reveal an important clinical dimension and implicit sociology.[61]

After I completed my thesis, the State of California's Department of Mental Health was persuaded that there was a sufficient enough link between friendship and mental health to fund an educational program that promoted the idea that "Friends Can Be Good Medicine." And since I completed my search of the literature relevant to the effect of friendship on mental health, Pat O'Connor did a similar and more recent review with a focus on British social science sources. Moreover, she raises several important issues, two of which I will briefly review in terms of an interview reported in this book.[62]

In the case of the style of "best-friend neighbor," we met Jean-Claude whose friendship with Pierre was "stress-buffering" in that when his sister decompensated and his parents had contributed to an atmosphere of fearfulness at home, his neighbor-friend's family provided him with shelter, food, and emotional support. At the same time, his friendship with Pierre was "assets-benefiting," in that his living with Pierre's family intensified their frequency of daily interaction over a period of years, in his being companionable with Pierre and being able to discuss with him almost anything. Besides the crucial importance of positive and enjoyable experiences in Jean-Claude's and Pierre's friendship, I reported the costs of maintaining this friendship, particularly around the issue of the break-up of Jean-Claude and Pierre's sister, Francine, and their dealing with their emerging sexualities. However, with a different take on this issue from O'Connor's, I stressed that part of these psychic costs derived from ambivalence toward the then newly-emerging, culturally-constructed norms surrounding sexuality. The scientific validity for these observations is closer to the ethnographer's procedures of replicability, internal consistency, providing enough detail for credibility of argument, and improvement than to the controlled experiment.[63]

Is Close Friendship Worse off Today?

In her lecture on "Love and Friendship in the '80s" at the University of California, Berkeley, on Wednesday, November 11, 1987, Lillian B. Rubin did not address the question of whether she thought the 1980s, with a popular image of being the age of "greed for the greater good," was less propitious for friendship until I pressed her on the issue. She was of the opinion that there was not a great distinction between the 1970s and the 1980s in regards to friendship.

Although I can speak only on the basis of my comparative experience of the two decades, it seems to me that there was a much greater caution and circumspection regarding forming friendships and the depth of personal disclosure a friend readily made to a close friend in the 1980s. It seems to me that people were more judgmental and realistic about the degree of material and time they committed to their friendships, often because large segments of the population experienced economic downward mobility, which led them to work harder to earn a living, which left them less time for friends and leisure. It seems that the extent to which close friends disagreed on the morality of the military build-up and revaluing of private enterprise, and its impact on the environment, pushed them into different socio-economic strata and classes, which, in turn, have tended to lessen their mutual esteem and similarities. Such experiences limited the amount of energy, trust, and love people into social movements were willing to invest in further close relationships.

Despite my pessimistic observations, a study of 3,530 French- and English-speaking Canadians between the ages of 15 and 19 found that in 1985 91% of young people considered friendship as being "very important" and 75% responded that they appreciated friendship "a lot." Comparing friendship with other important values, this survey found that love was important for 86%, freedom for 85%, an easy life for 78%, to be accepted by God for 43%, to have the esteem of one's peers for 39%, and to be popular for 21%.[64]

Two recent reports about friendship in the 1990s both suggest to me the decline of friendship in general with the possibility for the enrichment of friendships which remain. With the collapse of communism in the former Soviet Union and Eastern Europe, recent discussions and books suggest that extreme ethnic chauvinism and religious fundamentalism and control of the international market by multinational corporations are leading to a large underclass in the economically developed world accompanied by ethnic strife, leading to contained war in considerable parts of the economically developing world.

I share the communitarian concern that the social organization of the world's economy by multinational corporations is creating a structure that thrusts the individual to maximize his or her social bonds at the expense of community. Instead of the optimistic view of the promoters of the information highway, who see this new technology permitting the individual to work closer to his or her home and have more time for family and friends in a global village, I see fewer citizens having access to the means of earning an acceptable standard of living and a shattering of powerful, intermediate institutions, such as labor unions, between the state and the individual that have permitted larger segments of the population to participate in and enjoy the fruits of democracy in this century.

This observation implies that there will be increasingly large segments of the population composed of atomized individuals who will have to work harder to earn a lower standard of living and thus have even less time for friends. I see the major means of the economy still largely in the hands of the merchants of death, the industries allied to the military, despite recent, important attempts by the Clinton Administration to reorient the American economy in a more peaceful direction. Who is selling the armaments that fuel the many wars around the world, the drugs which anesthetize an increasingly large underclass and other socio-economic strata in the post-industrial countries, and the local arms that fuel these wars within the same societies? However, I stand to be corrected by the future work of sociologists who examine the link between the social organization of the multinational corporation and the state of friendship between human beings.

According to the United Nationals High Commissioner for Refugees, the spread of ethnic conflict since the end of the cold war "has pushed the number of refugees to 44 million people or more than one in every 130 inhabitants of the globe. The number of people qualifying as refugees because they have been driven across an international frontier has climbed steadily from 2.5 million in 1970 to 19. 7 million today ... ."[65]

In this context, Susan Rivers' touching story describes what happened to the friendship of Milan Oklopdzic, a 44-year-old Serbian novelist, who was arrested and had his family harassed in the spring of 1992 for opposing the nationalistic policies of Slobodan Milosevic. Oklopdzics' best known novel, *California Blues*, sold 100,000 copies and gained him notoriety and scrutiny in Serbia.[66] He, his wife, Brana, and their son Damian, 14, and daughter, Iva, 10, managed to slip out of his country with one suitcase. Mika Oklopdzic and his family ended up sharing an apartment with a Croatian friend in Castro Valley, California. When this friend "withdrew the welcome mat on a rainy night in January, the Oklopdzics were left literally in the street. They had $90 and an address book running low on names." Having been kicked out of his Croatian friend's, he called a woman he had known slightly from his days as a graduate student in Davis, where he did a master's degree at the University of California. She put him and his family up for 10 days and loaned him money to settle in Manteca. I totally concur with Milan "Mika" Oklopdzic's characterization of the change in friendships in California since his graduate student days 19 years ago. He finds,

> people have changed. Strangers are more suspicious of you, uneasy. I can't joke with people--they have too much on their minds." Friends are not the same, either, "They're worried about their jobs," he says. "They can't give much help."

I should add that I feel this example is particularly appropriate because the same article reports that others of the Belgrade intelligentsia have applied for asylum in Canada.

On a more hopeful note, I do not think that the *San Francisco Chronicle* would have published Art Hoppe's remarks on "Friendship's End" twenty years ago:

> I am writing this to tell my best friend I love him. I can't say it to him face to face. We heterosexual males cringe at the very thought of male love.
>
> I never admitted I love this man until he was diagnosed as having cancer. He was simply someone I was always glad to see; someone I was always comfortable with. Now the doctors give him a few months at most, and I realize how much I love him. It's time to tell him so.
>
> His name is Ken Wilson. He is a tall, solid man with an innate dignity, a fine mind, a refreshing modesty, a strong sense of justice and a self-deprecating sense of humor. He is a very good man. I'm proud that he's my best friend.[67]

Space does not permit me to recount the story of Hoppe's and Wilson's friendship as single and married men, but it does give me hope that even in an environmentally and socially deteriorating planet, there may still be a place for friendships of this caliber.

And it is a sign of hope that groups such as the Irish Children's Fund and Givat Haviva in Israel have helped foster real friendships across lines of religious and ethnic conflict in sensitive regions of the globe.

Studying Friendship

While not discounting the importance of the forces of personality and individual psychology, this book has concentrated on the cultural and social forces which help build friendship. I reported on Montrealers' complicated "cognitive maps" of friendship in the mid-1970s and, relying on a variety of secondary sources, I related how this pattern of meanings had been transmitted historically. Through many direct quotations from my interviews and clips from films, plays, newspapers, books, observations from friends' interacting, and interpretations of the aggregate results from my questionnaire data, I demonstrated how these inherited symbols were expressed in the Montreal of the 1970s. These made up the conceptions by which women and men communicated, perpetuated, and developed their knowledge about and attitudes toward friendship. In brief, these documents constitute, in Clifford Geertz's definition, the culture of friendship in Montreal in the mid-1970s.[68]

Drawing on the work of other sociologists of friendship, I found the notion of style of friendship a comprehensible analytical tool to summarize my interviewees' and respondents' complex definitions, real behavior in, experiences of, and normative expectations about friendship. These styles are, in George McCall's sense, an objectified social form in which there is a sense of collectivity, in which there is some role differentiation, and in which there exists a shared culture.[69] Even though I stressed that culture and social structures are constantly changing, I documented how the norm of a pluralist society that one should have friends from all ethnic, class, gender, civil status, and age groups is frequently governed by the social rule of homophily, of like-attracting-like, determining real world social interaction within friendship.

I attempted to present fairly the widely differing interpretations of the relationship of friendship by professional social scientists and related work in philosophy and the arts. As my work replicated a major work of a French psycho-sociologist, as most of the data were gathered in Montreal and as my graduate education was done at the French-speaking University of Montreal, I have given an important place in this book to presenting to the English-reading world French-speaking Quebec social scientists' interpretations and citizens' views about their experiences of friendship. I have also drawn on the accounts, questionnaire data, and other artifacts on English-speaking Montrealers' friendships and the works of English-language sociologists in Canada.

My work in Montreal and later groups I organized or facilitated in the United States of America provide evidence that friendships can be better understood and improved through clinical sociological interventions. Comprehending the constituents of the relationship of friendship and the forces that promote or destroy it enables the clinical sociologist to become engaged in enhancing the quality of human life by ameliorating existing friendships between individuals and groups or to invent strategies to build friendships where they do not exist.

Studying friendship required a mediation by a researcher and several interviewers. A social phenomenology, which demanded the integration of several empirical moments in a larger reduction, was used to grasp the meaning of friendship in secondary sources, questionnaires, essays, a telephone survey, personal observations, and conversations with teachers, associates, acquaintances, friends, and self. Some similar and other seemingly contradictory findings on friendship were weighed against one another, and what was left after this procedure tends toward the essential qualities of this relationship. However, like all other human understandings of friendship, the present account remains unavoidably an indexical expression.

Notes

1. Maisonneuve, Jean, *Psycho-sociologie des affinités* (Paris: Presses universitaires de France, 1966), 452.

2. Adams, Rebecca G. and Rosemary Blieszner, eds., *Older Adult Friendship: Structure and Process* (Newbury Park, CA: 1989); Allan,

Graham, *Friendship: Developing a Sociological Perspective* (Boulder, Colorado: Westview Press, 1989); Blieszner, Rosemary and Rebecca G. Adams, *Adult Friendship* (Newbury Park, CA: Sage Publications, 1992); Duck, Steve, *Friends, For Life: The Psychology of Close Relationships* (New York: St. Martin's Press, 1983); Duck, Steve and H. K. A. Sants, "On the Origin of the Specious: Are Personal Relationships Really Interpersonal States?" 1 *Journal of Social and Clinical Psychology*, 27-41; Eichenbaum, Luise and Susie Orbach, *Between Friends: Love, Envy, and Competition in Women's Friendships* (New York: Viking, 1988); Eisenstadt, S. N. and L. Roniger, *Patrons, Clients and Friends: Interpersonal Relations and the Structure of Trust in Society* (Cambridge: Cambridge University Press, 1984); Gouldner, M. and M. Symons Strong, *Speaking of Friendship: Middle-class Women and Their Friends* (New York and London: Greenwood Press, 1987); Graham, George and Hugh LaFollette, eds., *Person to Person* (Philadelphia: Temple University Press, 1989); Maas, James, *Speaking of Friends: The Variety of Man-to-Man Friendships* (Berkeley, CA: Shameless Hussy Press, 1985); McCall, George J., "The Organizational Life Cycle of Relationships," in *A Handbook of Personal Relationships*, eds. Steve W. Duck *et al.* (Chichester: Wiley, 1988); Meilaender, Gilbert C., *Friendship: A Study in Theological Ethics* (Notre Dame, Indiana: University of Notre Dame Press, 1981); Michaelis, David, *The Best of Friends. Profiles of Extraordinary Friendships* (New York: William Morrow and Co., 1983); Milardo, Robert M., "Personal Choice and Social Constraint in Close Relationships: Applications of a Network Analysis," in *Friendship and Social Interaction*, eds. V. J. Derlega and B.A. Winstead (New York: Springer, 1986); Oliker, Stacey J., *Best Friends and Marriage: Exchange among Women* (Berkeley: University of California Press, 1989); Nardi, Peter M., ed., *Men's Friendships* (Newbury Park, CA: Sage Publications, 1992). O'Connor, Pat, *Friendships between Women: A Critical Review* (New York: The Guilford Press, 1992); Pogrebin, Letty Cottin, *Among Friends: Who We Like, Why We Like Them, and What We Do with Them* (New York: McGraw-Hill Book Company, 1987); Rawlins, William K., *Friendship Matters: Communication, Dialectics, and the Life Course*

(New York: Aldine de Gruyter, 1992); Rubin, Lillian B., *Just Friends: The Role of Friendship in Our Lives* (New York: Harper & Row Publishers, 1985); Wadell, Paul J., *Friendship and the Moral Life* (Notre Dame, Indiana: University of Notre Dame Press); Wellman, Barry, "Domestic Work, Paid Work, and Net Work," in *Understanding Personal Relationships*, eds. Steve Duck and Daniel Perlman (London: Sage, 1985); Wiseman, J. "Friendship: Bonds and Binds in a Voluntary Relationship," *Journal of Social and Personal Relationships* 3 (1986):191-211.

3. I explore the connections between my religion, ethnicity, and socio-economic class more deeply in my novel, *Border of Lilies and Maples*. Jürgen Habermas's article, "The German Idealism of the Jewish Philosophers," helped me understand the importance of these connections. See his *Philosophical-Political Profiles* (Cambridge, Massachusetts: The MIT Press, 1983), 21-43. In relating "Friendship and the Moral Life: Why a New Model for Morality Is Needed," Paul J. Wadell, C. P., begins his book with "An Autobiographical Beginning." His personal revelations about friendship in his religious Catholic, American high school added depth, dignity, and a human sensitivity to his philosophical argument. See: Wadell, Paul J., *Friendship and the Moral Life* (Notre Dame, Indiana: University of Notre Dame Press, 1989).

4. See: O'Connor, Pat, *Friendships between Women: A Critical Review* (New York: The Guilford Press, 1982), 5.

5. Gitlin, Todd, *The Sixties: Years of Hope, Days of Rage* (New York: Bantam Books), 1987.

6. See: Robertson, Michael, "Dusting off the Doctorates: Can Yesterday's Victims of the Ph.D. Glut Resurrect Their Lost Careers?" *San Francisco Chronicle* 8 August 1990, B 3; B4; B 5.

6. Although the American Sociological Association attempted to deny the serious un- and under-employment among American sociologists when officers of the ASA encouraged readers of its newsletter, *Footnotes*, to discredit an article describing the severe decline in the discipline that appeared in the *New York Times*, few sociologists were fooled. See: Berger, J., "Sociology's Long Decade in the Wilderness," 28 May *New*

York Times 1989. As early as 1983, *Newsweek* pictured a former professor of sociology, Robert Tellander, painting houses after being laid off from California's Sonoma State University. See: Williams, Dennis, A., Pamela Abramson, and Lucy Howard, "Getting off the Tenure Track," *Newsweek*, 31 January 1983, 50. In August 1982 Edna Bonacich expressed a need for the formation of The Caucus on Underemployment in Sociology in an August 1982 article in *Footnotes* and the caucus was formed at the 1983 ASA meeting in Detroit. The November 1984 newsletter of that caucus stated that the ASA gave $750.00, the SSSP Board $500.00 from the Smigel Fund, and the Marxist Section of the ASA $100.00 to support the newsletter. See: Bonacich, Edna, "The Caucus on Underemployment in Sociology: A Brief History" and "The Caucus Today," in *Newsletter of the Caucus on Underemployment in Sociology*, (Clemson, South Carlina 29631: Department of Agricultural Economics and Rural Sociology, Barre Hall 219, Attention: Thomas Lyson - Clemson University).

Later Frederick R. Lynch commented:

> The American Sociological Association has issued reports that try to grapple with the limited statistics on the situation, which ignore the horrendous job applicant/job opening ratios (D'Antonio, 1987). In a report on employment patterns in sociology, Bettina J. Huber estimated that there would be a surplus of at least 2,500 sociology Ph.D.s during the 1980s (1985:18).
>
> In the August, 1988, edition of sociology's in-house newsletter, *Footnotes,* William D. Antonio cited a figure which indicated the gravity of underemployment in sociology. More than one thousand of the twelve thousand member ASA identified themselves as earning under $15 thousand annually. D'Antonio admitted that this was probably due to the presence of a large number of people who could gain no better than part-time employment in their profession.
>
> A more accurate description of the marketplace for sociologists was provided by a California department chairperson in 1987: "Insane." See: Frederick R. Lynch, *Invisible Victims: WhiteMales and the Crisis of Affirmative Action,* (New York: Praeger, 1991), 138.

Frederick R. Lynch attributes much of the woes of sociology to its strong support of affirmative action, which has led to reverse discrimination, which, in turn, has been viewed as unfair by the American electorate in surveys since the mid-1980s (Ibid., 119-139). Giving another explanation, Charles Cappell explains sociology's difficulties in terms of five major factors:

> 1. Sociology's problems are not different than those faced by other departments in the liberal arts--underfunding and student migration to "careerist" majors are the root of it all. 2. Attacks on sociology departments are caused by the confluence of several unlikely events, usually locally determined, such as the hostility of some "conservative" administrators or the bad luck of having multiple retirements during budget-cutting season. 3. Sociology is misunderstood; we have an image problem. Our colleagues and administrators lack a clear idea of what our work is about. 4. Fragmented sociological knowledge plus the eclectic interests of sociology faculty, especially evident in the curriculum, creates a perception of program anarchy or incoherence that invites attack. 5. Sociology departments are vulnerable to the extent that faculty research, teaching, and student performance fall below acceptable norms. See: Cappell, Charles, "Observations on the State of Academic Sociology," in *ISA (Illinois Sociological Association) Newsletter* ed. Prendergast Chris (Bloomington, Illinois: Department of Sociology, Illinois Wesleyan University), May 1993, 6-8.

While Berger, Lynch, and Cappell all identify factors that have contributed to sociology's current plight, I believe the discipline's downturn is much more complex and multivariate than their analyses. Pulitzer Prize-winning reporters of the *Philadelphia Inquirer* point to the deeper economic and political forces that underlie the decline of higher education [See: Bartlett, Donald L. and James B. Steele, *America: What Went Wrong?* (Kansas City, Missouri: Andrews and McMeel, 1992)]; a philosopher and psychologist identifies the psychological processes [See: Lerner, Michael, *Surplus Powerlessness: The Psychodynamics of Everyday Life ... And the Psychology of Individual and Social Transformation* (Oakland, CA: The Institute for Labor and Mental

Health, 1986); and sociologists record the psycho-social and spiritual forces that have shaped the current real crisis of sociology and other academic disciplines [See: Robert N. Bellah, Richard Madsen, William M. Sullivan, Ann Swidler, and Steven M. Tipton, *Habits of the Heart: Individualism and Commitment in American Life* (San Francisco, CA: Harper & Row, Publishers, (1985) 1986)]. As this book goes to press, a clinical sociologist has just published a new work that deals with this topic [See: Glassner, Barry, *Career Crash: The New Crisis and Who Survives* (New York: Simon and Schuster, 1994)].

It is informative that a senior Quebec sociologist, Guy Rocher, skirted Danielle Ouellet's question, "Have you attained the personal goal set for yourself at the beginning of your career, i.e. developing a Québec university milieu with a dynamic role for sociology?" From Professor Rocher's response, one is left in the dark about the current or recent condition of sociology in Quebec. See: Guy Rocher, "Benchmarks of a Changing Society," in *Forces: 1967-1992: Twenty-Five Years of Evolution in Québec: Education-Health-Economy-Culture-Society-Information-International Relations and Perspectives on the Future. Numéro 100, Hiver 1992-1993*, 22-25 (Montréal: la Société d'édition de la revue Forces), 25.

7. See: O'Connor, Pat, *Friendships between Women*, 5.

8. Ibid., 5.

9. Eisenstadt, S. N. and L. Roniger, *Patrons, Clients and Friends: Interpersonal Relations and the Structure of Trust in Society* (Cambridge; Cambridge University Press, 1984), 40.

10. Hess, Beth, "Foreword," in Adams, Rebecca G., and Rosemary Blieszner, eds., *Older Adult Friendship: Structure and Process* (Newbury Park, CA: Sage Publications, 1989), 9.

11. Seidler, Victor, J., "Rejection, Vulnerability, and Friendship," in *Men's Friendships*, ed. Peter M. Nardi (Newbury Park, CA: Sage Publications, 1992).

12. Lipset, Seymour Martin, *Continental Divide: The Values and Institutions of the United States and Canada* (New York: Routledge, 1990), 177-179.

13. This experience may have subconsciously motivated me to become active in the North American support group of Peace Now not long after its founding in 1978. On March 29, 1984, I was given the honor of moderating a discussion, "Israel and the Palestinians: Can There Be Peace in the Middle East?" between the then Israeli Colonel, now Minister of the Knesset, Mordecai Bar-on and Mr. Mohammed Milhem, former Mayor of Halhul, on the West Bank, at the University of Chicago. Segments of this show were broadcast nationally on Frontline on PBS.

14. Wade, Mason, *The French-Canadian Outlook: A Brief Account of the Unknown North Americans* (New York: The Viking Press, 1946), 125;136; Wade, Mason. *The French Canadians 1760-1945* (Toronto: The Macmillan Company of Canada Limited, 1955), 190;546;608;623;736;864;868;885;902;979;980;1010;1094.

15. Hughes, Everett C., *French Canada in Transition* (Chicago: University of Chicago Press, 1943), 212-219.

16. Shore, Marlene, *The Science of Social Redemption: McGill, the Chicago School, and the Origins of Social Research in Canada* (Toronto: University of Toronto Press, 1987), 244-245.

17. Curtis, James E., and Ronald D. Lambert, "Status Dissatisfaction and Out-group Rejection: Cross-cultural Comparisons within Canada," in *The Canadian Review of Sociology and Anthropology / La revue canadienne de sociologie et d'anthropologie* 12(2) 1975, 178-192.

18. Brazeau, Jacques, "Pertinence de l'enseignement des relations ethniques et caractérisation de ce champs d'études au Canada et au Québec," in ed. Juteau-Lee, Danielle, "Enjeux ethniques: production de nouveau rapports sociaux," *Sociologie et sociétés*, XV (2) octobre 1983), 136; Laferrière, Michel, "L'éducation des enfants des groupes minoritaires au Québec: De la définition des problèmes par les groupes eux-mêmes à l'intervention de l'état," in ed. Juteau-Lee, Danielle, ibid., 122-124.

19. Buckner, H. Taylor, "Attitudes towards Minorities: Seven Year Results and Analysis, June 1990," Presented at "Anti-Semitism around

the World," League for Human Rights of B'nai Brith Canada/*Ligue des droits de la personne de B'nai Brith Canada,* Montreal, Quebec, Canada, November 3-4, 1991, 34.

20. Ibid., 34.

21. Lerner, Michael, *The Socialism of Fools: Anti-Semitism on the Left* (Oakland, CA:Tikkun Books, 1992).

22. Cited in Richler, Mordecai, *Oh Canada! Oh Quebec: Requiem for a Divided Country* (New York: Penguin Books), 254.

23. Fletcher, Joseph F., "Canadian Attitudes toward Jews: Results from a Recent Survey," Prepared for a forum entitled, "Antisemitism in Canada: Perceptions and Realities," at The Triennial Meeting of The Canadian Jewish Congress, Montreal, Quebec, Canada, 7 May 1989.

24. See: Arnold, Abraham J., "Jews in Quebec," in *Jewish Currents: A Progressive Monthly* May (New York, 1989), 35-38 ; Gurdin, J. Barry, "Anti-Semitism in Canada," in *Jewish Currents: A Progressive Monthly* November (New York: 1989), 38-39; Also see: Abella, Irving and Harold Troper, *None Is Too Many, Canada and the Jews of Europe, 1933-1948* (Toronto: Lester & Orpen Dennys, 1982).

25. For an example of these reactions, see: Neamtan, Nancy. "Descendants de prostituées et antisémites congénitaux: Les anglophones du Canada doivent dénoncer Mordecai Richler," *Le Devoir,* jeudi 19 mars 1992, B-8.

26. Roy, Jean-Hugues. "L'Affaire Richler a relancé le débat: Le Québec est-il AntiSémite?" *Voir: 6:1992,* 5-6.

27. Parenteau, Éric. "Le Tableau de la Honte: L'antisémitisme au Québec, de 1807 à 1960. À noter qu'on retrouvait des racistes partout, tant à McGill qu'à l'Université de Montréal," *Voir* du 16 au 22 avril 1992, 10-11.

28. Singer, David and Ruth R. Seldin, eds., *American Jewish Year Book: A Record of Events and Trends in American and World Jewish Life* 92 (New York: The American Jewish Committee and Philadelphia: The Jewish Publication Society, 1992), 297. Also see: Block, Irwin, "The Bridge Builder," in *The Gazette,* Montreal, 28 August 1993, B3.

29. See: Lipset, Seymour Martin, *Continental Divide, 178.* Also see: Horowitz, Irving Louis, *The Decomposition of Sociology*, 92-93, who asserts that contemporary American sociology now finds itself enmeshed in anti-Semitism, which is a source of its decline.

30. Lerner, Michael, ed., *Tikkun: A Bi-Monthly Jewish Critique of Politics, Culture, and Society.* September/October, Volume 2/ No. 4, 1987; Lerner, Michael, *The Socialism of Fools,* 1992.

31. Abley, Mark. "A Troublesome Thesis: After a Year of Controversy, Esther Delisle Has Won a Ph.D. for Her Study of Lionel Groulx and Racism. It's out as a Book This Week. But She Can't Get a Job," *The Gazette*, Montreal, Saturday, September 1992, B 2. Also see: Block, Irwin, "Controversial Ph.D. Is a Best Seller," in *The Gazette*, Montreal, 28 August 1993, B3.

32. Noël, Lise, *L'intolérance: une problématique générale* (Montréal: Les Éditions du Boréal, 1989), 78, 100, 101, 103, 114, 130, 137, 139, 140, 152, 156, 242.

33. Ibid., 30.

34. Pogrebin, Letty Cottin, *Deborah, Golda, and Me: Being Female and Jewish in America* (New York: Doubleday, 1991), 1991:223.

35. Noël, Lise, *L'intolérance*, 59.

36. Frankiel, Tamar, *Voice of Sarah: Feminine Spirituality and Traditional Judaism* (San Francisco: Harper, 1990).

37. Clift, D. and S. M. Arnopoulos, *Le fait anglais au Québec* (Montréal: Éditions Libre Expression, 1979).

38. Singer, David and Ruth R. Seldin, eds., *The American Jewish Year Book: A Record of Events and Trends in American and World Jewish Life* 92 (New York: The American Jewish Committee, 1992), 97; Block, Irwin, "The Bridge Builder," in *The Gazette*, Montreal, 28 August 1993, B3; Csillag, Ron, "Jews by Faith up 7%; 'Ethnic' Issue Looms," in *The Canadian Jewish News Montreal Edition*," 10 June 1993, 1, 2, 10.

39. Fine, Morris, Milton Himmelfarb, and Martha Jelenko, eds., *American Jewish Year Book: A Record of Events and Trends in American and World Jewish Life* (New York: The American Jewish Committee, and Philadelphia: The Jewish Publication Society, 1968-1992) (1985),

193 and (1989), 261; Singer, David and Ruth R. Seldin, *The American Jewish Year Book: A Record of Events and Trends in American and World Jewish Life* 91 (New York: The American Jewish Committee, 1991; 1992).

40. Richler, Mordecai, *Oh Canada! Oh Quebec: Requiem for a Divided Country* (New York: Penguin Books, 1992), 212; Paré, Isabelle, "Montréal, capitale de la pauvreté: 22% des Montréalais vivent sous le seuil de la pauvreté; plus qu'à Saint-Jean, Terre-Neuve," *Le Devoir* 14 avril 1993, A-1, A-8.

41. See: Lipset, Seymour Martin, *Continental Divide*, 135.

42. Wisse, Ruth R., *If I Am Not For Myself... : The Liberal Betrayal of the Jews* (New York: The Free Press, 1992).

43. Ibid., 18.

44. Stern, Chaim, *Gates of Prayer: The New Union Prayerbook. Fifth Printing* (New York: Central Conference of American Rabbis, 1979), 18.

45. Wisse, Ruth R., *If I Am Not For Myself...* , 126-127.

46. See: Perel, Shloime and Henry Srebernik, "Signs of the Times," *The Jerusalem Post* 22 January 1982; Perel, Shloime and Henry Srebernik, "Signes des temps," *Le Devoir*, 17 février 1982, 9; Bissonnette, Lise, "Le Québec discrédité en Israël," *Le Devoir* 18 février, 1982; "Montreal Jews and the *Jerusalem Post* Affair," *Israel Horizons* September/October:12-15, 1982; Srebernik, Henry, "Les Juifs: Canadiens ou Québécois?" *Le Devoir* 30 mars: 1982, 7; Balikci, Asen, "Les <<souffrances>> des juifs montréalais! En marge de l'article du <<Jérusalem Post.>> *Le Devoir* 23 février 1982, 7; Benarrosh, Penny, Maurice Elmaleh, Joseph Lévy, Léon Ouaknine, et Victor Teboul, "L'article du Jérusalem Post," *Jonathan*, avril 1982, 6; Note that spatial limitations have forced me to cite only a few articles from a voluminous file on this "affair."

47. Halperin, Ian, "Canadian Paper Apologizes for Slander," *Washington Jewish Week* 30 January 1986, 29; Anonymous, "Srebrnik, Perel Get Le Devoir Apology," *The Canadian Jewish News* 23 January 1986, 13.

48. Gurdin, J. Barry, "Anti-Semitism in Canada," in *Jewish Currents: A Progressive Monthly* November (New York: 1989), 38-39.

49. Cohen, Eli (director), *The Quarrel*. Based on a short story by Chaim Grade, screenplay by David Brandes with the two main characters of Hersh Resseyner played by Saul Rubinek and Chaim Kovler played by R. H. Thompson (Los Angeles: Apple & Honey Film Corp).

50. See: O'Connor, Pat, *Friendship between Women: A Critical Review* (New York: The Guilford Press, 1992), 29.

51. Ibid., 122.

52. Ibid., 29.

53. O'Connor, Pat, *Friendship between Women*, 167.

54. See: Bloom, Allan, *Love and Friendship* (New York: Simon & Schuster, 1993), 543; 547; and 548. Also see: Stern, Michael, "*The Loss of Eros* [a book review of *Love and Friendship* by Allan Bloom, Simon & Schuster, 590 pages $25]" *San Francisco Chronicle Review* 4 July 1993, 5.

55. See: Duck, Steve and H. K. A. Sants, "On the Origin of the Specious: Are Personal Relationships Really Interpersonal States?" 1 *Journal of Social and Clinical Psychology*, 27-41.

56. See: Gouldner, M. and M. Symons Strong, *Speaking of Friendship: Middle-class Women and Their Friends* (New York: and London: Greenwood Press, 1987).

57. Mildardo, Robert, "Personal Choice and Social Constraint in Close Relationships: Applications of a Network Analysis," in *Friendship and Social Interaction*, eds. V. J. Derlega and B.A. Winstead (New York: Springer).

58. Wellman, Barry, "Domestic Work, Paid Work, and Net Work," in *Understanding Personal Relationships*, eds. Steve Duck and Daniel Perlman (London: Sage, 1985).

59. Wiseman, J. "Friendship: Bonds and Binds in a Voluntary Relationship," 3 *Journal of Social and Personal Relationships*, 191-211.

60. Gurdin, J. Barry, "The Therapy of Friendship," *Small Group Behavior* 17 (Newbury Park, CA: Sage Publications, 1986), 444-457.

61. Rhéaume, Jacques and Robert Sévigny, *Sociologie implicite des intervenants en santé mentale. Vol. 1, Les pratiques alternatives: du groupe d'entraide au groupe spirituel* (Montréal: Les Éditions Saint-Martin, 1988); Rhéaume, Jacques and Robert Sévigny, *Sociologie implicite des intervenants en santé mentale. Vol. 2, La pratique psychothérapeutique: de la croissance à la guérison* (Montréal: Les Éditions Saint-Martin, 1988).

62. See: O'Connor, Pat, *Friendship between Women*, 16-22; 107; 110-111; 176.

63. See: Schein, Edgar H., *The Clinical Perspective in Fieldwork* (Newbury Park, CA: Sage Publications, 1987), 51-54.

64. Anonymous, "Amitié, amour et liberté sont les principales valeurs des jeunes Canadiens," *Le Devoir* 22 January 1985.

65. See: Lewis, Paul, "Stoked by Ethnic Fighting, Refugee Numbers Grow," The New York Times 10 November 1993, A1.

66. Rivers, Susan, "Swelling Ranks of Refugees Seek Asylum: Increasingly Tough Fight Faces Those Who Claim to Be in Flight from Tyranny," *San Francisco Examiner and Chronicle* 27 June 1993, B1; B4.

67. Hoppe, Art, "Friendship's End," in *Sunday Punch, the San Francisco Sunday Examiner and Chronicle*, 27 June 1993; Hoppe, Art, "A Slow Death," in *Sunday Punch, the San Francisco Sunday Examiner and Chronicle*, 26 September 1993.

68. See: Geertz, Clifford, *The Interpretation of Cultures* (New York: Basic Books, 1973), 89.

69. See: McCall, George, "The Organizational Life Cycle of Relationships," in *A Handbook of Personal Relationships*, eds. Steve W. Duck *et al.* (Chichester: Wiley, 1988), 469.

Methods of Research

In isolating the empirical components which constitute friendship, researchers with a structural-functional perspective concurred that there had been a lack of attention paid to what was going on in the mind of the social actor as friend.[1] This concern for giving serious attention to interviewees' understanding of their own friendships is a central methodological issue from the points of view of symbolic interactionism, ethnomethodology, and social phenomenology.[2] Within these frameworks people could come to grips with their own friendships in their own words and have ideas about how their society and culture had gone into making up their friendships. However, their tales of friendships--often spun in an intricate logic--could be taken down only through a complicated interaction between an interviewer and an interviewee. Such were my major social scientific problems when I undertook my study of friendship. Yet, in reality, my own circumstances of being an activist against the War in Vietnam and dependent upon what meager earnings I could muster from odd jobs in a declining academic market, in a culture with which I was initially unfamiliar, and having a Rogerian for a dissertation advisor at a large French-language university, were equally important influences on how I arrived at my present account of friendship.

Aiming to preserve people's perspectives of their social world does not exclude contrasting their view of what they do with what an interpreter observes them doing; nor does it prevent an analyst from pointing out the presence or lack of coherence, congruence, and contradictions in interviewees' accounts or to similar contrasts in the aggregate data from questionnaire respondents and secondary sources. Relating what they do to what they think and locating this dual reality in particular situations in their specificity and generality takes on major importance to anyone who wants to understand human activity. Because I was constrained to respond to the concerns of the social sciences, I was limited in how I lifted an experience such as friendship out of consciousness and described how it is uniquely constituted. This procedure would have been closer to the original phenomenological project.[3]

If an interpreter of human friendships with these preoccupations wants to examine friendship from a sample of people reflective of larger trends in society, the written questionnaire, the recorded interview (i.e. a study of accounts), cultural artifacts like songs, television shows, literature, radio, and newspapers are good sources.[4] A small monograph of a subculture is an alternative which loses breadth in its depth of affording the cross-checking of accounts by participant observation.[5] Frame or dramaturgical analysis and a pure phenomenological reduction of the interpreter's own experience are other possibilities, which, of course, are likely to be biased by the limited view available from the analyst's own social stratum or subculture.[6]

First of all, most interpreters of a highly complex human experience such as friendship, love, or religious experience must make the decision for true statistical representativeness or in-depth analysis of the personal accounts of a limited number of human beings.[7] To some extent well-financed projects with a large, multidisciplinary research staff may take advantage of both possibilities; yet, even they at some point must integrate both perspectives.

Referring to Jean Maisonneuve's approach, I gathered a dissertation sample reflective of demographic groupings rather than a totally statistically representative sample. This result was was primarily due to my financial limitations rather than my intent. All the researchers I knew who worked with the Survey Research Center at the University of Montreal had access to lists based on representative samples upon which their studies could be undertaken. I believe this outcome was because they had research funds to pay for their samples, although I heard varying accounts about this matter from graduate students. After about six months of trying to compile my own survey sample, it became obvious to me that without the pre-established files of the Survey Research Center, it would take years to just compile my sample. At that point, I began to negotiate seriously to have access to the university's files to compile my own list. When I discussed my purposively selected in-depth interview and questionnaire sample of English Canadians with the member of the Survey Research Center, it was agreed that I should use it to compare with a group of French Canadians selected from the representative list from the Survey Research Center's files. In retrospect, given my financial limitations, I wish that I had been told to abandon the idea of doing a representative sample, and instead to concentrate on an ethnographic study of friendship in the neighborhood in which I was living. However, it is easy to speculate with hindsight about these matters.[8]

Then, I replicated the trends on ethnicity I had found in my purposive sample with a totally random, representative sample of the Montreal telephone directory. Finally, the cultural artifacts I gathered and the friendship development groups that I organized or facilitated must be considered parts of my sample (See Appendix B).

My Methodological Assumptions

When I interpret friendship, what am I doing? What methods and techniques am I using and why? My methodological assumptions answer these questions. In the following paragraphs, I will answer questions raised by Alfred Schutz and other phenomenologists in regards to the concrete life world of the contemporary social sciences.

When I listened to a cassette tape or read a typed transcription of a recorded interview, when I looked at written questionnaires or studied the calculated tables--produced by the transformation of the written questionnaire responses to data sheets, to IBM punch cards or tapes, or later to diskettes, and to the print-outs of the SPSS and later SYSTAT computer packages--I was dealing with completed acts. It could be that some or the great majority of the people interviewed are conducting their friendships in a very similar fashion to the way they described them in the interview situation. Phenomenologically, I understand that ***all of this material embodies meaningful, completed acts, rather than acts that are on-going***.

These data are considered as lived experiences guided by a plan or project arising from the subject's spontaneous experience. With the styles of friendship I have tried to describe the tendencies to act more or less as following a plan or project.

A particular act of attention distinguishes friendship from all other experiences. All the interviewees in the sample had something to write or say about either the written or the oral questionnaire. Not all of them answered every question. First of all, the interpreter distinguished friendship for the interviewees either directly or indirectly through the interviewers. By taking [(friend)/(ship)] out of the interviewee's inner stream of duration [*durée*], the continuous coming-to-be and passing away of hetereogeneous qualities, the interviewer's attention was focused on the closest friendships in their lives, thereby bringing friendship into the specialized, quantified, rendered-discontinuous homogeneous time.[9]

The written questionnaire compartmentalized friendship either to replicate or to be relevant to the literature, and the recorded questionnaire aimed at dialoguing around the same points. The interviewees were brought into this grid and were asked to situate their elapsed experiences of closest friendship into it. The questions sought out the specific or the intended meaning of friendship. ***In telling or*** *writing down their closest friendships, the interviewees provided me as interpreter with a series of polythetically constructed acts of friendship.*

An orthodox social phenomenologist would look at these friendship tales or written reports "with a single glance of attention" in order to place the series. In fact, I made many glances of attention while placing the series of friendship material in different contexts of meaning. First I explored the meaning of the lexical items of friendship from the pilot sample to determine to which extent the collectivity shared different notions of friendship. I began to ascertain their commonly held views of friendship after analyzing them by content and protothemes. When this original classification was done, I was attentive only to the subdivisions in the meaning of friendship as they varied by ethnicity. Then when the content analysis was done, I turned my attention to age, gender, and social class in relation to the responses. At the following stage, the external factors in the interview situation helped determine the written responses.[10]

Next the whole recorded interviews were taken as pregiven. Subsequently, my beam of attention was focused on the differences between what the respondents said about friendship and what they reported on doing in friendship. After this comparison, I paid attention to age, sex, class, kinship, and ethnicity insofar as they reflect trends in the calculated data. Then, these various steps in focusing attention were shifted to cultural artifacts--historical, literary, ethnographic, and mass media products--to put these contents of meaning in the larger context of meaning. Finally, I tried to make some sense out of the general patterns with the notion of styles of friendship.

All of the interviews done and small groups led for this work show that all the interviewees were capable of self-understanding of their own friendships to various degrees. Speaking of or writing about their friendships, they sorted out, identified, and recognized aspects of their friends and friendships.

The meaningful world of this analysis is intersubjective. It refers to the interviewee's world, to the interviewers' worlds, and to my world. The world of the friendship interviewee is a world of contemporaries. As the interpreter, I know them indirectly through the questionnaires, meetings, and cultural artifacts. I and the interviewee are thus in a they-orientation (*Ihrbeziehung*, lit., You-relationship) "because its object is not the thusness (*Sosein*)--or immediately apprehended qualities of another person but rather his whatness (*Wiesein*)--his being such and such a generalized type (*Gleichsam-sein*) ."[11] The more I conceptualized the interviewees' friendships, the less I was able to regard them as free agents. However, when I developed my friendship development groups, particularly the groups that I facilitated myself, the group participants and I were engaged in an emotionally close space and we regarded each other as relatively free agents, constrained by various social, cultural, and personality forces in our lives about which we became more aware through our group.

In the analysis of the tape recordings, written questionnaires, and cultural artifacts, I examined the occasional and actual meanings of friendship. This awareness moved me as social scientific interpreter to subject to a detailed analysis everything taken from the world of everyday life including my own judgment. Yet as social scientist, the interpreter is different, for he or she posits the friendships analyzed. When I considered all these meaning contexts, I constructed the total or highest context of meaning, often in dialogue with the work of other social scientists who had published about similar experiences in writing.

Truth Criteria

When I presented my thesis, I adopted a somewhat strict social phenomenological framework. In this point of view, Edmund Husserl had defined his truth criteria as "logical grounding" or "proof" (*Ausweisen*):

... that which truly or really (*Wirklich*) is and that which is rationally demonstrable (*Ausweisbar*) are intrinsically correlated ... .[12]

Since that time, while still harboring a desire to go back to friendship-in-itself, and still believing that you can gather much insight by using your own "intuition on the basis of very exact analysis," I have come to feel the eidetic and phenomenological reductions of friendship may be of less importance to understanding the *Lebenswelt* of friendship than a thorough qualitative description of data gathered from many different methods.[13]

Each time I go back and listen to my in-depth interviews, group transcripts or videotapes, and life experiences, I see something new which sheds some higher order understanding on friendship. And I do not think that I am any less exact than most social scientists I know. Rather I believe that human phenomena such as friendship are such that their understanding may defy being "absolute to consciousness in such a way as to manifest the impossibility of being given otherwise." Rather than saying that the absolute giveness and hence absolute being of friendship are available to a careful reflection on my acts of consciousness, I would rather say that an in-depth study of friendship constantly reveals new horizons to the researcher.[14] On the other hand, I do sense that in tying together all my observations of friendship I have rendered it "bodily present" in a manner of speaking. Since I did not pretend to formally know about friendship before conducting an exhaustive investigation, I do not think that friendship-intended and friendship-given are identical in this instance. However, I do have a sense that my intuition to study friendship has tended toward a rendition of friendship at a very deep level, even though not attaining friendship-in-itself.[15] For these reasons, I would claim that by having suspended or placed friendship in brackets, I have identified, described, and intuitively apprehended many deep aspects of friendship, and thus have provided a fresh approach.

To some degree naturalistic and cognitive sociology embody some of the social phenomenological concerns in a manner more applicable to contemporary social science. Field research and a study of social experience from consciousness can neither logically nor heuristically use the notions of validity and reliability as truth criteria unless their content is radically altered. Field research, because of cost, time, milieu, and design factors, is often "one-shot." Basically I financed the largest part of this work on the income of a part-time instructor. Some of the more sophisticated multivariate data analyses in this book were done several year later when I, as an assistant professor, paid for them out of my pocket. Moreover, the data were collected at a time when public opinion was negative towards similar social psychological studies. Thus, using Leonard Schatzman's and Anselm L. Strauss's qualitative tests of reliability and validity, my having had my dissertation accepted by a doctoral committee of the group about whom I was writing, and before friends, colleagues, and a TV audience, and having already found publishers who have judged aspects of my friendship research worthy of publication would serve as criteria of validity and reliability.[16] To these they would add that it was found acceptable because my propositions from field experience and the data were tested against further data, additional experience, and for logical consistency with my other propositions.[17]

Part of my relative success in communicating with North American audiences has been my incorporating some degree of measurement in my description of friendship. People want to know, "Well, how many of the people you studied had this or that aspect in their friendships?" In this methodological procedure, I was following the lead of Jean Maisonneuve.

Phenomenology and Statistics: A Contradiction?

While Maisonneuve claims his work to be phenomenological, he clearly dedicated a large part of his text to positivistic, descriptive statistics of the results of his questionnaires without explaining his methodological reasons for doing so. Maisonneuve is not alone, however. Like him, the closely related psychological sociology of symbolic interactionism has been divided between the empirical "Iowa School" and the non-empirical "Chicago School."[18]

Husserl wrote that the object of positive science is an abstraction and an artificial structure to the world of our original experience.[19] Nevertheless, there is no reason within Husserl's methodology to reject descriptive statistics from field work as a moment in a phenomenological reduction. To the contrary, if it is included, it can help ensure that the researcher's reduction that begins with the facts of the world stays close to the intentions of the subjective experience of friendship in one of its aspects. Reducing these facts becomes the job of the social phenomenologist. Intuitive or interpretive philosophies or sociologies have often misrepresented the feelings of the groups they purported to understand. In reaction to such errors, periods of various degrees of empiricism revolted against "non-empirical" approaches. By including an empirical moment in a larger phenomenological reduction, interpreters can reduce such distortion. They can assure that their interpretation is causally adequate in at least one stage of their interpretation.

The last consideration in establishing the grounds of truth for this project has to do with the question of adequacy on the level of meaning.[20] In Alfred Schutz's interpretation of Max Weber, interpretive sociology divides intended meaning into three classes. First is the meaning intended by an individual actor in a historically given case which I considered when I analyzed the recorded interviews and group transcripts which sketched various styles of friendships. When I correlated various encoded data on friends by age, civil status, class, sex, and ethnicity, I gathered the meaning intended on the average by a given group of several actors. After I related the cultural artifacts together with the meaning contexts from the former moments, I could derive the styles of friendship, akin to pluralistic types.[21] Even though Weber's concept of motive fails to distinguish between how the observer and the acting person interpret motives, by my clearly documenting the interview situation and by my carefully separating the interpreter's and the interviewee's interpretation, hopefully I have identified what these differences are and, hence, avoided Weber's error.

Ethnomethodology throws light on the many aspects entering into the analysis of recorded and written interviews of friendship. The documentary method and the systematic accounting of the indexicality of friendship expressions shows the myriad of subtleties in understanding the reporting of friendship, which, if omitted, would otherwise suggest a neatness and non-arbitrariness of social science methods.[22] Nevertheless, reporting these practices of the on-going accomplishment of researching and writing a book on friendship clarifies the difficulty and ease, short cuts and extensions, dead ends, personal and material blocks and supports and cutting and selecting the final documents which determine the present account. Of these practices leading questions in a few interviews and putting aside of the data gathered on the relationship of subjective alienation and personality to friendship contributed in secondary importance to my present account.

A final bracketing of friendship was undertaken when I reduced the contents of these notes and the printouts of the content analysis into a coherent text. The contingent factors which entered into my final composition are the notes, knowledge of field data, and the interview material, flashbacks onto particular illustrative cases, an examination of tendencies in the quantitative data based on the content analysis; my dialogue with articles and books being published about friendship; and conversations with people interrupting my reading, writing, and the general climate and atmosphere of the place of composition.

I can only speculate why these different steps in the construction of the present account led to different levels of meaning. Perhaps, the content analysis and questionnaire data, with all their bias, seemed to me to be more digestible to a North American readership. Maybe I had an unconscious preference to overly value the tendencies established through the figures backed up by verbal reports. It could be that my having been separated from the mainstream of the ethnomethodology movement due to my political exile had not provided me with the proper sensitivities or particular view for seeing the most salient meaning constitution in the place or in the interaction where these interviews on friendship were constituted.

Whatever may exhaustively explain the different degrees of perceived saliency will be left an open question. Open reporting of the general lines of these issues indicates my best description of how I accomplished the present account of friendship.

While I have been greatly inspired by ethnomethodology and cognitive sociology in doing this study, my work is not clearly in either current, for it employs some standpoints in procedure and reasoning which are anathema to the core members of those schools of thought. Specifically, the empirical moment in this work would not please orthodox ethnomethodologists, for they write:

> To obtain the computer print-outs and subsequent tables on which sociological explanations are built, the sociologist must first transform respondents' answers in quantifiable data. Such coding processes conceal the respondent's experience of the social scene that is being asked about. In addition, coding processes always necessarily mask the embodied symbolic character of the social interaction between the interviewer and the respondents that produced the answers in the first place.[23]

Throughout this work I have taken a great deal of concern to embody the ethnomethodologists' critique by describing the interviewers, interviewees, their interaction, the interview situation, other interactants, material, and thoughts which went into composing this book on friendship. On the other hand, I disagree with the prevailing view among ethnomethodologists that these instruments cannot be used with caution and as one, combined with other, perspectives to understand friendship. In more potent language, I understand their view as analogous to an earlier position in the phenomenological movement against which Maurice Merleau-Ponty argued in the following words:

> If experience should show me an image which does not correspond to what I have determined to be the essence, then of course, by definition, this is not an image. In the same way I may lay down a certain idea of social process. Then if I find a so-called social process in everyday history or in the past, which does not possess the essential

characteristics I have focused, I have the right to say that it is not a social process. Here we are certainly close to scholasticism. If one had followed this principle in practice, the whole of phenomenology would be an instrument for developing the definition of words.

But Husserl never thought in this way, and he was fully aware of the danger. Since his early articles on *"Philososphie als strenge Wissenschaft,"* he maintained that there was nothing in common between intuition, as he understood it, and a scholastic process which pretends to draw a real knowledge of things from the analytic judgement that one can make on the meaning of words. Husserl was, therefore, well aware of the danger of self-deception in proceeding by "eidetic intuition." It is possible for me to believe that I am seeing an essence when, in fact, it is not an essence at all but merely a concept rooted in language, a prejudice whose apparent coherence reduces merely to the fact that I have become used to it through habit. The best way of guarding against this danger would be to admit that though a knowledge of facts is never sufficient for grasping an essence and though the construction of "idealizing fictions" is always necessary, I can never be sure that my vision of an essence is anything more than a prejudice rooted in language--if it does not enable me to hold together all the facts which are known and which may be brought into relation with it.[24]

It could be that the bias against questionnaires and interviews as just one perspective among many others is particular to "California subjectivism," as Hans Gelner labels the ethnomethodological offshoot of phenomenology. Jean Maisonneuve's and David Triesman's work is influenced by phenomenology, and both either implicitly or explicitly argue for some empirical methods.[25]

Ultimately all language behavior embodies categorization so it is impossible to totally avoid categorization. The ethnomethodological position to the contrary is patently false. While wanting to avoid categorization of my friendship data, I was unavoidably led to categorize them to some extent. Underlying the ethnomethodological position is the belief that utimately no research is possible because there are no perfectly valid sources of data. Yet few human beings act as though they cannot understand human reality well enough to function in it because they lack valid perceptions. With all our weakness in understanding and with constant room for improvement, it is worth our effort to understand our realities and to record the limitations of the validity of our vision. This goal is the one I have tried to attain for friendship.

While revising this book, I have found myself pulled between trying to respond to the levels of meaning attributed to friendship by important researchers on friendship from a social scientific perspective on three continents who frequently disagree about many significant features of this relationship. Here I will comment on a few methodological issues that arise in their work which bear on the meaning I have reduced in this book.

Barry Wellman and S. D. Berkowitz concede that their structural analysis leaves "symbols, meaning and values" as a "derivative and often residual concern."[26] When this manuscript was accepted by McGill-Queen's University Press, my French-language reader commented that I needed to consult Francesco Alberoni's book on friendship--a good suggestion which I have incorporated into this revised work.[27] Alberoni's work emphasizes the symbols, meaning, and values that are underplayed by the structuralists. Hence, you have read even more about films, books, plays, and my ethnographic observations bearing on friendship in Quebec in this book than in the original work. For example, we learn much about the importance of the effect of politics on friendship in Quebec from what Canada's former Prime Minister, Pierre Elliot Trudeau, told Quebecers after the defeat of the referendum on sovereignty-association,

> To my fellow Quebecers who have been wounded by defeat, I wish to say simply that we have all lost a little in this referendum. If you take account of the broken friendships, the strained family relationships, the hurt pride, there is no one among us who has not suffered some wound which we must try to heal in the days and weeks to come.[28]

A signficant usage of the word, friend, by a former Montrealer, Philip Resnick, a professor of political science at the University of British Columbia in Vancouver, appears in *Letters to a Québécois Friend*:

> And yet, *cher ami* (and you are a friend, or even closer, what Baudelaire might have termed *un semblable, un frère*), something has changed in my sentiments towards you and I fear, those of many English-speaking Canadians, something which will leave an indelible mark on this country for a generation or more. ... [29]

Equally informative about the operation of close friendship in the circles of Quebec and Canadian politics is Mordecai Richler's chapter-long description of the friendship between Brian Mulroney, the former Progressive Conservative Prime Minister, and Lucien Bouchard, head of the *Bloc Québécois*. The then leader of the Liberal opposition, John Turner complained, "Mr. Bouchard had no known connection with the Conservative Party except that he is a close buddy of the prime minister ... ."[30] Later, when accused of betraying "his long-standing friend and patron," Lucien Bouchard protested that he was a "man of integrity" and "the victim of a biased Anglophone press."[31]

In my perspective, we learn as much about friendship from such qualitative secondary source material as we do from the structuralists focus "on *concrete* social relations among specific social actors."[32]

Both communitarian social theory and more philosophically rooted accounts of friendship embody a critical framework that assumes certain essential qualities as being necessary for meaningful friendship.[33] No doubt, Barry Wellman is exact in his observation that the streets were deserted because "East Yorkers were driving to friends' homes or were on the telephone," and that most of their "networks contain kin and friends, local and long distance ties, clusters and isolates, multistranded and specialized ties." And, having lived for a year and a third in Toronto myself, I believe he is accurate is recording that "comfortable coexistence of Saved kinship clusters and Liberated friendship ties" make "for low communal solidarity" but give "East Yorkers direct and indirect access to a wide spectrum of resources."[34]

Yet, should I disregard my ethnographic knowledge that Montrealers constantly told jokes about the quality of life in Toronto? The most frequently repeated joke was the old North American stand-by: a radio announcer offered a first prize of one week's vacation in Toronto; the second prize was two weeks vacation in Toronto. More seriously, I am disturbed by Wellman's glib cut that those who are concerned about the loss of community suffer from a "pastoral syndrome." By celebrating networks, Barry Wellman and other structuralists have avoided recording the decline in levels of community trust observed by the communitarians. This outcome is largely due to structuralists' failing to record the psycho-social-emotive depth of meaning attributed to bonds such as close friendship and love. They also escape identifying the impact upon social agents' future actions of breaking such intimate bonds. Finally, they neglect relating these collective experiences to the impact of the policies of dominant economic institutions such as multinational corporations.[35]

My last comment on method is a hopeful one for sociological practice. My experience in designing, facilitating, and grasping the meaning of friendship in groups for the development of friendship leads me to agree with Steve Duck that attempts at mastering "the right actions and activities at the right time" can help keep friendship alive.[36] At the same time, I have learned from the French psycho-sociologists and a German sociologist of roles that unconconscious forces may destroy this precious relationship. Thus, attention to such forces is essential in grasping the meaning of friendship and improving its chances to bloom in this difficult world.

Notes

1. Abelson, Willa D. and Elizabeth J. Weiss, "Psychological Studies of Friendship," in *Studies of Friendship*, ed. DuBois, Cora (Boston: Harvard University, 1953), 1-37.

2. Matthews, Sarah H., *Friendship through the Life Course: Oral Biographies in Old Age* (Newbury Park: Sage Publications, 1986);

Garfinkel, Harold, *Studies in Ethnomethodology* (Englewood Cliffs, New Jersey: Prentice-Hall, Inc., 1967); Sudnow, David, *Studies in Social Interaction* (New York: The Free Press, 1972); Cicourel, Aaron V., *Cognitive Sociology* (Harmondsworth: Penguin Books Ltd., 1973); Laing, R. D. and D. G. Cooper, *Reason and Violence. A Decade of Sartre's Philosophy* (London: Tavistock Publications, 1964); Laing, R. D. and A. Esterson, *Sanity, Madness and the Family*, (Harmondsworth: Penguin Books Ltd., 1970); Schutz, Alfred, *The Phenomenology of the Social World*, trans. George Walsh and Frederick Lehnert (London: Heinemann Educational Books, [1932] 1972), 22;215;220-221;223;235); Sartre, Jean Paul, *L'idiot de la famille. Gustave Flaubert de 1821 à 1857* (Paris: Gallimard, 1971).

3. Alberoni, Francesco, *L'amicizia* (Milan: Garzanti Editore s.p.a., 1984).

4. Denzin, Norman K., *The Research Act: A Theoretical Introduction to Sociological Methods. Second Edition* (New York: McGraw-Hill Book Company, [1970] 1978), 297.

5. Gans, Herbert J., *The Urban Villagers: Group and Class in the Life of Italian-Americans.* Forward by Erich Lindemann, M.D. (New York: The Free Press, A Division of Macmillan Publishing Co., Inc., 1962); Hannerz, Ulf, *Soulside* (New York: Columbia University Press, 1969); Boissevain, Jeremy, *Friends of Friends: Networks, Manipulators and Coalitions* (Oxford: Basil Blackwell, 1974).

6. Goffman, Erving *Frame Analysis* (New York: Harper Colophon Books, Harper and Row Publishers, 1974); Paine, Robert, "In Search of Friendship: An Exploratory Analysis in 'Middle-Class Culture.' " *Man, The British Journal of Social Anthropology*, January, 1970; Paine, Robert, "An Exploratory Analysis in 'Middle-Class' Culture," in *The Compact: Selected Dimensions of Friendship*, ed. Elliott Leyton (Toronto: University of Toronto Press [for Memorial University of Newfoundland], 1974), 117-137.

7. Lee, John Alan, *Colours of Love* (Toronto: New Press, 1973); Sévigny, Robert, *L'expérience religieuse chez les jeunes. Une étude*

psychosociologique de l'actualisation de soi (Montréal: Les Presses de l'université de Montréal, 1971).

8. Maisonneuve, Jean, *Psycho-sociologie des affinités* (Paris: Presses universitaires de France, 1966).

9. Schutz, Alfred, *The Phenomenology of the Social World*, trans. by George Walsh and Frederick Lehnert (London: Heinemann Educational Books, [1932] 1972), 45; also see: Wagner, Helmut R., ed., *Alfred Schutz: On Phenomenology and Social Relations Selected Writings* (Chicago: The University of Chicago Press, 1970).

10. Gurdin, Joseph Barry, "*Amitié*/Friendship: The Socio-cultural Construction of Friendship in Contemporary Montreal." Ph.D. diss., Department of Sociology, Université de Montréal, 1978, 189-216.

11. Schutz, Alfred, *The Phenomenology of the Social World*, 219.

12. Husserl, Edmund, *Ideas: General Introduction to Pure Phenomenology*, trans. by W. R. Gibson (London: Collier Macmillan Publishers, [1913] [1931] 1975), 136-138.

13. Lauer, Quentin, "Evidence," in *Phenomenology: The Philosophy of Edmund Husserl and Its Interpretation*, ed. J. L. Kockelmans (Garden City, New York: Doubleday Co., Inc., 1967), 151.

14. Ibid., 151.

15. Ibid., 153.

16. Schatzman, Leonard and Anselm L. Strauss, *Field Strategies for a Natural Sociology* (Englewood Cliffs, New Jersey: Prentice-Hall, 1973), 129.

17. Ibid., 133.

18. Triesman, D., "The Radical Use of Official Data," in Nigel Armistead, ed., *Reconstructing Social Psychology* (Markham, Ontario: Penguin Books Ltd., 1974), 295-313.

19. Kockelmans, J. J., ed., *Phenomenology: The Philosophy of Edmund Husserl and Its Interpretation*, 33-34.

20. Schutz, Alfred, *The Phenomenology of the Social World*, 231-232.

21. Schutz, Alfred, *The Phenomenology of the Social World*, 228.

22. Garfinkel, Harold, *Studies in Ethnomethodology* (Englewood Cliffs, New Jersey: Prentice-Hall, Inc., 1967), 78. Also see: Wieder, D.

Lawrence, in *Ethnomethodology*, ed. Roy Turner. Markham, Ontario: Penguin Books Ltd., 1974), 161-162.

23. Mehan, Hugh and Houston Wood, *The Reality of Ethnomethodology* (New York: A Wiley Interscience Publication John Wiley and Sons, 1975), 49.

24. Merleau-Ponty, Maurice, "Difficulties Involved in a Subordination of Psychology," in *The Primacy of Perception and Other Essays on Phenomenological Psychology, the Philosophy of Art, History, and Politics*, ed. James M. Edie (Evanston, Illinois: Northwestern University Press, 1964), 64-78;499-500.

25. Triesman, D., "The Radical Use of Official Data," in *Reconstructing Social Psychology*, ed. Nigel Armistead (Markham, Ontario: Penguin Books Ltd., 1974), 295-313.

26. Wellman, Barry and S. D. Berkowitz, eds., *Social Structures: A Network Approach* (Cambridge: Cambridge University Press, 1988), 5.

27. See: Alberoni, Francesco, *L'amicizia* (Milan: Garzanti Editore s.p.a., 1984); Alberoni, Francesco, *L'amitié*, trans. Nelly Drusi. (Paris: G. P. Ramsay, 1987).

28. Quoted in Richler, Mordecai, *Oh Canada! Oh Quebec: Requiem for a Divided Country*, (New York: Penguin Books), 125-126.

29. Quoted in Ibid., 155.

30. Quoted in Ibid., 163.

31. Quoted in Ibid., 169.

32. Wellman, Barry and S. D. Berkowitz, eds., *Social Structures*, 3.

33. See: Maurina, Zenta, *Verfremdung und Freundschaft* (*Alienation and Friendship. Essays*) (Memmingen/Allgau: Dietrich, 1966); Alberoni, Francesco, *L'amicizia*; Eisenstadt, S. N. and L. Roniger, *Patrons, Clients and Friends: Interpersonal Relations and the Structure of Trust in Society* (Cambridge; Cambridge University Press, 1984); Bloom, Allan, *Love and Friendship* (New York: Simon & Schuster, 1993).

34. Quoted in Kadushin, Charles, "Living up to Promises: Network Studies Come of Age," in *Contemporary Sociology: An International Journal of Reviews* 19 January 1990:136.

35. My observation has been framed as a more general, less critical question in a recent work: "What is it in our social and economic structure that allows non-institutionalized personal relationships to develop?" See: Allan, Graham, *Friendship: Developing a Sociological Perspective* (Boulder, Colorado: Westview Press, 1989), 5.

36. See: Duck, Steve, *Understanding Relationships* (New York: The Guilford Press, 1991),4-5.

The Samples

When lecturing part-time at a college in Montreal in 1972, I constructed a quota sample for the English Canadian population. While working in that milieu, I had an excellent opportunity to study Montreal's West Island's friendship patterns, so I drew up an initial pilot project sample of 156 questionnaires and a dialogue to be recorded on the basis of the written questionnaire. After I introduced the topic of interviewing and sampling as part of the class I was teaching, each of my students was given approximately ten questionnaires to direct filling out for the quotas based on age, sex, class, and ethnicity for part of their semester project. This pilot project led me to redesign entirely the recorded interview and to modify several aspects of the written questionnaire. The next semester another group of students was given the same number of questionnaires and in-depth interviews to complete following the same purposive sample as the students of the first semester. These interviews and questionnaires were selected from all over the island of Montreal where English Canadians who possessed the various attributes were chosen. In fact, I had to redo the interviews where the quality of interviewing and recording were unsatisfactory.

When I was provided access to the sample files of the Survey Research Center to compile a list of interviewees for the French Canadian sample, I followed the instructions of the chief researcher at the center who advised me to compare twenty-five French Canadian in-depth interviewees and twenty-five questionnaire respondents to be studied with the English Canadian sample I had already gathered. Given my time, personnel, and monetary restrictions, I followed this advice to the letter. From that point, Ms. Verrette and I worked for about a year to track down the fifty French Canadian interviewees and questionnaire respondents.

The actual content of Jean Maisonneuve's questions which I replicated, expanded, and modified for purposes of in-depth interviewing and small group work can be reviewed on pages 321 - 322 of this book. Jean Maisonneuve's questions, my translations of them, and their results in my research, are located on the following pages of this book: #1- pages 30, 44 - 50, 91 - 95; #2 - pages 117, 163, 213, 217 - 219, 270 [and related questions on 148 - 149]; #3 - pages 228, 232, 261 - 263; #4 - pages 261 - 263, 266 - 267; #5 - page 157; #6 - pages 141, 157; #7 - pages 142, 158; #8 - pages 228, 260, 270; #9 - pages 121, 155, 266; #10 - pages 121, 264; #11 - eliminated by Maisonneuve; #12 - pages 75, 88, 267- 268; #13 - page 88; #14 - pages 76, 143, 271; #15 - page 268; #16 - pages 155, 160, 328 - 329, 352; #17 - pages 284, 311 - 313; #18 - pages 284, 312; #19 - pages 129, 262; #20 - page 133; #21 - page 131; #22 - pages 130, 155; #23 - pages 353 - 354; #24 - page 314; #25 is analyzed in same places as #1. The question I added on ethnicity is found on page 98, and the questions on tactility and sexuality on pages 132, 296, 316 - 317, and 391 - 398. The items of the Bigelow and La Gaipa instrument are listed on page 51, and the factor analysis for these items of my data is found on pages 52 - 54 of this book.

These combined samples form the basis of the data upon which the first empirical moment of my study is based. They may be seen in the table on the next page.

The Principal Attributes Used in the Analysis of the 175 In-Depth Interviewees and Questionnaire Respondents in Montreal in the mid-1970s

Count Column %			Ethnicity								
Class	Sex	Age	English Canadian				French Canadian				
			Civil Status				Civil Status				
			Married with Children	Married without Children	Single Never Married	Divorced or Widowed	Married with Children	Married without Children	Single Never Married	Divorced or Widowed	Row Total
P R	M A	Old 61 - 75	1 2%	1 14%	0 0%	0 0%	2 9%	0 0%	0 0%	0 0%	4 2%
O F	L E	Middle 31 - 60	5 11%	0 0%	1 1%	0 0%	1 5%	0 0%	0 0%	0 0%	7 4%
E S		Young 15 - 30	1 2 %	2 29%	12 18%	0 0%	0 0%	0 0%	5 31%	0 0%	20 11%
S I	F E	Old 61 - 75	1 5%	0 0%	1 1%	0 0%	0 0%	0 0%	0 0%	0 0%	2 1%
O N	M A	Middle 31 - 60	8 17%	0 0%	0 0%	0 0%	2 9%	1 14%	0 0%	1 20%	12 7%
A L	L E	Young 15 - 30	2 4%	0 0%	14 21%	0 0%	0 0%	1 14%	1 6%	0 0%	18 10%
W	M	Old 61 - 75	3 6%	0 0%	0 0%	0 0%	0 0%	0 0%	0 0%	0 0%	3 2%
H I	A L	Middle 31 - 60	5 11%	1 14%	1 1%	1 25%	2 9%	0 0%	1 6%	0 0%	11 6%
T E	E	Young 15 - 30	1 2%	1 14%	9 13%	0 0%	0 0%	0 0%	6 38%	0 0%	17 10%
C	F	Old 61 - 75	3 6%	0 0%	0 0%	0 0%	0 0%	0 0%	0 0%	0 0%	3 2%
O L	E M	Middle 31 - 60	5 11%	1 14%	1 1%	2 50%	4 18%	0 0%	0 0%	0 0%	13 7%
L A R	A L E	Young 15 - 30	4 9%	0 0%	14 21%	0 0%	0 0%	1 14%	1 6%	0 0%	20 11%
B	M	Old 61 - 75	3 6%	1 14%	1 1%	0 0%	1 5%	0 0%	0 0%	0 0%	6 3%
L U	A L	Middle 31 - 60	3 6%	0 0%	1 1%	0 0%	2 9%	1 14%	0 0%	1 20%	8 5%
E	E	Young 15 - 30	0 0%	0 0%	6 9%	1 25%	1 5%	1 14%	2 13%	0 0%	11 6%
C O	F E	Old 61 - 75	0 0%	0 0%	0 0%	0 0%	1 5%	0 0%	0 0%	1 20%	2 1%
L L	M A	Middle 31 - 60	2 4%	0 0%	2 3%	0 0%	4 18%	1 14%	0 0%	2 40%	11 6%
A R	L E	Young 15 - 30	0 0%	0 0%	4 6%	0 0%	2 9%	1 14%	0 0%	0 0%	7 4%
Column Total			47 27%	7 4%	67 38%	4 2%	22 13%	7 4%	16 9%	5 3%	175 100%

Appendix C

Three Dimensional Smallest Space Analyses for the Respondents' and Their Six Closest Friends' Ethnicities by Low, Middle, and High Occupational Strata

The next empirical moment in my study consisted of compiling a random, representative sample of the personal entries in the Montreal telephone directory to inquire into the ethnicity of Montrealers' closest friends and their definitions of the lexical items, *Québécois* and *Quebecer*. Each of the students in my "Individual and Society" and "Sociology of Quebec" classes at the Loyola Campus of Concordia University in Montreal in the spring term of 1977 had to call 80 persons on his or her list for the semester project. These lists were compiled and checked in small groups in class. In Chapter Three, Note 3, I thank each of these students.

Toward the end of the course five student judges independently ranked the definitions of *Quebecer* and *Québécois* from universalistic to particularistic, according to Broom and Selznick's discussion which we operationalized.[1]

After eliminating data with collection errors (interviewers misunderstood instructions) or obvious coding or keypunching errors, 2371 interviewees remained. Of these 308 (13%) were unavailable because they did not answer the telephone after three attempts were made to call them; 591 (25% of the total sample; that is, 29% of those contacted, and 27% of those who agreed to participate in the questionnaire) were eliminated because their data contained an excessively large amount of missing data. The decision rule was that any interviewee who was missing more than four judges' ratings on any question or who was missing more than two reports of his or her friend's ethnicity was eliminated. Thus, 1082 interviewees with adequate data remained. From this pool three samples were drawn randomly: a sample of 206 French-Canadian subjects, a sample of 206 English-Canadian subjects, and a sample of 206 subjects who were neither French Canadian nor English Canadian. The entire sample was not used because the cost of computing the monotonicity coefficients for large samples is prohibitive, and because sufficient memory to store the matrix use in computations was not available. Since the computation of monotonicity coefficients requires a separate computation for each possible pair of interviewees, the central processing unit (CPU) time and memory needed to produce a coefficient escalates rapidly.

Later, using SAS's graphics program at UCSF where I used CPU Serial 013474 CPU Model 4381, I generated computer plots of three occupational groupings from the adequate data: "Low Status Occupation," "Middle Status Occupation," and "High Status Occupation." Although I am retaining all of the variables in the three dimensional graphic depictions in the following pages, here we are focusing on variable 2, "Ethnicity of the subject," and variable 4, "Friend 1's Ethnicity," through variable 9, "Friend 6's ethnicity." The data for Guttman-Lingoes' Smallest Space Coordinates for M = 3 (Semi-strong monotonicity) dimension by occupational grouping follow:

　　Amitié/Friendship

Low Status Occupation

Variable	Centrality Index	Dimension 1	Dimension 2	Dimension 3
1=Age of Subject	115.136	-58.839	-100.000	-100.000
2=Ethnicity of Subject	84.369	-90.122	-8.466	9.759
3=Sex of the Subject	119.104	-20.951	100.000	-49.643
4=Friend 1's Ethnicity	81.856	-95.468	-1.201	-14.803
5=Friend 2's Ethnicity	79.219	-91.660	6.818	-21.143
6=Friend 3's Ethnicity	83.941	-100.000	-14.623	-19.185
7=Friend 4's Ethnicity	82.162	-99.148	-17.919	-32.320
8=Friend 5's Ethnicity	72.252	-85.451	-34.007	-47.592
9=Friend 6's Ethnicity	85.559	-96.361	-31.072	-60.294
10=Judge 1's RankDef*Qué*[1]	76.827	54.280	4.726	-49.289
11=Judge 2's RankDef*Qué*	80.184	56.920	-5.950	-60.121
12=Judge 3's RankDef*Qué*	75.274	51.136	-2.841	-59.702
13=Judge 4's RankDef*Qué*	73.529	53.003	-9.008	-52.116
14=Judge 5's RankDef*Qué*	74.840	56.566	-17.767	-45.091
15=Judge 1's RankDistinct[2]	56.592	21.973	-42.745	1.140
16=Judge 2's RankDistinct	64.858	36.720	-34.113	1.084
17=Judge 3's RankDistinct	60.882	30.606	-39.071	0.007
18=Judge 4's RankDistinct	57.905	23.788	-38.639	4.019
19=Judge 5's RankDistinct	64.911	30.213	-48.876	0.441

[1]RankDef*Qué* for Judges 1 - 5 = Rankings of Definitions of *Québécois* and *Quebecer*.

[2]RankDistinct for Judges 1 - 5 = Rankings of the Distinctions between *Québécois* and *Quebecer*.

Guttman-Lingoes' Coefficient of Alienation = 0.03273 in 100 Iterations.

Kruskal's Stress = 0.02347

Low Status Occupation

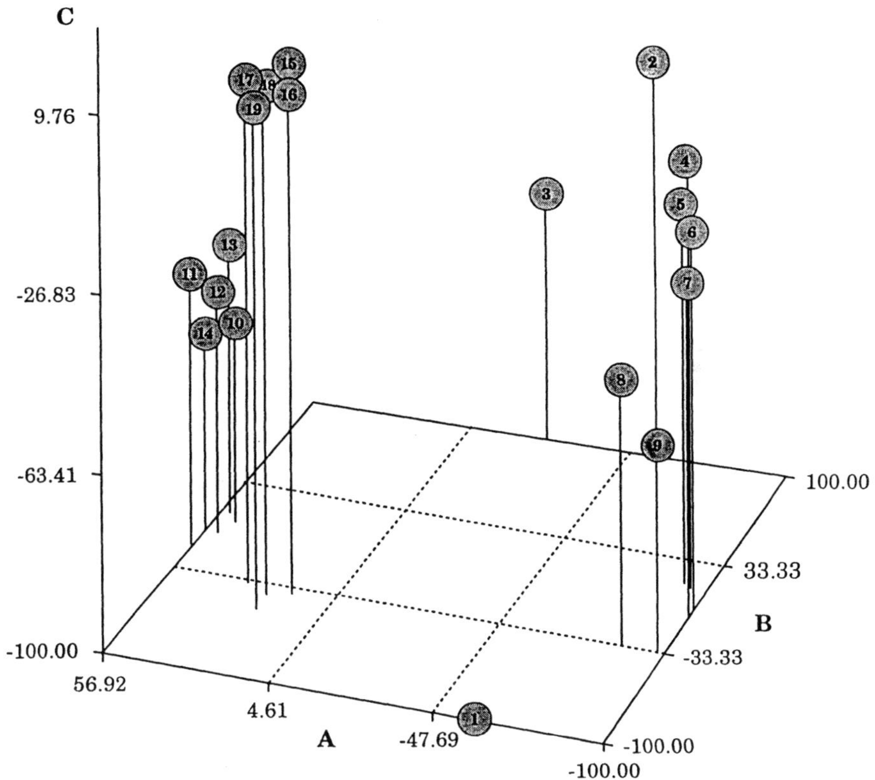

1	Age of subject
2	Ethnicity of subject
3	Sex of subject
4	Friend 1's ethnicity
5	Friend 2's ethnicity
6	Friend 3's ethnicity
7	Friend 4's ethnicity
8	Friend 5's ethnicity
9	Friend 6's ethnicity
10-14	Judges 1-5's rankings of the definitions of Quebecer/*Québécois*
15-19	Judges 1-5's rankings of the distinctions bet13 Quebecer/*Québécois*

Middle Status Occupation

Variable	Centrality Index	Dimension 1	Dimension 2	Dimension 3
1=Age of Subject	125.180	-59.833	42.160	-15.966
2=Ethnicity of Subject	100.817	-88.369	-97.530	-89.329
3=Sex of the Subject	116.779	-38.549	33.221	-100.000
4=Friend 1's Ethnicity	100.937	-100.000	-78.667	-70.565
5=Friend 2's Ethnicity	91.665	-91.409	-83.309	-61.412
6=Friend 3's Ethnicity	95.571	-95.532	-87.439	-44.519
7=Friend 4's Ethnicity	87.756	-82.163	-100.000	-35.198
8=Friend 5's Ethnicity	69.689	-66.276	-87.003	-29.429
9=Friend 6's Ethnicity	85.767	-84.923	-78.479	-27.081
10=Judge 1's RankDef*Qué*[1]	84.737	76.415	-51.848	-74.772
11=Judge 2's RankDef*Qué*	101.863	97.682	-52.480	-59.267
12=Judge 3's RankDef*Qué*	105.288	100.000	-83.282	-60.970
13=Judge 4's RankDef*Qué*	103.346	98.701	-75.947	-63.619
14=Judge 5's RankDef*Qué*	100.624	86.134	-97.055	-81.760
15=Judge 1's RankDistinct[2]	46.311	41.854	-63.894	-34.986
16=Judge 2's RankDistinct	67.143	45.463	-46.294	-4.473
17=Judge 3's RankDistinct	53.386	39.628	-66.739	-15.013
18=Judge 4's RankDistinct	54.326	40.952	-67.999	-15.315
19=Judge 5's RankDistinct	48.514	28.105	-86.967	-17.313

[1]RankDef*Qué* for Judges 1 - 5 = Rankings of Definitions of *Québécois* and *Quebecer*.

[2]RankDistinct for Judges 1 - 5 = Rankings of the Distinctions between *Québécois* and *Quebecer*

Guttman-Lingoes' Coefficient of Alienation = 0.06380 in 100 Iterations.

Kruskal's Stress = 0.05003

Middle Status Occupation

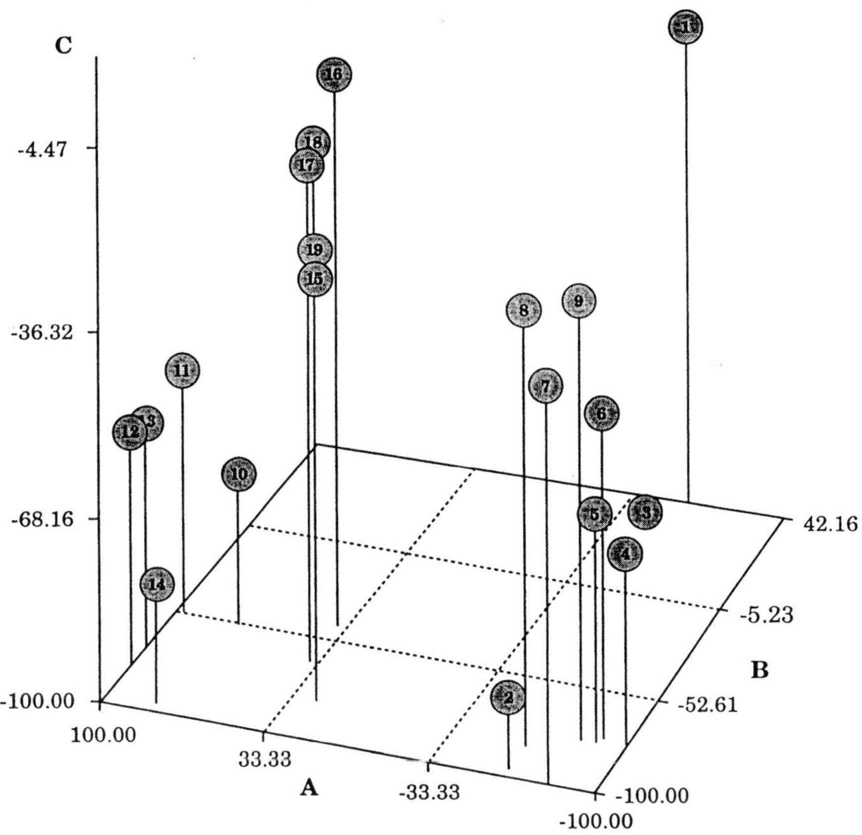

1	Age of subject
2	Ethnicity of subject
3	Sex of subject
4	Friend 1's ethnicity
5	Friend 2's ethnicity
6	Friend 3's ethnicity
7	Friend 4's ethnicity
8	Friend 5's ethnicity
9	Friend 6's ethnicity
10-14	Judges 1-5's rankings of the definitions of Quebecer/*Québécois*
15-19	Judges 1-5's rankings of the distinctions between Quebecer/*Québécois*

High Status Occupation

Variable	Centrality Index	Dimension 1	Dimension 2	Dimension 3
1=Age of Subject	124.127	54.595	-60.109	63.917
2=Ethnicity of Subject	67.012	41.226	-55.094	-88.517
3=Sex of the Subject	125.410	20.807	80.367	-100.000
4=Friend 1's Ethnicity	89.597	84.617	-51.058	-25.582
5=Friend 2's Ethnicity	102.776	100.000	-41.292	-25.305
6=Friend 3's Ethnicity	68.969	67.911	-35.387	-37.081
7=Friend 4's Ethnicity	96.152	92.684	-5.815	-45.490
8=Friend 5's Ethnicity	91.801	82.313	10.299	-43.127
9=Friend 6's Ethnicity	87.341	71.997	10.405	-71.131
10=Judge 1's RankDef*Qué*[1]	80.707	-74.063	-11.733	-14.632
11=Judge 2's RankDef*Qué*	94.573	-86.173	9.917	-34.178
12=Judge 3's RankDef*Qué*	104.249	-100.000	-0.376	-31.048
13=Judge 4's RankDef*Qué*	102.620	-89.213	11.233	-10.853
14=Judge 5's RankDef*Qué*	101.276	-83.993	24.735	-23.490
15=Judge 1's RankDistinct[2]	78.025	-31.866	-100.000	-52.926
16=Judge 2's RankDistinct	82.262	-38.272	-91.281	-81.585
17=Judge 3's RankDistinct	80.065	-47.189	-91.372	-62.262
18=Judge 4's RankDistinct	70.711	-35.767	-80.270	-76.915
19=Judge 5's RankDistinct	64.471	-39.829	-78.812	-55.397

[1]RankDef*Qué* for Judges 1 - 5 = Rankings of Definitions of *Québécois* and *Quebecer*.

[2]RankDistinct for Judges 1 - 5 = Rankings of the Distinctions between *Québécois* and *Quebecer*.

Guttman-Lingoes' Coefficient of Alienation = 0.08244 in 100 Iterations.

Kruskal's Stress = 0.07004

High Status Occupation

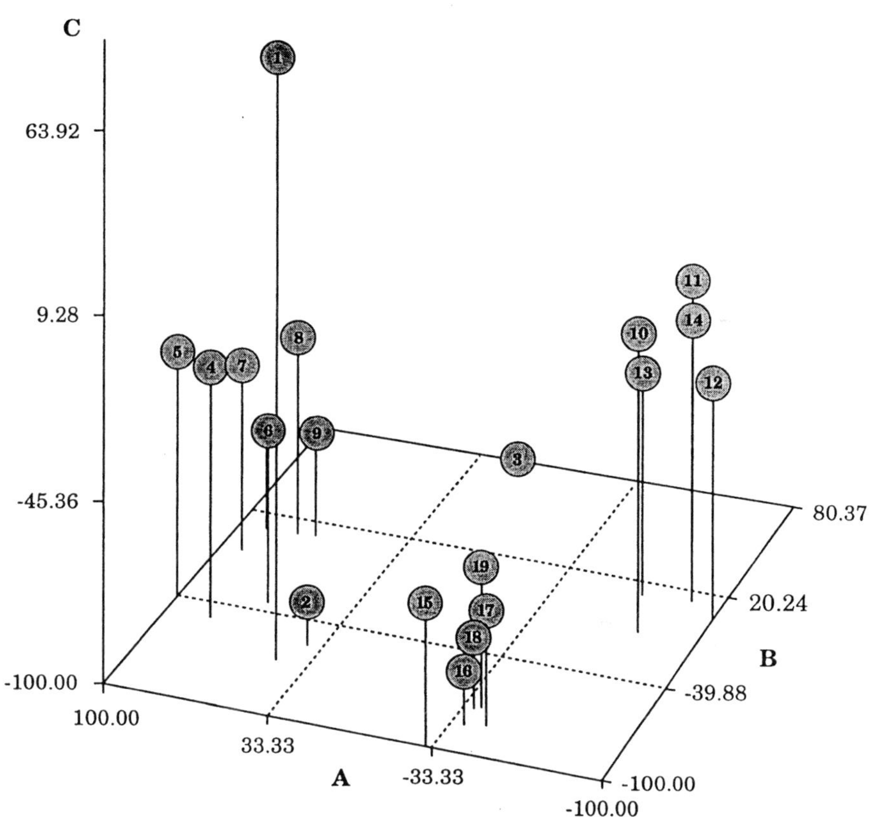

1	Age of subject
2	Ethnicity of subject
3	Sex of subject
4	Friend 1's ethnicity
5	Friend 2's ethnicity
6	Friend 3's ethnicity
7	Friend 4's ethnicity
8	Friend 5's ethnicity
9	Friend 6's ethnicity
10-14	Judges 1-5's rankings of the definitions of Quebecer/*Québécois*
15-19	Judges 1-5's rankings of the distinctions between Quebecer/*Québécois*

Notes

1. Gurdin, J. Barry, "Naturalistic Categories of Ethnic Identity in Quebec," Chap. 9 in *Culture, Ethnicity, and Identity: Current Issues in Research*, ed. Bill McCready (New York: Academic Press, 1983a), 150-152.

Multidimensional Scalogram Analysis of Friendship Styles by Item Plots and Three Dimensional Smallest Space Analyses for Montrealers' Definitions of Friendship and Styles of Friendship

Beyond the commentary already provided in this book, the reader may note the following trends in the multidimensional scalogram analysis' item plots which apply only to the in-depth interviewees.

Of the interviewees who were characterized by the style of "A1," the "Family-Oriented Friendship," eighty percent were married with children [16/20], only fifteen percent [3/20] were "single, never married," and one or five percent was divorced. Seventy percent of the people who displayed style A1 were of a middle age stratum, and only fifteeen percent were of an older or younger age stratum [3/20 each]. English Canadians [12/20 = 60 percent] had a "Family-Oriented Friendship" style more frequently than French Canadians [8/20 = 40 percent]. More professionals [10/20 = 50 percent], fewer blue collar [6/20 = 30 percent], and even fewer white collar workers [4/20 = 20 percent] had a "Family-Oriented Friendship" style. Somewhat more male [11/20 = 55 percent] than female [9/20 = 45 percent] in-depth interviewees enacted this friendship style.

"A3," the style of the "Sibling Friend," was more descriptive of English Canadians [9/15 = 60 percent] than French Canadians [6/15 = 40 percent]. Male in-depth interviewees [9/15 = 60 percent] reported having a sibling friend more often than females [6/15 = 40 percent]. Younger people between 15 and 30 [7/15 = 46.67 percent] displayed this style slightly more often than those between 31 and 60 [6/15 = 40 percent] and considerably more often than those between 61 and 76 [2/15 = 13.3 percent]. Similarly, interviewees who were "single, never married" [7/15 = 46.67 percent] had a sibling friend slightly more frequently than those who were married with children [6/15 = 40 percent] and much more frequently than those who were divorced [1/15 = 6.67 percent] or married without children [1/15 = 6.67%]. The sibling friend characterized the professionals [7/15 = 46.67%] more so than white collar [5/15 = 33.33 percent] or blue collars workers [3/15 = 20 percent].

Style "A4," the "Non-nuclear Family Friend," was observed most often in the middle age stratum, of those between 31 and 60, [9/13 = 69.23 percent], and considerably less often among the younger, 15 to 30 year-old, stratum [2/13 = 15.39 percent] or older, 61 to 76, stratum [2/13 = 15.39 percent]. Similarly, the style of the non-nuclear family friend characterized French Canadian and male [8/13 = 61.54 percent each] more so than English Canadian and female [5/13 = 38.46 percent each] friendships. People who were married with children displayed this style [7/15 = 53.85 percent] much more frequently than single people who had never married [3/13 = 23.076 percent] or those who were married without children [3/13 = 23.076 percent]. Class exerted the least influence on this style, with professionals [5/13 = 38.46 percent] having non-nuclear family friends somewhat more often than either blue or white collar workers [4/13 = 30.77 percent each].

Style "B1," the "Neighbor-Friend," characterized English Canadians and married people with children [12/26 = 53.846 percent each] somewhat more than French Canadians [12/26 = 46.154 percent] and people who were "single, never married" [10/26 = 38.46 percent]. This style was more typical of professionals [12/26 = 46.154 percent] than white collar [8/26 = 30.769 percent] and blue collar [6/26 = 23.08% workers. People of the middle age stratum [13/26 = 50 percent] more typically displayed the style of the "neighbor friend" than people of a younger [10/26 = 38.46 percent] or older [3/26 = 11.538 percent] age stratum. Married people without children and divorced people rarely [1/26 = 3.846 percent each] had "neighbor friends." Gender exerted no influence on this style, for male and female in-depth interviewees had neighbor friends to the same extent [13/26 = 50 percent each].

Style "B2," the "Best-Friend Proximity," was observed more frequently among females and English Canadians [4/7 = 57.14 percent each] than males and French Canadians [3/7 = 42.86 percent each]. Similarly, the younger age stratum [4/7 = 57.14 percent] displayed this style more often than the middle [2/7 = 28.57 percent] or older [1/7 = 14.29 percent] age stratum. The "Best-Friend Proximity" occurred as frequently among single people who had never married and white collar workers [3/7 = 42.86 percent each], but less frequently among professionals, blue collar workers, and people who were married without children [2/7 = 28.57 percent each]. It was even rarer among people who were married with children or divorced [1/7 = 14.29 percent each].

The style of "C1," the "Similar-Interest Close Friend" was much more common among male [22/29 = 75.86 percent] than female [7/29 = 24.14 percent] in-depth interviewees. This style was more typical for people who were married with children [15/29 = 51.72 percent] than for single people who had never been married [13/29 = 44.83 percent] or for married people without children [1/29 = 3.45 percent]. Professionals [14/29 = 48.28 percent] had similar interest close friends more often than did white collar [9/29 = 31.04 percent] or blue collar [6/29 = 20.68 percent] workers. Style C1 was about as frequent among interviewees of the younger age stratum [13/29 = 44.83 percent] as among those of the middle age stratum [12/29 = 41.38 percent] but less frequent among interviewees of the older age stratum [4/29 = 13.79 percent]. Ethnicity exerted little influence on this style, for only one more French [15/29 = 51.721 percent] than English [14/29 = 48.28 percent] Canadian displayed this style.

494

Style "D," the "Petit/e Ami/e, Boy-/Girl-Friend" was very prominent among interviewees who were "single, never married," male [7/9 = 77.8 percent each], and between 15 and 30 years of age [6/9 = 66.67 percent]. It was less marked among female and white collar workers [2/9 = 22.22 percent each], and even less noticeable among people who were married without children or divorced [1/9 = 11.1 percent each]. Interviewees between 31 and 60 and blue collar workers [3/9 = 33.33 percent each] displayed style D less frequently than interviewees who were of the younger age stratum and professional. Among the in-depth interviewees, there was little difference between English Canadians [5/9 = 55.56 percent] and French Canadians [4/9 = 44.44 percent] in this style of friendship.

In-depth interviewees who were male [6/8 = 75 percent], married with children, of the middle age stratum [5/8 = 62.5 percent each], and professional [4/8 = 50 percent] displayed style "E," "The Friend-in-Mind" in a noteworthy fashion. This style was much less marked among females, in the younger age stratum, who were either blue or white collar workers [2/8 = 25 percent each]. It was very infrequent among interviewees who were divorced or of the older age stratum [1/8 = 12.5 percent each]. The Friend-in-Mind occurred as frequently among French Canadians as English Canadians [4/8 = 50 percent each].

As the reader examines the item plots, it may be convenient to reread these brief descriptions. Due to the necessity of reducing the item plots in a quite small space, the graphic artist had to adjust the placement of the letters representing the individuals somewhat to be able to draw curves with a machine-sketched line. However, the relative positions of the individuals vis-à-vis one another is close to the computer generated print-outs.

Multidimensional Scalogram Analysis
50 Interviewees' Friendship Styles

*(The shaded area represents the designated
space of the friendship style.)*

A1 = Family-oriented Friendship

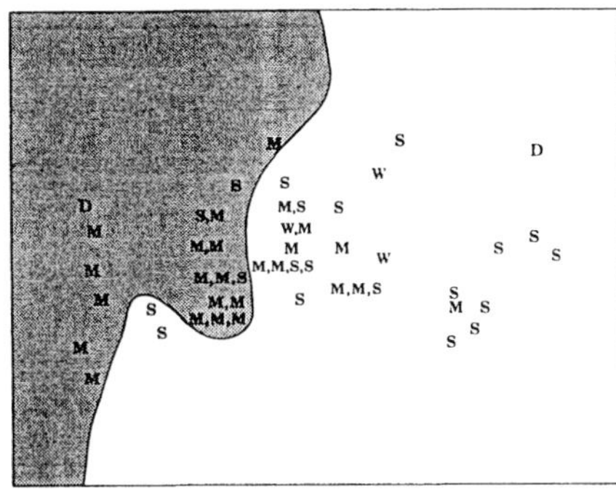

M = Married with Children
S = Single, Never Married
D = Divorced
W = Married without Children

A3 = The Sibling Friendship

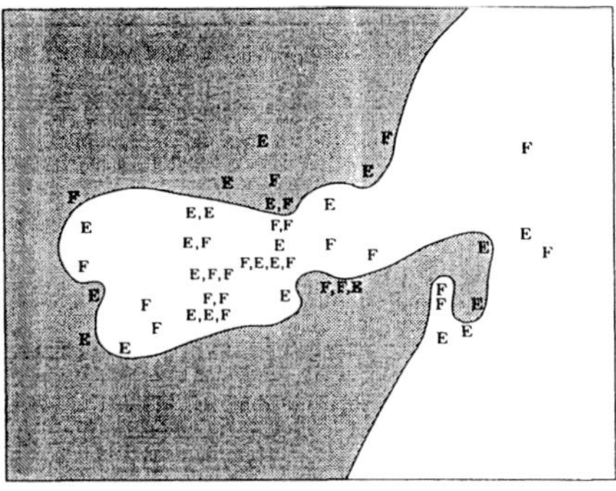

E = English Canadian
F = French Canadian

A4 = Non-nuclear Family Friend

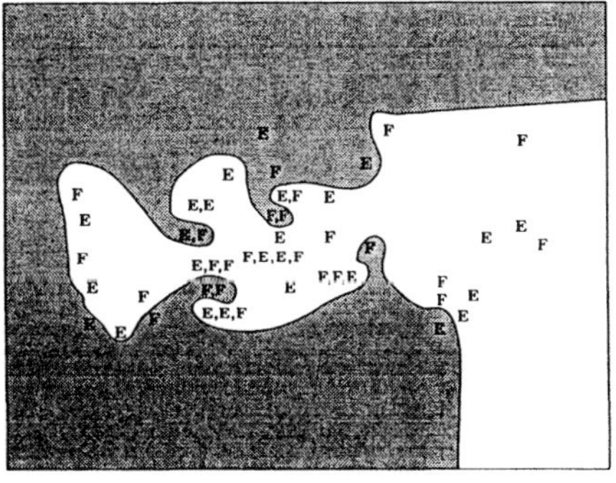

E = English Canadian
F = French Canadian

B1 = Neighbor-friend

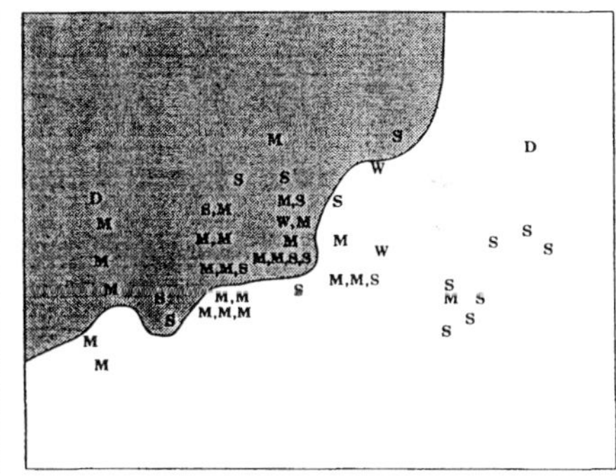

M = Married with Children
S = Single, Never Married
D = Divorced
W = Married without Children

B2 = Best-friend Proximity

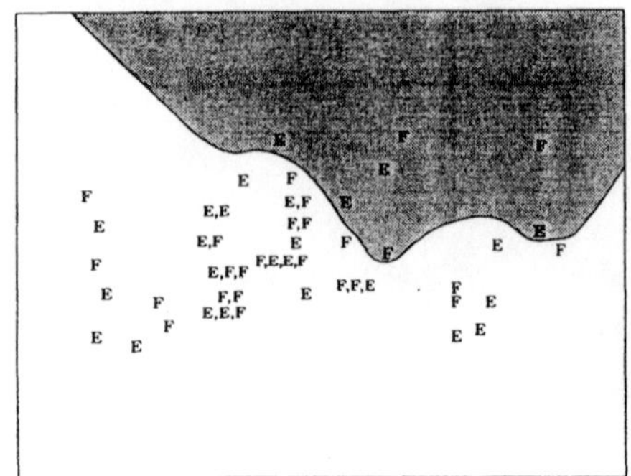

E = English Canadian
F = French Canadian

C1 = Similar-interest Close Friend

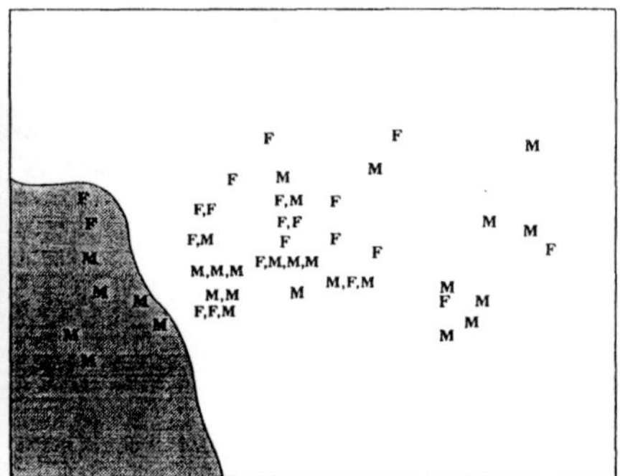

M = Male
F = Female

D = The Girl-friend / Boy-friend, Petit / e Ami / e

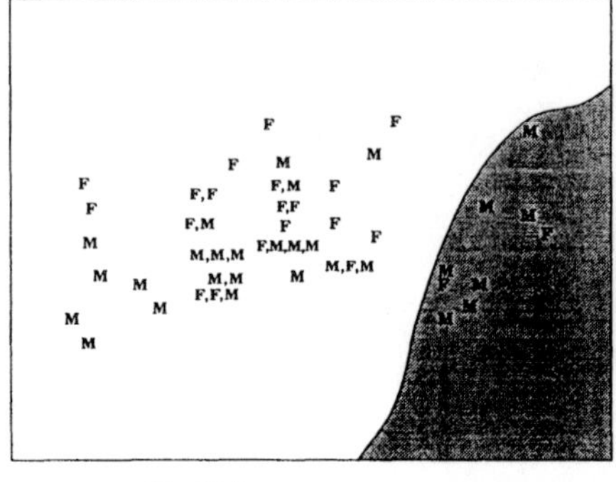

M = Male
F = Female

E = The Friend-in-Mind

M = Male
F = Female

Styles of Friendship

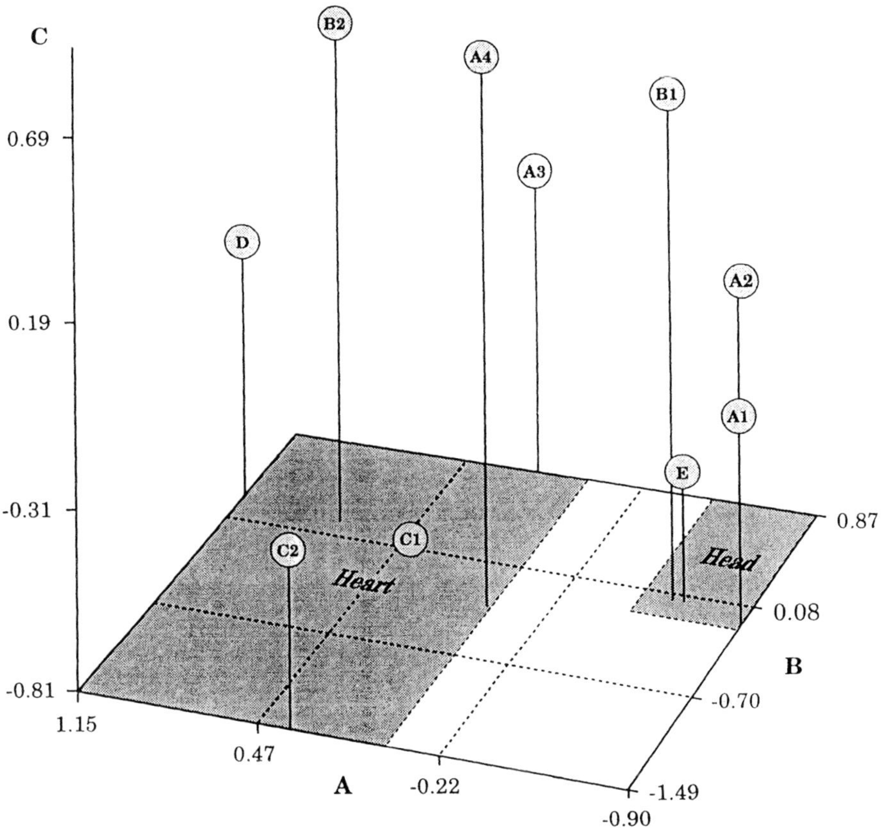

A1	Family-oriented Friendship
A2	Friendship after the Break-up of the Family
A3	The Sibling Friendship
A4	The Non-nuclear Family Friendship
B1	The Neighbor-friend
B2	Best-friend Proximity
C1	The Similar-interest Close Friend
C2	The Buddy-*Copain-Copine* Phenomenon
D	The Girl-friend/Boy-friend, *Petit/e Ami/e*
E	The Friend-in-mind

*See: Chapter Two, Note 14, for Similarities Coordinates in Three Dimensions
and Guttman / Lingoes Coefficient of Alienation in Three Dimensions.*

Definitions of Friendship

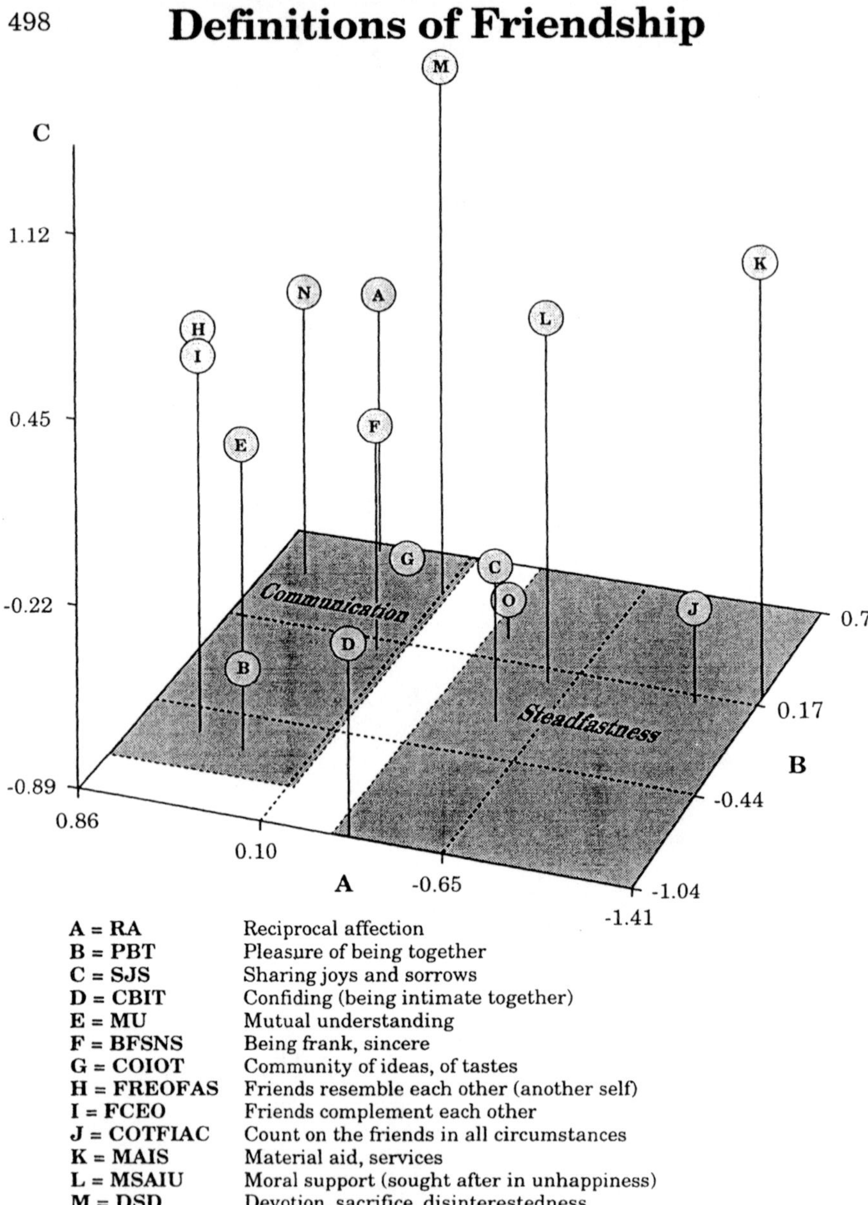

A = RA	Reciprocal affection	
B = PBT	Pleasure of being together	
C = SJS	Sharing joys and sorrows	
D = CBIT	Confiding (being intimate together)	
E = MU	Mutual understanding	
F = BFSNS	Being frank, sincere	
G = COIOT	Community of ideas, of tastes	
H = FREOFAS	Friends resemble each other (another self)	
I = FCEO	Friends complement each other	
J = COTFIAC	Count on the friends in all circumstances	
K = MAIS	Material aid, services	
L = MSAIU	Moral support (sought after in unhappiness)	
M = DSD	Devotion, sacrifice, disinterestedness	
N = TL	Trust, loyalty	
O = CPFIH	Constancy, perenniality (friendship is holy)	

See: Chapter Two, Note 16, for Similarities Coordinates in Three Dimensions, Guttman / Lingoes Coefficient of Alienation in Three Dimensions, and μ2 Coefficients for the Maisonneuvean Content Analytical Categories.

Bibliography

This bibliography lists all the works to which I have referred directly in this book and, in addition, other literature which has inspired my research on friendship but which I do not cite explicitly in this work. For dictionary and encyclopaedia items listed under anonymous in the chapter notes, I have followed a modified version of *The Chicago Manual of Style: Thirteenth Edition, Revised and Expanded* in this bibliography, where they are alphabetized under the name of the reference work. The exact entry follows s.v. (*sub verbo*) "under the word." In older works I have added such information as volume, date of publication, and publisher to help the reader locate these sources. I have followed generally *The Chicago Manual of Style*'s rules for French titles.

Abella, Irving and Harold Troper. *None Is Too Many, Canada and the Jews of Europe, 1933-1948*. Toronto: Lester & Orpen Dennys, 1982.

Abelson, Willa D. and Elizabeth J. Weiss. "Psychological Studies of Friendship." In *Studies of Friendship*, ed. Cora DuBois, 1-37. Boston: Harvard University, 1953.

Abley, Mark. "A Troublesome Thesis: After a Year of Controversy, Esther Delisle Has Won a Ph.D. for Her Study of Lionel Groulx and Racism. It's out as a Book This Week. But She Can't Get a Job," *The Gazette*, Montreal, 19 September 1992, B-2.

Adams, Rebecca G., and Rosemary Blieszner, eds. *Older Adult Friendship: Structure and Process*. Newbury Park, CA: Sage Publications, 1989.

Aelred of Rievaulx. *Spiritual Friendship*, trans. Mary Eugenia Laker. Kalamazoo, Michigan: Cistercian Publications, 1977.

Alberoni, Francesco. *L'amicizia*. Milan: Garzanti Editore s.p.a., 1984.

------. *L'amitié*, trans. Nelly Drusi. Paris: G. P. Ramsay, 1987.

Albert, R. S. and T. R. Brigante. "The Psychology of Friendship Relations: Social Factors." *Journal of Social Psychology*, 1962.

Allan, Graham. A., *A Sociology of Friendship and Kinship*. London: George Allen & Unwin, 1979.

------. *Friendship: Developing a Sociological Perspective*. Boulder, Colorado: Westview Press, 1989.

Allen, Vernon L. "Self, Social Group, and Social Structure: Surmises about the Study of Children's Friendships." In *The Development of Children's Friendships,* ed. Steven Asher and John M. Gottman, 53-90. Cambridge: Cambridge University Press, 1981.

Anderson, Margare, ed. *Mother Was Not a Person*. Montreal: Content Publishing Co., 1972.

Altman, Irwin and Dalmas A. Taylor. *Social Penetration: The Development of Interpersonal Relationships*. New York: Irvington Publishers, Inc., 1973.

An Anglo-Saxon Dictionary, s.v. "Freond, friond, es, freondscipe," London: Oxford University Press, 1964.

Anonymous. "Amitié, amour et liberté sont les principales valeurs des jeunes Canadiens," *Le Devoir*, 22 January 1985.

Anonymous. "Srebrnik, Perel Get Le Devoir Apology." *The Canadian Jewish News*, 23 January 1986, 13.

Anonymous. *The Status of Women in Canada*. Royal Commission Report. Ottawa: Information Canada., 1970.

Anonymous. *Women in the Labour Force - Facts and Figures*. Labour Canada, 1975.

Anonymous. *Women Unite*. Toronto: Canadian Women's Educational Press, 1972.

Aquinas, St. Thomas. *Summa Theologica I/II. Vol. 20 of Great Books of the Western World*, trans. Fathers of the English Dominican Province. Revised by Daniel J. Sullivan. Toronto: Encyclopaedia Britannica, 1952.

Arendt, Hanna. *The Origins of Totalitarianism*. Twelfth Printing. New York: A Meridian Book World Publishing, [1951] 1972.

Aristotle. "7. Friendship between Unequals." In *Nicomachean Ethics*, Book VIII, trans. Martin Ostwald. Indianapolis: The Bobbs Merrill Company, Inc., 1962.

Armistead, Nigel, ed. *Reconstructing Social Psychology*. Markham, Ontario: Penguin Books Ltd., 1974.

Arnold, Abraham J. "Jews in Quebec." *Jewish Currents: A Progressive Monthly*, May 1989, 35-38.

Asher, Steven R. and John M. Gottman, eds. *The Development of Children's Friendships*. Cambridge: Cambridge University Press, 1981.

Aublet, Y., ed. *Gay Montréal*, Novembre, No. 16. Montreal: Le Journal Gay Montréal, 1976.

Augustine, St. *The City of God*, Volume 18 of *Great Books of the Western World*. Trans. Marcus Dods. Toronto: Encyclopaedia Britannica, 1952.

Babin, Vedi P. *Friendship*. New York: Herder and Herder, 1967.

Balikci, Asen. "Les <<souffrances>> des juifs montréalais! En marge de l'article du <<Jérusalem Post.>>" *Le Devoir*, 23 février 1982, 7.

Barkas, J. L., *Friendship: A Selected, Annotated Bibliography*. New York: Garland Publishing, Inc., 1985.

Bartlett, Donald L. and James B. Steele, *America: What Went Wrong?* Kansas City, Missouri: Andrews and McMeel, 1992.

Bassett, Isabel. *The Parlor Rebellion*. Toronto: McClelland and Stewart Ltd., 1975.

Beauvoir, Simone de . *La vieillesse: essai*. Paris: Gallimard, (1970) 1972.

Bell, Robert R. *Worlds of Friendship*. Beverly Hills, California: Sage Publications, Inc., 1981.

Bellah, Robert N., Richard Madsen, William M. Sullivan, Ann Swidler, and Steven M. Tipton. *Habits of the Heart: Individualism and Commitment in American Life*. San Francisco: Harper & Row, Publishers, [1985] 1986.

------. *Individualism & Commitment in American Life: Readings on the Themes of Habits of the Heart*. San Francisco: Harper & Row, Publishers, [1987] 1988.

------. *The Good Society*. New York: Vintage Books, A Division of Random House, 1991.

Benarrosh, Penny, Maurice Elmaleh, Joseph Lévy, Léon Ouaknine, et Victor Teboul. "L'article du Jérusalem Post." *Jonathan*, avril 1982.

Bentham, Jeremy. *The Works of Jeremy Bentham*, Volume 6. ed. John Bowring. New York: Russell and Russell Inc., [1838-1842] 1962.

Benveniste, Émile, *Le vocabulaire des institutions indo-européennes: économie, parenté, société*. Paris: Les Éditions de Minuit, 1961.

Berger, J. "Sociology's Long Decade in the Wilderness." *New York Times*, 28 May 1989.

Berger, Peter and Thomas Luckmann. *The Social Construction of Reality: A Treatise in the Sociology of Knowledge*. Garden City, New York: Anchor Books Doubleday and Co., 1966.

Bibby, Reginald W. "The State of Collective Religiosity in Canada: An Empirical Analysis." *The Canadian Review of Sociology and Anthropology/La revue canadienne de sociologie et d'anthropologie* 16(1)(1979): 105-116.

Bigelow, Brian. J. "Children's Friendship Expectations: A Cognitive-developmental Study." In *Child Development*, 18 (1977).

Bigelow, Brian J. and John J. La Gaipa. "Children's Written Description of Friendship: a Multidimensional Analysis." *Developmental Psychology*, II, (1975) 857-858.

Bissonnette, Lise. "Le Québec discrédité en Israël." *Le Devoir*, 18 février 1982.

Black, H. *Friendship*. New York: Fleming H. Revell Co., 1904.

Blais, Marie-Claire. *Une saison dans la vie d'Emmanuel*. Saint-Lambert, Québec: Éditions internationales Alain Stanké: Les Presses de Payette & Simms Inc.

Blieszner, Rosemary and Rebecca G. Adams. *Adult Friendship*. Newbury Park, CA: Sage Publications, 1992.

Block, Irwin. "The Bridge Builder," *The Gazette*, Montreal, 28 August 1993, B3.

------. "Controversial Ph.D. Is a Best Seller," *The Gazette*, Montreal, 28 August 1993, B3.

Block, Joel D. *Friendship*. New York: Macmillan Publishing Co., Inc., 1980.

Block, Marc. *The Growth of Ties of Dependence*. Volume 1 of *Feudal Society*. Trans. L. A. Manyon. Chicago: University of Chicago Press, 1964.

Blom, Jan-Peter. "Some Impressions and Hypotheses Concerning The Source, Quality and Relevance of Friendship." Draft of a paper read at the Colloquium on the Comparative Sociology of Friendship, Institute of Social and Economic Research, Memorial University of Newfoundland, March 1969.

Bloom, Allan. *Love and Friendship.* New York: Simon & Schuster, 1993.

Bloom, B., S. Asher, and S. White. "Marital Disruption as Stressor: A Review and Analysis." *Psychological Bulletin* 85 (1978): 867-94.

Blum, Alan and Peter McHugh, eds. *Friends, Enemies, and Strangers: Theorizing in Art, Science, and Everyday Life.* Norwood, New Jersey: Ablex Publishing Co., 1979.

Blumer, Herbert. "Sociological Analysis and the 'Variable'." In *Symbolic Interaction. A Reader in Social Psychology*, 2nd ed. by J. G. Manis and B. N. Meltzer. Boston: Allyn and Bacon, Inc., 1956 (1972).

Boissevain, Jeremy. *Friends of Friends: Networks, Manipulators and Coalitions.* Oxford: Basil Blackwell, 1974.

Boldt, Edward D., Neil E. Lindquist, and G. Anne Percival. "The Significance of Significant Others." *The Canadian Review of Sociology and Anthropology / La revue canadienne de sociologie et d'anthropologie* 13(3)(1976): 345-351.

Bol'shaia Sovetskaia Entsiklopediia Publishing House (Great Soviet Encyclopedia). 1962, s.v. "Druzhba (Friendship)."

------. 1962, s.v. "Druzhba narodov (Friendship of Peoples)."

Bonacich, Edna. "The Caucus on Underemployment in Sociology: A Brief History" and "The Caucus Today." In *Newsletter of the Caucus on Underemployment in Sociology.* Clemson, South Carlina 29631: Department of Agricultural Economics and Rural Sociology, Barre Hall 219, Attention: Thomas Lyson - Clemson University.

Bonin, Jacques. "La socialisation." Chap. 9 in *Aliénation et idéologie dans la vie quotidienne des Montréalais francophones.* Vol. 2, eds. Yves Lamarche, Marcel Rioux, et Robert Sévigny, 637-793. Montréal: Les Presses de l'université de Montréal, 1973.

Bonin, Jacques and Jules Duchastel, "Vie privée vie publique," in *Aliénation et idéologie dans la vie quotidienne des Montréalais francophones.* Vol. 2, eds. Yves Lamarche, Marcel Rioux, et Robert Sévigny, Montréal: Les Presses de l'université de Montréal, 1973.

Booth, George. *A Friend Is Friendly!* Norwalk, Conn.: The C. R. Gibson Co., 1981.

Borg, Ingwer. *Multidimensional Data Representations: When & Why.* Mathesis Press: Ann Arbor, Michigan, 1981.

Borowitz, Eugene B. "Friendship." In *Encyclopaedia Judaica*, Volume 7, Fr-Ha, 195. Jerusalem: The Macmillan Co., 1971.

Boswell, James. *The Life of Samuel Johnson*. Volume 44 of *Great Books of the Western World*. Toronto: Encyclopaedia Britannica, 1952.

Brain, Robert. *Friends and Lovers*. New York: Basic Books, Inc., Publishers, 1976.

Brazeau, Jacques. "Pertinence de l'enseignement des relations ethniques et caractérisation de ce champs d'études au Canada et au Québec," In *Sociologie et sociétés*, ed. Juteau-Lee, Danielle, 133-146. Montréal: Les Presses de l'université de Montréal.

Brenton, Myron. *Friendship*. New York: Stein and Day Publishers, 1974.

Broom, L. and P. Selznick. *Sociology. A Text with Adapted Readings*. Fifth Edition. New York: Harper and Row, 1973.

Brown, Michael. *Jew or Juif? Jews, French Canadians and Anglo-Canadians 1759-1914*. Philadelphia: Jewish Publication Society.

Browning, C. and W. A. Wallace. "Friendship," "Friendship, Particular," and "Friendship, Spiritual." In *The Catholic Encyclopaedia*, Volume 6, Fra-Hir, 203-206. Washington, D. C.: The Catholic University of America, 1967.

Buckner, H. Taylor. "Attitudes towards Minorities: Seven Year Results and Analysis, June 1990." Presented at "Anti-Semitism around the World," League for Human Rights of B'nai Brith Canada/*Ligue des droits de la personne de B'nai Brith Canada*. Montreal, Quebec, Canada, November 3-4, 1991.

Butkowski, Bill. *The Company They Keep: Friendship in Childhood and Adolescence*. Cambridge University Press, in press.

Cappell, Charles. "Observations on the State of Academic Sociology." In *ISA (Illinois Sociological Association) Newsletter*, ed. Chris Prendergast, 6-8. Bloomington, Illinois: Department of Sociology, May 1993.

Cappell, Charles L. and Thomas M. Gutterbock. "Visible Colleges: The Social and Conceptual Structure of Specialties." *American Sociological Review* 27(2)(1992): 266-273.

Carrier, Roch. *Il n'y a pas de pays sans grand-père*. Saint-Lambert, Québec: Éditions internationales Alain Stanké; Les Presses de Payette & Simms, Inc., 1979.

Cass, Connie. "Most U.S. Spouses Are Faithful, Study Finds." *San Francisco Examiner*, 19 October 1993.

Cicero, Marcus Tullius. *Essay on Friendship. Laelius De Amicitia.* Trans. with Notes by Alexander J. Inglis. New York: The Platt & Peck Co., 1908.

Cicourel, Aaron V. *Method and Measurement in Sociology.* Glencoe: The Free Press, 1967.

------. *Cognitive Sociology.* Harmondsworth: Penguin Books Ltd., 1973.

Centineo, E. "Amicizia." In *Enciclopedia Filosofica. Interamente Rielaborata I A-Conoscenza.* Second Edition. Firenze: G. C. Sansoni Editore, 1967.

Clift, D. and S. M. Arnopoulos. *Le fait anglais au Québec.* Montréal: Éditions Libre Expression, 1979.

Cohen, Eli (director). *The Quarrel.* Based on a short story by Chaim Grade, screenplay by David Brandes with the two main characters of Hersh Resseyner played by Saul Rubinek and Chaim Kovler played by R. H. Thompson. Los Angeles: Apple & Honey Film Corp.

Cohen, Theodore, F. "Men's Families, Men's Friends: A Structural Analysis of Constraints on Men's Social Ties." In *Men's Friendships*, ed. Peter N. Nardi, 115-131. Newbury Park, CA: Sage Publications, Inc., 1992.

Cohen, Yehudi. *Social Structure and Personality: A Casebook.* New York: Holt, Rinehart, and Winston, 1961.

Cooley, C. H. *Human Nature and the Social Order.* Introduction by Philip Rieff. Forward by Herbert Mead. New York: Schoken Books, 1964.

Cooper, John Irwin. *Montreal: A Brief History.* Montreal: McGill-Queen's University Press, 1969.

Corsaro, William A. *Friendship and Peer Culture in the Early Years.* Norwood, New Jersey: Ablex Publishing Co., 1985.

Coulon, Jocelyn. "L'industrie militaire au Québec. Plus de 100,000 personnes travaillent pour ce secteur." *Le Devoir*, 2 fevrier 1987.

Couture, Marcel, ed., *Forces: Economic, Social and Cultural Quarterly*, Montréal: la Société d'édition de la revue Forces, 100 (Hiver 1992-1993).

Crothers, S.M. *The Book of Friendship.* New York: The Macmillan Co., 1910.

Crozier, Michel. "Les relations interpersonnelles et intergroupes et le problème de la routine." In *Le phenomène bureaucratique.* Paris: Le Seuil, 1963.

Crysdal, S. "Family and Kinship in Riverdale." In *The Underside of Toronto,* ed. W. E. Mann, 97-108. Toronto: McClelland & Stewart Ltd., 1970.

Csillag, Ron. "Jews by Faith up 7%; 'Ethnic' Issue Looms." *The Canadian Jewish News Montreal Edition*, 10 June 1993.

Curtis, James E. and Ronald D. Lambert. "Status Dissatisfaction and Out-group Rejection: Cross-cultural Comparisons within Canada." *The Canadian Review of Sociology and Anthropology/La revue canadienne de sociologie et d'anthropologie* 12(2) (1975): 178-192.

Davidson, Lynne R. and Lucile Duberman. "Same Sex Friendships: A Gender Comparison of Dyads" (Paper delivered at Session 153 on His and Her Perspectives on Intimacy at the 74th annual meeting of the American Sociological Association, Boston, 1979).

------. "Friendship: Communication and Interactional Patterns in Same-sex Dyads." *Sex Roles* 8 (1982): 809-822.

Davis, Murray S. *Intimate Relations*. New York: The Free Press, 1973.

Délude-Clift, C. and E. Champoux. "Le conflict des générations." In *Recherches sociographiques*. 14 (1973).

Denzin, Norman K. *The Research Act: A Theoretical Introduction to Sociological Methods. Second Edition.* New York: McGraw-Hill Book Company, [1970] 1978.

Derber, Charles, "Coming Glued: Communitarianism to the Rescue," *Tikkun: A Bimonthly Jewish Critique of Politics, Culture & Society*, Oakland, CA: the Institute for Labor and Mental Health, July/August 1993, 27-30; 95-99.

Derber, Charles, Mary Edsall, Peter Gabel, Ruth Rosen, and Michael Sandel. "Roundtable," *Tikkun: A Bimonthly Jewish Critique of Politics, Culture & Society*, Oakland, CA: the Institute for Labor and Mental Health, September/October 1993, 19- 26; 87- 89.

Desbiens, Jean-Paul. "Looking to the Future," *Forces: Economic, Social and Cultural Quarterly*, ed. Marcel Couture, Montréal: la Société d'édition de la revue Forces, 100 (Hiver 1992-1993), 54-55.

Devroede, G. "Le Québec de 1977 vu par un immigrant en quête de racines," *Le Devoir*, 20 juin 1977, 5.

Dictionnaire alphabétique et analogique de la langue française, s.v. "Ami - amitié," Paris: Société du Nouveau Littré, 1960.

Dofny, Jacques. *Les ingenieurs canadiens français et canadiens anglais à montréal.* Documents de la commission royale d'enquête sur le bilinguisme et le biculturalisme 6, 1970.

Dolment, M. and Marce Barthe. *La femme au Québec*. Ottawa: Les Presses Libres, 1973.

Douglas, Jack D. *Understanding Everyday Life. Toward the Reconstruction of Sociological Knowledge*. Chicago: Aldine Publishing Co., 1970.

Douglas, Mary. "Part 3: The *a priori* in Nature." In *Implicit Meanings*. London: Routledge & Kegan Paul, 1975.

Dreitzel, Hans Peter. *Childhood and Socialization 5*. New York: Macmillan Publishing Co., Inc., 1973.

Driedger, L. "In Search of Cultural Identity Factors: A Comparison of Ethnic Students." *The Canadian Review of Sociology and Anthropology / La revue canadienne de sociologie et d'anthropologie* (1975): 150-162.

DuBois, Cora, ed. *Studies of Friendship*. Boston: Harvard University, 1953.

------. "The Gratuitous Act: Introduction to the Comparative Study of Friendship Patterns." In *The Compact: Selected Dimensions of Friendship Patterns*, ed. Elliot Leyton, 15-32. Toronto: University of Toronto Press [for Memorial University of Newfoundland], 1974.

Duchesne, Louis. *Annuaire du Québec 1979-1980*. Gouvernement du Québec. Ministère de l'Industrie et du Commerce. Bureau de la statistique du Québec. Québec: L'Éditeur officiel du Québec, 1980.

Duck, Steve. *Friends, For Life: The Psychology of Close Relationships*. New York: St. Martin's Press, 1983.

------. *Personal Relationships and Personal Constructs: A Study of Friendship Formation* (New York: John Wiley and Sons, 1973).

Duck, Steve and Robin Gilmour, eds. *Personal Relationships*. Vols. 1-6. London: Academic Press, 1981-1985.

Dufresne, Francine. "Devrait-on faire l'amour avec ses amis?" *Nous* 2 mai 1975, 65-66.

Durham, Lord. *The Gazette*, Montreal, 4 December (1839) 1976.

Durkheim, Émile. *The Division of Labor in Society*. New York: The Free Press, A Division of Macmillan Publishing Co., Inc., 1933.

Édition abrégée dictionnaire canadien français-anglais anglais-français, s. v. "Ami, e, amitié." Toronto: McClelland and Stewart.

Eichenbaum, Luise and Susie Orbach. *Between Friends: Love, Envy, and Competition in Women's Friendships*. New York: Viking, 1988.

Eisenstadt, Shmuel N. and Luis Roniger. *Patrons, Clients and Friends:
Interpersonal Relations and the Structure of Trust in Society.* Cambridge:
Cambridge University Press, 1984.

Elliott, Jaques. "The Method of Social Analysis in Social Change and Social
Research." *Clinical Sociology Review* 1 (1982).

Engels, Friedrich. *The Origin of the Family, Private Property, and the State.* New
York: International Publishers, 1972.

Enriquez, Eugène. *De la horde à l'état: Essai de psychanalyse du lien social.*
Mayenne: Éditions Gallimard, 1986.

Epstein J. L. "Reexamining Theories of Adolescent Friendships with
Longitudinal Data" (Paper delivered at Session 199, on Socialization, at the
74th annual meeting of the American Sociological Association, Boston, 1979).

Etzioni, Amitai, "On Communitarianism and Its Inclusive Agenda." *Tikkun: A
Bimonthly Jewish Critique of Politics, Culture & Society,* Oakland, CA: the
Institute for Labor and Mental Health, September/October 1993, 49-51.

Farnsworth, Clyde H. "An Uneasy Peace -- And No Peace of Mind: In Quebec,
Indians Look back in Anger at Oka Crisis," *San Francisco Sunday Examiner and
Chronicle,* 6 February 1994, *Sunday Punch.*

Fennario, David. *Nothing to Lose.* Play produced the Centaur Theater Company,
November 11, 1976. Directed by Guy Spring; designed by Barbara Matis;
lighting designed by Harry Frehner; stage manager, Michael Benoit. Volume 2,
Issue. Montreal: Rosenfield Printing Co. Ltd., 1976.

Fitchen, Allen, Catharine Seybold, and Bruce Young, eds. *The Chicago Manual of
Style: Thirteenth Edition, Revised and Expanded.* Chicago: The University of
Chicago Press, 1982.

Field, Tiffany; Jaipaul L. Roopnarine, and Marilyn Segal, eds. *Friendships in Normal
and Handicapped Children.* Norwood, New Jersey: Ablex Publishing Corporation,
1984.

Fields-Meyer, Thomas, "This Year's Prophet: With *Tikkun,* His Magazine of the
Jewish Left, and His Catch Phrase 'the Politics of Meaning,' Michael Lerner Has
Become the Clintons' Norman Podhoretz," *The New York Times Magazine,* 27
June 1993, 28-32; 35-36; 61-62.

Fine, Morris, Milton Himmelfarb, and Martha Jelenko, eds. *American Jewish Year
Book: A Record of Events and Trends in American and World Jewish Life.* New

York: The American Jewish Committee, and Philadelphia: The Jewish Publication Society, 1968-1992.

Firth, Raymond William and Judith Djamour. "Kinship in South Borough." In *Two Studies of Kinship in London*, ed. Raymond Firth. University of London: The Athlone Press, 1956.

Fischer, Claude S. *To Dwell among Friends: Personal Networks in Town and City*. Chicago: The University of Chicago Press, 1982.

Fletcher, Joseph F. "Canadian Attitudes toward Jews: Results from a Recent Survey." Prepared for a forum entitled, "Antisemitism in Canada: Perceptions and Realities," at The Triennial Meeting of The Canadian Jewish Congress, Montreal, Quebec, Canada, 7 May 1989.

Fortier, Theodore L. "On Friendship: Its Nature, Kinds, and Effects in Human Life." Ph.D. diss. Quebec City: l'Université Laval, 1970.

Fortin, Andrée. *Histoires de familles et de réseaux: La sociabilité au Québec d'hier à demain*. Montréal: Saint-Martin, 1987.

Fraisse, Jean-Claude. *Philia: La notion d'amitié dans la philosophie antique: Essai sur un problème perdu et retrouvé*. Paris: Philosophique J. Vrin, 1974.

Frankiel, Tamar. *Voice of Sarah: Feminine Spirituality and Traditional Judaism*. San Francisco: Harper, 1990.

Freud, Sigmund. *Group Psychology and the Analysis of the Ego*. Trans. and ed. James Strachey. New York: W. W. Norton and Company, 1959.

Fritz, Jan, W. Maesen, and Pat See, eds. *Clinical Sociology Review* 1 (1982).

Fromm, Erich. *Sigmund Freud's Mission: An Analysis of His Personality and Influence*. New York: Harper & Bros. Publishers, 1959.

The Gage Canadian Dictionary. s.v. "Chum" and "friend - friendship." Toronto: Gage Educational Publishing Ltd., 1973, 203; 467.

Gagnon, N. "Un nouveau type de relations familiales." *Recherches sociographiques* 9 (1968):59-66.

Gallagher, Nora. "Women as Friends," *Playgirl*, May 1976, 46-47, 52.

Gallant, Mavis. "The Doctor," *The New Yorker*, 20 June 1977, 33-42.

Gans, Herbert J. *The Urban Villagers: Group and Class in the Life of Italian-Americans*. New York: The Free Press, A Division of Macmillan Publishing Co., Inc., 1962.

Garfinkel, Harold. *Studies in Ethnomethodology*. Englewood Cliffs, New Jersey: Prentice-Hall, Inc., 1967.

Garigue, Phillipe. *La vie familiale des Canadiens français*. Montreal: Les Presses de l'université de Montréal, 1962.

-----. *Famille et humanisme*. Ottawa: Leméac, 1973.

Gaskell, Jane S. "The Sex-role Ideology of Working-class Girls." *The Canadian Review of Sociology and Anthropology/La revue canadienne de sociologie et d'anthropologie*, 12, 4 (1975): 453-461.

Gautier, Hervé. *Évolution démographique du Québec*. Office de planification et de développement du Québec, 1977.

Gay, Francis. *The Friendship Book*. London: D.C. Thomson & Co., Ltd., 1975.

Geertz, Clifford. *The Interpretation of Cultures*. New York: Basic Books, 1973.

Gelven, Michael. *Winter, Friendship, and Guilt: The Sources of Self-Inquiry*. New York: Harper and Row, Publishers, 1972.

Gibson, D. *et al.*, eds. *Body Politic Gay Liberation Journal*, 25 (July-August) 1976, Pink Triangle Press.

Giordano, Peggy C., Stephen A. Cernkovich, and M.D. Pugh. "Friendships and Delinquency," AJS Volume 91 Number 5 (March 1986): 1170-1202.

Gitlin, Todd. *The Sixties: Years of Hope, Days of Rage*. New York: Bantam Books, 1987.

Glassner, Barry. *Career Crash: The New Crisis and Who Survives*. New York: Simon and Schuster, 1994.

Glassner, Barry and Jonathan A. Freedman. *Clinical Sociology*. New York: Longman, Inc., 1979.

Glazer, Nathan and Daniel P. Moynihan, eds. *Ethnicity: Theory and Experience*. Cambridge, Mass.: Harvard University Press, [1975] 1976.

Glossarium Mediae et Infimae Latinitatis, Tomus 1. s. v. "amiabilis - amicus." Conditum a Cardo du Fresne Domino du Cange: Niort, L. Favre, 1883.

Goethe, Johann Wolfgang von. *Elective Affinities*. Trans. R. J. Hollingdale. Harmondsworth: Penguin Books Ltd., [1809] 1971.

Goffman, Erving. *Relations in Public. Microstudies of the Public Order*. New York: Harper Colophon Books, Harper and Row Publishers, 1971.

Goffman, Erving. *Frame Analysis*. New York: Harper Colophon Books, Harper and Row Publishers, 1974.

Gold, Gerald L. and Marc-Abelard Tremblay. *Communities and Cultures in French Canada*. Toronto: Holt, Rinehard, & Winston, 1973.

Gouldner, Alvin W. *The Coming Crisis of Western Sociology*. New York: Avon Books, 1970.

Gouldner, M. and M. Symons Strong. *Speaking of Friendship: Middle-class Women and Their Friends*. New York and London: Greenwood Press, 1987.

Graham, George and Hugh LaFollette, eds. *Person to Person*. Philadelphia: Temple University Press, 1989.

Grandmont, Pierre de, ed. *Annuaire du Québec 1974*. 54e édition. Gouvernement du Québec. Ministère de l'Industrie et du Commerce. Bureau de la statistique du Québec. Quebec: L'Éditeur officiel du Québec, 1974

------. *Annuaire du Québec 1977/1978*. Gouvernement du Québec. Ministère de l'Industrie et du Commerce. Bureau de la statistique du Québec. Québec: L'Éditeur officiel du Québec, 1979.

Greeley, Andrew M. *The Friendship Game*. Garden City, NY: Doubleday Image Books, 1971.

Green, Mary Jean. "Writing in a Motherland." French Department, Dartmouth College, Hannover, N.H., 1984.

Gurdin, Joseph Barry. "*Amitié*/Friendship: The Socio-cultural Construction of Friendship in Contemporary Montreal." Ph.D. diss., Department of Sociology, l'université de Montréal, 1978.

Gurdin, J. Barry. "Themes from *Amitié*/Friendship: The Socio-cultural Construction of Friendship in Contemporary Montreal" (Brief Report on Recent Research, Session 321, delivered at the 78th annual meeting of the American Anthropological Association, Cincinnati, 1979a), 31.

------. "Friendship between Nurses and Their Patients--An Atypical Case Study" (Paper delivered as part of the session on "Bridging the Gap from Hospital to Home," Fifth Annual Conference ARN/RNI, Association of Rehabilitation Nurses, Chicago, 1979b).

------. "Quebecer and *Québécois:* Same Meaning?" (Paper delivered at the Session on the Lexicon, 79th annual meeting of the American Anthropological Association, Washington, D.C., 6 December 1980).

------. "Friendships" and "Friendship and Mental Health." Theta Cable 12. Interviewer: Margaret Thurmond. Los Angeles, March 12 and 27, 1982a.

Gurdin, J. Barry. "Groups for the Development of Friendship" (Paper and audiovisual presentation delivered at the 31st annual meeting of the Society for the Study of Social Problems, San Francisco, 1982b).

------. "Demonstration of a Friendship Development Group." (Presentation at the annual meeting of the Clinical Sociology Association, Burlingame, California, 1982c).

------. "Naturalistic Categories of Ethnic Identity in Quebec." In *Culture, Ethnicity, and Identity: Current Issues in Research*, ed. Bill McCready, 149-180. New York: Academic Press, 1983a.

------. Book review of Robert Bell's *Worlds of Friendship. Qualitative Sociology* 6 (Winter 1983b): 365-369.

------. "The Therapy of Friendship." *Small Group Behavior* 17 (1986): 444-457.

------. "Groups for the Development of Friendship." *Small Group Behavior* 19 (1988): 57-66.

------. "A Friendship Demonstration." On Artists Embassy International Television Program. Channel 25. San Francisco, 1988.

------. "Styles of Friendship" (Paper delivered at Session on Intimacy and Friendship at the Eighty-fourth annual meeting of the American Sociological Association, San Francisco, 12 August 1989a), 57.

------. "Anti-Semitism in Canada," *Jewish Currents: A Progressive Monthly*, November 1989b): 38-39.

Gurdin, J. Barry and Horst Hutter, "Some of My Best Friends Are ...: The Relationship of Ethnicity to Close Friendship" (Paper delivered at the Thirty-second annual meeting of the Society for the Study of Social Problems, Detroit, 27-30 August 1983b).

Gurdin, Joseph Barry and Horst Hutter. "Some of My Best Friends Are ...: The Relationship of Ethnicity to Close Friendship." *Quebec Studies* 3 (1985): 101-112.

Gurdin, J. Barry, Deena Nardi, Janet R. Reohr, and David Schroder. "The Influence of Propinquity on Urban and Underclass Convalescent Center Residents" (Paper nd videotape presentation delivered at the International Conference on Personal Relationships at the University of Wisconsin-Madison, 1984).

Gurvitch, Georges. *Les cadres sociaux de la connaissance.* Paris: Presses Universitaires de France, 1966.

Guttman, Louis. "A General Nonmetric Technique for Finding the Smallest Coordinate Space for a Configuration of Points." *Psychometrika*, 33 (1968): 469-506.

Habermas, Jürgen. "The German Idealism of the Jewish Philosophers." In *Philosophical-Political Profiles*. Cambridge, Massachusetts: The MIT Press, 1983.

Hagoel, Leah. "Urban Friendships: Qualitative and Quantitative Aspects of Primary Relations in an Urban Community Context." Ph.D. diss., University of Minnesota, 1980.

Handlin, Oscar. *Race and Nationality in American Life*. Garden City, New York: Doubleday Anchor Books, 1950.

Halperin, Ian. "Canadian Paper Apologizes for Slander," *Washington Jewish Week*, 29 (30 January 1986).

Hamer, Dean H., Stella Hu, Victoria L. Magnuson, Nan Hu, and Angela M. L. Pattalucci. "A Linkage Between DNA Markers on the X Chromosome and Male Sexual Orientation," *Science*, 16 July 1993, 321-327.

Hannerz, Ulf. *Soulside*. New York: Columbia University Press, 1969.

Hayes, Robert B. "The Development and Maintenance of Friendship." *Journal of Social and Personal Relationships* 1 (1984): 75-98. London: Sage Publications, Ltd.

Hess, Beth. "Friendship." In *Aging and Society: A Sociology of Age Stratification* 3, eds. Matilda White Riley, M. Johnson, and A. Foner, 357-393. New York: Russell Sage, 1972.

Hess, Beth. "Foreword." In *Older Adult Friendship: Structure and Process*, eds. Adams, Rebecca G., and Rosemary Blieszner, 7-9. Newbury Park, CA: Sage Publications, 1989.

Hill, Frederick I., ed. *Canadian Urban Trends*. Vol. 2 (of 3 Vol.) Toronto: Copp Clark Publishing, 1976.

Historisches Wörterbuch der Philosophie. Band 2. D-F, ed. Joachim Ritter, 1104-1114, s.v. "Freund/Feind" and "Freundschaft." Verlag. Base/Stutgart: Schwabe and Co., 1972.

Hoppe, Art. "Friendship's End," *San Francisco Sunday Examiner and Chronicle*, 27 June 1993, *Sunday Punch*.

Hoppe, Art. "A Slow Death," *San Francisco Sunday Examiner and Chronicle*, 26 September 1993, *Sunday Punch.*

Horowitz, Irving Louis. *The Decomposition of Sociology* (New York: Oxford University Press, 1994).

Hume, David. *A Treatise on Human Nature. Book III. Of Morals*. London: Oxford University Press, [1740] 1973.

Husserl, Edmund. *Formale und transzendentale Logik. Versuch einer Kritik der logischen Vernuft (Formal and Transcendental Logic)*. Halle: a. S. Max Nijmeyer, 1929.

------. *Ideas: General Introduction to Pure Phenomenology*. Translated by W. R. Gibson. London: Collier Macmillan Publishers, [1913] [1931] 1975.

Hutchins, R. M. *The Great Ideas. A Syntopicon of Great Books of the Western World*, Vol. 1. Toronto: Encyclopaedia Britannica, 1952.

Hutter, Horst. "The Symposium: Eros, Philia, and the Doctrine of Political Harmony in Plato" (Paper delivered at the Canadian Political Science Association's Annual meeting, Quebec City, June, 1976).

------. *The Politics of Friendship* [This is the original manuscript], 1977.

------ *Politics as Friendship*. Waterloo, Ontario: Wilfrid Laurier University Press, 1978.

Ishwaran, Karigoudar, ed. *The Canadian Family: A Book of Readings*. Toronto: Holt, Rinehart & Winston of Canada Ltd., 1971.

Issacs, Harold R. "Idols of the Tribe: Group Identity and Political Change." In *Ethnicity: Theory and Experience*, eds. Glazer, Nathan and Daniel P. Moynihan, 29 -52. Cambridge, Mass.: Harvard University Press, 1976.

James, Muriel and Louis M. Savary. *The Heart of Friendship*. New York: Harper & Row, Publishers, 1976.

Jaques, Elliott. "The Method of Social Analysis in Social Change and Research." *Clinical Sociology Review* 1 (1982): 50-55.

Jean, Michèle, Jacqueline Lamothe, Marie Lavigne, and Jennifer Stoddart. "Nationalism and Feminism in Quebec: The 'Yvettes' Phenomenon." In *The Politics of Diversity*, eds. Roberta Hamilton and Michèle Barrett. London: Verso, 1986.

Johnson, David W. and Frank P. Johnson. *Joining Together. Group Theory and Group Skills*. Englewood Cliffs, New Jersey: Prentice Hall, 1975.

Jones, Sir H. S. *A Greek English Lexicon. A New Edition*, Vol. 2. Oxford: Oxford at the Clarendon Press. [1934] 1951.

Juteau-Lee, Danielle, ed. "Enjeu ethniques: production de nouveau rapports sociaux." *Sociologie et sociétés*, Vol. XV, 2 (octobre 1983).

Kadushin, Charles. "Living up to Promises: Network Studies Come of Age." *Contemporary Sociology: An International Journal of Reviews* 19 (January 1990): 135-137.

Kant, Emmanuel. *Fundamental Principals of the Metaphysic of Morals. Great Books of the Western World*.Vol. 42. Trans. Thomas Kingsmill Abbott. Toronto: Encyclopaedia Britannica, [1785] 1952.

Kardiner, Abraham. *My Analysis with Freud: Reminiscences*. New York: W.W. Norton, 1977.

Kaufman, Sharon R. *The Ageless Self: Sources of Meaning in Late Life*. Madison: University of Wisconsin Press, 1987.

Kelley, H.. H., E. Berscheid, A. Christensen, J. H. Harvey, T.L. Huston, G. Levinger, E. McClintock, L. A. Peplau, and D. R. Peterson. "Analyzing Close Relationships." In *Close Relationships*, H. H. Kelley *et al.*, 20-67. New York: Freeman, 1983.

Kemper, Theodore D. *A Social Interactional Theory of Emotions*. New York: Wiley, 1978.

------ "Love and Like and Love and Love" (Paper delivered at the American Sociological Association, 1983).

King, Henry Churchill. *The Laws of Friendship: Human and Divine*. New York: The Macmillan Company, 1921.

Kockelmans, Joseph J., ed. *Phenomenology: The Philosophy of Edmund Husserl and Its Interpretation*. Garden City, New York: Anchor Books Doubleday and Company, Inc., 1967.

Kohn, Melvin L. *Cross-National Research in Sociology*. Newbury Park, CA: Sage Publications, 1989.

Koulack, David and Daniel Perlman, eds. *Readings in Social Psychology. Focus on Canada*. Toronto: Wiley Publishers of Canada Ltd., 1973.

Kupers, Terry A. "Menfriends: Others Shy away from and Define as 'Too Needy' the Man Who Wants to Build Close Male Friendships." *Tikkun: A BiMonthly Jewish Critique of Politics, Culture & Society*, March/April 1993, 54.

Lacaze-Duthiers, Gérard de. *Les chemins de l'amitié*. Paris: Les amis de
     l'artistocratie, P. Clairac, Éditeur, 1948.

Laferrière, Michel. "L'éducation des enfants des groupes minoritaires au
     Québec: De la définition des problèmes par les groupes eux-mêmes à
     l'intervention de l'état." *Sociologie et sociétés*, Vol. XV, 2 (octobre 1983), ed.
     Danielle Juteau-Lee, (1983), 117-132.

La Gaipa, John J. "A Systems Approach to Personal Relationships." In *Personal
     Relationships: 1. Studying Personal Relationships*, ed. Steve Duck and Robin
     Gilmour, 169-189. New York: Academic Press, 1981.

------. "Rules and Rituals in Disengaging from Relationships." In *Personal
     Relationships. 4: Dissolving Personal Relationships*, ed. Steve Duck, 189-210. New
     York: Academic Press, 1982.

La Gaipa, John J. and Brian J. Bigelow. "The Development of Childhood
     Friendship Expectations" (Paper delivered at the meeting of the Canadian
     Psychological Association, 1972).

La Gaipa, John J. and H. Diane Wood. "Friendship in Disturbed Adolescents." In
     Personal Relationships. 3: Personal Relationships, in Disorder, ed. Steve Duck and
     Robin Gilmour, 169-189. New York: Academic Press, 1981.

Laing, R. D. *The Voice of Experience*. New York: Pantheon Books, 1982.

Laing, R. D. and D. G. Cooper. *Reason and Violence. A Decade of Sartre's
     Philosophy*. London: Tavistock Publications, 1964.

Laing, R. D. and A. Esterson. *Sanity, Madness and the Family*. Harmondsworth:
     Penguin Books Ltd., 1970.

Laliberté, Robert. "Étude comparative des parents et des enfants de différentes
     classes sociales." Chap. 4 in *Aliénation et idéologie dans la vie quotidienne des
     Montréalais francophones*. Vol. 1, eds. Yves Lamarche, Marcel Rioux, et Robert
     Sévigny, 173-276. Montréal: Les Presses de l'université de Montréal, 1973.

Lamarche, Yves, Marcel Rioux, et Robert Sévigny, eds. *Aliénation et idéologie dans la
     vie quotidienne des Montréalais francophones*. Vol. 2. Montréal: Les Presses de
     l'université de Montréal, 1973.

Lambert, Wallace E. "What Are They Like, These Canadians? A Social-
     Psychological Analysis." In *Readings in Social Psychology. Focus on Canada*, eds.
     Koulack, P. and D. Perlman, 30-48. Toronto: Wiley Publishers of Canada Ltd.,
     1973.

Langevin, Serge. "L'amitié homme-femme, ça se peut!" 4, 9 *Nous* Montreal: Nous Magazine Limitée, 1977, 51, 71-72.

Larson, Hal. *You Are My Friend: A Celebration of Friendship*. San Francisco, CA: Halo Books.

Larson, L. E. *The Canadian Family in Comparative Perspective*. Scarborough, Ontario: Prentice-Hall of Canada Ltd., 1976.

Lasch, Christopher. *The Culture of Narcissism: American Life in an Age of Diminishing Expectations*. New York: Norton, 1978.

Latham, R. E. "Amicus." In *Revised Medieval Latin Word List from British and Irish Sources*. London: Oxford University Press, 1965, 18.

Lauer, Quentin. "Evidence." In *Phenomenology: The Philosophy of Edmund Husserl and Its Interpretation*, ed. J. L. Kockelmans. Garden City, New York: Doubleday Co., Inc., 1967.

Lazure, Jacques. *Le jeune couple non-marié: une nouvelle forme de revolution sexuelle*. Montréal: Presses de l'Université du Québec, 1975.

Leacy, F. H. *Historical Statistics of Canada: Second Edition*. Ottawa: Statistics Canada, 1981.

Lee, John Alan. *Colours of Love*. Toronto: New Press, 1973.

Leefeldt, Christine and Ernest Callenbach. *The Art of Friendship*. New York: Pantheon Books, 1979.

Lejeune, Jean Paul, "The Economy--between the Boom Times and New Expansion: Interview with Jean Guertin, Director, École des Hautes Études Commerciales, Montréal," *Forces: Economic, Social and Cultural Quarterly*, ed. Couture, Marcel, 78-81. Montréal: la Société d'édition de la revue Forces, 100 (Hiver 1992-1993).

Lepp, Ignace. *Les chemins de l'amitié*. Paris: Bernard Grasset Éditeur, 1964.

Lerner, Michael, ed. *Tikkun: A Bi-Monthly Jewish Critique of Politics, Culture, and Society*, September/October, Volume 2/ No. 4, 1987.

Lerner, Michael. *The Socialism of Fools: Anti-Semitism on the Left*. Oakland, CA: Tikkun Books, 1992.

------. *Surplus Powerlessness: The Psychodynamics of Everyday Life ... And the Psychology of Individual and Social Transformation*. Oakland, CA: The Institute for Labor and Mental Health, 1986.

Levy, Shlomit and Louis Gutttman. "On the Multivariate Structure of Wellbeing." In *Multidimensional Data Representations: When and Why*, ed. Ingwer Borg, 125-52. Mathesis Press: Ann Arbor, Michigan, 1981.

Levy, Shlomit and Louis Gutttman. *Structure and Level of Values for Rewards and Allocation Criteria in Several Life Areas*." In *Multidimensional Data Representations: When and Why*, ed. Ingwer Borg, 153-192.. Ann Arbor, Michigan: Mathesis Press, 1981.

Lewis, Edward and Robert Myers, eds. *To Be a Friend*. Kansas City, Missouri: Hallmark Cards, Inc., 1967.

Lewis, Paul. "Stoked by Ethnic Fighting, Refugee Numbers Grow," *The New York Times*, 10 November 1993, A1.

Lexicon Totius Latinitatis Tom 1. s.v. "Amicabilis, e - amicus." AB Aeugidio Forcellini: Arnaldus Forni Excudebat Bonoiae Gregoriana Edente Patavii, 1965.

Leyton, Elliott, ed. *The Compact: Selected Dimensions of Friendship* Toronto: University of Toronto Press [for Memorial University of Newfoundland], 1974.

Liebow, Elliot. *Tally's Corner. A Study of Negro Streetcorner Men*. Boston: Little, Brown and Company, 1967.

Lindsey, Karen. *Friends as Family*. Boston: Beacon Press, 1981.

Lingoes, James C. "The Multivariate Analysis of Qualitative Data." In *Geometric Representations of Relational Data: Readings in Multidimensional Scaling*, eds. James C. Lingoes, Edward E. Roskam, and Ingwer Borg, 575-608. Ann Arbor, Michigan: Mathesis Press, 1979.

Lingoes, James C., Edward E. Roskam, and Ingwer Borg. *Geometric Representations of Relational Data: Readings in Multidimensional Scaling*. Ann Arbor, Michigan: Mathesis Press, 1979.

Lipset, Seymour Martin. *The First New Nation. The United States in Historical and Comparative Perspective*. Garden City, New York: Doubleday, 1967.

------. *Continental Divide: The Values and Institutions of the United States and Canada*. New York: Routledge, 1990.

Lipsiae in aidibus, Vol. 1, s.v. "Amicabilis, e - amicitia, ae," and "amicus - amicus," B. G. Tevbner, 1900.

Littré dictionnaire de la langue française, Tome 1, s.v. "Ami, ie - amitié." Monte Carlo: Édition du Cap, 1970.

Litwak, E and I. Szelenyi. "Primary Groups, Structures and Their Functions: Kin, Neighbors and Friends," *American Sociological Review* 34 (1969): 465-81.

Lucas, R. A. *Minetown, Milltown, Railtown. Life in Canadian Communities of Single Industry*. Toronto: University of Toronto Press, 1971.

Luckman, Thomas, ed. *Phenomenology and Sociology: Selected Readings*. Harmondsworth: Penguin Books Ltd., 1978.

Lukes, S. *Emile Durkheim. His Life and Work: An Historical and Critical Study*. Harmondsworth: Penguin Books Ltd., 1973.

Lynch, Frederick R. "Chapter 9: Affirmative Action, The University, and Sociology." In *Invisible Victims: White Males and the Crisis of Affirmative Action*, 119-139. New York: Praeger, 1991.

Lynch, J. J. *The Broken Heart: The Medical Consequences of Loneliness*. New York: Basic Books, 1977.

Lytton, Hugh and David M. Romney. "Parents' Differential Socialization of Boys and Girls: A Meta-Analysis." *Psychological Bulletin* 109 (1991): 267-291;287.

Maas, James. *Speaking of Friends: The Variety of Man-to-Man Friendships*. Berkeley, CA: Shameless Hussy Press, 1985.

MacDonald, D. "Sex and Social Participation," *Chatelaine*, March 1974.

MacLennan, Hugh. *Two Solitudes*. Toronto: Macmillan Company, 1945.

Maisonneuve, Jean. *Psycho-sociologie des affinités*. Paris: Presses Universitaires de France, 1966.

Maisonneuve, Jean and Lubomir Lamy. *Psycho-sociologie de l'amitié*. Paris: Presses Universitaires de France, 1993.

Marsan, Jean-Claude. *Montreal in Evolution: Historical Analysis of the Development of Montreal's Architecture and Urban Environment*. Montreal: McGill-Queen's University Press, 1981.

Martineau, Richard. "Gilles Carle: le facteur temps," *Voir* du 16 au 22 avril 1992, 12.

Marty, Martin E. *Friendship*. Allen, Texas: Argus Communications, 1980.

Marx, Karl. *Manuscrits de 1844*. Paris: Ed Sociales, 1844.

Marx, Karl and Friedrich Engels. *Karl Marx Friedrich Engels Werke*. Band 31. Berlin: Dietz Verlag, [1864-1867] 1965.

Maslow, Abraham H. *Religions, Values, and Peak Experiences*. Columbus, Ohio: State University Press, 1964.

Matthews, Sarah H. *Friendship through the Life Course: Oral Biographies in Old Age.* Newbury Park: Sage Publications, 1986.

Maurina, Zenta. *Verfremdung und Freundschaft (Alienation and Friendship. Essays).* Memmingen/Allgau: Dietrich, 1966.

McCall, George J. "The Social Organization of Relationships." In *Social Relationships,* ed. George J. McCall, 3-34. Chicago: Aldine, 1970.

McCall, George. "The Organizational Life Cycle of Relationships." In *A Handbook of Personal Relationships,* eds. Steve W. Duck *et al.* Chichester: Wiley, 1988.

McFeat, Tom. *Small-group Cultures.* New York: Pergamon Press, 1974.

McGregor, Gaile. *The Wacousta Syndrome: Explorations in the Canadian Landscape.* Toronto: University of Toronto Press, 1985.

McKenna, Brian and Susan Purcell. *Drapeau.* Markham, Ontario: Penguin Books, Ltd., 1980.

Mehan, Hugh and Houston Wood. *The Reality of Ethnomethodology.* New York: John Wiley and Sons, 1975.

Meilaender, Gilbert C. *Friendship: A Study in Theological Ethics.* Notre Dame, Indiana: University of Notre Dame Press, 1981.

Merleau-Ponty, Maurice. "Difficulties Involved in a Subordination of Psychology." In *The Primary Perception and Other Essays,* ed. James M. Edie, 64-78; 499-500. Evanston, Illinois: Northwestern University Press, 1964.

Metzger, N.J. and G.M. Phillips. *Intimate Communication.* Boston: Allyn and Bacon, 1976.

Michaelis, David. *The Best of Friends. Profiles of Extraordinary Friendships.* New York: William Morrow and Co., 1983.

Milardo, Robert M. "Personal Choice and Social Constraint in Close Relationships: Applications of a Network Analysis." In *Friendship and Social Interaction,* eds. V. J. Derlega and B.A. Winstead. New York: Springer, 1986.

Miller, Stuart. *Men and Friendship.* Boston: Houghton Mifflin Company, 1983.

Miner, Horace. *St. Denis: A French Canadian Parish.* Chicago: University of Chicago Press, 1939.

Mitchell, W. E. "Amicatherapy: Theoretical Perspectives and an Example of Practice." *Community Mental Health Journal,* Vol. 2, (Winter 1966).

Montagu, Ashley. *Touching: The Human Significance of the Human Skin*. New York: Columbia University Press, 1971.

Montaigne, Michel de. *Essays*, trans. J. M. Cohen. Harmondsworth: Penguin Books Ltd., [1580] 1958.

Moreux, Colette. *Fin d'une religion? Monographie d'une paroisse canadienne-française*. Montréal: Presses de l'université de Montréal, 1969.

Myers, Robert and Edward Lewis. *To Be a Friend: Sayings and Verses Celebrating the Beauty of Friendship*. Kansas City, Missouri: Hallmark Cards, Incorporated, 1967.

Naegale, Vedi K. "Friendship and Acquaintances: An Exploration of some social distinctions." *Harvard Educational Review* 28 (1958): 232-253.

Nagel, Joane and Susan Olzak. "Ethnic Mobilization in New and Old States: An Extension of the Competition Model." *Social Problems* 30 (1982): 127-143.

Nardi, Peter M., ed. *Men's Friendships*. Newbury Park, CA: Sage Publications, 1992.

Nardi, Peter M. "Sex, Friendship, and Gender Roles among Gay Men." In *Men's Friendship*, 173-152. Newbury Park, CA: Sage Publications, Inc., 1992.

Natanson, Maurice. "Phenomenology: A Viewing." In *Literature, Philosophy, and the Social Sciences*. The Hague: Nijhoff, 1962.

Neamtan, Nancy. "Descendants de prostituées et antisémites congénitaux: Les anglophones du Canada doivent dénoncer Mordecai Richler," *Le Devoir*, 19 mars 1992, B-8.

Newman, Peter C. *The Canadian Establishment*. Toronto: McClelland and Stewart Limited, (1975) 1977.

Newman, Philip L. *Knowing the Gururumba*. New York: Holt, Rinehart & Winston, 1965.

Noël, Lise. *L'intolérance: une problématique générale*. Montréal: Les Éditions du Boréal, 1989.

O'Connor, Pat. *Friendships between Women: A Critical Review*. New York: The Guilford Press, 1992.

The Oxford Dictionary of English Etymology, ed. Charles Talbut Onions. Oxford: Clarendon Press, 1966.

The Oxford English Dictionary Being a Corrected Re-issue with an Introduction, Supplement, and Bibliography of a New English Dictionary on Historical Principles Founded Mainly on the Materials Collected by The Philological Society,

Volume 4, F-G, s.v. "Friend, friendship." Oxford: Oxford at the Clarendon Press, 1933.

OED. *The Oxford English Dictionary*. Oxford: Clarendon Press, 1961.

Oliker, Stacey J. *Best Friends and Marriage: Exchange among Women*. Berkeley: University of California Press, 1989.

Ouaknine, Serge. "De la haine de soi à l'obscurcissement d'autrui," *Le Devoir*, 19 mars 1992, B-8.

Ouellet, Danielle. "An Interview with Guy Rocher, Sociologist. Benchmarks of a Changing Society," *Forces: Economic, Social and Cultural Quarterly*, ed. Couture, Marcel, 22-25. Montréal: la Société d'édition de la revue Forces, 100 (Hiver 1992-1993).

Ouellet, Danielle. "Bilan de société: Repères pour une société en mutation, avec le sociologue Guy Rocher," *Le Devoir*, 6 Février 1993, A 11.

Packard, Vance. *The Status Seekers: An Exploration of Class Behavior in America*. London: Longmans, 1959.

Paine, Robert. "In Search of Friendship: An Exploratory Analysis in 'Middle-Class Culture.' " *Man, The British Journal of Social Anthropology*, January, 1970.

------. "An Exploratory Analysis in 'Middle-Class' Culture." In *The Compact: Selected Dimensions of Friendship*, ed. Elliott Leyton, 117-137. Toronto: University of Toronto Press [for Memorial University of Newfoundland], 1974.

Paré, Isabelle. "Montréal, capitale de la pauvreté: 22% des Montréalais vivent sous le seuil de la pauvreté; plus qu'à Saint-Jean, Terre-Neuve." *Le Devoir*, 14 avril 1993, A-1, A-8.

Parenteau, Eric, "Le Tableau de la Honte: L'antisémitisme au Québec, de 1807 à 1960. À noter qu'on retrouvait des racistes partout, tant à McGill qu'à l'université de Montréal," *Voir* du 16 au 22 avril 1992, 10.

Parsons, Talcott. *Essays in Sociological Theory Pure and Applied*. Glencoe, Illinois: Free Press, 1954.

Perel, Shloime and Henry Srebernik. "Signs of the Times." *Jerusalem Post*, 22 January 1982.

------. "Signes des temps." *Le Devoir*, 17 février 1982, 9.

------. "Montreal Jews and the *Jerusalem Post* Affair." *Israel Horizons*, September/October 1982, 12-15.

Perlman, Daniel. "The Sexual Standards of Canadian University Students." In *Readings in Social Psychology: Focus on Canada*, eds. Koulack, David and Daniel Perlman. Toronto: Wiley Publishers of Canada Limited, 173, 139-160.

Perlman, Daniel and Letitia Anne Peplau. "Toward a Social Psychology of Loneliness." In *Personal Relationships. 3: Personal Relationships, in Disorder*, ed. Steve Duck and Robin Gilmour, 31-56. New York: Academic Press, 1981.

Petit, Paul. *La Paix Romaine*. Paris: Presses universitaires de France, 1971.

Petrowski, Nathalie. *Notes de la salle de rédaction*. Montréal: Les Éditions coopératives Albert Saint-Martin de Montreal, 1983.

Piddington, R. "A Study of French Canadian Kinship." In *Readings in Kinship in Urban Society*, ed. C. C. Harris, 71-98. Toronto: Pergamon Press, 1970.

Plato. *The Works of Plato: A New and Literal Version, Chiefly from the Texts of Stallbaum*. Bohn's Classical Library. Vol. 4 of 6 Vols. Trans. George Burges. London: G. Bell & Sons, 1854-1911.

Pogrebin, Letty Cottin. *Among Friends: Who We Like, Why We Like Them, and What We Do with Them*. New York: McGraw-Hill Book Company, 1987.

------. *Deborah, Golda, and Me: Being Female and Jewish in America* New York: Doubleday, 1991.

Pool, Robert. "Evidence for Homosexuality Gene: A Genetic Analysis of 40 Pairs of Homosexual Brothers Has Uncovered a Region on the X Chromosome That Appears to Contain a Gene or Genes for Homosexuality," *Science*, 16 July 1993, 291-292.

Porter, John. *The Vertical Mosaic. An Analysis of Social Class and Power in Canada*. Toronto: University of Toronto Press, [1965] 1968.

------. *The Vertical Mosaic: An Analysis of Social Class and Power in Canada*. Toronto: University of Toronto Press, [1975] 1976.

Postgate, D., K. McRoberts, and J. Biggs. *Quebec Social Change and Political Crises*. Toronto: McClelland and Stewart Ltd., 1976.

Rafky, David M. "Phenomenology and Socialization: Some Comments on the Assumptions Underlying Socialization Theory." In *Childhood and Socialization*, ed. Hans Peter Dreitzel. New York: Macmillan Publishing Co., Inc., 1973.

Ramsoy, O. "Friendship." In *International Encyclopedia of the Social Sciences*, Vol. 6, ed. David L. Shills. New York: Macmillan Co. and The Free Press, 1968.

Rawlins, William K. *Friendship Matters: Communication, Dialectics, and the Life Course.* New York: Aldine de Gruyter, 1992.

Ray, D. Michael, ed. *Canadian Urban Trends.* Volume 2. Toronto: Copp Clark Publishing, 1976-1977.

Reisman, John M. *Anatomy of Friendship.* New York: Irvington Publishers, Inc., 1979.

Reisman, John M. and T. Yamokoski. "Psychotherapy and Friendship: An Analysis of the Communications of Friends." *Journal of Counseling Psychology* 21 (1974).

Reiss, Ira.L. "The Role of Sexuality in the Study of Family and Fertility" (Paper delivered at the conference on "Family and Fertility," sponsored by the Center for Population Research and the National Institute for Child Health and Human Development, Belmont, Elkridge, Maryland. Mimeographed, June 13-16, 1973).

Reohr, Janet. "The Place of Reciprocity in Friendship." Ph.D. diss., Boston University, 1978.

Rhéaume, Jacques and Robert Sévigny. *Sociologie implicite des intervenants en santé mentale.* Vol. 1, *Les pratiques alternatives: du groupe d'entraide au groupe spirituel.* Montréal: Les Éditions Saint-Martin, 1988.

------. *Sociologie implicite des intervenants en santé mentale.* Vol. 2, *La pratique psychothérapeutique: de la croissance à la guérison.* Montréal: Les Éditions Saint-Martin, 1988.

Richler, Mordecai. *Oh Canada! Oh Quebec: Requiem for a Divided Country.* Toronto: Penguin Books, 1992.

Rioux, Marcel. *Les québécois. Le temps qui court.* Bourges: l:Imprimerie Tardy Quercy Auvergne, 1977, 87-113.

Rioux, Marcel and Yves Martin. 1964. *French Canadian Society.* Toronto: McClelland and Stewart Ltd.

Rivers, Susan. "Swelling Ranks of Refugees Seek Asylum: Increasingly Tough Fight Faces Those Who Claim to Be in Flight from Tyranny." *San Francisco Examiner and Chronicle,* 27 June 1993, B1; B4.

Robertson, Michael. "Dusting off the Doctorates: Can Yesterday's Victims of the Ph.D. Glut Resurrect Their Lost Careers?" *San Francisco Chronicle,* 8 August 1990, B 3; B 5.

Rocher, Guy. "Benchmarks of a Changing Society," *Forces: Economic, Social, and Cultural Quarterly*, ed. Couture, Marcel, 22-25. Montréal: la Société d'édition de la revue Forces, 100 (Hiver 1992-1993).

Roloff, Michael E. and Charles R. Berger. *Social Cognition and Communication*. Beverly Hills, California: Sage Publications, 1982.

Ronquist, Eyvind. "Friendship in Lawrence of Durham" (Paper delivered at the Concordia University Colloquium on Friendship, March, 1977).

Ronquist, Eyvind. "Friendship in Laurence of Durham." In *Classica et Mediaevalia: Revue. danoise de philologie et d'histoire* 35 (1984): 191-213.

Roy, Jean-Hugues. "L'Affaire Richler a relancé le débat: Le Québec est-il AntiSémite?" *Voir* du 16 au 22 avril 1992, 5-6.

Roy, Jean-Hugues. "Bonsoir Shalom: Quatre ans après l'affaire de la synagogue de la rue Durocher, les communautés hassidique et francophone d'Outremont croisent le fer à nouveau. Le prétexte: une synagogue <<clandestine>>, qui loge dans une ancienne épicerie," *Voir* du 16 au 22 avril 1992, 8-9.

Ryerson, Stanley B. *French Canada*. New York: International Publishers, 1943.

Rubin, Lillian B. *Intimate Strangers. Men and Women Together*. New York: Harper and Row Publishers, 1983.

Rubin, Lillian B. *Just Friends: The Role of Friendship in Our Lives*. New York: Harper & Row Publishers, 1985.

Rubin, Zick. *Children's Friendships*. Cambridge, Massachusetts: Harvard University Press, 1980.

Runcie, J. F. "Participant Observation of a Small Group." In *Experiencing Social Research Revised Edition*. Homewood, Illinois: The Dorsey Press, 1980.

Saint-Exupery, Antoine de. *Le Petit Prince*. Paris: Librairie Gallimard, 1946.

Salaman, G. *Community and Occupation: An Exploration of World Leisure Relationships*. Cambridge: Cambridge University Press, 1974.

Sales, Arnaud. *La bourgeoisie industrielle au Québec*. Montréal: Les Presses de l'université de Montréal, 1979.

Sancton, Andrew. *Governing the Island of Montreal: Language Differences in Metropolitan Politics*. Berkeley: University of California Press.

Sartre, Jean Paul. *Critique de la raison dialectique*. Paris: Gallimard, 1980.

------. *L'idiot de la famille. Gustave Flaubert de 1821 à 1857*. Paris: Gallimard, 1971.

Scanzoni, Letha and John Scanzoni. *Men, Women, and Change: A Sociology of Marriage and Family*. New York: McGraw Hill Book Company, 1976.

Schatzman, Leonard and Anselm L. Strauss. *Field Strategies for a Natural Sociology*. Englewood Cliffs, New Jersey: Prentice-Hall, 1973.

Schofield, Janet. "Complementary and Conflicting Identities: Images and Interaction in an Interracial School." In *The Development of Children's Friendships,* ed. Steven Asher and John M. Gottman, 53-90. Cambridge: Cambridge University Press, 1981.

Schofield, W. "The Psychotherapist as Friend." *Humanitas Journal of the Institute of Man* [Issue: Personal Growth Through the Friendship Encounter] , Vol. 6, 2 (Fall, 1970): 211-223.

Schur, Edwin M. *The Awareness Trap: Self-absorption instead of Social Change*. New York: Quadrangle Books, 1976.

Schutz, Alfred. *The Phenomenology of the Social World*, trans. George Walsh and Frederick Lehnert with an introduction by George Walsh. London: Heinemann Educational Books, [1932] 1972.

Seidler, Victor, J. "Rejection, Vulnerability, and Friendship." In *Men's Friendships*, ed. Peter M. Nardi, 15-34. Newbury Park, CA: Sage Publications, 1992.

Selman, Robert L. "The Child as a Friendship Philosopher." In Chap. 9: *The Development of Children's Friendships*, eds. Steven R. Asher and John M. Gottman, 242-272. Cambridge: Cambridge University Press, 1981.

Sévigny, Robert. *L'expérience religieuse chez les jeunes. Une étude psychosociologique de l'actualisation de soi*. Montréal: Les Presses de l'université de Montréal, 1971.

------. *Le Québec en héritage: La vie de trois familles montréalaises*. Laval, Québec: Éditions coopératives Albert Saint-Martin, 1979.

Sévigny, Robert and Pierre Guimond. "Psycho-sociologie de l'actualisation de soi. Quelques problèmes de validation." *Sociologie et sociétés* 1-2 (1969-70). Montréal: Les Presses de l'université de Montréal.

Sharabany, R. "Girlfriend, Boyfriend: Age and Sex Differences in Intimate Friendship." *Developmental Psychology*, 17 (1981): 800-808.

Sheldon, Michael. "Francophone Women Are Different." *The Montreal Star,* September 25, 1976, Business Today, Section H-I.

Shore, Marlene. *The Science of Social Redemption: McGill, the Chicago School, and the Origins of Social Research in Canada.* Toronto: University of Toronto Press, 1987.

Shragge, Eric, Ronald Babin, and Jean-Guy Vaillancourt. *Roots of Peace: The Movement against Militarism in Canada.* Toronto: DEC Book Distribution, 1986.

Shye, Samuel, ed. *Theory Construction and Data Analysis in the Behavioral Sciences: A Volume in Honor of Louis Guttman.* San Francisco: Jossey-Bass Publishers, 1978.

Silver, A. "Friendship in Commercial Society: Eighteenth-Century Social Theory and Modern Sociology." In *American Journal of Sociology*, 95, 1474-1504, cited in *Adult Friendship* by Rosemary Blieszner and Rebecca G. Adams, 30-31. Newbury Park: Sage Publications, 1992.

Simmel, Georg. *The Sociology of Georg Simmel*, trans. and ed. Kurt H. Wolff. New York: Free Press, [1908] 1964.

Singer, David and Ruth R. Seldin, eds. *The American Jewish Year Book: A Record of Events and Trends in American and World Jewish Life* 92. New York: The American Jewish Committee, 1992, 97.

Sirois, Antoine. *Montréal dans le roman canadien.* Montréal: Marcel Didier, 1968.

Skolnick, Arlene. *The Intimate Environment. Exploring Marriage and the Family.* New York: Little, 1973.

Slater, Philip. *The Pursuit of Loneliness: American Culture at the Breaking Point.* Boston: Beacon Press, 1970.

Smith, Adam. *Theory of Moral Sentiments.* New York: Garland Publishing Inc., [1759] 1971.

Spinoza, B. *Ethics and De Intellectus Emendatione.* Trans. A. Boyle. New York: Dutton, [1632-1677].

Srebernik, Henry. "Les Juifs: Canadiens ou Québécois?" *Le Devoir* 30 mars 1982, 7.

Srole, Leo, Thomas Lagner, Stanley T. Michael, Marvin K. Opler and Thomas A. C. Rennie. *Mental Health in the Metropolis: the Midtown Manhattan Study.* New York: Blakiston Division, McGraw Hill, 1962.

Stählin,G. *Theological Dictionary of the New Testament.* Trans. and ed. Geoffrey W. Bromiley; ed. Gerhard Friedrich, 113-171. Grand Rapids, Michigan: William B. Eerdmans Publishing Co., 1974.

Stephenson, Marylee, ed. *Women in Canada.* Toronto: New Press, 1973.

Stern, Chaim, *Gates of Prayer: The New Union Prayerbook. Fifth Printing*. New York: Central Conference of American Rabbis, 1979.

Sternberg, David. *How to Complete and Survive a Doctoral Dissertation*. New York: St. Martin's Press, 1981.

Stoler, Peter. "Land of Hope and Hustle," *Time Magazine*, 5 October 1987, 37-38.

Strauss, A. L. *The Contexts of Social Mobility: Ideology and Culture*. Chicago: Aldine Publishing Co., 1971.

Sudnow, David. *Studies in Social Interaction*. New York: The Free Press, 1972.

Sutherland, S. L. and E. Tanenbaum. "Rokeach's Value Survey in Use." *The Canadian Review of Sociology and Anthropology / La revue canadienne de sociologie et d'anthropologie* 75, 12 (November, 1975): 551-564.

Suttie, Ian D. *The Origin of Love and Hate*. London: Kegan Paul, Trench Trubner and Company, Ltd., [1935] 1939.

Suttles, Gerry D. "Friendship as a Social Institution." In *Social Relationships*, ed. George McCall *et al.*, 95-135. Chicago: Aldine Publ. Co., 1970.

Tönnies, Ferdinand. *Community and Society*. Trans. Charles Loomis East Lansing: Michigan State University Press, [1887] 1957.

Tremblay, Michel. *L'Impromptu d'Outremont*. Leméac, collection Théatre Leméac, numéro 86, 1980.

------. *Les anciennes odeurs*. Leméac, collection Théater Lemeac, numéro 106, 1981.

Trésor de la langue française. Dictionnaire de la langue du XIXe et du XXe siècle (1789-1960). Centre National de la Recherche Scientifique. Centre de Recherche pour un Trésor de la Langue Française-Nancy. Tome Deuxième: Affinerie - Anfractuosité. ed. Paul Imbs. Paris: Éditions du Centre National de la Recherche Scientifique, 1973.

Triesman, D. "The Radical Use of Official Data." In *Reconstructing Social Psychology*, ed. Nigel Armistead, 295-313. Markham, Ontario: Penguin Books Ltd., 1974.

Troyat, H. *An Intimate Friendship (Une extrême amitié)*, trans. Joyce Emerson. London: Redman, 1967.

Tuma, N.B. and M.T. Hallinan. "The Effects of Sex, Race, and Achievement on Schoolchildren's Friendships." *Social Forces* 57 (June, 1979): 1265-1283.

Tumin, Melvin M. *Readings on Social Stratification*. New Jersey: Prentice-Hall, 1970.

Turner, Roy, ed. *Ethnomethodology*. Markham, Ontario: Penguin Books Ltd., 1974.

Vaz, E. W. "Middle-Class Adolescents' Self-Reported Delinquency and Youth Culture Activities." *The Canadian Review of Sociology and Anthropology / La revue canadienne de sociologie et d'anthropologie*, 2 (February, 1965).

Verbrugge, Lois M. "Multiplexity in Adult Friendships." *Social Forces* 57 (June, 1979): 1287-1309.

Vinter, R.D., R.M.C. Sarri, and P. Glasser. *Individual Change through Small Groups*. New York:Free Press, 1974.

Wade, Mason. *The French-Canadian Outlook: A Brief Account of the Unknown North Americans*. New York: The Viking Press, 1946.

------. *The French Canadians 1760-1945*. Toronto: The Macmillan Company of Canada Limited, 1955.

Wadell, Paul J. *Friendship and the Moral Life*. Notre Dame, Indiana: University of Notre Dame Press.

Wagner, Helmut R., ed. *Alfred Schutz: On Phenomenology and Social Relations Selected Writings*. Chicago: The University of Chicago Press, 1970.

Wallace, Clement. *The Canadian Corporate Elite: An Analysis of Economic Power*. Toronto: McClelland and Stewart Limited, 1975.

Wallace, Samuel E. *The Urban Environment*. Homewood, Illinois: The Dorsey Press, 1980.

Weber, Max. *Economy and Society: An Outline of Interpretive Sociology*, eds. Guenther Roth and Claus Wittich. Berkeley, California: University of California Press, 1978.

------. *The Protestant Ethic and the Spirit of Capitalism*. Trans. Talcott Parsons. New York: Charles Scribner's Sons, 1958.

Weisberg, D. Kelly. "The Stages of Friendship Formation." In *Examples of Grounded Theory: A Reader*. Mill Valley, CA: Sociology Press, 1993.

Wellman, Barry and S. D. Berkowitz, eds. *Social Structures: A Network Approach*. Cambridge: Cambridge University Press, 1988.

Wilkinson, Leland. *System Systat Statistics*. Evanston, Illinois: Systat, Inc., 1984.

Williams, Dennis, A., Pamela Abramson, and Lucy Howard, "Getting off the Tenure Track," *Newsweek*, 31 January 1983, 50.

Wirth, Louis. "Clinical Sociology." *The American Journal of Sociology* 37 (1931): 49-66.

Wiseman, J. "Friendship: Bonds and Binds in a Voluntary Relationship," *Journal of Social and Personal Relationships* 3 (1986): 191-211.

Wisse, Ruth R. *If I Am Not For Myself ... : The Liberal Betrayal of the Jews*. New York: The Free Press, 1992.

Wolff, G. "It's 1977. Do You Know Who Your Friends Are?" *Esquire* 87, 5: 1977, 81-93, 138-148.

Wolff, K. H. *The Sociology of Georg Simmel*. Toronto: The Free Press, 1950.

Xenophon. IV *Memorabilia and Oeconomicus*. Trans. E. C. Marchant. Cambridge: Massachusetts: Harvard University Press, 1979.

Youniss, James and Denise L. Haynie. "Friendship in Adolescence." In *Developmental and Behavioral Pediatrics* 13 (1992): 59-65.

Znaniecki, F. *Social Actions*. New York: Farrar and Rinehart, Inc., 1936.

Zucker, Marvin and June Callwood. *The Law is Not for Women*. Toronto: Pitman Publishing, 1976.

Zvulun, Eli. "Multidimensional Scalogram Analysis: The Method and Its Application." In *Theory Construction and Data Analysis in the Behavioral Sciences*, ed. Samuel Shye, 237-264. San Francisco: Jossey-Bass Publishers, 1978.

Zylberberg, Jacques. "L'enfer c'est les autres: à propos des minorités religieuses (Hell Is the Others: about Religious Minorities)," *Le Devoir*, 5 mars 1985, vii.

Author Index

Author Index

Author Index

Subject Index